THE
CORPORATE
CLOSET

THE
CORPORATE
CLOSET

The Professional Lives of
Gay Men in America

JAMES D. WOODS
with Jay H. Lucas

THE FREE PRESS
A Division of Macmillan, Inc.
NEW YORK

Maxwell Macmillan Canada
TORONTO

Maxwell Macmillan International
NEW YORK   OXFORD   SINGAPORE   SYDNEY

The Free Press
A Division of Macmillan, Inc.
866 Third Avenue, New York, N. Y. 10022

Maxwell Macmillan Canada, Inc.
1200 Eglinton Avenue East
Suite 200
Don Mills, Ontario M3C 3N1

Macmillan, Inc. is part of the Maxwell Communication Group of Companies.

Printed in the United States of America

printing number

1   2   3   4   5   6   7   8   9   10

Library of Congress Cataloging-in-Publication Data

Woods, James D.
    The corporate closet: the professional lives of gay men in
America / James D. Woods with Jay H. Lucas.
        p.   cm.
    ISBN 0-02-935603-2
    1. Gay men—Employment—United States.   2. Corporate culture—
United States.   3. Sex in the workplace—United States.
4. Professional employees—United States.   I. Lucas, Jay H.
II. Title.
HQ76.2.U5W66   1993
305.38'9664—dc20   93-19898
                                                      CIP

Dedicated to my many patient and gifted teachers

To be nobody-but-myself—in a world which is doing its best, night and day, to make you everybody else—means to fight the hardest battle which any human being can fight, and never stop fighting.

—e. e. cummings

Contents

Acknowledgements

OVER THE PAST three years, more than a hundred gay men were kind enough to spend an afternoon or evening with a couple of strangers toting a tape recorder and notepad, who took a seat in their living rooms and promptly began asking personal questions: "Where do you work?" "What are your plans for the future?" "At what age did you first consider yourself gay?"

These men served as our guides on a tour of corporate America, pointing and explaining, leading us to the conclusions that now fill the book. For their kindness and hospitality Jay Lucas and I are sincerely grateful, as we are for their willingness to trust, to explore, and to speak candidly. From their stories emerges a highly subjective portrait of the working world, of its daily humiliations and accommodations, and of the search for meaning in a career. For many, these were difficult stories to tell. They touch on fundamental questions about a man's sexuality, relationships, and ways of presenting himself to the world. They force him to revisit some of the most complex decisions he will encounter in the course of his career. Too few of them have happy endings.

In the text, I was obliged to cloak these men in pseudonyms, which prevents me from thanking them by name. My hope, however, is that they will find our insights helpful, our criticisms fair, and our note-taking at least reasonably accurate. We also offer them the assurance that by making their stories known, by stepping forward, they help bring an awareness of sexual diversity to men and women whose lives will be enriched by it—that is to say, to *all* of us.

Behind these men stands an enormous cast of supporting players to whom we owe a significant debt. The initial fieldwork was supervised by my doctoral committee at the Annenberg School for Communication, University of Pennsylvania, including Professors Carolyn Marvin, Charles Wright, Paul Messaris, and Vicky Smith. With their thoughtful reviews, Roy Cain and Barry Adam paved the way for the conversion of the dissertation into a book. At the Free Press, Joyce Seltzer was a gifted editor and teacher, as were many other friends and colleagues who graciously applied their red pencils to early drafts of the manuscript: Miriam Cardozo, George Custen, Loretta Denner, Jeff Escoffier, Michael Goff, Justin Hecht, Jeff Hoover, Mark Kaplan, Sue Llewellyn, Denis Lucey, Toni Lucey, Ann Miller, Leslie Mitchner, Nancy Morris, Dave Roche, Andrew Sullivan, Chérie Weitzner, and my inordinately patient literary agents, Charlotte Sheedy and Ellen Geiger. We are also indebted to Ed Bergman, David Blum, Jim Bryson, Gray Coleman, Brian Gould, Dean Putterman, Pat Rose, Hunter Runnette, and the many others who opened their little black books, introducing us to the men who took part in the study. Countless others helped in small but significant ways: performing an introduction, supplying an anecdote, untangling a sentence.

In the pages that follow, I've written about the role of mentors and benefactors, about the importance of having footsteps to follow. I speak from considerable firsthand experience. By hiring me as his research associate, Stephen X. Doyle made it possible for me to finish graduate school and taught me much of what I know about being myself at work. Larry Gross chaired my dissertation committee and shepherded me through my graduate studies. The project would never have seen the light of day without Larry's wisdom, enthusiasm, and unfailing good humor. Finally, I owe an incalculable debt to my family, who encouraged, supported, and otherwise indulged me over the several years it took to complete the project. More than anyone, these remarkable people put wind in my sails: my parents, Patricia Lynn Woods and James D. Woods, Jr., and my partner, Paul Young.

Prologue

A FEW WEEKS SHORT of a college degree, with a new suit and fresh haircut, I tried to seem calm when the woman in personnel called me back into her office. I had the job, she told me, an entry-level position with an advertising agency known for its beer, burger, and soft drink commercials. She extended a hand and invited me to ask any last-minute questions. I consulted my mental list: "What time do people usually come to work?" "Do people work on weekends?" "Where do I pick up my paycheck?" The woman in personnel had heard these questions before. "Everything will fall into place after you start," she assured me, steering me back toward the elevators. "Your first day will be a real learning experience."

On July 8, 1985, a few minutes before nine, I met my new boss in the upstairs lobby. She whisked me into an office, and we ran through the preliminaries: identification card, benefits, vacations, how to find the men's room. Then she explained, with a smile, that I would be working on the men's razor account, an assignment she thought "would be perfect for a young man like you." But first there was something we had to discuss. "Before I introduce you to anyone else," she began, "we should decide what you're going to be called."

I share the name James with my father and grandfather, and as the third James in the family, I'd been given the nickname Trey long before I had any say in the matter. I had included it at the top of my resume, and explained during the interview that except on the first day of each school year, I had never been called anything else. My boss smiled and folded her arms. "Well," she began, "it's your decision, but you may want to reconsider. It's important that people take you seriously." This struck me as odd. No one had ever questioned my nickname before. In the Texas farming town where I grew up there had been half a dozen Treys, and to my knowledge none of us gave the seriousness of the name much thought. But here I was, talking to a woman who held my career in her hands, afraid that I had already blown it. "Well, Jim is fine with me," I replied. "That's probably a good idea," my boss said, opening the office door. "It sounds a bit more masculine."

Over the next few hours, I was escorted around the agency and introduced to some of the key people I needed to know. First I met Sharon, who had joined the company the week before. She worked on the fast food account and seemed as nervous as I was. I liked her at once. When she mentioned that she, too, had grown up in Texas, I was tempted to seek her opinion on the nickname question but decided against it. "Let's have lunch," she suggested, "so I can share my vast experience with you." I agreed and continued my tour of the agency. (Later that week, my boss warned me that Sharon was off limits. "I know what you're thinking," she said, quite spontaneously, "but intrafucking is strictly against the rules.")

We moved on through the various offices and meeting rooms, where I met the writers, producers, media planners, and brand managers I'd be working with. After each ritual introduction, we exchanged a few vital statistics. I asked how long they had been with the agency, what accounts they worked on, how they liked New York. They wanted to know where I'd gone to college, where I lived, and if I was married. When I assured them I was neither married nor "otherwise involved," one of the men told me about the weekly singles night in the cocktail lounge on the second floor. "I'll be there," I said.

After lunch I was taken to a tiny screening room, where my boss had arranged for me to see a reel of television commercials for competing brands of men's razors. She also wanted me to see the current campaign for our brand, which featured clean-shaven young men laughing and playing, having a great time in cars, on beaches, and at basketball games. The new campaign, which was scheduled to air in a few weeks, featured rock music and a college dormitory setting. The old stuff, she told me, was "really faggy."

As five o'clock approached, I was introduced to one of the head writers, an older man named Don. He reminded me of my grandfather, with his wispy white hair and gentle, amused eyes. His office was littered with toys and old movie paraphernalia. Though I didn't notice it at the time, Don was the first person who didn't ask the usual questions about my personal background. Instead he showed me a script he was working on and insisted that I visit a certain restaurant, an old favorite of his, in an obscure corner of my new neighborhood. "How do you like New York?" he wanted to know. "Do you enjoy the theater?" "Have you been to Chinatown?" Leaving Don's office, I remarked, "He seems like a nice guy." My boss was amused. "I'm sure he thinks *you're* nice, too." Don had been with the company a long time, she told me, and was an important person to know, "especially if you want to have a homosexual fling." She caught my eye, and we shared a chuckle.

Walking home, I felt the curious mix of exhaustion and exhilaration that follows an extended dose of adrenaline, the relief an actor must feel when he steps offstage after a performance. Nothing disastrous had happened, and it seemed to me that I had performed quite well during the introductory small talk. My boss had impressed me as someone who would make a stern but effective teacher, someone who had my best interests at heart, concerned as she was with the subtleties of my public image. To make sure I was sending the right signals, she had even persuaded me to run with her and several others in the annual Corporate Challenge, a five-mile road race in Central Park. "You want people to see you as a team player," she had explained. I agreed at once, grateful that she would want me on her team.

Joining a college friend at a gay bar later that evening, I spoke glowingly about my first day. I showed off my new sweat shirt and tote bag, complete with company logo. Out of loyalty to my new client, I vowed to abandon my electric shaver for the twin-bladed, pivot-headed razors I would now be charged with selling to Middle America. It never entered my mind, as I shared all this with my friend, that there was any reason to doubt my employer's good intentions. Surrounded by other gay men in suits and ties, it didn't occur to me, not even for a moment, that my initiation into the working world had been hostile or demeaning. On the contrary, Monday struck me as a typical day at the office. My first day of work felt like countless other experiences I had been through over the years: beginning the school year, moving to a new town, entering a roomful of strangers.

Years later I see the situation differently. I now recognize the countless ways I was told—formally and informally, in word and in deed—that I was unwelcome in this organization. Like the company's other lesbian and gay employees, I sensed the moral judgment implicit in social invitations for "you and a girlfriend," in the occasional joke about who was or wasn't a queer, and in the seductive advertisements, depicting heterosexual romance and love, that I would be helping to create. I filled out personnel forms that recognized only one kind of domestic relationship and that promised health insurance and other benefits to the families of those checking the "married" box. I learned the rules about dating: "Homosexual flings" and heterosexual "intrafucking" were forbidden, even as it was taken for granted that I would desire the latter. I discovered that there were other people like me in the company, *single* people who gathered on Fridays in the hope of solving that particular problem. Finally, I had been told that "fagginess" was undesirable in any form: in nicknames, in product advertising, and in people.

My response, as the weeks passed, was to adopt what I now call a "counterfeiting" strategy. I went to the company's singles night and spoke vaguely about past girlfriends. I was conspicuous about my friendships with women. I told (or at least laughed at) the right jokes and didn't say too much about my interest in theater. On a friend's suggestion, I read the sports section of the *New York Times* and at least twice dragged myself to Yankee Stadium. For a time, I even hid a small notepad in my desk on which I scribbled key biographical information about "Heather," a quite imaginary young woman with brains, looks, and the good sense to have dated me in college. Heather had unfortunately moved to Maine.

Like my lesbian and gay coworkers, I learned to "manage" my identity at work. I paid close attention to my presentation of self, to the people with whom I was seen, to nuances of appearance and gesture, and to the information about my personal life that circulated through the hallways. I became skillful in assembling the necessary props and supporting players. A few months after I began work, Don began to complain of a mysterious ailment with an array of puzzling symptoms. When someone commented, "He's a faggot, so it's probably AIDS," I bit my tongue. Don ultimately died, but in the weeks that followed I was careful not to show too much concern for him, not even to ask what had killed him. In short, I claimed an identity as a heterosexual man, the identity that was expected and rewarded in my organization.

I'll never know if the strategy worked. Walking home one afternoon, I realized that I would ultimately be forced to abandon it, that my counterfeit identity had an expiration date. Before long coworkers would find my simple evasions less convincing. One expects a single twenty-one-year-old to be vague about his life plans, but unanswered questions give rise to suspicion and mistrust when he turns thirty, forty, fifty. Perhaps my peers would express their curiosity more directly, seeking more convincing (or at least more recent) evidence of my heterosexuality. Looking above me in the hierarchy, I saw no one whose life resembled mine. My boss was married and was planning to have a baby. Her boss had several kids my age. The president of the company was having a very public affair with his secretary and, later, with the summer intern whose office was next to mine. Looking ahead, I saw social pressures I didn't know how to handle, promotions (and thus visibility) I wasn't sure I wanted. The conclusion was unavoidable: In the long run, there was no place for me in this organization. Something snapped, and with that I began polishing my résumé, planning my escape. Exactly one year after my first day of work, I left the company to begin graduate school.

On my last day of work, several of my peers threw a small farewell party. Fittingly, I was given a bagful of souvenirs—bottles of mouthwash, tubes of toothpaste, a package of razors—to commemorate the advertising campaigns I had worked on over the past

year. There was also the obligatory gag gift that accompanied all
such promotions or departures—in my case an inflatable, anatomi-
cally correct "love doll" intended to keep me company during
those long nights in graduate school. I was suitably embarrassed
but curiously flattered and put at ease by the gesture; a few months
earlier, the man renowned as the office Casanova had received a
similar gift when he transferred to the Chicago office. As the party
wound down, my boss said something nice about the professional
potential I had demonstrated, assuring me that "there will always
be a place for you here." I thanked her and said my goodbyes.

Almost seven years later, I imagine an alternative ending to the
story. How would my boss have responded if I had told her, on the
spot, that I was gay? How would others have responded? Given
their eagerness to believe otherwise, my announcement would undoubtedly have come as a surprise. At the time, however, it didn't
even occur to me as an option. Like many gay men, I had fallen almost without thinking into a pattern of deception and evasion, my
desire to be truthful overwhelmed by my fear of the consequences.
My response was to hide, to seek safety in the camouflage I had
worn since childhood, and—when that no longer seemed a de-
pendable solution—to flee. It wasn't until years later that the alternatives became apparent. Faced with a similar dilemma, other men
have made different choices—if such accommodations can indeed
be viewed as choices.

I told my story to Jay Lucas several years later, as we laid the
groundwork for *The Corporate Closet.* Jay was a management consultant with Deloitte & Touche, a top accounting firm, and his
predicament was similar to mine in many respects, complicated
somewhat by the fact that he was farther along in his career. Over a
series of Chinese dinners, we pondered what he should do—and
what I should have done—returning again and again to the same
questions: How should a gay man handle information about his
sexuality at work? What should he take into account when deciding how, when, and whom to tell? Our own experiences told us
that gay men had devised a number of different strategies for managing information about their sexual lives, disguising and revealing
themselves in many different ways. But which of the strategies was

most effective? What were the costs and consequences of using any particular one?

The strategies quickly became the focus of our study, and as we told friends about the undertaking, there was an outpouring of recollections, confessions, and complaints. Just as every gay man has a "coming out" story, all have stories about the way they handled a homophobic boss, an inquisitive client, or a supportive coworker. We took notes, gradually turning our questions into a lengthy questionnaire. In the spring of 1990, we began with a series of informal group meetings in which we asked professional friends to tell us about the decisions they had made about self-disclosure. Whom had they told? What had been the response? We then asked them to introduce us to friends and friends-of-friends in San Francisco, Houston, Washington, Philadelphia, and New York who might be willing to talk with us. It was through this network of contacts that we ultimately located the core group of seventy strangers—"the men" described in the Appendix—each of whom spent several hours telling us about his life and career. We conducted our first full-length interview in July 1990 and spent the next seven months on the road, contacting, screening, and interviewing gay men. Then, with the interviews completed, I began the task of analyzing, organizing, and writing.

From time to time, meanwhile, I heard news of my former employer. My boss resigned soon after I did to spend six months trekking through Tibet. She now has a daughter. Most of my lesbian and gay coworkers have moved on to other jobs in other agencies, and one of them, a young copywriter, died of an AIDS-related illness last spring. I hear that the firm's nondiscrimination policy was ultimately expanded to include sexual orientation, and I assume without being told that the firm still employs a large (if unknown) number of lesbians and gay men. Sources also tell me that, perhaps humbled by the loss of several key clients, the macho atmosphere has broken down. If this is so, my former employer is like many of its competitors. It is slowly awakening to the sexual diversity of its work force, struggling to disentangle its demand that workers be creative, productive, and efficient from its desire that they also be heterosexual.

Today the lesbians and gay men who walk through the company's doors have options that were unavailable even a few years ago. They face different penalties for coming out and pay a different price for remaining in the closet. There is still no single, ideal solution, and in choosing a particular strategy, they inevitably reject one configuration of problems only to accept another. Yet the trade-offs have become more apparent. Eight years ago, on my first day of work, I responded reflexively, resigning myself to invisibility in a way that fewer and fewer gay professionals do. Increasingly these men recognize that there are drawbacks to life on either side of the closet door. Like me, they have begun to question the environment that presents us with such limited choices, making closets necessary in the first place.

1

Dimensions of the Closet

"BY THE TIME I get to an interview, they already know I can do the job," says Stuart, an attorney in his mid-thirties who is currently looking for a new job. "They have seen my resume. They know where I went to law school, and they know the kind of expertise I have. They've already decided that I have the right qualifications. So the whole point of the interview is to see if we have the right chemistry. Do I look like them? Will we get along? Can we spend long days and nights working together? Interviews are not at all about qualifications. They never test my *abilities* during an interview."

Stuart began his job search shortly after he marked his fifth anniversary with his current employer, a Boston firm known for its strong ties to the Ivy League. Two years short of partnership, having grown up in a nearby suburb, Stuart felt it was time to move on. He began quietly to circulate his resume, to read the Help Wanted section of the *New York Times,* and to network with friends from Harvard Law School. The recession meant that openings for real estate attorneys were relatively scarce, but within a few months Stuart had scheduled a handful of interviews. "My goal in the interviews is to make the other person as comfortable as possible with me," he says. "Interviews are just social performances. Nothing else is being tested during an interview."

One of the first calls came from a large, respected firm in midtown Manhattan. The firm had grown substantially during the booming real estate market of the 1980s and was now expanding into general commercial work. Stuart considered it a promising lead. "The people were known for being unusually smart, and I had always heard that they were committed to cultivating a diverse work force." A classmate from law school had interviewed with the firm and described the people as "interesting and quirky." Through a recruiter the firm asked Stuart to send a transcript and a writing sample, calling him several days later to schedule a first round of interviews. Several weeks later, after much anticipation and several visits to the firm, Stuart was invited back for a final round. He was scheduled to meet with several attorneys, including the hiring partner who would make the final decision.

Just before he was scheduled to meet with the hiring partner, however, Stuart was diverted into the office of a senior associate, a woman in her mid-forties. The hiring partner was running late, she explained, offering to keep Stuart company until her boss got off the phone. Stuart took a seat. The associate seemed friendly and direct, and something about her manner put Stuart at ease. Scanning the office, he noticed a bulletin board filled with family photographs. Propped on her desk was a picture of her fourteen-year-old son. Stuart also noticed that she had arranged her office so that the desk faced the wall. "She didn't use her desk as a barricade, the way a lot of lawyers do. We were sitting about two feet apart." Stuart began to relax. "She began the interview by saying, 'Look, I'm sure you've already answered all the standard questions. I'm sure you've already heard the stock information about the firm. Now's the time to ask the "tough" questions.' "

The hiring partner stayed on the phone for almost an hour. Stuart ran through his list of questions, asking the associate about the social atmosphere at the firm, the chances of making partner, and the kind of schedule he would be expected to keep. She described the firm as a supportive and relaxed group of people, emphasizing the "quality of life" it would afford him. She also pointed out that in her case the firm had given her a flexible schedule so that she could work at home and attend to family needs. Stuart took this as an invitation. "I wanted to hear more about the social atmosphere in the firm, so I asked her if she would describe the firm as a 'diverse' group of people. It was my way of getting her to talk about the kind of social relationships they had, the way they got along in the office. I suppose it was also a way of coding my real question. I was hoping that she would give me some hint that the firm was also a tolerant place for a gay man."

The associate started to answer, telling Stuart about a partner who had traveled through Asia. She also mentioned a junior associate who had taken several years off to travel before starting work at the firm. Then, after a moment, a look of confusion crossed her face. "She had been very poised during the interview," Stuart recalls, "but now it seemed to dawn on her that she wasn't really answering my question. She stopped, and then she began to reinterpret the question, without any help from me. She said the word 'diverse' aloud a couple of times. I started to get scared at this point, because I had no idea where she was going with the question."

" 'Well,' she said, after a pause, 'if I understand your question correctly, everyone here is Jewish. Does that pose a problem?' " Stuart was horrified. His last name clearly marked him as a WASP, but at the moment his religious background was the last thing on his mind. As the associate grappled with the question, Stuart tried to intervene, to pull the conversation back on track, but found that it was no use. "At this point, my self-image began to interfere with my ability to conduct the interview," he recalls. "I refused to have my question understood as an anti-Semitic remark, so I interrupted her. I said, 'Look, I'm gay. What effect will that have on my career at this firm?' "

The associate seemed puzzled by the question. "She obviously hadn't expected this," says Stuart, "but she answered right away. She said that the firm didn't discriminate. She insisted that it wouldn't be a problem. In fact, she didn't seem to understand why I would bother to bring it up in the first place." To reassure Stuart the woman also mentioned another attorney in the firm who was rumored to be gay. "Everybody assumes he's gay," she told him.

"We could go by his office, if you'd like, and you'll see what I mean. He has a lot of antiques. Maybe you'd like to talk to him?" Stuart declined, explaining that under the circumstances it might be a rather awkward encounter. He asked instead if the firm had a nondiscrimination policy. The associate wasn't sure but could not recall hearing or reading about one.

"I realized right away that I had made a terrible mistake," says Stuart. "I didn't get any useful information out of her. I opened my-self up for all kinds of trouble, and I made both of us nervous. In one fell swoop, I became somebody she simply couldn't identify with." The conversation sputtered along, and after another half hour, the hiring partner finally got off the phone. Stuart moved on to the next interview, rattled and exhausted. "They made me talk to three more people that afternoon, and those final interviews were the most bor-ing of my entire life. I was afraid of making the same mistake again, so I was guarded and cautious. I was also tired. It was so traumatic for me to give up my heterosexual facade that I just wanted to go home. I had done more than a day's work just by coming out."

A few days later the firm declined to make Stuart an offer, with-out offering any explanation. "I'll never make that mistake again," he says. "In a way it's really a shame. I can never be myself in the interviews, which means that an employer never gets to know me. That chemistry that they're always looking for is never going to be there, unless it's artificial. So the person they hire is not me, it's someone I've made up. At the same time, I never get to know them, so I can never figure out how we're really going to interact on a personal level."

For gay professionals the story is an achingly familiar one. A gay man faces a decision every time he sets foot in a work environ-ment, whenever he is in the presence of a boss, client, secretary, customer, or some other professional peer. At all times he must bal-ance a whole host of considerations—worries that are largely un-known to his heterosexual peers: How should he handle information about his sexuality? What will be the consequences of coming out? Of remaining in the closet? Of trying to avoid the issue altogether? The decision is not one he can afford to take lightly.

For many employers, however, the scenario is new and unfamiliar. American business is only now waking up to the presence of its lesbian and gay employees, and the awakening has brought the resistance, misunderstanding, and social clumsiness we would expect to accompany so fundamental a change. Lesbians and gay men represent a challenge to some of our most entrenched ideas about the separation of work and sexuality; their mere presence seems to upset our conventional beliefs about privacy, professionalism, and office etiquette. Because they can often disappear, they differ from "traditional" minorities, whose problems are better understood. And because they have historically remained invisible, American business has little idea how numerous they really are.

A curious paradox results. Working under cover, lesbians and gay men are both widely integrated and almost entirely ignored. With the right disguise, they have already been admitted to a club that still formally excludes them. They view the nation's banks, law firms, hospitals, and charities not as outsiders clamoring to be let in, but as insiders afraid to make their presence known. Their collective contributions, productivity, and satisfaction have serious implications for the bottom line. Moreover, their significance to American business is way out of proportion to their actual numbers. As individuals lesbian and gay professionals influence and interact with a much larger circle of peers: the men and women, both gay and straight, who share their offices and secrets, who become their friends and adversaries, who sometimes hire and fire them. As a group they symbolize some of our most basic beliefs about privacy, professionalism, and the role of sexuality in the workplace.

Yet until recently, almost nothing has been said about their role in American business, nor about the changes that must come if they are to participate as full and equal partners. Sexual diversity is a new concept to most companies and as such it requires a certain amount of explaining. Employers too rarely recognize the destructive trade-offs they impose on lesbian and gay workers, and only now are they beginning to see the personal and economic consequences of heterosexism. Even lesbian and gay workers who inhabit the corporate closet are often unaware of its full size and depth. Like their heterosexual peers, they accept certain conventional ways of doing business, blind to the inequities embedded within them. A few preliminary definitions are thus in order.

Heterosexism at work

Though lesbians and gay men are assumed to make up some 10 percent of the population (a figure that has been subject to much recent debate), there is no reliable way to estimate their numbers in the professional workforce.[1] Neither do we know very much about the particular kinds of jobs they hold. Professions like design, travel, and arts management seem to employ a large number of gay men, and popular lore also has them clustered in the world's flower shops, hair salons, and gourmet emporiums. Gay waiters and hairdressers are stock sitcom characters. And who hasn't, on occasion, made assumptions about a male flight attendant, nurse, or ballet dancer?[2]

Indeed, the visibility of gay men in certain professions prompts the frequent claim, usually accompanied by anecdotal evidence, that there are in fact "gay industries." In his 1974 essay "The Homosexual Executive," Richard Zoglin remarks that "certain more 'creative' fields such as advertising and publishing have traditionally had a higher incidence of homosexuality," especially when compared to "the most conservative segments of the business community," like insurance, banking, and the utilities.[3] A recent article on the Condé Nast publishing empire, published in the *Advocate,* suggests that the fashion and design industries would virtually grind to a halt without gay men. According to Raul Martinez, art director at *Vogue,* the magazine "could be put together without gay men, but it would be a nightmare. The majority of the fashion magazine world is gay—hair and makeup people, stylists, top photographers like Steven Meisel, Herb Ritts, and Matthew Rolston, and, of course, the people who make the clothes." Having said all this, Martinez reflects for a moment. "Wait a minute," he adds. "Maybe all of this *can't* be done without gays."[4]

In other industries, for whatever reason, gay men seem virtually absent. Writing in *Commentary* in 1980, Midge Decter expressed doubt that homosexuals "have established much of a presence in basic industry or government service or in such classic professions as doctoring and lawyering, but then for anyone acquainted with them as a group, the thought suggests itself that few of them have ever made much effort in these directions."[5] Scott, a gay insurance agent, says that "there are absolutely no other gay people in my industry," while Matt, an executive with Ford Motor Company, assures me that "there aren't too many gays in my business." Darren, a New Jersey dentist, feels that homosexuality is "real uncommon" in his line of work. "It's just one of those professions in which you don't see it that often. You see a lot more gay doctors."

Given the ease with which appearances can be (and are) manipulated, however, they are almost certainly deceptive. Like most myths, the notion of "gay industries" sprang from a seed of truth: Gay men are indeed invisible in many professions. The problem is that the myth mistakes invisibility for rarity. Because lesbians and gay men must identify themselves to be counted, their visibility is an unreliable measure of their presence. A quick scan of a particular company or industry may tell us something about the willingness of gay employees to identify themselves, but reveals comparatively little about their actual numbers. Indeed, it is quite plausible that the "most conservative segments" of the business community are fully saturated with gay professionals who simply keep a lower profile than do men in the arts, advertising, and travel.

None of which is to say that gay professionals are distributed evenly across all occupations, companies, or geographic areas— this, too, seems unlikely. Yet there is ample evidence that the true distribution of gay professionals, if known, would be surprising. According to a 1991 survey of 6,075 lesbians and gay men conducted by Overlooked Opinions, a Chicago market research firm, more lesbians and gays are in science than in food service, and more work in finance than in the arts. Among gay men the three most common job categories were management, health care, and education.[6] Whatever the actual distribution and numbers, we can also rest assured that *no* field is entirely devoid of lesbian and gay workers. Certainly anyone who claims that they cannot be found in medicine, banking, or insurance too readily accepts conventional wisdom. "I used to think there were no gay stockbrokers," says a Wall Street veteran, now in his fifties. "Then I got my first job in a brokerage, and little by little they came out of the woodwork. Now I wonder why I didn't see them in the first place."

Under the circumstances, it is hardly surprising that lesbian and gay professionals often elect to remain invisible. While they have always worked in the nation's offices, classrooms, and laboratories, they've never been at home in them. Since 1980 some two dozen studies have documented hiring, promotion, and compensation practices that discriminate against lesbian and gay workers.[7] Of the thousands of gay men surveyed in these reports, roughly one in three believed he had experienced some form of job discrimination. The most recent of these reports also suggest that as lesbians and gay men have become more visible in recent years, the rates are climbing. In a typical survey, conducted in Philadelphia in 1992, 30 percent of gay men (and 24 percent of lesbian women) reported that they had experienced employment discrimination at some point in their careers.[8] A sizable number (12 percent of the men and 9 percent of women) said that it had occurred within just the past twelve months. The lowest rate reported by any study, for men and women, was 16 percent; the highest was 44 percent. (For a summary of these studies, see the Appendix).

The numbers, however, are conservative. Because gays often disguise themselves precisely to *avoid* discrimination, we can only guess how its incidence would soar if they made themselves easier targets.[9] The same 1992 survey of Philadelphians found that 76 percent of gay men (and 81 percent of lesbians) remained in the closet at work. Seventy-eight percent of the men (and 87 percent of the women) feared they *would* be the victims of job discrimination if their sexual orientation were known to others.[10] A 1981 study of lesbians came to much the same conclusion. In that report it was found that "nearly two out of three respondents felt that their jobs might be jeopardized if their sociosexual orientation were known. Clearly disclosure in one's work environment is perceived by lesbian women as a high-risk event."[11]

Moreover, actual discrimination is not always recognized as such. With some notable exceptions, most employers avoid the awkward (and increasingly illegal) practice of explicitly denying jobs to homosexuals on the basis of their sexual orientation.[12] Gay men don't always know why they were fired or denied a promotion and can't say for sure what prejudices lurk beneath the generic refusals they are often given: "lack of experience," "overqualified," "job already filled," "wouldn't fit in."[13] While in most cases they can only second-guess an employer's motives, an important study of employers in Anchorage, Alaska, suggests that their fears are well founded. Of the 191 employers who responded to the 1987–88 survey, many said that they would fire (18 percent), not hire (27 percent), or not promote (26 percent) someone they thought to be homosexual.[14]

Even the definitions of discrimination are conservative and narrow to the point that they ignore what may be the most common ways in which lesbian and gay workers are penalized. Surveys of gay professionals typically ask respondents if their sexuality has at any point cost them a job or promotion. Others put the question more broadly, asking respondents if they've ever encountered "any problems at work." The answers reflect the particular way in which the question has traditionally been framed. When he reports discrimination, a gay man usually has in mind an unjust termination, a negative evaluation, a job offer that never materialized, or a promotion that was denied. The question encourages him to think in terms of specific homophobic incidents or individuals—those that can be clearly identified and labeled as such.

Yet discriminatory incidents are just the tip of the iceberg. Even when the most blatant, episodic forms of bias are eliminated, one can identify a process that excludes lesbian and gay professionals in other, more subtle ways. In prejudicial compensation practices, the forced invisibility of gay employees, the social validation of heterosexual mating rituals, the antigay commentary and imagery that circulate through company channels, even the masculine nature of bureaucratic organization itself, a certain kind of heterosexuality is routinely displayed and rewarded. The traditional white-collar workplace is "heterosexist" in the sense that it structurally and ideologically promotes a particular model of heterosexuality while penalizing, hiding, or otherwise "symbolically annihilating" its alternatives.[15] Like racism, sexism, and other isms, heterosexism encompasses not only blatant, isolated displays of prejudice (a bigoted remark, a hate crime) but also the more subtle, unseen ways in which lesbians and gay men are stigmatized, excluded, and denied the support given their heterosexual peers.[16]

When the definition of discrimination is expanded to include these *systemic* forms of heterosexism, the rate soars. When *Out/Look* asked readers if their sexual orientation ever creates "stressful situations at work," 62 percent said that it was "always" or "often" a source of stress, 46 percent said it had influenced their choice of career, and 27 percent thought it had influenced their choice of a particular company.[17] Among the seventy men in my own sample, five (or 7 percent) were convinced that they had lost a prior job due to the prejudice of a boss or client. Another ten (14 percent) feared that they *would* be fired or encouraged to resign if their secret were known. And virtually all (97 percent) thought their sexuality had, at some point, cost them a promotion, a raise, or a relationship with a potential mentor.[18]

Unjust compensation practices are also ignored by traditional measures of discrimination. According to the U.S. Chamber of Commerce, employee benefits like health insurance, relocation expenses, and other perquisites now account for roughly 37 percent of payroll costs.[19] Although married employees routinely receive these benefits for children, husbands, and wives, gay workers are almost always denied them. Neither are they usually granted bereavement, medical, or maternity leave to take care of an unmarried partner. In a 1991 survey by *Partners* magazine, only 8 percent of lesbians and gay men said that employers provided their partners with an employee benefit of some kind. Only 5 percent had company health insurance that covered a partner.[20] As insurance premiums soar and compensation through benefits displaces real wages—having already climbed from 33 percent to 37 percent in just a few years—lesbian and gay workers are being compensated less and less.[21]

A comprehensive definition of discrimination should also take into account the many subtle ways in which heterosexism can distort a career. Even when he is spared an unjust termination or negative evaluation, a gay man faces obstacles that are largely unknown to heterosexual peers. Heterosexism takes its toll across the span of an entire lifetime, and may be visible only in retrospect. Consider Martin, an account executive at Ogilvy & Mather. "After college I wanted to be in New York because I thought it would be a tolerant city," he says, "and I guess I assumed the same thing about advertising. I thought that advertising meant 'creative people, liberal atmosphere, lots of gay men.' To some extent that's proven true." Martin feels that most of his coworkers are "terrific, smart, fun people," and thinks that he's treated reasonably well. Still, he is not untouched by heterosexism. Shortly after joining the company, Martin carefully avoided an assignment that would have required extensive after-hours socializing with a particular client. A few years later he turned down a promotion that would have taken him to a smaller city, one in which he feared it would be "harder to be gay." Then there is the matter of his lover, a physician, who is denied the benefits and social invitations a wife would receive automatically.

Martin also worries about his long-run prospects with the company. He has the reputation of being somewhat aloof and enigmatic at work, someone who doesn't attend all the company parties or outings. He is formal with his superiors and has carefully segregated his personal and professional activities, friends, and identities. "I have a limited relationship with my boss," he explains, "which means I don't always get the mentoring I need." Nor does Martin find himself eager to go the extra mile, to devote long hours to a company that doesn't seem to value him. "My career is less fulfilling than it might be," he says. "I turn to other activities for sustenance."

Even so Martin thinks that by staying in the closet, he has largely avoided discrimation. He recognizes that his sexuality has influenced many of his choices, stunted certain professional relationships, even drawn him to a particular city and line of work. Eventually it may lead him out of advertising and into his own, private consulting practice. Yet he considers himself lucky. "I can't really say I've been the victim of discrimination," he says. "At least not that I'm aware of."

Many of the men we interviewed tell some version of this story. At countless junctures heterosexism has guided their professional trajectories.[22] Craig, a vice president at American Express, says that it was probably his reason for leaving the army. John thinks it made the priesthood attractive to him as a young boy and later encouraged him to accept a position with an urban congregation. For Duane it was a reason to attend graduate school and to select Columbia over a smaller school in a rural setting. Burt, Chip, and Henry were all fired from previous jobs and are certain that an employer's prejudice was part of the reason. When asked by the *Advocate* if being gay had influenced his decision to enter show business, media mogul David Geffen said that it had been one of his chief considerations. "When I realized as a teenager that it was possible that I might be gay—I wasn't sure until my 20s—I thought, *What kind of career can I have where being gay won't make a difference?* I thought about it a lot, and I decided that the entertainment business was a profession in which being gay was not going to be unusual or stand in my way."[23]

Over time the incessant tug of heterosexism leads these men down paths that diverge from those taken by straight peers. On the one hand they are drawn away from large companies, from jobs that require extensive socializing with clients or peers, from companies with traditional, family-oriented cultures, from vaguely defined managerial roles that emphasize social skills, and from environments that they consider homophobic. On the other they are drawn toward technical, clerical, sales, and other skilled positions that tolerate greater diversity and measure performance in more concrete, objective terms. Many are drawn into gay ghettos within their own companies, surrounded by others who have been marginalized for one reason or another. A sizable number abandon large organizations altogether, to work for smaller companies, for gay-run businesses, or for themselves. Until now the migrations of this vast talent pool have attracted little notice.

Even when they are blind to the embedded, structural forms of heterosexism, lesbians and gay men are only too familiar with the more immediate, interpersonal mode of its expression: homophobic behavior. Homophobia, in this sense, is the fear or hatred of homosexual people, the expression of heterosexism in prejudicial attitudes and behavior.[24] While a man may not recognize the full scope of cultural and institutional heterosexism, he can scarcely ignore the way his boss makes fun of a particular client, the one they say is "just a bit odd." He may not view questions about marital status as a degrading ritual but knows that "sissy" jokes are. Because a man's response to homophobia depends on his perception of it, he must be attentive to the various signals and cues given off by those around him. By necessity he becomes skilled at detecting homophobia. He does so in a number of different ways.

When a man is openly gay, coworkers may express their homophobia directly. Darren, a dentist in New Jersey, remembers the one and only time he revealed himself to someone at work. While Darren was attending dental school, he and his lover Bob became friendly with Rick and Renee, two of Darren's classmates. "They were just wonderful, wonderful people," Darren recalls. "We mixed socially a couple of times a week." As the friendship warmed, Darren thought it was safe to come out. "One night we were out at a club, dancing. Somehow it came up that I lived with Bob, and maybe we were gay. Renee was laughing like it was crazy, a joke. I said, 'Why is that a joke? What's so outrageous about that?' And she says, 'Well, what do you mean?' So I said, 'Well, we *are* gay. We've been lovers for four years.' "

The relationship soured immediately. "The next day Renee called me up and said, 'I need to talk to you.' So she came over, and she says, 'Would you please come out to my car and speak with me?' I didn't know what it was about, so I walked out to the car. She left the motor running, and I remember that she didn't look me in the face. She says, 'Well, I just wanted you to know that Rick and I have talked it over and we've decided—and this isn't a hundred percent because of what you told me last night—that we can't see you or Bob anymore. We can't be your friends anymore.' " Ten years later Darren is still troubled by the episode. "It was like being hit in the face with a sledgehammer," he says. "This was the first person I had ever come out to." Though Renee tried to apologize a few months later, Darren felt it was too late. Today he is guarded and secretive at work. "When you stick your finger in the fire," he says, "you don't put it back in again."

Such episodes leave little doubt that a particular work setting is hostile. But not all gay men have had experiences like these; quite often they base their assessments on more oblique or secondhand evidence of homophobia. Rather than expose himself directly to the climate of opinion, for example, a man may instead observe the way *other* gay men and lesbians are treated at work. Tom, an elementary school teacher in New Jersey, hears comments about the school librarian. "He's real obvious," Tom says. "The kids mimic him, and everybody knows who he is." In Dave's office it is the copier repairman who gets the attention. "He's a real flamer," says Dave, the credit manager for a Philadephia fuel supply company. "He comes in and everybody talks about how 'flowing and diaphanous' he is. When he asks people for something, they say, 'Honey, it's over there, honey,' as a joke." For Todd, a human resources manager at Bell Atlantic, making personal judgments like these is part of the job. Todd has participated in hundreds of hiring and firing decisions and knows that his staff routinely discriminates against gay candidates; he's seen them do it. "In some departments," Todd says, "a candidate will simply be ruled out if he's known to be gay." Not surprisingly these men consider their work environments hostile. All are in the closet.

George has been on both sides of the hiring process, first as a flight attendant and now as a training executive with a large European airline. "In-flight is *so gay*," he says. "I mean, male flight attendants are like hairdressers. Everybody knows that, and so there's a fear in management. I know that we actively discriminate against gays in the recruiting process. I know it for a fact; they'll terminate them in training for that. I don't think they care if someone's gay or not. They care about how effeminate you are. They really don't care what you *do*, but if you're a flamer—I mean I'm not butch, but if you really were a flamer, they'd have you out of there in a heartbeat. It varies by airline, too. I'm friendly with a recruiter at another airline, and she told me that the head guy in Chicago called her and said, 'Stop sending me all these queers.'" George took this as a warning. Everyone at work knows that he is gay, but he rarely talks about it. He tries not to seem too obvious.

Others describe gay coworkers who found their effectiveness

compromised, their authority undercut, when word got out that they are gay. Nick, a consultant with a large firm in New York, remembers a former boss who was ultimately forced to transfer to another office. "He had a problem managing people," says Nick. "He was a little bit effeminate, and people didn't always take him seriously, especially on the customer side. He couldn't go out and do much with them. I remember this one lady, she was just vicious. She'd come in and say things about him, 'Oh, I saw him and his *boyfriend* down in the Village over the weekend.' Those type things. People respected him to his face, but they did say things behind his back." Andy, a Houston attorney, describes a partner in his firm who recently came out at work. "It became a limiting factor because some people chose not to work with him," says Andy. "Fortunately, there are clients who know he's gay and work with him anyway. There's a significant number of attorneys who work with him and have no problem with it, and so on balance it works out fine. But I'm privy to criticisms and comments from time to time."

Conversations about AIDS are another context in which homophobia is often expressed. "If you're gay," says Tip, a surgical resident at a large Manhattan hospital, "the other surgeons just assume you're HIV-positive. The comments are always negative, and they're always about how they would rather not operate on someone who's gay. A black boy came in as a patient recently, and he had a nasal deformity. He was gay, a little effeminate. I would have done it; I would have been happy to do the surgery. But the chief resident and one of the other residents talked about it in the hallways, walking by after clinic, and they said, 'Hell no, we're not going to do that surgery. He's a flamer. I mean, why expose ourselves to that?' "

Even when they have not directly overheard comments like these, most gay men have heard rumors or secondhand accounts of harassment.[25] Most can recall comments, jokes, or company folklore that betray underlying opinions. Most can name a gay friend or acquaintance who was fired under suspicious circumstances. And virtually all have read public accounts of lesbians and gay men fired from other companies, the military, or from positions as teachers or priests. Keith has heard, for example, that his employer, a diversified energy company in Houston, has an unwritten rule against articles of men's clothing that it considers effeminate. "Supposedly, there's a hidden law, or hidden rule, that if you come in for an interview with an earring, and you're a man, your application is automatically thrown away." Asked how he had learned of this secret policy, Keith thought for a moment. "I think my boss told me that."

It may be no more than a joke, comment, or anecdote that sets the tone. In its 1990 survey of lesbian and gay journalists, the American Society of News Editors found that in just the twelve months preceding the survey, 81 percent of respondents had heard derogatory comments about gays or lesbians in general, and nearly half had heard comments directed at a particular gay or lesbian employee. Twenty percent of respondents didn't think their newsrooms were a good environment for lesbians or gay men.[26] Among my own seventy respondents, more than half could recall a specific homophobic remark or incident at work; one in five said that such comments were frequent.

Tip says that he has "lost count" of the homophobic remarks made by Dr. Thomas, the head of surgery. "Dr. Thomas is an ultraconservative Republican type who thinks I share the exact same goals that he has," says Tip. "He took a sailing trip recently where they were fogged in and had to take port in Provincetown. You'd have thought he had ended up in Saudi Arabia, the way he described it. 'Jesus,' he said, 'you couldn't believe it. All these bullish looking girls walking around together, a very unattractive group of people, strange men holding hands. A disgusting display. This is where our country is headed, can you believe this?' Dr. Thomas was saying this on the elevator, to two other professors."

Comments like these are also standard on the construction sites in northern California where Geoff works as a supervisor. "In my business homosexuals are something you put underneath a slab. That's a generalization, but most of these guys are very redneck, macho. They're not bad people, but they have very distinct views about how the world should operate." According to Rodney, a former trader at Morgan Guaranty, Wall Street isn't much different. "There's a locker-room mentality on the trading floor," he says. "Lots of infantile, high school, locker-room banter. Tons of antigay jokes and AIDS jokes." Rodney remembers one man who was especially vocal. "He made a remark one time about one of the top traders in the bond market. He was talking about how bizarre it was, like, 'This guy's a fucking faggot, and he's still trading.' " Under the circumstances, there was little incentive for Rodney to come out. "This guy's level of homophobia was enough to keep us all in the closet," he says. For Matt, an executive at Ford, the comments come from his boss. As Matt describes him, his boss is the "last of a dying breed," a man known in the office for his "truck driver mentality" who is given to frequent displays of prejudice against ethnic and racial groups. "He's the most overbearing person I've ever met in my life, a real pound-on-the-table-and-scream manager," says Matt. Indeed, during our interview, Matt's fear of his boss was almost palpable. To protect himself Matt declined even to give the man's name, insisting that we refer to him during the interview by a nickname. "Let's just call him Attila."

In other work environments, explicit antigay remarks are largely unknown. Whatever people think about homosexuality, no one actually *talks* about it. Perhaps there are no other (visibly) gay employees at work. Perhaps the subject has just never come up. If a man is new on the job, he may not yet be privy to conversations at the water cooler. Even if he has been with a company for many years, a man who assiduously avoids personal conversations may have established a climate that encourages others to do likewise. He ensures that conversations about personal and sexual matters will take place out of his earshot.

In these settings a man's assessment of his work environment may be based entirely on indirect evidence: the type of industry he is in, the ages or personal backgrounds of peers, perhaps the way they handle other kinds of unconventional behavior. "I know five or six men who are cheating on their wives or wives who are cheating on their husbands," says Derek, a senior vice president who sees this as evidence of a progressive sexual atmosphere at his firm. "I don't want to say we're *loose*, but people just do their own thing and feel free to discuss it." Brent, too, thinks that his boss is "very liberal when it comes to sexuality. She's divorced and has a boyfriend at the moment. I think the boyfriend was in the picture before the divorce happened. My perception of her is that she's very liberal and open about sex." When asked if this necessarily made her progay, Brent thought for a moment. "Her children are not mainstream children. They've been raised to make their own calls and make their own decisions. Her daughters didn't subscribe to a lot of the things women subscribe to as far as shaving their legs and underarms, that sort of thing. I just see her as very liberal and open. She's not hung up on what people think about her or care about her. She's not a person who gets embarrassed easily."

Others cite the ages, religious beliefs, or personal backgrounds of coworkers. Grey says that his company is "a very conservative, navy suit, white shirt, real estate developer." To him that portrait includes conservative sexual values. Dave says that the average age at his company is around forty-five. "It's a very old company, with a lot of southerners. They didn't even want to hire black people." Although homosexuality is never mentioned at work, Dave assumes that attitudes are negative. "I can't imagine any of the executives appreciating the fact that they have a gay employee. I'm sure AIDS would probably come up. I'm sure people would probably be worried that, 'Oh my god, he's a gay man.' Who knows what people would do?"

Mark saw evidence of homophobia in the type of work his company, a consulting firm headquartered in New York, was doing for its clients. The firm specializes in the design of compensation and benefits packages, and many of its clients had expressed concern about rising health care costs, especially those associated with AIDS. Several years ago a memo appeared in the firm's electronic mail system. "There was a flyer saying that the firm had put together an addendum of benefits-plan language to minimize costs for prescription drugs or disability or alternative treatment modes or home health care," Mark recalls. "There was a whole laundry list of ways to exclude AIDS. I mean, how much more blatant could you be?"

The type of work or the general reputation of an industry may also be a consideration. Tom, a high school teacher, feels that his profession is conservative by nature. As evidence he recites the familiar myths about gay people: that they "recruit" from the ranks of the young, that they are all pedophiles. He points to the periodic campaigns to remove gay teachers from the classroom—California's "Briggs Initiative" and Anita Bryant's "Save Our Children" campaign, to name two famous examples.[27] He recognizes that there is widespread anxiety about homosexuals who work with children. "In the position I'm in, with kids, you have to worry about it," Tom says. "We've had male teachers accused of molesting the little girls, so you hesitate even putting your arm around a little girl and giving her a hug. And, being gay, you have to be twice as careful because you have to watch out for little boys, too. In that respect being gay is a double-edged sword. So if a kid does something good, you think twice about giving him a hug and saying, 'You did a good job.' It could be misinterpreted." Tom doesn't think he's been the victim of discrimination and hears only an occasional homophobic comment at work (usually directed at the school librarian). Yet he is certain that explicit acknowledgement of his sexuality would be unwelcome.

In situations like these, when there is little concrete evidence of their coworkers' attitudes, gay men tend to play it safe. They hold on to beliefs formed in childhood, attitudes exhibited by family and friends. They import what are usually negative assumptions, formed earlier in life, into the workplace. Perhaps this is why Derek, who describes his own family background as "somewhat tense," remains so nervous around the other men and women at work. He claims to have experienced no job-related discrimination and considers his coworkers a reasonably tolerant group. His boss already knows that Derek is gay and at one point even told him that he's perfectly happy to have a gay man working for him. Even so, Derek is reluctant to lower his guard. "I'm starting to relax," he says, "and I'm going to get happy for the first time I can remember, and I'm not comfortable with that. You know, you're just too vulnerable. When you're most vulnerable, you don't *think* you are. I'm so comfortable now, that I keep thinking, 'You're on borrowed time, darling.' "

Derek's paranoia speaks to the pervasiveness of homophobia both in and out of the workplace. In a homophobic society there is a tendency simply to *presume* that a particular coworker, too, will be intolerant; without compelling evidence to the contrary, one treads lightly. "If I were going for a job interview, I probably wouldn't say, 'By the way, I'm gay,' because of the perception that it could result in my not getting the job," says Jim, a Philadelphia software engineer. "Remember, that's after *years* of having it beat into me that people will react negatively. I've never had a negative experience personally. Every single one has been positive. You could say that I should have learned by now. But I still have the perception that it's negative."

Sex at Work?

An obvious solution presents itself: Why not simply keep sexuality out of the workplace? If homosexuality offends or antagonizes one's coworkers, then why bring it to work?

This was apparently what Judith Martin had in mind when she scolded a correspondent to her "Miss Manners" column for bringing his "private life" to work. Professionals must learn not to confuse the two, she sniffed. "And now look what has happened. We are having a variety of unseemly public debates in which fitness for one's professional life—the very opposite of private life, requiring quite different abilities and attractions—is measured in terms of one's sexual conduct or sexual orientation." Her advice was to keep it out of the office. "If you open your personal life to debate, you cannot then become indignant because not everyone agrees with the way you conduct it."[28]

Gay men are often eager to accept this line of thinking, to believe that sexual and professional roles can be disentangled. A familiar refrain, heard from many, is the question: "What does being gay have to do with my career?" Michael, who runs a Philadelphia consulting firm, posed the question early in our interview. He spoke candidly about his job, his plans for the future, and how he felt about his boss and coworkers. But when asked how he managed his sexuality at work, Michael looked apologetic. "I guess I'm not the right person to answer that question. I keep them totally separate. I keep my private life private, and I don't let sexuality interfere with my work."

Not only is sexuality unrelated to work, the men say, but it also reveals little about them *as people*. Dan, the head of a psychiatric clinic in Houston, says, "Everyone on the staff knows who's gay and who's not. Some are more verbal about it than others. But it doesn't matter to anybody. They're people first, and sexual orientation comes second." Scott, a marketing representative with Blue Cross, says that, "My sexuality is secondary to who I am as a person and as a professional. It's really a separate issue." And Keith, a records clerk in a large Houston company, says, "If someone at work knows I'm gay, I'd like to think they can overlook that, that it's secondary to the person I am."

Sexuality is thus described as a superficial trait, one that can be detached from a man's personhood, one that fails to explain who he "really is." Beneath it lies a core "self" that is more essential and encompassing. A 1978 survey of English Department chairpersons found that gay respondents (who represented 21 percent of the total sample) often resisted the idea that sexual orientation was an important part of a man's identity.[29] When asked to describe their sexuality in a few words, gay respondents often chose generic labels like "unique" or "human." Some insisted that they "don't like to be identified" by sexual orientation at all, or that they were "fed up with crap like this." They saw sexual orientation as a trait to which one was "reduced," one that failed to represent them as complete, complex individuals. "I happen to be gay," says George, "but I'm a lot more than that. That just happens to be the card I was dealt. I'm not living because I'm gay, that's not my reason for *being*. That's not *who I am*." Eric, a bank officer in Delaware, agrees. "It doesn't change me as a person," he says. "What difference does it make whether I'm gay or not? I'm still *me*."

Yet for all their eagerness to detach sexuality from work and to distinguish the sexual (and superficial) from the personal (and essential), gay men find the task a difficult one. Personal and professional roles are firmly entwined, and the reason for this is largely beyond their control: Work is a social activity. In the first issue of the *Harvard Business Review*, Daniel Starch made the commonsense observation that "business consists of human reactions and relations because business is done by human beings, and in that broad sense business is psychological in nature."[30] To this it might be added that humans are also sexual creatures, that our social interactions are always colored by sexual possibilities, expectations, and constraints. We can't help but bring these capacities to work.

Indeed, offices are profoundly sexual places. Inside them sexuality is continuously on display, explicitly or implicitly part of the innumerable interpersonal exchanges that together constitute "work." Sexuality is alluded to in dress and self-presentation, in jokes and gossip, in looks and flirtations. It can also be found in secret affairs and dalliances, in fantasies, and in the range of coercive behaviors that we now call sexual harassment. Even when these more blatant manifestations are excluded, sexuality is part of every professional relationship.[31] No one seriously believes that secretaries spend much time on their bosses' knees or that many executives have really slept their way to the top. Actual sexual contact is the exception rather than the norm, and jokes aside, most work relationships are centered on the tasks at hand. Yet sexual possibilities affect the way professionals perceive themselves and others. Sexual assumptions and attractions can be found in the jokes they tell, the clothes they wear, and the courtesies they extend or deny one another. A sexual subtext is often the basis for such intangibles as rapport, familiarity, and "chemistry." It can generate intense feelings of loyalty and personal commitment. Professional relationships often have the contours of, and are experienced as being like, seductions.

Most jobs involve some degree of socializing, which leads to countless situations that involve sexuality in one way or another. Wives or girlfriends are routinely invited to company outings, to dinners with clients, or to informal stops at the local bar. Even more often, they turn up as subjects of conversation. Dan recalls the excitement a nurse stirred up at the clinic when she announced her plans to have a baby. Her efforts to become pregnant, even her ovulation status, became a regular feature of the office small talk. Another man recalls a formal lunch at which a female coworker described, to an enthusiastic audience, the experience of "breaking water" before she gave birth.

It is not uncommon for companies to have a "singles club," and it is virtually *de rigueur* for office dating games to be played on an informal basis; as single professionals know only too well, there is always an office busybody with an unmarried cousin, neighbor, or daughter. Todd recalls a recurrent situation involving one of his clients. "We have an office in Florida that I go down to a couple of times a year. The branch manager there is very, very friendly and a very, very nice guy, and he always asks me to come over to his house. And he just *assumes* that I will bring someone down with me. When I say, 'No, I'm by myself,' he says, 'Oh, you left your little lady at home?'—or whatever quaint thing he would say. I just nod. One time he and his wife took me and a woman friend to dinner. Things like that happen all the time."

In some cases overtly sexual contexts are a regular part of doing business. Bars, taverns, and strip joints are places in which important organizational information is exchanged and decisions made.[32] So are men's locker rooms. Traditionally male activities like fishing trips, sporting events, and fraternity parties become opportunities to do business. Though gay men are not necessarily unwelcome in any of these settings, they may find themselves unable (or unwilling) to take part in the sexual banter that often accompanies them. "There's a lot of male camaraderie involved in sex that you're not sharing," according to Roy, an executive at Time-Warner. "You're not making comments about the secretary, and there are lots of ways that you don't play the same game they're playing. Spouses and kids is a huge one." Other men recount jokes and anecdotes, office pranks, and "shared, meaningful glances" at women that are part of professional fellowship.

As a result sexual information is routinely used to make tacit judgments about a man's professional performance.[33] Much "work" is in fact the management of relationships, which means that workers are obliged to notice the social qualifications of their peers. "The decision to hire a lawyer is a chemical one," says Milton, a Washington attorney. "After you pass a certain level of competence, it's a chemical decision, and you tend to work with people with whom you feel most comfortable." Randy, a Wall Street broker, agrees. "Transaction after transaction, deal after deal, new idea after new idea, clients eventually say, 'Well, whenever Randy says something in a certain way, we know we can believe him.' Trust is a very important thing in our business."

Because our society reads such significance into sexual behavior, trust inevitably has a sexual dimension. "One of the things that comes up in any relationship that lasts is personal life," says Randy. "People want to talk to someone they have something in common with. They want to talk to someone who's forthcoming in many ways, including about his personal life. They introduce you to their wives, bring you into their lives, and they want to be brought into yours. It's a reciprocal thing. And if they feel they're giving of themselves, letting down their professional defenses, then you should too. It's only fair." Yet Randy has never discussed his sexuality with clients and doesn't always respond to their social overtures. "When you don't," he says, "you risk a little bit of their confidence in you. Outside of work, they may feel that you don't have that much in common, and they may prefer chatting and having conversations with someone else. Or, at worst, they'll just decide, 'I don't trust him.' "

A man's sexuality is thus unavoidably part of his "work." Because it plays a role in all work relationships, sexual identity becomes an informal part of the job description.[34] In a man's sexual biography, potential employers look for clues to his worldview. Judging it to be unusual or unacceptable, they may doubt that he's the right person for the job. When selecting successors or peers, they reflexively seek candidates who share their social characteristics, and this sort of "homosocial reproduction" tends to keep a certain type of person in power.[35] Some 86 percent of management jobs are never advertised through public channels but are filled by word of mouth, encouraging the evolution of restrictive hiring practices and exclusive information loops.[36] Family status becomes symbolic of other shared life experiences, encouraging male executives to hire "family men" who, like them, understand the pressures of feeding a wife and kids. Those who break the mold seem unfamiliar, enigmatic, and less likely to perceive situations in the same way. They cannot be trusted.

Tip learned this lesson the hard way when he began his surgical residency. He was shocked, at first, by the number of social events he was expected to attend as part of his "training." Several times each month, he was invited to a barbecue, a weekend excursion, or a formal dinner at the home of another surgeon. His boss, the chief of surgery, tried to arrange dates for him; he even told Tip to trim his sideburns so that he would look "more professional." "They wanted to know everything about my personal life," Tip explains, and "it was just part of being a team, part of the job."

Tip worries that by rejecting these overtures, he may have damaged his professional credibility. "When the general surgery resident asked me to his house for dinner, he said I had to bring a date. I said, 'Fine, then I won't go.' So I didn't, and now I don't feel like I fit in there. I've had numerous invitations from other good friends of mine. Fred, another resident, was a good friend and has asked me to his house so many times. Finally he quit asking, and then you drift apart socially. That was my choice, and I'm cognizant that that was going on. But I'm glad it's over."

Learning to Manage

Entering the workplace, a gay man faces a host of decisions. The head of personnel wants to know what kind of guy he is: How does he spend his time? What sort of skills and interests will he bring to the company? Will he get along with the others who work there? His officemates will invite him to the local tavern, to the baseball game, or to the Monday morning chat about their weekend conquests. As he climbs the corporate ladder, those above will want to know if he shares their values, if he faces the same demands from home and family, if he can be trusted. And from the guy next door, he'll hear all about a favorite niece or neighbor, a truly remarkable woman who just happens to be single. . . .

Given the heterosexism that pervades most workplaces, it's little wonder that a gay man often assumes a disguise—sheltering himself, as it were, in a vast and crowded corporate closet. He satisfies their curiosity with fabrications. He laughs at their jokes and listens attentively to their stories, trying to act like one of them. He demurs on social invitations. He cultivates a reputation as an eccentric, a liberal, or as an exceedingly private man. He permits them to assume, incorrectly, that he is a heterosexual. However he hides, we say that he is "in the closet."

The closet. At least since the Stonewall riots, the 1969 confrontation from which we chronicle the contemporary drive for lesbian and gay rights, the closet has been the principal metaphor by which gay men have thought and spoken about sexual identity. To be "in the closet" is to misrepresent one's sexuality to others, to encourage (or at least permit) them to draw a conclusion that one knows is false. A quarter century after the Stonewall riots, conversations about self-disclosure remain shackled to this binary metaphor, one that severely limits our understanding of what is at stake.

Some version of the metaphor infiltrates virtually all discourse on the subject. The shelves in gay bookstores are crowded with titles like *The Final Closet, The Vinyl Closet, The Celluloid Closet,* and *The Contested Closet,* to name but a few. Gay magazines bear such titles as *Out/Look, Outweek,* and *Out.* My own title, *The Corporate Closet,* was suggested by countless friends. Put two lesbians or gay men in a room, and you'll be likely to have a conversation about "coming out," the need to remain "closeted," or the ethics of "outing" gay celebrities.[37]

One encounters some rather baroque elaborations of the metaphor. Over the past two years, I heard about men who "banged into the coat hangers" while trying to pass as heterosexuals. Others, after years in the closet, have "locked the door and lost the key." A Houston executive says that he "came running out" at an early age and "left the dresses swinging in the breeze." Still another described his efforts at self-disclosure as if they were a plan for home improvement. "I was totally closeted in college, and I realized I had to have more space. It was cramped, and I just couldn't live in there. So I started adding a few windows, told a few of my closest frends. It didn't make the closet any bigger, but it gave me a better view."[38]

To be sure, the closet is often an apt way of thinking about the subject. Most closets are cramped and dark, spaces in which one can hide but in which no one wants to live. They conceal those articles that seem unfit for larger, more important rooms. While hiding in a closet, one is invisible to those outside it. Working in it, one has little room to move about.

But despite its apparent suitability, the "closet" actually misrepresents the ways gay men reveal and conceal themselves in social settings. A sexual identity encompasses far more than a man's sexual orientation, yet the closet implies that it is a simple, discrete bit of information (like eye color or height) that one could, with a single word or deed, *reveal.* It further depicts the construction of an identity as a choice between possible end states (in the closet, out of the closet), while ignoring the means by which a man arrives at either. Consequently, when we speak of someone who has "come out," we've said almost nothing about what actually took place. What did he reveal? An affinity for other men? For a particular sexual act? For a lover of many years? Closet language collapses these various disclosures into a single, undifferentiated act—an exit from the closet. As Marny Hall points out in her study of lesbian professionals, " 'Coming out' is not an end point in the strategy of adjustment. Rather, it is a conceptual short cut, an abbreviated way of thinking which fails to encompass the extremely complex process of managing discrediting information about oneself."[39]

At the same time the closet casts secrecy in passive terms (to disguise himself, a man simply "stays" in the closet), which fails to encompass the countless lies, conversational dodges, and petty deceptions such stasis actually requires. To stay in the closet, a man might fabricate girlfriends or sexual exploits. He might avoid all discussions of sexuality, insisting that others respect his privacy. Or he might complain about his status as a confirmed bachelor, as someone unlucky in love, as someone with an old war wound. Staying in the closet can be a bit like staying on a treadmill.

Closet language makes it impossible to talk about the way a man's sexuality is actually disguised or revealed in any of these situations. When asked if he had "come out" at work, Martin shrugged at the question. "I'm not sure how to respond," he began. "You'll have to tell me what you mean by 'come out.' I worry not only about who knows I'm gay, but how they know, what else they know, and how I have to behave as a result. Do I tell them I'm gay and then drop the subject, or do we make this part of our daily conversation? And what about my love life or about sex? Do we talk about that? The gay pride march I went to? My favorite gay author? Coming out is the beginning of the story." When asked the same question, a Boston executive was more blunt. "There are so many ways to be 'out.' Tell me what the term means, and I'll tell you if I fit the bill."[40]

What is needed is a rhetoric that hovers nearer the lived experiences of gay professionals, a vocabulary that allows us to describe their specific interpersonal maneuvers and countermaneuvers. By necessity gay men become adept at thinking about self-disclosure and learn, sometimes at great cost, that different sexual identities bring different social consequences. They become self-conscious. They learn to control and monitor outward appearances, to distort them when necessary. They learn to dodge. For many the result is a calculating, deliberate way of approaching social encounters. One can say, as I intend to, that they *manage* their sexual identities at work.

Unlike other stigmatized groups for whom identity management is a necessity, sexual minorities usually have the option of remaining invisible.[41] Because sexual orientation does not manifest itself on the body, there is no direct perceptual access to a defining "trait."[42] Unlike a man's gender, age, or race, it is not physiologically evident; unlike class or ethnicity, there are no learned behaviors to be disguised.[43] Lesbians and gay men are distinguished by a category of forbidden thoughts and deeds and, like political and religious outlaws, have no identifying marks or physical characteristics.[44] Even the personal mannerisms assumed to betoken homosexuality—effeminacy in men, mannishness in women—are unreliable signifiers. All of them can be managed. Milton made the obvious comparison to race. "Every white gay man and every white lesbian can at some point choose not to correct people when they say homophobic things, to cross their legs a little bit differently, to walk into a room differently, to be silent, to hide. As a person of color, I don't have that choice."

Instead sexual orientation is usually inferred from behaviors that do not themselves constitute sex. In employment situations, people communicate *about* sexual behaviors more often than they display them. We symbolize, represent, and talk about sexual orientation. We hear secondhand accounts of actual, intended, or desired sexual contact. We are introduced to girlfriends, boyfriends, and spouses and accept the sexual implications of these labels. We hear that a male coworker saw a new movie—the one about two straight people falling in love, the one featuring the sexy starlet, the one he attended with the single woman in accounting—and discern the multiple, entwined heterosexual scripts that were performed that evening. We also notice that a man has a firm handshake and an impressive knowledge of baseball trivia, and interpret these as signs that he is a masculine man, and thus a heterosexual as well. We make judgments about the sexual behavior of others, in other words, without having observed it.

For gay men, the resulting gap between psychic and social reality poses countless decisions—to display or not to display, to tell or not to tell, and in each case, to whom, how, when, and where—that become central to their navigation of the world. Gay lives and careers are characterized by a preoccupation with self-disclosure and skill in the management of sexual identity.[45] "Coming out" stories figure prominently in gay folkore, and there is an elaborate argot within gay communities for talking about self-disclosure and its consequences.[46] Few other decisions are a source of such intense, recurrent concern.[47]

Even when their coworkers seem sympathetic and supportive, even when they have the "perfect" work situation, gay men must manage their identities. Arthur, a New York attorney, says that his coworkers are largely "indifferent" to his sexuality. "That's part of the reason people like to live in New York," he says. "It's not that people are accepting, and say, 'Oh, there he is with his male lover. I embrace that. I support that.' They just don't *give* a damn, and that's different. I *love* their indifference. I would rather have their indifference than their soulful eyes."

Having recently made partner, Arthur has considerable job security and is well liked by the senior partners in his firm. Several have met his lover, Tim, and have been to their home for dinner. Arthur seems to have every reason to feel secure. Yet the indifference of his coworkers, however comforting, has *not* made him less self-conscious about his sexual identity. When spending time with clients or coworkers, he isn't always sure how to talk about "personal" subjects. When discussing his lover at work, he wonders what is appropriate, how much is enough. He still feels uncomfortable bringing Tim to company events.

For gay people the self-consciousness begins long before their careers and extends well beyond the workplace. Professional experiences often replicate situations that are familiar from relationships with family, neighbors, and friends. An office is not unlike a living room, playground, church, or supermarket. All are sites in which identity must be managed, and this strategic disposition, once learned, is not easily lost. As Martin explains, "When you've been set apart, held up for criticism or ridicule, and told you're illegal, unnatural, inappropriate, or immoral *because of this one trait,* your sexuality will never be irrelevant to the way you view yourself in social settings. It will always be somewhere in the foreground."

Sexuality becomes an overriding concern for these men, not because it is more essential to their lives than it is for others, but because heterosexism forces them to perceive it as an issue, a recurrent source of tension. The perpetual threat (if not the reality) of discrimination compels self-consciousness and wariness in those at risk; at all times even the slightest threat must be monitored. However a man defends himself—with deception and disguises, avoidance of the issue, or direct confrontation of homophobic peers—he has little choice but to monitor his behavior, to worry that he's made the wrong decision, and to wonder what its consequences will be. Managing his sexual identity becomes one of the central projects in his career.

Even so, employers often misunderstand the reasons lesbian and gay workers have begun to reveal themselves and to demand that their special concerns be recognized. When a man comes out at work, the reaction from others is often discomfort and bewilderment. They are puzzled that he would bother to raise the issue in the first place. They suspect that by speaking out he has only succeeded in making additional trouble for himself. Imagining a simple solution, they pose a familiar question: What does his sexuality have to do with work?

2

The Asexual Professional

IN 1980 IT WAS revealed that Mary Cunningham, then vice president of strategic planning at Joseph E. Seagram & Sons, was having an affair with the chairman of its parent company, William Agee. The result was an unprecedented flurry of speculation and criticism in the national press. Although she was an honors graduate of the Harvard Business School, Cunningham was portrayed as a sexual opportunist. She had won a string of promotions and raises since joining the company in 1979, and these were now subject to intense scrutiny. Why had she been promoted so quickly? Had she been rewarded for professional performance or for her extraprofessional dealings with her boss? Agee, meanwhile, was accused of behavior unbefitting a chief executive officer. The relationship with Cunningham wasn't the issue, according to his critics; the problem was the lapse in judgment it reflected. Dogged by these accusations, her credibility in question, Cunningham resigned.[1]

The Agee-Cunningham affair, like countless others that attract less attention, highlights one of our most cherished beliefs about the workplace: that it is, or at least should be, asexual. Whether it's a company, law office, hospital, or charity, an organization is usually described as a structure, as a hierarchy of abstract "slots" to be filled by generic, asexual "workers." Activity within is organized around getting something done—managing an activity, manufacturing a commodity, providing a service—and behavior not relating to that central endeavor is kept at the fringes. Sexuality, when acknowledged at all, is assigned one of several labels: It's a friendly social diversion, an imprudent distraction, or an unwanted (and in the case of harassment, illegal) intrusion. Whatever it is, it's not official business.

Indeed, the legitimacy of bureaucratic authority is grounded in its apparent asexuality. Bureaucratic principles emphasize formal chains of command and official channels through which power and influence are presumed to flow. Few circumstances invite more resentment or are more discrediting to a manager than the appearance that he or she acquired a position of power "unfairly"—that is, by establishing romantic or sexual ties to those above. "Even when decision-makers actually remain uninfluenced by personal loyalties, the appearance of impartiality that a bureaucracy must maintain to preserve its legitimacy can be threatened if intimate relationships are publicized."[2]

Because they appear to short-circuit formal lines of authority, relationships like the one that developed between Agee and Cunningham are seen as threats to the organization. Eleven years after the liaison was made public, Standley H. Hoch's resignation as president of the General Public Utilities Corporation suggests that the rules have changed very little. In the summer of 1991, word traveled through the company that Hoch was having an affair with Susan Schepman, the company's vice president of communications. The only difference this time was who paid the penalty: It was the senior officer, Hoch, who was forced to resign. As the *New York Times* noted in its headline to the story, "The Boss Who Plays Now Pays."[3]

The Asexual Imperative

Our most powerful metaphor for the workplace is the machine, a comparison that encourages us to judge organizations according to their efficiency, productivity, and the smoothness of their output. We imagine that work is a rational activity and that workplaces depend on order. Sexuality, in contrast, is perceived as a threat to all that is rational and ordered, the antithesis of organization. It is part of an animal nature—biologically or psychodynamically driven, irrational, innate—that exists prior to (and is at war with) civilization, society, and the forces that would repress or tame it.[4]

With their emphasis on the rational, goods-producing side of work, organizational theorists have traditionally ignored sexuality in the workplace.[5] As a topic of study, sex is largely neglected in textbooks and journals concerned with organizational theory.[6] Except when it can be commodified and made part of the output (as it is, for example, by models, entertainers, and others for whom physical appeal is explicitly part of the job),[7] sexuality has no place in traditional organizational theory.[8] In most cases this means that sexuality is viewed as an external threat to an organization, something that interferes with its primary purpose—something that must be regulated, prohibited, or otherwise held at the company gates. Our dominant ideologies and images of organization make sexuality an outsider.

Indeed, one can identify an array of policies and informal rules designed to eliminate "personal" considerations like sexuality from business. Most organizations have official or unofficial rules against nepotism, and some forbid fraternizing with clients. Managers are usually expected to absent themselves from decisions involving coworkers who are also friends, just as judges routinely disqualify themselves from trials involving people to whom they have personal ties. Employment statutes distinguish private and professional roles by prohibiting an interviewer from asking questions about an applicant's ancestry, national origin, marital status, parental status, birthplace, spouse, children, or other relatives. Implicit in these restrictions is the assumption that such matters have no impact on a candidate's ability to do the job; an employer presumably cares only about the "worker" who lies beneath the various "personal" characteristics on the surface. Even when violated, these rules establish an ideal type, an expectation about the proper way of doing business.[9]

When sex does appear, the informal policy in most organizations is to look the other way. A 1987 survey of thirty-seven
Fortune 500 companies found, for example, that only two had
formal policies on romantic relationships at work (though sixteen
had policies on nepotism).[10] When personnel managers were asked
how they handled relationships in the office, most replied that
they either "tried to overlook them" (36 percent) or "felt the
problem [would] resolve itself" (18 percent). Only two (6 percent) gave new employees any kind of orientation or instruction
on the matter of romantic involvements at work. Asked at what
point they would have "a sense of responsibility" for their subordinates' sexual behavior, the managers replied that they would
step in only when it "blatantly interfere[d] with their credibility
with other employees," "[became] a source of gossip so that others
might avoid the person," or "became offensive to others or disrupted the normal flow of business."[11] Likewise, when asked by
Business Week to describe his company's policy on in-house romance, a senior manager at Leo Burnett Co., an advertising
agency, explained that his company didn't have one: "As long as
the relationship doesn't affect our ability to get out ads, it is none
of our damn business."[12]

As a result sexual liaisons in the office are more often governed
by informal custom and taboo than by company policy. Explaining
the absence of a formal etiquette on sex between coworkers, for example, Letitia Baldrige advises in her *Complete Guide to Executive
Manners:* "There is no book of sexual manners in the office, because sex simply doesn't belong in the office. It exists, in lesser and
greater degrees, but the greater the degree becomes, the closer the
situation approaches disaster."[13] Indeed, when sexuality is acknowledged in employee manuals and hiring policies, it is usually to
guard the organization against it. Policies that prohibit nepotism,
fraternizing with clients, and immodest clothing all take the form
of organizational prophylaxis; office romances can be stopped before they start (an implicit purpose of most dress codes) or firmly
escorted outside company doors. When coworkers marry, for example, one of them is usually asked to leave.

Most often, however, sexuality goes unacknowledged until someone files a charge of sexual harassment, a matter on which most
companies now have an explicit policy.[14] The prescribed solution is
usually the same: The sexual offender is simply expelled from the
organization. Consequently, while some researchers have explored
the definition of what constitutes harassment,[15] most have attempted only to gauge the frequency and effect of particular ha-
rassing behaviors: "There is little systematic description of
non-harassing sexual behavior at work and few attempts to understand sexuality at work aside from determining whether some particular class of behavior is or is not harassment."[16] While useful for
policymakers and law enforcement officials, this approach scarcely
suggests the protean role sexuality plays at work.

Sexuality is thus seen as the transgression of asexual actors into
sexual territory, not as an inherent component of organizational
behavior.[17] The official, top-down view of a company classifies sexuality as an extraorganizational phenomenon. Formal and informal
policies acknowledge it only when it seems to trespass on company
grounds. When organizations do acknowledge sexuality, they define it narrowly, as a category of discrete "acts" (innuendos, affairs,
flirtations), not as a broad subtext to all organizational behavior
(sexual identities and sex-appropriate behaviors and assumptions).[18]
Indeed, if sexuality were rightly seen as an inherent component of
all human interaction—something constitutive of, rather than
threatening to, a professional relationship—formal policies on the
matter might serve very different ends. Rather than simplistic pro-
hibitions on sexuality, we might have an etiquette that sought to
shape and police it.

The resulting sex-work dichotomy means that when professionals step into their offices, they cross an important cultural boundary. They leave the private world and assume their public roles as
bankers and doctors, lawyers and teachers; sexuality stays behind in
the realm of pleasure and emotion. They imagine that sex and
work utilize different skills and satisfy different appetites. Each is
given its characteristic time slots (the workday versus evenings and
weekends) and its intended spaces (offices versus bedrooms).

Geographically, temporally, and ideologically, we keep them apart. Social space is partitioned accordingly, permitting us to distinguish professional and social friends, work and leisure clothing, official and unofficial business.[19] However it is expressed, the dichotomy implies that there is a public, work-producing, professional "self," one that can be shorn of its sexuality during office hours.

And that's how it *should* be, according to most professionals, both gay and straight. When asked to describe the role their sexuality plays at work, gay men often volunteer the conclusion that it is entirely fair and proper that the two be kept apart. In addition to formal policies that ignore or attempt to expel sexuality, they cite informal rules and normative beliefs that define sexuality as marginal, inappropriate organizational behavior. In office hallways one hears the familiar remarks: Sexuality is a private matter and doesn't belong in the office; it isn't relevant to the task at hand; people shouldn't be that intimate at work; it's impolite, a breach of office etiquette. Office decor is expected to be in "good taste," and off-color jokes are usually off limits. The cumulative message is loud and clear.[20]

Taken together these entwined beliefs about privacy, professionalism, and office etiquette comprise an "asexual imperative," a multilayered argument that sexuality doesn't belong in the workplace at all. Gay men did not invent the imperative; on the contrary, their defense of conventional notions about privacy and professionalism merely echoes the values of the larger culture, which have a long and tangled history.[21] But if they did not invent the imperative, they make special and insistent use of it. Like their straight peers, they often believe that sexuality has no place at work; unlike them, however, they use the imperative to protect themselves, to rationalize their own visibility. Recognizing the penalites they might pay for being openly gay at work—fearing they cannot be candid about their sexuality—they embrace the idea that they should not be, that it would be unprofessional, rude, disruptive, or tacky. The asexual imperative, although voiced by gay and straight professionals alike, is therefore most meaningful to those whose sexuality has been a source of stigma.

"My sex life is private"

Without thinking, we often use the terms *sex* and *private life* interchangeably.[22] When asked if they've come out at work, for example, gay men often answer in euphemisms: "My boss doesn't know about my private life," or, "I haven't told her about my personal situation." Steve, an accountant with a Houston firm, remembers his dismay when a coworker moved into the same apartment complex. "He used the stairwell that runs right up to my front door," Steve recalls. "So I had to be careful. I kept my personal life—my personal life didn't come to my apartment. I went out for my personal life." Because romantic encounters were now arranged off site, Steve felt that his "personal life" no longer took place at home.

Offices, by contrast, are defined as public places, and the result is a familiar syllogism: Sexuality is private; offices are public; therefore sexuality doesn't belong in the office. When asked why he was reluctant to tell coworkers about his lover, Martin invoked the same binary logic: "Sex belongs in the bedroom, not the boardroom." Brent, a Houston manager in his late twenties, attributes the same thinking to his employer: "I think management would probably look at my coming out as a conflict of interests, in other words, that I'm bringing my personal life to work and I shouldn't be." Brent expects to be promoted within the next few years, provided "my life isn't becoming a problem with the job I'm doing."

Sexual secrecy can thus be justified as a matter of boundary maintenance, as gay men try to keep private behavior in its proper domain. In a 1992 survey by *Out/Look,* 36 percent of lesbians and gay men cited the "desire for privacy" as a reason they have remained secretive with one or more coworkers.[23] "There are lines you don't cross, says Carter, a sales representative with Hilton Hotels. "Personal matters, private matters, just don't belong in the office. You have to be aware of those boundaries." Glen, the general counsel at a large Houston company, agrees. "I need to have balance, he says. "I don't need to be socializing more with the people I work with. Likewise, I don't particularly need for my parents to know more of the details of my private life than they already know. It's *mine*. Privacy has a function, it seems to me. I've got an equilibrium that I'm comfortable with." Glen's "private life" is thus posed as something distinct from (and opposed to) his work, something that can be balanced against the counterweight of work. As he explains it, one must seek "equilibrium."

Sometimes it may be an influential boss or coworker who draws the boundaries. Jeff is one of three analysts in a small Philadelphia investment firm. Though he considers his coworkers liberal and open minded, he is reluctant to talk about sexuality at work. I don't think they'd have any problem with it," he says. "I think about telling my boss sometimes. I'm just not sure what the reason would be. I know his attitude is that he really keeps his private life private. He doesn't talk much about his wife and kids. I'd be bringing my private life into the office, to a degree." In keeping his sexuality a secret, Jeff feels he's merely taking his cue from his boss. "We all keep our social lives pretty separate," Jeff says.

With this conceptual framework in place, even the most elaborate efforts to mislead coworkers can be justified in the interest of privacy. Louis, a lawyer in his mid-forties, recalls his first few years at one of Boston's most prestigious firms. With a growing client base and considerable expertise in tax law, Louis was considered one of the firm's rising stars. Other associates found him easy to work with, and in a few years he was considered a likely candidate for partner. The word in the hallways was that Louis was going places.

There were others, however, who considered him something of an enigma. He rarely attended office social events, and although invitations were often extended, no one at the firm had met his wife and family. She never called him at work. One Christmas Louis had invited several of the partners to a holiday party for which a lavish meal had been prepared, but even then his wife had been unexpectedly called away and was unable to meet the guests. An otherwise friendly, sociable man, Louis avoided conversations about his home life and would sometimes protest that he "wanted to keep private matters private" or that it was "unprofessional" to bring family concerns to work. When a secretary asked where Louis and his wife would be spending a summer vacation, he replied, half jokingly, that it was a secret.

His notion of privacy seems somewhat strict until one learns—as the partners ultimately did, after Louis made partner—that the wife in question was actually a man, a lover of many years who had been carefully kept out of sight, disguised in countless conversations, and excluded from office gatherings and parties. Louis's wedding ring was a family heirloom, and the photographs on his desk were of a college girlfriend long since married to someone else. At the mysterious dinner party, Louis's lover had dutifully prepared the meal and hidden in the garage until the guests were gone. While the other attorneys were surprised by the news, Louis says that they understood his reasons for doing what he did. The scheme had been an attempt, Louis explains, "to set up some boundaries and mark off a little space for my private life."

"I don't want to be that intimate with coworkers"

Most of us learn early on to associate sexuality with intimacy.[24] Sex, we are taught, is to be shared by those who are emotionally or conjugally attached; sex between strangers, even when morally condoned, is considered an indulgence, a substitute for the real thing. The same can be said about conversations on the subject. We are usually reluctant to discuss our sexual lives with strangers and are encouraged to reserve the topic for chats with lovers, close friends, or therapists of one sort or another.[25]

As a result explicit sexual conversations often serve as milestones in the development of an intimate friendship. By withholding information about our sexuality, we place limits on the growth of a relationship. Terry, a Houston attorney, feels that being secretive about his sexuality has made him "a bit colder than I might otherwise be at work." Tony, who works for a Philadelphia financial services firm, is also somewhat distant at work. "Coming out might make us closer," he says. "It might open up the opportunity for us to become close friends. In fact, I might be blocking it." The converse is also true. By coming out at work, men invite coworkers to treat them as intimates, sometimes without intending to. Sean, who works for a large public relations firm in New York, remembers coming out to his secretary. "Suddenly she assumed she knew me really well, that we were really close friends, just because she knew that I was gay."

Professional asexuality is often justified on precisely these grounds. Gay men imagine that relationships with coworkers are categorically different from friendships. A "strictly professional" relationship encompasses only the work at hand, which means that when confidences are exchanged, they should be of a business nature. "It's not as if I have a personal friendship with most of these people," says Randy. "I've socialized once with three or four of them, but we're not close friends." Work relationships that grow more intimate, as many do, are said to have "crossed over" from one category to another. As Charles, a travel agent in Virginia, explains: "After a while, somebody's not your coworker, they're your friend—someone who's stepped over the boundary from coworker to friend. They have a new definition in your life."

To keep their distance, some men avoid all mention of sexuality at work. "I just don't think it's proper behavior in the office," says Roland, an art director for a small Manhattan advertising agency. "I don't come here to socialize with everybody. I work with these people, and if I like them, fine. And if we get along, great. But I'm not going to do it on a regular basis." Many fear that if the lines are blurred, if professional relationships become too intimate, they won't be able to do their jobs. "I have too many other things on my mind during the course of the day," says Arthur, who insists: "It isn't appropriate to get that involved in other people's personal lives." Dan warns: "There's the potential for it to get too loose, too comfortable, too friendly," when coworkers are open with one another. "It's real nice to have that comfortable feeling, he says, "but you can't cross the line. People start personalizing and not being objective."

Often they fear that their judgment will be compromised by intimate knowledge of a coworker's life. Glen refers to office friendships as a form of "modified nepotism." Brent avoids even casual lunches with coworkers. "I just think you have a better workplace if people keep their private lives to themselves," he says. "If they bring too much of it to the office, if I know too much about a person's social life, it's going to influence my decisions on merit increases or disciplinary actions, that sort of thing. Specifically, if I know that someone has gone through a divorce, and it's an unpleasant divorce and there are children involved, I'm going to be more sympathetic in my treatment of that person. And that really shouldn't impact what goes on in the office. You leave that outside the door at 8 A.M." Les, the business manager of a technical high school in Pennsylvania, lives by the same rule. "There's an old adage," he says. "You never dip your pen in the company inkwell. There must have been half a dozen times in my life when I wanted to. But I'm always glad that I didn't, because eventually I'd have to fire someone, or there'd be some static or something."

"Professionalism" is the term often invoked in defense of these boundaries. In the survey of *Out/Look* readers, 15 percent of lesbian and gay respondents said they would consider it "unprofessional" to come out at work.[26] Dan insists that the gay men on his staff be discreet about their sexuality in the presence of clients, and last year threatened to fire a male therapist who came to work wearing an earring, attire that Dan considered "unprofessional." When asked if female therapists were allowed to wear earrings in the clinic, Dan confessed that there was a double standard. The problem wasn't the earring per se but the message it might send to patients. "On a man an earring will arouse suspicion that he's gay, and that poses a problem from a professional point of view," according to Dan. "A mental health professional has to be a blank screen, so that a client can project whatever they have on you. If you disclose something inappropriate about yourself, that makes the process less clean and effective than it could be. I try to maintain the professional atmosphere you need in this society." Patrick's boss has a similar rule. Herself a lesbian, she heads a small staff of personnel trainers, including Patrick, at a large teaching hospital in Washington. "She thinks that trainers should be anonymous," Patrick says. "It would be inappropriate to come out at work, because that draws attention to yourself." Brent agrees. "It could become dangerously unprofessional around here if people found out that I'm gay," he says.

Chip, who manages the information systems in a Houston company, received a harsh lesson in professionalism. Several years ago, he confronted a former coworker when she made a negative remark about gay people and AIDS. In the ensuing argument, Chip revealed that he is gay. Although he thought the disagreement had ended amicably, he received notice several days later that he had been fired. The official explanation: "unprofessional behavior."

"My sexuality isn't relevant to work"

Like arguments about privacy and intimacy, the relevance argument is grounded in the notion that "work" and "sexuality" are distinct classes of activity. It assumes that the separation of spheres is natural and normal, that the boundary between them should be breached only when there is a compelling reason. "I don't think that personal knowledge about one's sexuality is necessary for working relationships," says George, a senior airline executive, and "if there's no reason to bring it up, then why go to all the trouble?" Roland offers a similar explanation. "I'm not one of those people to go around advertising my sexuality because I don't think it's necessary. What's necessary is what I do for a living, and the job is not who I sleep with or who I date."

Typical of this view is an emphasis on the job itself and the insistence that all other matters, including sexuality, are of secondary importance. When asked if coworkers know that he is gay, Les assured me that it makes no difference. "I do my job. I'm competent. I treat them fairly. My sexuality is irrelevant." Matt, an executive at Ford, says that his boss "doesn't care if people come to work in their fucking pajamas, as long as they do the job." Jerry, a securities trader, is even more adamant. "On Wall Street, a place of work, it really isn't a place to discuss sexuality. With your friends, on non-work time, it's perfectly fine to discuss sexuality. And if your friends happen to be coworkers, when you're not on work time, if you want to discuss sexuality, that's fine. But in a business setting there really isn't any reason to gossip." "You want to be judged on your accomplishments," says Grey, the public relations director for a Houston mall, "not on your relationships."[27]

In saying that sex has nothing to do with work, these men imagine that asexuality is a man's natural, initial state of being. Asexuality is his status by default, the role he assumes passively. Until he indicates otherwise, he simply *remains* asexual. Jason, a senior executive at Johnson & Johnson, remembers speaking to a friend at a meeting of the gay physicians' group in Philadelphia. The woman asked if Jason thought she should tell a potential employer, a local hospital, that she is a lesbian. "I told her that if somebody came into my office with that information, applying for a job in our organization, I would wonder, 'Why are you telling me this?' I would question their judgment. People don't come in and tell me they're heterosexual or bisexual or homosexual. That's not a part of the employment interview." Implicit in Jason's advice is the notion that workers are asexual—not heterosexual, bisexual, or homosexual—until they affirm otherwise. In a working environment, he says, such affirmations are a sign of poor judgment.

If sexuality is indeed irrelevant to work, then "coming out" can be made to appear trivial, even laughable. Milton says that "if someone ever said to me 'Are you gay?' my immediate response would be, 'Well, why on earth are you asking me?' " Jim imagined this scenario: "I've thought about it a couple of times—actually coming out at work—but I don't see how it's relevant. I don't need to go round saying, 'I'm gay, I'm gay,' and write a memo to everyone saying, 'Oh, by the way, I'm gay.' It doesn't seem like it's really important." Others described equally unlikely situations. "Unless you're a prostitute or a porn actor," asks Martin, "what does your sexuality have to do with work?"

Joel, who runs his own consulting firm in Washington, says that the same applies to most of his friendships. "Sometimes people need to know everything about you to be your friend, but I don't feel that that's the basis for friendship. My friends are not Republicans, or Lutherans, or rich people, or gay people. They're *all* people. I have lots of minorities, straights, non-Lutherans as friends. So it won't enhance our relationship for them to know that I'm gay." Only under unusual circumstances, Joel says, does he reveal his sexuality to any but close friends. As an example he describes an encounter that took place several years ago. A member of a local church organization, Joel frequently hosts dinners for students from Georgetown, American, and other universities in the

Washington area. "They come in and have dinner here and social-ize," he explains. After one of these dinners, one student in particu-lar seemed eager to talk. "He said to me, as he discussed his life, that he was gay. He wanted to talk to me. He was a graduate stu-dent, and he taught Bible studies. And as I listened to him, my sense was that he needed a gay friend. He was really reaching out for help."

For Joel this at last was ample "reason" to reveal himself. "So I told him that I was also gay and invited him to go with me to get a broader range of experience in gay life in Washington." Joel admits that he rarely finds himself in situations like this, but says that "when there's a need, I'm happy to address my sexuality. But if there's no need, I'm not prepared to take the risk."

"It's rude to talk about sex"

It can also be objected that sexual disclosures constitute a breach in office etiquette, that they are rude or tacky. Talking about sex, gay or otherwise, is potentially offensive, intrusive, or rude. Coworkers may find the subject distasteful, and their sensitivities must be taken into account.

Gay men are aware that sexual topics are often unwelcome, that coworkers may be upset by even the intimation of sex. "I put a joke on the messaging system once," says Chip. "The question was, 'What has a thousand teeth and eats weenies?' The answer is 'a zip-per.' One of the guys called me and said he didn't think that was appropriate, because women were on the system." Arthur feels that "lawyerly etiquette" prohibits such jokes at his firm. "I think lawyers have it easier than any other profession," he says. "It's just not an inquisitive profession. We're paid to ask questions, and when it comes to our intramural relations, we just don't. It would be unseemly for me to ask another single associate—I might ask what he did over the weekend, and he'd say, 'I saw *Postcards from the Edge*.' But it would be unseemly to say, 'Well, did you go with a girl with big tits, and did you, you know, *do it?* "

Conversations about homosexuality, in particular, are off limits. "I always find them—because of my southern background—to be a bit crass," explains Chris, an arts management consultant in New York. "You know, as southerners we don't talk about things like that. We just do them." Dave, likewise, is certain that his secretary knows his secret. "But she would *never* bring it up. She knows that it would make me uncomfortable, so she wouldn't do it. She would consider it inappropriate."

The list of examples could go on. The asexual imperative is a central, pervasive feature of professional culture, and some version of it was reported by all of the men to whom we spoke. It was defended in different ways, sometimes as a matter of privacy, productivity, or professionalism, sometimes as plain "good manners."

However it is articulated, asexuality becomes the model against which professionals judge their own behavior, a norm they observe even in the breach. The particular arguments made on its behalf differ in certain respects but are joined at the base in the shared assumption that "work" (and its corollaries "organization," "professional," and so forth) and "sexuality" (or "personal life") are inherently distinct.

Marginalizing Sex

But what happens when sexuality *does* find its way through the office door? How do professionals respond to behavior, at work, that they *do* interpret as being sexual?

One need not look far to find countless work situations that involve sexuality in one way or another. As we've already seen, sexuality suffuses the workplace. At the personal, social, and symbolic levels of organizational life, one invariably finds sexual attractions and impulses, roles and appearances, flirtations and jokes, expectations and assumptions. They range from sexual feelings, fantasies, and innuendos right through to sexual relationships, sexual acts, violations, and harassment.

On a day-to-day basis, few of these activities are categorized as sex. When they are, however, the asexual imperative supplies the conceptual framework with which we label, evaluate, and make sense of them. The imperative ensures, in particular, that while we may sometimes acknowledge sexuality in work settings, we never see it as an inherent component of work. We recognize that sexual and professional activities may at times overlap—temporarily, accidentally, illegally—but believe that we can nonetheless tell them apart, disentangling them when necessary. Indeed, even in work environments that are overtly and explicitly sexual, the imperative encourages us to see sex as the perpetual visitor, external to the true life and purpose of the organization. As workers, we signal one another that sex is (or should be) marginal to work.

One tactic is to trivialize sexual displays. We devalue work environments in which physical attractiveness is emphasized and are reluctant to assign "professional" status to those whose jobs require them to be physically attractive. Recent efforts to "professionalize" some jobs, for example by turning "stewardesses" into "flight attendants" or "secretaries" into "office managers," are often little more than campaigns to desexualize them.[28] Professional women, especially, find it insulting to be told that their appearance is part of the job. Because we imagine a distinction between "real work" and sex appeal, such compliments are seen as a trivialization of their professional skills.[29] Workers who do acknowledge their use of sexuality are usually deemed nonprofessional or are criticized for being unprofessional.

We frame sexual discussions as jokes or distractions and use special labels to distinguish sexuality from the flow of "real" work. When sex is the subject of conversation, we are trading "gossip" or "just kidding around." "We joke about it, you know," according to Ralph, an executive with an oil and gas exploration company in Houston. "We'll say, 'So, did you get any sex this weekend?' Or, 'I'm gonna go out and get some sex this weekend.' I'll ask Perry, this guy at work, when's the last time he and his girlfriend Jackie had sex. You know, we joke about that a lot."

Sometimes the discussion is accompanied by a disclaimer, a protestation of surprise that denotes its forbidden status. "It's *amazing* what people will tell you if you ask them," says Peter, a Philadelphia realtor who claims to know "a lot" about the private lives of his coworkers. Matt adds, "I'm always *astounded* that people

will engage in that sort of locker-room talk" about their sexual conquests. Others confess a sort of guilty pleasure in talking about sex
while at work. "It's terrible," Peter says, "but we shock each other
by saying outrageous things, just to pass the time when the market
is slow." Scott, who works for Blue Cross in Philadelphia, agrees.
"You'd be amazed—or maybe you wouldn't—at what people will
ask after they've had a couple of beers or a couple of drinks. And
how forward people will get!"

When work environments are especially matter-of-fact about
sexuality, they are usually described as being "unusual" in this respect. George feels that his company is unique because most of its
senior executives are Scandinavian. "People talk about sex in
Scandinavia like they talk about going to the store. They just don't
have the hangups we have in America. It took some getting used
to." Others say they don't appreciate the sexual candor. Burt, a
paralegal for a large Philadelphia firm, has no patience for the
"constant heterosexual jokes" he hears at work. "As I'm taking
notes, my boss will say things like, 'Did you see the piece of ass on
that chick?' To me that's just gross. There's no place for that kind
of talk in the office." Whether they are deemed amusing or offensive, trivial or inappropriate, sexual conversations are thus seen as a
sort of lived exception to the asexual imperative. They are considered surprising or shocking, an indulgence or a distraction. By labeling sex in these ways, professionals signify its tenuous status in
the organization.

Professionals also tend to limit their discussion of sex to those
below or beside them in the hierarchy. Like other discrediting or
"unprofessional" behavior, sex talk travels downward along the
chain of command. Of the men we interviewed, only one felt that
he could discuss sexual matters openly with his superior. "With
people below you in the hierarchy, no problem," Burt adds, to clar-
ify his earlier comment. "You can joke and have a good time, you
can do whatever you want. But there are lines of demarcation
about what you say to people above you." The result is a tendency
to save one's sexual puns or confidences for those who are less powerful, those who share one's status, or those who are discredited.
Steve shares a series of "secret nicknames" with the other junior ac-

countants in his Houston firm (like 'The FF Look," for the "fresh-fucked look"). Grey regularly "cruises" the aisles of the mall during his lunch hour, usually with the women in his secretarial pool.

Some men even suggest that sexual conversations are typical of a category of person, usually those of lower status within the organization. "My boss is a professional, and my colleagues are somewhat professional," according to Brent. "Everyone else is clerical, so it's a different kind of person. They tend to be busybodies, discussing people's personal—you know, gossiping and that sort of thing, not as serious about their work." Like most men, Brent says that sex talk isn't something a rising executive should indulge in.

The formal hierarchy is further supplemented in most organizations by a gender hierarchy, which makes it easier for gay men to confide in women than in other men. Gay professionals sometimes accumulate a coterie of female subordinates (nurses, secretaries, and so forth) with whom they share their secrets. Tip has this sort of relationship with the support staff at his hospital. Though he avoids sexual topics with his various supervisors, Tip is close to several of the female nurses. "Because of the intensity of the emergency room and operating room, you bond with everyone," he explains. "The nurses that I run into know that I'm gay—I seek them out. I go down there when I have nothing to do and visit. We chat and discuss relationships."

In short, sexual banter is considered a trivial activity and is generally reserved for trivial people. Professionals feel they are being casual or frivolous when talking about sex, and are reluctant to take this tone with those who are more senior. "A lot of flirting goes on at our office," says Darren, whose clinic employs a number of young, female dental hygienists. "As you can imagine, there are so many young women in our office, and I'm the only unmarried man there. So you have a lot of women between twenty and thirty, and flirting with me is a big part of their lives."

The asexual imperative further compels professionals to marginalize sexuality, to grant it the sort of limited access one accords any visitor: only to certain physical areas and at certain times, usually when "normal" office activities have been temporarily suspended (during lunches, breaks, travel, or special events). Overtly sexual behaviors are thus confined to the temporal and spatial margins of "work," permitted only in personal spaces or during specks of personal time.

In the most obvious sense, personal time commences when the workday ends, during the transition from business hours to social or leisure time. The restraint that coworkers show during the day dissolves over drinks or dinner, and after-work outings often raise sexual or romantic possibilities (for many gay men, a compelling reason to avoid them). "If you want to talk about sex, you should talk about it after work or some other time," says Roland. "If a coworker said to me, 'Can we go out after work and talk about X, Y or Z?', I'd say 'Sure.' " Jerry makes the same distinction. "With your friends, on nonwork time, it's perfectly fine to discuss sexuality. It's also fine if your friends happen to be coworkers, when you're not on work time."

Blocks of personal time or space can also be snatched at other times during the day, provided official duties have been temporarily suspended. Sometimes, a verbal cue signals the transition. Martin remembers feeling a "pang of fear" when his boss at Ogilvy & Mather suggested that they "have a friendly chat." "I knew that meant he wanted to talk about personal stuff, which made me uncomfortable." Other men chuckle at the tendency of their coworkers to whisper when talking about personal matters, as if they were sharing a dirty secret. "They don't say, 'She works in respiratory therapy and she happens to be gay,' " according to Patrick. "It's more like [he whispers and points], 'She's gay.' " Verbal ("Let's get back to work") or nonverbal cues (withdrawing eye contact, shuffling papers) can signal the end of a personal moment.

At other times the transition is spatial. Coworkers may seek the refuge of a private office or call one another "aside" in the hallways before trafficking in sexual information. Men's restrooms become "personal space," in which the usual restrictions on sex talk are suspended. Business travel occupies a hazy gray area, bringing coworkers together in settings (hotels, airports) that mingle the personal and the professional. Company picnics, dinners, and outings are in fact designed for this purpose, to encourage social relationships between those who might otherwise know each other only on a limited, professional basis. As any corporate caterer knows, nothing kills a company party more quickly than the decision to hold it on company grounds. Perhaps because the spatial location (work space) is at odds with its temporal location (after work) and purpose (nonwork), the frequent result is ambiguity about appropriate social behavior and a lousy time for all. The move from company space signals a transition to personal time.

When coworkers encounter one another unexpectely in such settings, the boundaries can become fuzzy. Martin ran into his secretary at a gay disco, and was distressed the following Monday when she complimented him on "the shirt I was wearing on Saturday night." Though no one else overhead their exchange, he felt she had "intruded" on his social life. Arthur remembers running into Robert, one of the firm's paralegals, at a concert. "I've known for a long time that Robert is gay," says Arthur. "You know, I see him sitting on the Long Island Railroad, getting off at the right stops, that kind of stuff. He's seen me with all-male groups; I've seen him with all-male groups, having dinner or going to the movies. We never really talked about it. Then I went to a performance of the Gay Men's Chorus, and there he was, singing baritone. At first I was afraid to congratulate him on a wonderful concert, but then I realized that that's a very public sort of thing, to get up there on stage. I mean, Carnegie Hall, that's pretty public. And so I told him I enjoyed the concert, and since then we've been friendly."

The distinction between personal and company time is further eroded in those exceptional institutions that establish no such boundaries. Most organizations permit some segregation of professional and personal lives, however vague or shifting the boundary.[30] It is a different matter, however, when the "total" quality of an organization precludes such distinctions. "My boss has this view of officers as representatives, twenty-four hours per day, of the company," says Jeff. As evidence of this he cites a story he heard about the director of human resources, a man named Greg, shortly after he joined the company. "I've never asked Greg whether this is true or not, but somebody told me that the president of the company told Greg that he didn't want him seen coming out of the all-male theater, the Tom Cat bookstore. Apparently Greg had been seen going in there a couple of times."

Tip complains that he has no personal time. As a surgical resident he is accustomed to long hours and frequent nights on call. Even when not at the hospital, he is at the beck and call of the hospital—practically and symbolically affirmed by the pager he wears. "My boss doesn't like you to take vacations," he says, "even though it's allowed. He feels you're wasting your time. If you come in with a tan, he'll give you grief about the fact that you weren't at home reading." Other organizations, like churches and the military, argue that their members are always on the job, that one simply *is* a soldier or priest.[31] In dismissing thousands of lesbian and gay men, the military has argued that their sexual behavior falls within its broad jurisdiction, even when it takes place off site and after hours.

But such organizations are unusual. In most cases the question is not if but *where* the boundary between the public and private shall be placed. The asexual imperative, having insisted that such a divide is possible, ensures that work and sex will be on opposite sides of it. The imperative is neither unconditional nor universally imposed (or self-imposed); indeed, it varies in strength from one setting to the next, even within the same organization. Yet virtually all gay men articulate it—and quite often defend it—in one form or another.

It is easy to see why the asexual imperative might appeal to gay men. Describing it, they are sometimes emotional, often passionate. They adopt a tone of voice reserved for sensitive subjects, and it is clear that they have used these same words before. In their comments one often hears what appear to be contradictions, as they articulate their wishes (the hortatory "Sexuality *shouldn't* matter") in the form of observations or statements of fact (the declarative "Sexuality *doesn't* matter"). Yet the repeated insistence—that sexuality *doesn't* matter, *doesn't* belong in the workplace, *is* a private matter—scarcely conceals the men's recognition that it is not always so.

The asexual imperative insists that workers be judged on the quality of their work, that professional interactions be stripped of their sexual component. For men whose sexuality has been stigmatized, criminalized, medicalized, morally condemned, and subjected to interpersonal penalties of all sorts, this is a powerful idea. Seen in this way, the invocation of the imperative is an appeal for fairness; it demands that "work" be defined narrowly, that it not be confused with the social or sexual characteristics of the individual doing it. "It's not a perfect world," says Terry. "Sexuality should have no impact on the people you work with, on clients, or on business development and all of that." But Terry knows that this isn't the case. "I know some people in town who have that situation, but there are damn few."

The imperative is appealing for another reason. By demanding that workers be asexual, it permits gay men to rationalize the painful efforts they sometimes make to misrepresent themselves at work. As they worry about the necessity of misleading coworkers, as they speak to them of imaginary lovers or take pains to disguise actual ones, they often believe that they are acting on principle. Strict beliefs about privacy and professionalism are comforting; they supply a justification, other than self-protection, for sexual secrecy. "Even if coming out were easier, if you weren't worried about losing your job or something, I don't think I would do it," says Glen. "Even if gay people were in the majority, I would want a certain amount of privacy. I don't think I'd want everyone at work to know my business." But beneath his statement of principle lies another motive. "It would be nice," he adds, "to have the choice."

3

The Sexual Double Standard

As HIS SIXTY-FIRST birthday approaches, Jason is understandably proud of his long marriage, grown children, and impressive career in medicine. In 1980, after twenty-five years as a pediatrician, he took a desk job at Johnson & Johnson and quickly soared into the ranks of senior management. Last year he took over the development of several important new products, a promotion that brought with it a substantial raise. When he retires in a few years, he and his wife plan to open a small bed-and-breakfast in Maine. He isn't sure what changes the move will force on his relationship with Richard, his lover of many years.

Jason speaks highly of his employer, a company that he says "really lives up to its reputation as the 'guy in the white hat.' Given the company's history, public image, and product lines, there is a heavy emphasis here on family activities." Jason often takes his wife to company events, and coworkers regularly ask about his children. Some even seek his advice on marital problems. "This guy named Tom used to report to me," he recalls, "and he loves to talk. Tom would come in and tell me all about his marriage, his parents, his father's death, his friends. It's almost as if I'm part of the family."

The company also provides a number of services for its employees, from on-site day care to seminars on stress management and the care of aging parents. An upcoming seminar on AIDS includes videos featuring C. Everett Koop. Past programs have dealt with sexism and sexually transmitted diseases. "In the employee benefits program there's always family stuff coming up," Jason says. "When we have big company parties, it's not just 'employee day' or 'employee recognition day'—it's *family day.*' Bring the kids, bring the grandparents, we're going to have a big family party."

Yet when asked what role his sexuality plays at work, Jason insists that private and professional matters be kept apart. "It's a raised consciousness kind of company," he says, "one in which sexuality really has no place." Jason reserves the term "sexual" for explicit, forbidden acts—those that take place outside the institution of marriage. His own identity as a married heterosexual is described as a social status, as a configuration of responsibilities involving children, property, and vacation plans. When talking about gay coworkers (and his own relationship with Richard), Jason uses the terms "sexual" and "private life." Describing those who are married, he speaks of "family." As a result, Jason sees no inconsistency in bringing his wife to company events while insisting that his sexuality "isn't an issue" at work. "I couldn't care less who my coworkers are sleeping with, when, where, or why. That's none of my business."

How do we explain the curious double standard in Jason's thinking? He describes a company suffused with sexuality, even as he insists that it is irrelevant to his work. In private conversations with coworkers, in official company policies and programs, in social events that include spouses, even in his ability to thrive in a culture that he describes as "family-oriented," Jason trades on his identity as a married heterosexual. Yet it is only his homosexual behavior—behavior that he insists is private, nonprofessional, irrelevant, and worth keeing a secret—that receives a "sexual" label.

(Hetero)sexual Presumption

Heterosexuality is taken for granted in most work situations. The "model professional" brings to mind a heterosexual (male), an ideal that turns gay men (and women) into exceptions or deviations.[1] Homosexuality disrupts the expected pattern, which means that unless he provides evidence to the contrary, a professional man is usually presumed to be heterosexual.[2]

The presumption is most evident in the routine questions people ask about marital or romantic status. Sooner or later, all professional men are asked if they are, or plan to be, married. "I'm the only one in the department that's still single," says Tip. "Out of the whole group, they're all married, every single one of them. That was clear the first day I got here four years ago. There was a barbecue the day before the internships began. Everyone showed up with their wives. The question to me wasn't, 'Are you married?' but 'Where's your wife?' I got that like six times. And I was thinking, Goddamn. Where is she? Where's *who?* I don't have a wife."

In fact questions about marital status are a matter of course in professional circles, part of the accepted get-acquaintanced ritual. "We had this discussion at work on marriage and how I don't believe in it," says Steve. "Michelle, one of the other accountants, says, 'The right girl hasn't come around yet.' And I'm thinking to myself, 'Okay, fine, you know, whatever. Marriage is not for Steve.'" Tony remembers a similar conversation. "The senior VP is such a character," he says. "The second day I was at the company, I ran into him coming from the parking lot after lunch, and he said, 'Well, Tony, are you married or are you single?' I said, 'I'm single.' And he looked at me with a smile, and said, 'Give these women a year, and you'll be married.' When I told him that I didn't think so, he just said, 'I wouldn't doubt their tenacity.'"

Even when coworkers are not overtly homophobic, they may be blind to the possibility that a man is gay. "Most attorneys, male attorneys especially, they're real nice guys, but they just would never *think* of it," says Al, a Philadelphia attorney. "It's just not something that would have entered their heads even if you never mentioned girlfriends, blah, blah, blah. They just don't think about things like that." Al says that he makes no attempt to mislead his coworkers, most of whom know that he lives with another man. "I even talk like I have a spouse," he says. Yet no one seems to know that he is gay. "It doesn't mean that they're opposed or homophobic or anything," he says. "It just never would have entered their heads that I'm gay."

The presumption is at times so strong that even in the face of conflicting evidence, coworkers continue to assume that their peers are heterosexual. Justin, a college professor in the Washington area, was certain that his students "at least suspected" the truth about him. Several years ago he received a grant from the Centers for Disease Control to study AIDS-prevention behaviors among gay men. At the outset Justin assumed that his involvement with the project might encourage rumors about his own sexuality. "I thought it was pretty clear," he says. "The grant was CDC-sponsored, and it was announced that awards were given to community-based organizations. This one was given to a local gay organization. It seemed to me that my situation would be pretty clear." But a few months later, when he ran into a former student in a gay bar, Justin learned otherwise. "He was just shocked; he was really, really surprised. After he got over that, after I ran into him a couple more times, we chatted a little bit. He said it just didn't cross his mind that I was gay, even though we were working on this survey about gays. He said, 'I assumed that since you had so much experience, this was just another consulting job you happened to get. And since it was such a big project, anybody would grab at it.' That surprised me. I thought it was more obvious."

Russ, a claims negotiator with a Philadelphia insurance company, found that his coworkers were equally oblivious. One evening he took his boyfriend, Ed, to a baseball game with several clients. "I have a car, but Ed always drives it, so we went to the stadium in my car. I handed Ed the keys. My client kind of lifted his eyebrows at that. Someone said, 'Wait, I thought this was your car,' and I said, 'Well, yes it is, but he's driving.'" Russ realized later that his clients have no idea who Ed is. "Spouses communicate in a certain way. It's very intimate. Even if it's not physically intimate, maybe it's the way they glance at each other. But since these lawyers aren't in the mind-set to perceive that these are two gay men going to the baseball game, they may not have picked it up. I doubt that they did." As another man joked, "For some people, I would have to show a videotape of my boyfriend and me engaged in sex before it would occur to them, 'Hey, this guy just might be gay.' "

The presumption of heterosexuality is thrown into further relief by those rare instances in which it is reversed. Harry, the director of development for an AIDS service organization, says that "probably 80 percent of the men in the office are gay." Disclosure is no longer an issue for the gay employees, he says. It's now the scattered heterosexuals who find themselves the exceptions. "When someone straight joins the organization," Harry laughs, "they have to come out, or everyone will just assume they're gay." A year earlier one of the men produced a wife at a company function, and his "disclosure" came as a complete surprise to many.

The circumstances are rare, however, in which one must "come out" as a heterosexual. With few exceptions it is homosexuality that must be actively disclosed; it is a status one moves *to,* never a starting point. We signify that it is unexpected even in the way we talk about it. Gay men don't conform to our model of "the professional," so we employ special linguistic tags to identify them. We speak of the gay accountant, the lesbian engineer, the homosexual teacher.[3] Patrick worries that "people at the hospital see me as the gay trainer, as opposed to the trainer who happens to be gay." Chris imagines the following newspaper headline: "Chris Jones, President of Jones Consulting Group, *Gay.*"[4]

The presumption ultimately becomes self-confirming. Expecting their peers to be heterosexual, professionals see nothing else. Conflicting evidence is simply ignored or overlooked. Blinders on, they remain unaware of the sexual diversity that surrounds them, diversity that might if noticed shatter their assumptions. "People imagine that they work in these exclusively straight, heterosexual clubs," says Martin. "That's what they expect, so when they look around, that's what they see."

If homosexuality is invisible because it is unexpected (and often disguised), heterosexuality is invisible for precisely the opposite reason: because it is so ubiquitous, so public, so deeply embedded in social behavior. Indeed, it is a paradoxical habit of perception that we often fail to notice that which has become most familiar.[5]

Because heterosexuality is implicit so many social rituals, it becomes the Great Unsaid of our sexual culture, continuously displayed though rarely named.[6] Heterosexuality becomes part of the furniture, encoded in everything from our modes of dress (wedding rings) and terms of address ("Mrs." to designate a married woman) to our most deeply held beliefs about masculinity and work ("You have to be tough to survive in this business"). Because displays of it are so common, and in most cases confirm what we already take for granted, we are only tacitly aware of their symbolic content. They merely corroborate the expected.

Consequently the veneer of asexuality is itself built on masculine, heterosexual principles. "The abstract, bodiless worker, who occupies the abstract, gender-netural job, has no sexuality, no emotions, and does not procreate," is in fact a deeply sexualized figure.[7] Male sexual imagery, language, and speech patterns pervade most organizations, as do military and sports metaphors that serve to legitimate a certain model of professional competence. In our notions of "rationality" and "efficiency," one can identify traditional masculine ideals of control, competition and the suppression of emotion. Even our belief that "jobs" are distinct from those who do them is a masculine construction, the myth of those who have traditionally been masters of their material circumstances.[8] Yet in work environments that until recently have been populated largely by (ostensibly) heterosexual men, these sexual underpinnings are largely invisible.[9] Masculinity and heterosexuality are relational phenomena, defined in contrast to other phenomena, and are difficult to see when only the masculine and heterosexual are present.[10]

As a result masculine, heterosexual values and behaviors have been cloaked. They are perceived as belonging to categories other than sexuality and thus remain invisible *as sexuality*. As Barbara Gutek has observed, "Sexual pursuits and conquests, jokes and innuendos can be subsumed under the stereotype of the organizational man—goal-oriented, rational, competitive and assertive, which are expected and recognized as male traits. Men may make sexual overtures in an assertive, competitive manner. Likewise, sexual jokes, metaphors and innuendos may be seen as part of competitive male horseplay. Thus the traits of competitiveness, assertiveness and power-orientation are noticed, whereas the sexual component is not."[11]

Nowhere are heterosexual values more deeply embedded than in what may be our single most conspicuous social institution: the family. In work settings the family is on display in countless social rituals and symbolic objects, in company imagery and rhetoric, and in interpersonal exchanges that involve spouses and children. Indeed, assumptions about family life are inescapable in most work settings. One of George's company's programs requires the trainers to share personal stories about their "families" with new trainees. "In the seminar the trainer has to tell stories about his family, but the stories are all made up. The trainees don't know it, but all of the trainers talk about the same 'Marvin' and 'Eliot' and 'Shirley.' They use them as examples during the sessions." The training program thus incorporates a rather quaint, limited notion of what constitutes a family, one that its trainers are forced to uphold. For some of the men, George included, this poses a problem. "The gay guys are expected to go back to their bases and teach this stuff. I have to stand up and talk about my wife, 'Shirley,' and my son, 'Eliot.' "

Yet few would say that this constitutes a sexual display. When a man speaks of his wife in a professional setting, others interpret this as a statement about his social role (as husband), not his sexual performance (as heterosexual). Their interest is centered on the history or length of the marriage, the wife's occupation or personality, or the couple's children. Because marriage is a legal as well as a religious institution, others think of the relationship in terms of kinship or social status, not sex.[12] Homosexuals have no corresponding public institutions; they are denied the legal and social recognition accorded heterosexual marriages. As a result family imagery and values become an ostensibly "asexual" means of advertising one's heterosexuality, one's membership in the sexual elite. Consider Jason once more. When speaking about gay coworkers (and his own male lover), Jason uses the terms "sexual" and "private life." But when describing his married coworkers, he speaks of "family."

Alternatives to the traditional family are thus exoticized as "exceptions" or trivialized as "choices," "preferences" and "life-styles." Jeff knows a wealth of details about his boss, Jack. He knows where Jack's kids attend school, their ages, even the fact that the youngest daughter is dyslexic. He remembers where Jack's wife spent her last three vacations. "It's all very superficial stuff," Jeff says. Yet for three years Jeff has carefully avoided revealing anything about his weekend plans, the bars or clubs that he frequents, even the fact that he is single. "That would be bringing my personal life-style into the office," he says. Arthur remembers using the same words when he came out to a man in his firm, a senior partner whom he describes as "part mentor, part Dutch uncle." While the two were eating dinner, the partner noted that "there are things you and I never talk about." Arthur knew what he was referring to. "I was sort of looking down at my veal parmigiana thinking, 'Are we gonna have that conversation now?' And I thought, 'Fuck it, why not? It's exactly the time we ought to have it.' So I just looked up and said, 'Are you talking about personal inclinations and social-life choices here?' He said yes, and then he got sort of pink." Arthur's relationship with Tim, his lover of many years, is thus reduced to a "personal inclination."

The resulting double standard compels the sexual silence of some while condoning the ceaseless displays of others. Heterosexual assumptions and attractions become part of a man's job, even as official ideologies render him asexual. "Work" and "sex" appear to be separated, even as they suffuse one another. Traditionally masculine principles (rationality, competitiveness) masquerade in gender-neutral garb. Heterosexual institutions (the family) appear asexual. For men like Jason, the result is the inability to see their coworkers' marriages, spouses, and children in sexual terms. They see them as social roles, as personal arrangements or obligations, as family matters. In work environments it is their alternatives that receive a sexual label.[13]

It has been said that nothing is sexual, but naming it makes it so. Thus, to determine if a gesture or word is "sexual," one must turn from the behavior itself to the beholder, to the one who assigns the categories and attaches the labels.[14] A warm, inviting smile may be sexual (in the context, say, of flirtation). But can the same be said when it takes place during a medical examination? During a graduation ceremony? During an act of violence? The distinctions lie not in the smile itself but in the different meanings we assign it.

The labeling is done by those with the cultural authority to do so, of course, and their means of constructing the category itself reveal much about the sexual behaviors they wish to regulate, stigmatize, and prohibit. The virtually unchallenged authority of heterosexuality ensures that its numerous manifestations have vanished into a vast background of expected, ostensibly asexual behavior. Thus we claim to categorically forbid "sex" during work, reserving the term for those behaviors we find repugnant.

(Homo)sexual Outlaws

Only when one enumerates all the possibilities does it become clear how narrowly white-collar culture has defined what constitutes acceptable sex. Male homosexuality is only one of many stigmatized alternatives. Indeed, most of the options on the heterosexual menu, including such common practices as extramarital affairs and sex with prostitutes, are deemed unfit for public mention. Promiscuous heterosexuals find that they must be discreet if they are to maintain respectability at work. Bisexuals are encouraged to reveal considerably less than the whole truth about their sexual interests. And a self-identified pedophile would almost certainly find himself unwelcome in most office settings.

Although it may be small comfort to lesbians and gay men, they have not cornered the market on forbidden sex.[15] On the contrary, they are but one of several constituencies who find themselves devalued and stigmatized in the workplace. There are in fact several levels to our system of sexual castes. As Gayle Rubin has argued:

> Modern Western societies appraise sex acts according to a hierarchical system of sexual value. Marital, reproductive heterosexuals are alone at the top of the erotic pyramid. Clamoring below are unmarried monogamous heterosexuals in couples, followed by most other heterosexuals. Solitary sex floats ambiguously. . . . Stable, long-term lesbian and gay male couples are verging on respectabil-

ity, but bar dykes and promiscuous gay men are hovering just above the groups at the very bottom of the pyramid. The most despised sexual castes currently include transsexuals, transvestites, fetishists, sadomasochists, sex workers such as prostitutes and porn models, and the lowliest of all, those whose eroticism transgresses generational boundaries.[16]

Men whose behavior stands high in this erotic "pyramid" are granted visibility, social acceptability, and the labels "natural" and "normal." Those at the bottom are regarded with scorn.

The derision is only encouraged by the fact that sexual outlaws are numerically in the minority. Even if *all* gay men were visible, they would remain relatively uncommon in most work settings; under present circumstances their apparent number is dramatically reduced by the many who remain in hiding. The resulting proportions ensure that gay men, when visible, grab a disproportionate share of the group's attention. Like the lone black in a crowd of whites or the token woman in a roomful of men, an openly gay man is an anomaly in the vast majority of professional settings. The apparent scarcity of other gay men (coupled with the forbidden nature of his sexuality), ensures that he will stand out. Others respond accordingly. To coworkers, a gay employee is often a novelty. The men and women in his office may be unaccustomed to having a gay person around. They worry that they do not know how to talk about him, think about him, or work with him. He captures a high "awareness share" simply by being different.[17]

Having revealed himself, a gay man is thrust into the spotlight. Even routine activities are now noticed, remembered, and scrutinized by others. ("Did you hear the joke he told in front of the clients?" "Did you see the tie he was wearing?" "Why do you suppose the boss took him to lunch?") The situation is familiar to anyone whose gender, race, or background has placed them in the minority; the "few" will always stand out against the background of the "many." But with sexual minorities the spotlight has an especially unsettling consequence: the mere revelation that a man is gay will often be seen as an attempt to "flaunt" or "promote" homosexuality. Certainly no one accuses black or Asian professionals of "flaunting" their racial background when they make no attempt to disguise it. Nor do we assume that female executives are "making a statement" when they are identifiable as such. Our belief in professional asexuality virtually guarantees, however, that *any* evidence of homosexuality will seem like too much. Its relative scarcity—and frequent invisibility—ensure that even the slightest hint of it will overwhelm.

Even the most subtle disclosure can provoke the objection that a gay man is "making an issue" of his sexuality. Wary of this accusation, gay men are often vague and restrained in their comings out. "I've left room for people to think I'm gay, but I'm not open," says Dave. "I really don't want to come out and *say it*. I feel like I've struck a good balance." Kirk, a Philadelphia obstetrician, was similarly evasive when applying for internships at several hospitals. "I certainly didn't say 'girlfriend' or 'she' during the interviews," he says. "I said 'significant other' or 'partner,' and if they picked up on it, they picked up on it. I wouldn't have been coy about it, had they actually asked me. I just felt uncomfortable bringing it up in an interview with people I was meeting for the first time."

Even men who are openly gay feel they must be discreet. "The biggest problem for me is realizing that there's a difference between accepting my sexuality and flaunting it," says Jack, the VP of human resources at a Washington publishing company. Jack came out to his coworkers in 1978, and although he is generally comfortable talking about the subject, he remains guarded. "I make some people uncomfortable by alluding to my sexuality unnecessarily, and I have to be careful about that," he says. When talking about his lover, for example, Jack tries to strike a balance. "For years, I put up with the frustration of having my male drinking buddies talk openly about what was going on sexually with them. By God, now that I'm open, I'm going to discuss my life as openly as they discuss theirs! I don't see any reason that I shouldn't. But I have to stop short of deliberately rubbing people's noses in my sexuality when I don't have to and when it can make them uncomfortable. It's not an easy line to walk." Striking a balance, for others, means avoiding self-disclosure altogether. Terry says he is reluctant to come out because he doesn't want to make his sexuality "a cause" or "wear it as a badge." "I don't choose to let it be the dominant issue in my life," he says.

Some men distinguish "knowing about" from actually seeing evidence of gay sexuality. "It's fine if you're gay," says Mitch, a New York estates attorney, "but I don't know that anybody would be pleased if I brought my lover to the firm's dinner dance. As long as it doesn't interfere on a day-to-day basis, or make them feel uncomfortable, it's fine. But it would create problems if I suddenly started wearing ACT-UP pins." Harry says that his former boss was reasonably tolerant of his sexuality until he encountered him one night on the street, while taking a walk with his lover, Alan. "Alan was somewhat of a femme," Harry says, "and that bothered my boss quite a bit. I mean, I think that's when he probably *saw* it for the first time. It's one thing to know about it, but I think a lot of straight people have problems with it when it goes beyond a certain point. There's a threshold, I think." Milton tries to stay within that threshold by downplaying his involvement with a local AIDS clinic. Though the other partners in his firm know about his community work, Milton discreetly removes articles about the clinic from the file of press clippings that circulates throughout the firm. "On some level it gets to be too much," he says. "Beyond a point it's best neither to confirm nor deny."

Overvisibility is implicit even in the figurative language of self-disclosure. When they speak of coming out, gay professionals worry that they are "making an issue of it," "shouting it from the rooftops," "flaunting it," or "letting the whole world know." They liken disclosure to "wearing a badge" or "carrying a sign." Others talk about not wanting to "volunteer it" or "blurt it out," as if their sexuality were an interruption, beside the point.[18] Sean drew this comparison: "There was a political cartoon in Canada, when one of the members of Parliament declared his homosexuality in the Calgary newspaper. There was a picture of him coming through customs, standing on this little box, holding up a sign that said, 'I'm a homosexual,' and another sign, 'I'm gay, hooray!' And the caption read, one customs inspector talking to another, 'I only asked him if he had anything to declare.' I always think of that cartoon, because I don't stand up on a box and declare my homosexuality. But it's not something that I push under the carpet either."

Gay men also attract a particular kind of attention. Because it is sexuality that distinguishes a gay man from his heterosexual peers, it is his sexuality that attracts their notice. In homogeneous groups sexual orientation rarely becomes an issue. When only heterosexuals are present, there is little need to explicitly acknowledge the trait that everyone has in common; it is simply understood. The presence of even one gay man changes all this. Now the group's attention is drawn to the subject of sexuality. It seems to divide them, to define distinct subgroups whose differences are now exaggerated and polarized. Heterosexuals who might never have thought of themselves as a group become self-conscious about their alikeness, sensitive to what it is that sets them apart from the homosexual token. Whatever differences do in fact exist between the groups, they now eclipse those traits that both have in common.[19]

The so-called "contrast effect" is especially powerful in the case of sexuality. As Jeffrey Weeks has argued, "the deeply rooted injunctions against homosexual sex have had the effect, especially amongst gay men, of focusing attention upon the act of sex itself."[20] Prevailing stereotypes about gay men (that they are hypersexual, promiscuous, indiscriminate) further emphasize the sexual aspects of their lives.[21] The result is a tendency to hypersexualize gay men, to allow their sexuality to eclipse all else about them, even to see sexual motives or intentions where there are none.[22] As Marny Hall observes in her study of lesbian professionals: "An obvious and intense flirtation between two heterosexual colleagues may not elicit actual censure until the two are discovered *in flagrante delicto* in the staff lounge. In contrast, the person known to be homosexual must do nothing in particular in order to be perceived in terms of excessive eroticism."[23]

The resulting double standard ensures that an identical disclosure made by two men—one gay, the other straight—will be interpreted in radically different ways. If both acknowledge having a "spouse," for example, one disclosure will be viewed as evidence of the man's affections, his future plans, his family, his marital status, and his good character. The other will conjure an image of tangled and twisted sheets and will be viewed as a lurid and inappropriate statement about his erotic life. Men and women who would passionately deny that a marriage license is a sexual contract (for the exclusive use of a spouse's genitals), or that baby pictures are pornographic (as evidence of specific ejaculatory practices), nonetheless scrutinize gay relationships in precisely this way.[24]

Gay professionals have quite often internalized this reductionist logic. Like their heterosexual peers, they often make only vague distinctions between homosexual orientation, identity, fantasy, and practice.[25] Statements about a man's sexual orientation, about who he *is,* are misread as statements about what he *does* during actual sexual encounters. The resulting logical trap often ensnares gay men as they make decisions about self-disclosure. Burt has worked for years with a woman named Judy and came out to her shortly after they both joined the company. But when Judy shared Burt's secret with another woman in the office, he was furious. "She can get a little too open about my sexual preference at times when she should not—I mean, I don't talk about her yeast problems, okay?" Glen says the same thing about his straight peers. "I don't particularly need for people to know the details of my private life. I'm not sure that somebody who's dating women or is in a marriage and has sexual problems should discuss all those details with his colleagues either." In the first example Burt equates his sexual orientation with a vaginal infection. In the second Glen's sexual orientation is compared not to another man's marriage—presumably a sign of *his* orientation—but to "all those details" of his sexual dysfunction. Terry explains that "being gay is not something I wear on my sleeve. When I was straight I didn't run around the office talking about what woman I'd slept with last night. Now I don't go in the office and talk about what man I slept with."

Barry faced precisely this dilemma when he decided to come out at his firm. "I didn't know exactly how to do it," he says. "You know, one of the partners doesn't come in and sit down and pick his coffee up and say, 'By the way, I like my wife to get on top.'" Barry's solution, ultimately, was to be indirect. "There was a guy in the tax department who I was very friendly with, and he had the biggest mouth, *the biggest mouth.* So I took him home and introduced him to my then-lover, and I knew the next day it would be all around the firm. So that's the way I handled that." Fearing that the other lawyers would accuse him of "talking about sex," Barry engineered a disclosure that was as unobtrusive and generic as possible.

White-collar culture thus observes a veiled but far-reaching double standard, one both imposed on and propagated by gay professionals.

A series of absurd and unjust situations result. When asked how much he really knows about his coworkers' lives, Glen replies: "I know that they all belong to country clubs, play a little golf on the weekends, take the wife to dinner, take nice vacations, and have cute and smart kids and send them to all the right schools, and that's really as much of their private lives as I want to know." But when the question was turned around—How much do they know about *you?*—Glen admits that they know nothing about his lover of many years. They don't even know that he is gay. "They think I live alone," he says, "and I don't think they would take it much further than that." Steve finds himself in a similar situation. "I don't think I'd be fired, and I don't think I'd be harassed if I came out at work," he explains. "I think my bosses would probably call me in and the two of them would say, 'It doesn't matter, we all keep our personal lives out of the office.'" But as Steve thinks about it, he recognizes that this isn't quite true. "When Dana is dating someone that works two offices down, and Jay is dating Tamara and someone else is dating an auditor—I mean, aaaaaaargh!—people are bringing their personal lives into the office whether they like it or not. It's 'The Love Connection' around here."

Whether they recognize the double standard or not, gay men often live by it. They believe that their sexuality is a private activity, one that should rightly be excluded from public spaces, even as heterosexual coworkers wear wedding rings, display baby pictures, and parade wives and girlfriends at company functions. They protest that self-disclosure will invite unwanted intimacy, yet watch office friendships develop all around them, and see promotions and perks go to better-liked peers. They argue that sexual orientation isn't relevant to their work but seem to know, or presume to know, the orientation of every heterosexual in the place. They feel it would be unprofessional to disclose their sexuality but are surrounded by professional men and women who make little effort to disguise their heterosexuality. And they sense that office etiquette forbids personal disclosures, even as they fabricate romantic lives and relationships that can be disclosed.

Our cultural authorities defend the same double standard in the name of propriety, privacy, and good manners. Etiquette doyenne Judith Martin once received the following question from a reader. "Dear Miss Manners: How should I handle people who ask if certain of my friends are gay?" Her suggested reply—"I have no idea. I wouldn't dream of asking them anything so extremely private"— comes from a woman who has written entire books outlining the polite and proper ways to hold a wedding, raise a child, and inquire about a friend's divorce.[26]

It is here that the real function of the imperative becomes apparent. By concealing different standards for heterosexuals and homosexuals, the imperative has the general effect of delegitimizing sexual self-disclosure for gay men.[27] Our prevailing image of the "professional" is of a rational (male) individual who keeps his emotions in check and his personal matters out of the office (unless special circumstances warrant otherwise).[28] Sexual banter is deemed unbefitting such a person—it is something professional people do only in their spare time, but which "spare" people do on professional time. Even the most casual or subtle disclosures are thus made to seem overt and unnecessary; they must be reconciled with beliefs about privacy, intimacy, and professionalism that seem to forbid them. Some special justification is always required before a man reveals that he is gay, one that would never precede the mention of his birthplace, taste in wine, astrological sign, or marriage.

As a result, a gay man's effort to appear asexual is in fact something quite different: an attempt to assimilate, to leave the presumption of heterosexuality intact. The double standard ensures that bringing a female date to an office party is organizationally expected behavior; bringing a male date is not. Either companion might constitute a "statement" about a man's sexuality, but only the former can be justified as an attempt to appear asexual, to keep private matters private, to be professional, or to be polite. Gay men's efforts to *de*sexualize are in fact efforts to *hetero*sexualize.

It seems curious that the double standard would be embraced by the men it penalizes; when they defend conventional definitions of privacy and professionalism, gay men support the very ideologies that compel their invisibility. Yet there can be little doubt that these ideologies owe much of their power to the acquiesence of gay men. In social scientific language, the term used to describe this sort of arrangement is *hegemony,* a system of oppression that maintains itself with the consent of the oppressed.[29] As historians and political theorists have observed, force is a relatively inefficient way for one group to control another. From the perspective of those in power, it is more efficient to engineer the consent of those ruled by supplying beliefs and definitions of the situation that justify the imbalance. They can be given interpretations, even justifications, for the contradictions they confront daily, in particular for the fact that one group constitutes the powerful and another the powerless.[30] By enabling the oppressed to believe that their status is normal and natural, a hegemonic system reproduces itself. Invisibility is the ultimate measure of its success.

The hegemony of heterosexuality ensures that when they defend conventional beliefs about privacy and professionalism, gay men perceive them not as opinions or values but as "common sense" or "normal reality." The sexual inequities with which they live are experienced simply as "the way things are." Heterosexual hegemony persists because, knowingly or not, in countless subtle ways, we all consent to it. Though few Americans live in heterosexual marriages that are truly fidelitous, virtually all join the public celebration of the ideal of monogamy.[31] Few men look like Schwarzenegger or Stallone, but many collaborate in sustaining these men as models of masculinity.[32] By accepting conventional beliefs about privacy, office etiquette, and professional behavior, gay professionals support the very ideologies that confine them to the lower levels of the erotic pyramid.

Heterosexual hegemony also fuels their sense of impoverishment. Under the circumstances, gay men cannot but feel that their lives are shameful, unworthy of public display, something that should be kept out of view. To reveal that one is gay is to talk about "who you're sleeping with"—nothing more—while heterosexuality is expanded to encompass friendship, love, and family. Phil, a senior consultant in New York, says that he wouldn't want to work in an all-gay environment. "I don't like to be in a ghetto situation," he explains. "I'm really not that kind of person." When asked if he would work for an all-gay company, Jim didn't think so either. "I like having straight coworkers. It helps me feel part of the human race, which I might kind of lose contact with if I were in a totally gay environment."

In an article in *Out/Look,* Michael Denneny supplied this anecdote. "A couple of weeks ago, I watched an almost classic liberal, Bill Moyers, on his television show ask August Wilson, 'Don't you ever get tired of writing about the 'black experience?' A question of such breathtaking stupidity that even Wilson paused. Would Moyers ask John Updike whether he gets tired of writing about the white experience? Would he ask Dostoevsky if he ever gets tired of writing about the Russian experience?" As Denneny goes on to point out, Moyers's question contains a remarkably chauvinistic assumption—namely that somebody else's life is of smaller consequence, capable of more limited expression. "The implication is that 'the black experience' is somehow limited, is something one could get tired of, is not inexhaustible the way life is. After all, one can't quite imagine even Moyers asking, 'Don't you ever get tired of writing about the human experience?' I mean, what else is there to write about?"[33]

Professional culture invites gay men to believe that the "professional experience" is a uniquely heterosexual one, that the "office" is a heterosexual space. At different levels and in different ways, they are aware of this double standard. But quite often their will to challenge it is sapped by the belief, deep down, that sexuality really doesn't belong in the workplace. They have largely bought the conventional wisdom that a man must be a consummate professional, that like his straight peers, he must be "asexual" at work. Attempts to say otherwise invite the criticism that he is being unprofessional, that he is embarrassing or provoking others, or that he is "making an issue" out of something that shouldn't be one. Shamed into silence, gay professionals help sustain the source of their shame—the very system that renders them powerless.

4

Playing It Straight

THE FIRST TIME Ed fell in love, it was with a woman he met during his freshman year at UCLA. "I was introduced to Patty in the library, and we spent almost every night together for the next two weeks," he recalls. "It was very passionate." By Ed's twentieth birthday, he and Patty were living together in Los Angeles, planning to marry when Ed graduated in the spring. Ed took an entry-level sales job with IBM, and a few weeks later they announced a date for the wedding.

In March of that year, Ed met a young man at a party, and the two began to correspond. Before long they were in love. The man urged Ed to be cautious, but certain details slipped his mind. "Like a fool I left this card on my dresser, and Patty found it," Ed recalls. "It was very incriminating. It sounded like we did all these things and we really hadn't." A period of estrangement followed, during which Patty decided to relocate to San Diego. A few weeks later, Ed's boyfriend sent him another card, this time informing him that their relationship was over. "And so within the same month, the two great romances of my life ended," says Ed, with a laugh. "At the time I thought I would never recover."

Eighteen years later Ed shares a house with a lesbian friend in Santa Monica. "Karen and I bought the place about ten years ago, partially because it made sense for tax reasons, but partially because we both needed to maintain appearances. We figured that 'living in sin' was a better appearance than 'single and available,' so we started looking at real estate." In many ways, Ed points out, "we're like a traditional couple. We mow the yard, shop for groceries, and fight over the chores." Ed manages a regional sales office at IBM and is "happily involved" with a man who lives nearby. Karen is an attorney with the city of Los Angeles. At work their arrangement provides the perfect cover. "Because I live with a woman," he says, "people don't even suspect."

Ed's reputation is further safeguarded by his behavior in the office. Ed hobnobs with the women at work, complimenting them on their hair and clothing. He is quick with a suggestive remark. On business trips he frequently entertains female clients, a habit that has earned him a reputation as the office "superstud." "I never give my coworkers any concrete indication that I fool around on my trips," he explains. "It's just that I'm a very friendly person. I like women, and I'm very close to the females I work with. I probably go overboard sometimes. I treat them nicely, and I think they like that. A lot of people think I'm womanizing."

His reputation notwithstanding, Ed worries that he will be exposed. He goes to great lengths to keep his various social worlds apart, to ensure that coworkers know only a few details about his relationship with Karen and even less about his relationships with gay men. He fears that some day he will misplace another incriminating letter or phone number. "It produces a lot of stress," Ed says. "You're always trying to keep the two apart—you know, I'm straight here, I'm gay here—so that they don't come together and get mixed up somehow. You've always got to be on top of things so you don't screw up."

Ed also worries that the stress has physical consequences. Asked to explain, he lifts his shirt to reveal a long red scar. "Well, I've lost twenty-four pounds since June," he begins. "I was thin to begin with; I mean, I'm not a heavy person. I have a lot of headaches. I've had severe ulcers. I've had half my stomach removed due to ulcers that were definitely a result of being gay and straight all at the same time. It definitely affects me inside, physically. Sometimes I get depressed because of it." As Ed looks ahead to the rest of his career, it is with apprehension. "It's not that I wish I weren't gay," he says. "I just wish I could do one or the other."

When he counterfeits an identity, a gay man invites others to believe that he is a heterosexual. He knows that they will base their impressions on the things he says and does, so he tries to say and do the things they expect of straight men. To be known as a heterosexual, he tries to act like one.

But what, exactly, do straight men do? The answer at first seems obvious: They have, desire, or fantasize about sex with women—that's why we call them hetero*sexuals*. But on closer inspection, this definition has little to do with the ways we actually make social judgments about others. Sexual identities, heterosexual or otherwise, are rarely determined by actual sexual contact. Except in the unlikely case that we've caught someone with his pants down, we routinely accept alternate, circumstantial evidence of his sexual orientation. Our assumptions about the sexual practices of friends, bosses, and landlords are rarely based on firsthand observation. Indeed, the paradigmatic heterosexual act, sexual contact with a person of the other sex, is the one we are least likely to see.

When personal traits are inferred rather than directly perceived, there is always the opportunity for false inferences. Because the behaviors and symbols that signify sexual orientation can usually be hidden or fabricated, one can counterfeit a sexual identity through the manipulation of its various signifiers.[1] The term *counterfeit* is useful in this context because it stresses the active nature of the task, distinguishing it from strategies that permit the performer to be more passive. The counterfeiter actively constructs and asserts a false identity, marshaling whatever props, settings, and supporting players are necessary. The term also takes into account his awareness that the performance is an attempt to mislead, that he is not being "himself." He knows that his public persona is "just an act."[2]

Virtually all gay men counterfeit an identity at some point in their lives. While only a handful of our participants (fifteen of the men, or 21 percent) were currently using this strategy at work, all had used it at some point in the past.[3] In one situation or another, all had permitted or encouraged a professional peer to believe that they were heterosexual. Their collective repertoire includes several basic moves.

Inventing a Sexual Life

Some men counterfeit an identity by supplying evidence of sexual relationships or fantasies that do not, in fact, exist. Through direct or indirect means, they disseminate a sexual biography that is essentially a work of fiction.

In its most direct form, this tactic involves women, real or imagined, who are presented as girlfriends or lovers. In a 1992 survey by *Out/Look*, 4 percent of the men reported that they sometimes discuss fictional girlfriends at work (though many more have undoubtedly used the tactic at some point in the past).[4] Miguel, a senior resident at a large Philadelphia hospital, found himself in a typical situation. Early in his residency Miguel's coworkers took an aggressive interest in his social schedule. Miguel was attractive and shy and had only recently moved to the United States from Puerto Rico. His coworkers took this as their cue to arrange his social life, to introduce him to the female nurses in the hospital, to show him around town. On a few occasions Miguel agreed. "If you go out with a nurse," he explains, "the next day all of them would know, so it was really good. I went out with one, and the next day I thought, 'Well, nobody's going to bother me anymore. No one's going to have the suspicion that I'm gay.' "

By his second year the frequent invitations had become more than Miguel could handle. As long as he remained single, he was fair game for any single female who needed a date. One time, to avoid one of these invitations, Miguel made a passing reference to "Kathy," a woman he hinted had become "sort of special." The name stuck, and to Miguel's horror Kathy quickly became the center of attention at the hospital. "Suddenly people were asking me about the famous Kathy, who didn't exist. 'What does Kathy do? Where is she from? Why don't you come over for dinner—and bring Kathy?' " The pressure to date had been alleviated, but it was replaced by pressure to elaborate Kathy's life history, to bring her to social events, and to explain why she was always too busy to attend. Miguel spun the entire relationship out of thin air.

Clay, an executive secretary in his fifties, has refined the technique somewhat. On his application forms he noted that he was "divorced," and word quickly spread that he had been married. Periodically Clay grumbles something about his ex-wife or recounts some episode for their past life together. When someone asks he simply says, "I'm divorced. She's in New York. I see her every once in awhile, and that was twenty years ago." Sometimes he updates the story a bit. "I go on vacations, and my boss will say, 'Oh, going up to New York to see the ex?' I just say, 'Yeah.' " No one pushes Clay for more information on what they probably imagine is a painful subject.

Other men begin with some shred of fact—an actual person, an actual event—and make this the basis for a fictive love life. "People ask me a lot about this girl I met at one point," says Ralph. "About a year ago, when I lived in this high-rise apartment building, I knew a girl there who kept calling me up. I didn't really know anything about her; I knew that she worked at Texas Commerce Bank, but that's about it. I used to see her out by the pool. So I told people, 'Oh, this girl keeps calling me,' and I finally said that I'd gone out with her once. Then people asked *all the time:* 'What does she do? Where does she live?' That was really uncomfortable, given that I hate having to lie, and you always wonder if you *look* like you lied; I mean, even in my mind, I made up a biography of her, where she worked, how old she was, and stuff like that." Then, after about a month, Ralph gave the romance a conventional ending, telling coworkers that he wasn't going to call her anymore. "They thought I'd just kind of blown her off," he says.

Fictional lovers can be surprisingly demanding, however, and in most cases such elaborate fabrications are unnecessary. Rather than invent an intricate, long-standing romance, men often settle for brief and uncomplicated "dates" with women. To be effective "strategic dating" need only be conspicuous. "I'm waiting for the next time we all get together," says Clay, who frequently goes to dinner with the other secretaries in his office. "Then I'll bring a date. Of course it'll be fun. We'll really create an impression. They'll be talking about it for days." Tip maintained a conspicuous romantic life by dating women who worked at his hospital, women who were highly visible—the nurse who ran the paging system, for example, renowned for her "big mouth and big tits." After an evening at a club or restaurant, "we would go back to the hospital, and people would be saying, 'Oh, I heard you two went out.' That meant security that you're straight." As Martin explains, these dates "are like any other staged media event. There's no point in doing it if no one hears about it. It's like the mayor kissing babies and opening shopping malls. You do it for the publicity, but instead of a photo op, it's a gossip op."

Quite often the opportunity is supplied by the intended audience itself. Especially when the counterfeiter is young and single, coworkers may be eager to furnish him with dates and equally eager to accept these dates at face value. Ralph says that his boss supplies a steady stream of these women. "He always knows some girl who's in the neighborhood, and who he thinks would be good for me," says Ralph. "He always starts by saying, 'Now, I don't want you to feel obligated, but I know this girl, and she's really cute.' That's kind of how it starts out. The first time I didn't know what to say. He caught me off guard, and so I said, 'Sure, just give me her name and number.' She was an Australian girl who lost her visa before I actually called her, which was lucky."

When dates are furnished by coworkers, however, the women are usually unaware that they have become part of a counterfeiting operation. For this reason intraoffice relationships are usually limited to one or two dates, at which point the counterfeiter moves on. Because he ultimately has no interest in a romantic relationship, third dates are considered risky. Charles is in the habit of taking female escorts to social events in his small Virginia town. Sometimes there are romantic complications. "Never in my career have I lied to anyone," he says, "but there are always single women who enjoy going out without getting serious. You don't always make the right choices, though, and sometimes you have to say, 'Whoa, let's back off here.' But there are times when you have to have an escort of the opposite sex."

Because of the potential for such complications, Matt is no longer willing to engage in this sort of strategic dating. "I'm at the point now where I don't want to have any more intimate relationships with women," he says. "I know where I am now, and would probably feel more comfortable in the future dating lesbian women. It's not fair to the dates, because when the relationship comes to a point where she's getting serious, I tend to run away like a scalded rabbit, especially when she starts talking about marriage or something. That usually ends the relationship." In the spring of 1990, Matt became involved with a flight attendant in her mid-forties and soon found that he couldn't carry on. "Her time clock was running out, and she was getting serious," he says. "Obviously it wasn't fair for me to continue leading her on. It would have been an ethics issue to let her continue to think that there was a possibility of a marriage."

As the relationships inevitably end, men who engage in strategic dating often become the subject of public scorn. Especially when the unwitting accomplice is a coworker, her anger or disappointment may find its way to the company grapevine. After a string of such dates, Geoff, who is thirty-three, has earned a reputation in his office as a "bad catch." "I'm known as the swinging bachelor who never has a date for more than three nights," he says. "I'm out every night partying and all that, and friends think I just can't find the right woman. If I take someone to a party and everyone meets her, then they don't see her again, they'll ask: 'Oh, what happened to Mary Ellen? Where's Maria?' And I always say, 'Oh, we broke up.' So in their minds I'm this basically irresponsible person who can't keep dates." Yet while the publicity has been negative, Geoff considers it better than no publicity at all. His reputation as a "swinging bachelor" is a useful smokescreen, deflecting the more damning identity of homosexual.

Strategic dates rarely provide a long-term cover, however, because "dating" is itself a temporary status. The heterosexual model of romance implies forward motion toward either marriage or separation, and makes it unacceptable to "just date" indefinitely. This became clear to Gary, who works in the tax department of Bell

Atlantic, when his "arrangement of mutual convenience" began to expire. Coworkers made comments about his female friend and asked why he didn't marry her. "I thought, I've got to rotate these women. I can't be seen taking the same one every year." Dan anticipates the same problem "Every time some social event comes up, I think, 'What am I going to do for a date?' People expect me to be single because I'm younger. But as I'm growing older, I find that people wonder when I'm going to get married. How come I'm not dating anybody? That type of thing. And I know that as time goes on, if I keep bringing somebody different, or if I keep bringing the same girl for forty years, they're going to wonder, 'What's going on here?' "

Although both men are in their thirties, Gary and Dan realize that their status as "eligible bachelors" will soon expire. In the fall of 1990 Gary changed jobs, which made it possible to begin a new round of strategic dating. He isn't sure what he'll do when this round ends. If he continues to use the same tactics, he'll ultimately have no choice but to adopt one of several longer-term roles: confirmed bachelor, lothario, or married man.

Not all counterfeiting operations require imaginary girlfriends or strategic dates, however. Indeed, total fabrications are often unnecessary. In most work settings, workers anticipate a typical, unremarkable sexual identity—heterosexuality, in most work environments—permitting gay men to remain undetected provided they do not upset these assumptions. Counterfeiting, in these cases, involves presenting oneself as being "just like everybody else" by hiding whatever evidence exists to the contrary.

In its simplest form, this approach involves the suppression of discrediting information. Details about a gay man's sexual life are disclosed selectively, perhaps stripped of their context, so that they do not upset his implicit claim to be straight. The classic example is that of a married man whose counterfeit identity is based on a series of partial truths. His reputation can be established through public displays of a wife, children, and countless other symbols of marriage, while aspects of his sexual life that would discredit this identity—his gay relationships, fantasies, or intentions—are kept out of sight.

Phil recently divorced his wife and began a new life in New York City. Coworkers know that he is divorced, and his family has been the subject of numerous conversations. "I have pictures of the kids in my office," he says, "so even if I meet someone who doesn't know my background, they walk in and see the kids and they think either you're married or divorced. This past week, a girl who works on my floor, who I don't know very well, walked in and wanted to borrow my paper. She saw the picture, and said, 'Oh, are these your kids?' So, typically, I tell people that I'm divorced. They usually don't ask a lot of questions once you say you're divorced, about whether you're gay or whatever, or why you got a divorce. It just seems to be a closed chapter." Though Phil has never intimated to coworkers that he has any interest in dating or remarrying, they have no idea that he is gay. He talks with them about his plans to visit his children, his adjustment to bachelorhood, his decision to leave North Carolina. What he doesn't mention is the *reason* he left his wife, or the lover with whom he now lives.

Other men discuss romances from their heterosexual past while saying as little as possible about the gay present. "If there was some funny anecdote that I could bring up from some past relationship, I brought it up," according to Greg, a Philadelphia architect. "But that was about it. I was just telling them what my past life was like. 'I had a girlfriend once who did this,' or something like that." When asked about his current living situation, Greg avoids mentioning the lover with whom he now shares a house. His sexual identity at work is based on biographical details that are almost ten years old.

The tactic is less effective, however, with audiences who recognize it (perhaps because they've used it themselves). Martin recalls a situation in which a counterfeiting operation failed. "I remember going to a Christmas party with one of the people in my office, a guy in his mid-thirties. The talk got kind of raunchy, and before long Joe was talking about his old girlfriends, their pet names for him, their idiosyncrasies. And then it hit me: This guy's talking about women he dated *fifteen years ago*. I knew right away, just like that, that he was gay."

Sometimes the suppressed information involves a current friend or lover. By omitting a few key details, for example, gay men reduce lovers to roommates, and friends to mere acquaintances. Ralph found himself in this situation when coworkers began to inquire about his bachelor roommate. For almost three years Ralph has lived with his lover, Jack, and worries that the situation may ultimately spoil his efforts to counterfeit. "I think thirty is kind of a threshold," Ralph says. "I mean you hit *thirty*, and then all of a sudden it starts clicking in people's minds. 'Gosh, he's thirty and he's not married and he's not bad looking, and he's doing well. Why isn't this guy married? Or, why isn't this guy living with a girl?' And then what do you do? 'Why does this guy have a roommate? He doesn't *have* to have a roommate. He can afford to live wherever he wants, but he doesn't. And why is his roommate thirty-five?' "

To protect his own identity, Ralph tells coworkers as little as possible about Jack. He doesn't talk about the time they spend together, their home, or their plans for the weekend. Sometimes he goes even further, inventing a sexual life for Jack. "I tell everyone he's got a girlfriend," Ralph explains. "He used to live with a girl for three or four years, and I act like she's still his girlfriend. I volunteer the information, like, 'Yeah, I have a roommate, but he pretty much lives with his girlfriend. He's never there.' "

In other situations the information withheld is the gender of a friend or acquaintance who figures prominently in a man's life. Rather than admit that he went to the movies with a male friend, for example, Steve told coworkers that he went "with a group of friends from college." Michael uses a similar tactic. "One of my clients said, 'You're single, right?' And I said, 'Yeah, I guess.' So he said, 'When you're in Boston next summer, I'm going to fix you up with a girl, a nice Jewish girl.' And I said, 'Look, you really don't have to do that, I'm really quite taken.' The two men exchanged meaningful glances and let the matter drop; the client apparently took for granted that the unnamed third person was a woman. In subsequent conversations he has referred simply to Michael's "better half."

Vague labels can also be used to disguise gay friends and lovers. An evening with a special someone—whose name, if offered, might be remembered—is turned into "just a quick dinner." A party with gay friends becomes "a little get-together" with "somebody I know from the neighborhood." Brent is similarly vague about the vacations he takes with his lover. "Whenever I take a trip, everyone wants to see pictures, so I censor the pictures," he explains. "There will be photographs of things and other people, but none of my roommate, whom I traveled with, or of my roommate and me together. One of my employees finally noticed. 'These are nice pictures of you,' she said, '*whoever* took them.' "

For many, such evasions have become second nature. Nick, a consultant with a firm in New York, routinely deflects personal questions in this way. "People ask if I'm seeing someone, and I always answer them truthfully, except that I leave out the gender. If I'm seeing someone, I'll tell them. If they say, 'What does she look like?' I'll say, 'blond hair, blue eyes.' If they say, 'What does she do?' I'll tell the truth. I just never say whether the person is male or female." Hearing these evasions, one sometimes wonders if lesbians and gay men didn't in fact pioneer the (mis)use of the third-personal plural "they" to replace the singular, gendered "he" and "she." "You can always tell a guy is gay when he refers to his dates as 'they,' " says Martin. "He'll say, 'I was in a relationship years ago, but they got too demanding.' Yeah, right. I mean, he was dating several people at once? Or is he trying not to say whether 'they' is a girl or a boy?"

The ruse is facilitated, however, by the almost uncanny eagerness of coworkers to believe that a man is straight. The presumption of heterosexuality is often so strong that coworkers sometimes interpret even nonsexual matters in a sexual way, seeing elaborate romantic plots in the most mundane of situations. In a typical scenario, Tony capitalizes on his friendship with Carol, the president's secretary, who is widely assumed to be his girlfriend. Because the two of them live downtown, they often find it convenient to spend time together on the weekends. "We do things socially," he says, "and I think that's kind of helped me maintain an image. My boss knows that Carol and I do things socially, and I guess he thinks we're dating. People in the company think that we've dated, and I don't do anything to change their assumptions. People come up to me and say, 'When are you gonna marry Carol? I think you guys should get married.' "

Russ is often visited at work by a girlfriend from college. "People just assume that we're going out," he says. "And I must say, that's kind of convenient. It stopped people from asking questions. A few years ago, we went to a party at the College of Physicians, and I took her. I was renovating my house at the time, and she was living there. It was very easy for us to act like spouses. People would ask about our house, never specifically about *us,* but about how the renovations were going." In these situations the goal, for Russ, was to do as little as possible to disrupt the presumption of heterosexuality. By selectively hiding information about himself, he deceived by omission.

It is not necessary, in many cases, for the object of a man's affection to have even a name, face, or address. She can be merely suggested, implied into existence with a well-chosen word or glance. Even oblique symbols of sexual activity can be used to counterfeit an identity. Rather than display the partner herself, for example, gay men can allude to her with photographs, birthday cards, and other props. Martin adopted the habit of wearing a wedding ring to his local gym (to fend off advances from both men and women). Geoff uses a photograph. "I've got a picture of me and my friend Mary on my desk, and I talk about her," he says. "Anybody who asks, I say, 'Yeah, that's my girlfriend.' I mean, she is a girl*friend* of mine." Whenever Geoff reports to a new construction site, he displays the photograph. "The new superintendent will come into my office, and he always asks, 'Who's this gorgeous woman?' And I say, 'Oh, it's the woman I'm dating right now.' Once the superintendent knows, he spreads it through the crew that I'm okay."

In some cases even a minor display of sexual interest is sufficient. Sexual jokes, innuendos, and feigned displays of attraction can be used to demonstrate heterosexual intentions, if not experiences. Men who supply no evidence of an actual relationship (imaginary or otherwise) can make it known that they are at least thinking about one. Chip, who is in his mid-twenties, recalls a series of practical jokes he played on Phil, a straight friend at work. In an adult bookstore, Chip found a photograph of a naked woman, on her knees, with a lewd caption. "It was really tacky," he says. "So I bought it. I thought, Phil needs this." He sent the photo through interoffice mail with a brief note, signing the name of the company president. Phil apparently took it in stride, and a few days later Chip received an obscene letter and a photo of a big-busted woman dressed up as Pocahontas. It was signed, "Love, Simone." Chip pinned them to his office wall and plotted his next move. To others in the office, the ensuing string of practical jokes looked like a fraternity prank—well within the bounds of adolescent, boys-being-boys heterosexuality.

Other men employ meaningful glances and comments to similar effect. "If I find a woman who's beautiful and attractive, I say so," according to Scott. "I just comment on how nice she's looking. I may even inquire, 'Who is she?' and God knows because I'm a single man, if you ask about a girl like that, it sends out waves of rumors. My questions and my interests are sincere, but I never carry it to the point of getting myself in trouble."

Playing Against (Stereo)type

A heterosexual identity can also be established through the display of traits that, while largely independent of a man's sexual orientation, are routinely interpreted as signs of it. Because we expect heterosexual men to dress, walk, and talk in traditionally masculine ways, we tend to accept these outward behaviors as evidence of a man's sexual orientation.

Conventional definitions of masculinity conflate heterosexuality with a potentially unrelated criterion: gender conformity. Our image of the "real man" incorporates assumptions about both sexual orientation and gender. Sexual deviation (homosexuality) is thus expected to correlate with gender nonconformity. Homosexual males are assumed to be effeminate (that is, like women). Heterosexual men, conversely, are expected to behave in traditionally masculine ways, a naive assumption that places yet another set of symbols and appearances at the disposal of the counterfeiter.[5]

We all have an image of the stereotypical gay male, with his mincing ways, effeminate speech, and flamboyant dress. This characterization is woven through much of our sexual culture, and supplies the key imagery with which the mainstream continues to represent and identify gay men. The "telltale signs" of homosexuality are such familiar targets for ridicule that most adolescents have learned them even before leaving grade school.

Among most gay professionals, mention of the sterotype evokes a cool response. Some men flinch at even the suggestion of effeminate behavior, flamboyance, or camp; it makes them uncomfortable, and they are careful not to let it creep into their own behavior. One often hears someone else described as a "screaming queen," and it is rarely meant as a compliment. "We're not all like that," one man assured me, shaking his head in frustration. "That's what most people don't understand." Many explain that this is in fact their key motivation for coming out at work, so that coworkers will realize, as one man explains, "that we're not all flaming faggots."

The trouble is, many gay men *are* effeminate, flamboyant or "stereotypically gay." Writing about film, Richard Dyer has pointed out: "It might be inaccurate of straight movies and television to make out that all gay men are screaming queens and that that is something frightful to be, but plenty of gay men do enjoy a good scream."[6] Our stereotypes of gayness may be a distortion of the truth or truthful for only a tiny proportion of men, but they are not in any simple sense "untrue." The problem, rather, is that they purport to represent more than they do.

For gay professionals these crude assumptions represent an opportunity. Stereotypes are often so inaccurate that they identify only the smallest part of a group; while some men fit the popular image of the "fag," most do not.[7] The resulting gap between perception and reality permits men to disguise themselves with simple displays of "manly" interests or abilities. Scott finds it especially easy. At six foot two, with broad shoulders and a muscular frame, Scott fits the popular image of an athlete. When he joined Blue Cross, he was immediately invited to join the company's baseball team and to represent it in corporate sporting events. Scott thinks that being an athlete counters any suspicion that he is gay. "I was an athlete for years," he points out, "and in the straight world you put someone on a pedestal for that. Not only that, but I'm a very *good* athlete. They've seen that in the Battle of the Corporate Stars because I did very well in the track-and-field and swimming events. They also know that I was an athlete in college, and when someone finds out about that it spreads—especially among the guys, you know. I have a big advantage in that sense. It throws off even the slightest hint that I'm a homosexual."

It is easiest to play against gay stereotypes, of course, when they are clearly defined. Common, familiar images of homosexuality can supply a sharp point of comparison, a model against which a heterosexual identity can be shaped. The task is made even easier when this countermodel comes in the form of an actual person. "If anybody brings up the topic of being gay," says Eric, "I just go right along with them. There's an attorney that works for us and they say he's a little bit strange or gay. One time my boss said, 'Watch out. He's a great attorney, but watch out for him because he's gay.'" Eric gave his boss a nod. "I just said, 'Okay, I'll make sure I watch out for him.'"

Ralph seized a similar opportunity. At twenty-seven, Ralph is tall and attractive, and frequently takes part in company athletics to bolster his "jock" image. At the company volleyball tournaments and football games, he also takes part in a running joke about another man in his office, a man who is known to be gay. As Ralph explains, "Whenever you do something kind of gay, somebody will say, 'We're going to set you up with David Miles.' People make comments like that a lot. Anything gay—like in volleyball, if you go for a spike and you don't spike it as hard as you should have or something, they'll say, 'Oh hell, Miles, that's too bad.' Last Wednesday, I got really hyped up—the ball was coming to me— and I yelled something like, 'Set me up, babe!' And everyone said, 'Oh, man, set me up, babe, *babe!* Then someone made a comment about David Miles."

An image of nonmasculinity is thus made concrete in the person of an effeminate coworker. By participating in the collective criticism of David Miles, Ralph reinforces a particular standard of masculinity and aligns himself with it. "I've made jokes before when I thought someone else said something kind of gay," he recalls. "Like my friend Perry, he always notices everything about people. He'll make comments about people, at volleyball or whatever, like, 'Hey, look at that guy's muscles,' or 'Wish I had a body like that guy's.' And I'll come back with something like, 'Maybe I can set you up with him.' Just stuff like that, never anything derogatory about gay people."

Other men cultivate specific traits or behaviors that can be used to forestall suspicion that they are gay. By highlighting the ways in which he differs from David Miles—by avoiding soft spikes and comments like 'Set me up, babe'—Ralph drives a wedge between his own identity and his friends' credulous image of gayness. Gary describes a similar tactic. "I really like sports," he explains. "I especially like football, so I can have a conversation with anyone about that. I'm not doing it to mislead them—I *enjoy* it—but I think most people think the typical gay male has no interest in those things. I don't do anything on purpose; I don't do it self-consicously. I think that living out in the suburbs, buying a house—maybe there's a subconscious effort there to say, 'Look, I'm not a typical gay male, living in the city in an apartment.' "

Counterstereotypical behavior is thus a way of capitalizing on the naïveté of peers. "I love football and I have a good memory for statistics, players, scores," says Martin. "Most people take that as a sign that I'm 'one of the guys.' You don't associate that with gay people." Jeff says that although his secretary has a number of gay friends, she clings to a fairly narrow vision of what being gay means. "She used to be a dancer in New York," he explains, "and I think she assumes—the gay men she knew must have been very effeminate, because she assumes that all gay men are going to be that way. It never crosses her mind that she could be working in a small investment company in the suburbs of Philadelphia and run across a gay man there. She associates gayness with this artistic environment in New York." By talking about sports, Jeff throws her off the track. Counterstereotypical traits are thus used to keep an unwanted label from sticking. In Goffman's language, they are "disidentifiers" that break up what might otherwise be a coherent picture.[8]

To counterfeit an identity, however, a gay man must do more than invoke masculine symbols and topics of conversation; he must also avoid behaviors that signify effeminacy, behaviors that *do* fit the stereotype. Not all are skilled performers. Some find it difficult to manipulate their outward appearances, making it impossible for them to hide.[9] Especially when his mannerisms are stereotypically "gay", a man may lack the confidence to pretend otherwise.[10] "Nobody ever called me faggot or anything like that," says Rodney. "But I just assumed they knew. I mean I have a slight lisp, and I was a loner." Another man was more to the point. "I'm a big ol' *queen*," he explained, with a toss of the arm. "Nobody mistakes me for Mel Gibson. If they don't at least *assume* I'm gay, it's because they're sound asleep."

Even men who consider themselves "straight acting" may be uncomfortable playing the role. "I don't know what straight guys do at lunch, when they're single," says Phil. Lacking practice, he isn't sure he makes a credible bachelor. "All my coworkers are married, so they don't talk about the women they met over the weekend, that kind of stuff. They know I'm single, so I'm never sure what to say." Despite his interest in sports, Martin feels he has a similar problem. "I have no idea what straight guys talk about," he says. "Car repair? Bad furniture? I never know how to act around them."

Of the outward behaviors that we associate with gender role, vocal mannerisms are among the most noticeable and hardest to control. "I really demonstrate gayness in my voice," says George. "I wish I could have a different speech pattern and just be able to fade into the woodwork when I want to. But I don't." At least in the United States, George feels he has little choice but to come out in work settings. It's a different story, however, when he does business abroad. "By American standards I'm more effeminate than your average businessman. But internationally that gets lost. You're suddenly an American, and there are so many other issues of difference that this pales in comparison." In part this explains George's decision to work for an airline that is headquartered in Europe. "My esteem is much better internationally," he says. "I probably speak German with a gay twang, but nobody seems to notice."

Tip is also frustrated by his voice, which has become a recurrent issue at the hospital. "I'm soft spoken, especially when I'm put on the spot," he explains. "Maybe my voice trails off or something." Tip first grew concerned when the comment turned up in his evaluations at Tulane Medical School. "The head surgeon showed me a departmental evaluation, and it kept popping up that I'm 'soft spoken,' which of course means 'gay.' They wrote 'soft spoken' in quotation marks. To me that meant I was gay and they didn't want me." Years later, during his residency in New York, Tip encountered the same criticism. "In my evaluation here, all the professors were happy about my speed, precision, etc. My supervisor's comment, his *only* negative comment on my evaluation, was 'You're meek.' I mean, I *hate* that. He's saying I'm not like him in some respects, that I should be tougher. He always comes up and slaps you on the back and says, 'Come on.' You know, 'Get tough.' "

Indeed, the macho standards of the surgical staff have become a source of constant tension for Tip, who feels he must cultivate a hypermasculine image to be accepted. he tries to play along. "After he said I was meek, you know what the next question was? This is during an evaluation of my job performance. His next question was, 'Have you ever been in a fistfight?' I just wanted to go, 'Yeah, how about right now?' I *hated* that. I said, 'Yeah, I've been in a fistfight. I actually broke some guy's nose in the subway, and I got arrested for it.' So he liked hearing that story. Of course you can beef it up if you want, you know. It's just like talking pussy. Disgusting, the whole thing. That's the worst part of my job." Tip's reluctance or inability to effect a macho exterior has led him to take several steps. His masculinity in doubt, he compensates by using other, more direct counterfeiting maneuvers. He invents girlfriends and sexual exploits, dates women in the hospital, and actively cultivates a reputation as a promiscuous "party boy."

Other men disguise interests and hobbies they fear will throw their masculinity into question. Taste in clothing and design, an interest in the arts, and extensive travel, are all cited as signs of a gay lifestyle. "If I'm in the office and I'm talking to somebody, I'll try not to be as cynical or sarcastic about gay things as I might be," according to Joel. "I try not to be campy." Paul, an executive with British Airways, fears that his personal tastes have "given him away." "I'm fifty-five years old and single and living in New York and go to Lincoln Center twice a week," he says. "Given what I like to do, what interests me—and everyone who knows me knows—I assume they've put two and two together."

Martin jokes that he is afraid to come to work with "a glorious suntan," because it might invite questions about his summer house, which is located in the Fire Island Pines, a well-known gay resort. Keith even finds it necessary to feign ignorance about gay activities that are dear to him. A coworker, a woman in her mid-twenties, let it be known that she was a drag-show afficionado. "She started talking to me, saying that she has lots of friends that are gay," he recalls. "She goes out to the gay bars every once in a while. And I'd say, 'Why would you go there?' You know, I just played very dumb. 'We'd watch the drag shows.' And I'd say, 'Drag shows?' and raise an eyebrow and cock my head like I don't understand." Later Keith made a point of cultivating more traditionally masculine interests, periodically scanning the newspaper "so I can talk sports if I have to."

For many AIDS is also closely associated with homosexuality, given its early and ongoing devastation of the gay male population. Indeed, even the mention of AIDS can sometimes interrupt the construction of a traditional masculine facade, encouraging some gay men to avoid conversations on the subject. When he asked for time off to attend a friend's funeral, Clay worried that the request would arouse suspicion. "I know what was going through my boss's mind," he says. "It was flashing at me as she was talking. She says, 'Oh, I have a friend who's in the hospital, who's sick.' Right away she wanted to know what my friend died of. 'Oh, I think he died of liver failure or something.' They didn't have it in the paper; she read the whole article, and it mentioned nothing about AIDS. But she was hoping that it would come up." While it seems likely that Clay's boss is sympathetic on the issue, Clay is reluctant to speak openly about it. He avoids giving the impression that he is especially knowledgeable or concerned about AIDS.

A counterstereotypical cover only works, however, when the necessary assumptions are in place. Coworkers must equate sex role with sexual orientation if the former is to signify the latter; one can't play against a stereotype when it doesn't exist. Duane, the president of an oil exploration company in Houston, finds that for this reason his cover doesn't work with everyone in the office. Older coworkers are the most credulous. "It doesn't occur to them that I'm gay," he says, "because my geologists are all men in their fifties. It's a little trickier if we hire younger people. The people in their fifties, unless they know someone specifically, have a stereotype of what a gay person is. I don't equal that stereotype, therefore I'm not gay." His office manager, a lesbian in her late sixties, uses a similar strategy. Because she doesn't fit the image of the "typical" lesbian, "people would never dream in a million years that Shirley is a lesbian. She's a widow and grandmother. She has four children, and goes to see her daughters- and sons-in-law on weekends. It never occurs to anyone that she's gay."

But when stereotypes are weak, or when coworkers have first-hand experiences that negate them, counterstereotypical behavior may be an ineffective disguise. Martin says that for this reason he is "wary of women who know too many gay men, because they see through the cover. It takes more than a little sports talk to throw them off the track."

Performance Anxiety

By definition, when a man counterfeits an identity, he plays a role that is at odds with his sense of who he really is. However practiced or convincing to the audience, his performance is still an act. The most skillful performer, playing a role for the thousandth time, is still performing.[11]

The dramaturgical metaphor is appropriate here because it helps explain the concern most often cited by men who counterfeit sexual identities. Identity performances, like theatrical ones, require planning. A plausible plot must be devised, the needed props and settings arranged. The performer must remember lines and cues. A cast must be assembled (with or without their consent), and the necessary steps must be taken to ensure that the performance will be credible. Because much of it will be improvised, the performer must closely monitor his audience, gauging their reaction, making whatever adjustments are needed along the way.

For the gay man, thrust into the combined role of playwright, director, and performer, the result is stress. He becomes conscious and calculating in his behavior, hyperattentive to the impression he is making. He must avoid the missteps that could bring the performance crashing down, which means he must be "on" in social situations that others take for granted.[12] He must be careful, in particular, to keep track of the plot. Imaginary people and events, once elaborated, take on a social life of their own. The audience, for its part, may reasonably expect a man to supply further installments: "Whatever happened to so-and-so?" "Have you heard from what's-her-name?" Or, quite often: "I know someone who works at that same company. Maybe she knows your friend so-and-so." The survey by *Out/Look* found that 62 percent of lesbians and gay men considered these hassles a major incentive to come out at work.[13]

The more complicated the drama, the more difficult it is to perform effectively. In some cases, when the cast of characters becomes too large or the narrative too complicated, the drama can become a comedy of errors. Tip learned this lesson several years ago when his stories began to get out of hand. Among the residents at his hospital, Tip has become famous for his conspicuous romances, most of which have been loosely based on actual events. When asked if he is dating, Tip tries to avoid specifics, describing only the basic outline of his social life. "I always use generic terms in an effort not to lie," he says. "But you can only do that so long. You have to give someone a name sooner or later. So Annette, one of the nurses, will pick out the names that I use. She does that instantly. I tell her about a date and she'll say, 'We'll call this one Jenny.' " Two years ago Tip became involved with a man who worked for the New York City Ballet. Annette renamed the boyfriend "Amy"—coincidentally the name of a principal dancer in the company. As word spread through the hospital, Tip and Amy's romance became legendary.

Tip was involved with Amy for a year and a half, and found their relationship remarkably easy to document. Through his boyfriend Tip obtained a steady supply of tickets and publicity shots of the real Amy, which he distributed throughout the hospital. On several occasions he accompanied the ballet when it toured. "We went to Paris twice and to Hawaii twice," he recalls. The ruse was only threatened once, when one of the senior physicians, Dr. Wu, suggested that he and Tip go to the ballet together. To avoid an awkward situation, Tip made certain that he and Dr. Wu weren't seated together. Amy knew that she was part of Tip's cover and had been warned that she might be called upon to help after the performance. "She was sharp enough not to blurt out anything stupid," Tip says. During the intermission Tip told Dr. Wu that he was going to slip backstage to say hello to Amy. He hid in a men's-room stall until the performance resumed.

Geoff used a similar tactic until his fabrications collapsed under their own weight. After several years in the same office, Geoff had invented a sexual life with a particularly large cast of characters, and found it increasingly difficult to keep track of them all. His biggest problem, he says, was "keeping this imaginary life going. It's difficult. I'm going out with some guy who's named Brian, he'll become Brenda. I try to find a name that I can attach well enough that I won't get it confused. Ken becomes Karen, that kind of thing. But it's very difficult to keep an imaginary life alive, keeping all the facts straight. I need to keep notes on my continuing saga." Several years ago, as Geoff grew increasingly careless with the details, one of his coworkers took notice. "There was a guy at the developer's office who had an unbelievable memory; he would remember all the details. And he'd say, 'Well, wait a minute. You said *this* and then you said *that*. The stories don't jibe.' When I'm drunk I'm trying to keep this imaginary life going, and I'm not remembering the details. And here's this guy who's filtering everything through his computer." Ultimately Geoff realized that his act was no longer convincing. Several months later the man asked if Geoff was gay.

Miguel learned a similiar lesson when his stories about "Kathy" got out of hand. "I would never do that again," he says. "The Kathy thing was a mistake. That was last year, and it's just a three-year program. Most of the people who were working with me then are gone. I was glad when they left. The new people don't know about Kathy, because I decided I don't want to do that again. So the only people who know about Kathy are third-year residents, or they're on my same level." After graduating Miguel plans to use a different strategy. "I'm just trying to play that topic down," he explains, "because it was a mistake I made at one point, while I was trying to find a solution."

While complicated dramas bring high levels of anxiety, the level of stress is usually lower for men whose identities are not based on overt fictions. Men who disguise themselves behind a masculine facade, for example, experience considerably less performance anxiety. Likewise there is less stress for men who need only hide discrediting facts rather than invent fictions. When he first moved to San Francisco in the early seventies, Carl met a woman named Lisa, and ultimately moved in with her. Meanwhile he continued to have sexual relationships with men. "The relationship with Lisa was stormy," he explains. "She wanted me to be straight, and I wanted her to be a man. It was doomed." Carl's coworkers were not given the whole story, however. "I didn't have to lie or make up stories about doing things with women so that I could pass, because I *was* doing things with the woman I lived with." Rather than invent a sexual life, Carl hid a few details about his relationship with Lisa, namely that he found the sex unsatisfying.

But even those who complain most bitterly about performance anxiety acknowledge that they can, if necessary, pull off the act; most gay men have learned, at one time or another, to counterfeit. Raised (almost always) in heterosexual environments, coached (by parents, peers, teachers) to behave as heterosexuals, and warned (in numerous ways) that there are penalties for straying from the prescribed path, most lesbians and gay men go under cover when they first acquire a sense of being different.[14] A gay man spends his formative years in the homes of people who assume he is like them, who school him in traditions that will ultimately exclude him, and who teach him, quite often, to despise the person he will become. By the hour of his sexual awakening, he has learned to disguise himself.

After years of rehearsal the performance may cease to feel unnatural. "I was always very comfortable in the closet," says Rodney. "I didn't have a lot of angst about it. I had arguments with gay friends who said, 'Oh, it's great to be out of the closet,' and stuff like that. 'You should do it.' But I said, 'Well, listen, where I'm working and with the family I have, I don't need the grief.' I wasn't suffering from being in the closet. If I had been in a position of great angst, then yeah, I would have said there are some trade-offs here. But there really wasn't a lot of stress involved."

Ethical Dilemmas

All forms of counterfeiting, from the occasional substitution of "she" for "he" to the complete fabrication of a heterosexual life, place the gay man in a tenuous moral position. His actions are intended to mislead, and these intentions conflict with the beliefs he (probably) holds about honesty. The gay community, meanwhile, increasingly views such behavior as an act of cowardice, even as a betrayal of the struggle for equal rights. Not only is a man denying what he knows to be true, but he may also be ignoring the strong exhortations of his peers to come out.[15] In the *Out/Look* survey, the vast majority of lesbians and gay men cited ethical issues as one of the key criteria that influenced their choice of strategy. Eighty-one percent cited "the desire to feel honest" as a major incentive to come out.[16]

Although gay men often invoke ethical concepts to explain their choice of strategy, there is no consensus about the ethical implications of these choices. Like their straight counterparts, gay men hold a wide range of ethical beliefs. They disagree about what constitutes "truth" and "lying." Asked to describe their relationships with coworkers, they frame their behavior in moral terms, but struggle to find the proper words. Steve described a situation in which he felt he had been dishonest. "We went to the beach one day," he recalls. "I had a date that night, and I'd come to the conclusion that if anyone asked me what I was doing, I would tell them. And so Jay asked me what I was doing that night, and I said, 'I have a date.' And he said, 'Oh, yeah, how'd you meet her?' Well, I didn't bother to correct Jay. I just said, 'Through a friend.' I didn't say 'her' anywhere; I was very careful. I know that's deception, but still . . ."

Others recount situations in which they "lied," only to quickly retract the term. "It's not really lying," says Milton. "I don't think it's lying when you're put on the spot like that. Or if it's anything, it's a white lie." Other men take a stricter view, holding that any deceptive situation or behavior is ethically questionable. "Most people assume I'm straight, without me indicating anything one way or the other," says Martin. "I never said anything to that effect, but it's still dishonest. I don't think it's lying, necessarily, but maybe it is. Other people might think so, anyway."

There is confusion about the terms because our beliefs about deception and honesty are shrouded in a definitional fog. One person's lie is clearly another's ambiguous remark or misleading half-truth. One can deceive in any number of ways—through omission or commission—with words, gestures, smoke signals, or any of the other codes with which we communicate. One can also deceive through silence. Indeed, within the larger category of deception, we must distinguish the concealment of information from the revelation of misinformation. The latter category, misinformation, encompasses all statements of one form or another that are intended to mislead, including "lies" in the conventional sense. The former category, concealment, is less clearly defined. It includes that which is true, but which we have deemed unsuitable for expression to others (a shameful secret, a concealed fact). It includes something about an individual that he or she has simply forgotten or neglected to mention (an irrelevant fact, a private nickname). It also includes information that, if revealed, might prevent a deception (by clarifying a misunderstanding or correcting a false assumption).

Although behavior in either category can lead to deception, few gay professionals view the concealment of information as outright lying. Because concealment often permits the counterfeiter to be passive, he may excuse himself of moral wrongdoing when using this tactic. Phil uses this distinction to explain his own behavior. Because he is recently divorced and continues to visit his children in North Carolina, Phil finds it easy to counterfeit a sexual identity. "I don't feel that I'm not being true to myself," he says. "I don't feel like I'm scheming just to project an image. And I really get the sense that the people that I work with don't really care. If anyone ever pressed me on it, I would not lie to them. I don't have to do anything other than what I normally do."

Phil thinks that he will eventually come out at work and anticipates a series of questions from coworkers, along the lines of, "Is that why you divorced?" and "Is that why you didn't move back to North Carolina?" Yet Phil doesn't worry that he will be called a liar. "I don't think they could really say anything about it, because I've never gone overboard in saying that I'm not gay. It's not like

I've really tried to deceive them. I just don't come out and tell them what I do at home in my bed, just like they don't tell me what they do in theirs." Phil's moral position is thus based on the distinction between active and passive deception. His conscience is clear because he didn't really "try" to deceive anyone. One can mislead, as he discovered, with statements that are essentially truthful.

For Scott statements of this sort have become an important part of the repertoire. When coworkers ask about his private life, Scott responds with true, albeit misleading, statements. "I say I don't want to date," he explains, "which is true. Sometimes I border on a white lie, but on the whole, I would say I'm telling the truth. I just don't want to date." When coworkers try to arrange blind dates for Scott, he sometimes plays along. "I'm attracted to women, and I may make comments about a particular person, but I never follow up." He describes a typical conversation: "They'll say, 'Don't you like her?' I say, 'Yes, I do.' 'Why don't you go and ask her out?' And I'll say, 'I don't want to.' That's a little white lie. Or I'll say, 'She's not really my type.' That'd be a little white lie, too."

Like Scott, Terry is also troubled by the ethical ambiguities associated with omission and deception. In general, however, his rule is to avoid situations in which he must "affirmatively misrepresent" himself. "There are times when I get tired of lying to people," he says. "I get tired of being two-faced about it, two-faced in the sense of not admitting that I'm gay, or not standing up to somebody who makes some derogatory comment about homosexuals." When asked if he had ever heard such comments or made them himself, Terry is adamant. "I don't do that," he says. "It's not like I live a complete lie, 'Go hang all the queers that are marching in the street,' or something like that." Instead, Terry limits himself to more subtle maneuvers, like an occasional date at a company party or a conspicuous friendship with a woman he knows from college. But even these tactics make Terry uncomfortable, and he tries to avoid them. "You tend to shut other people out of your life if you are a little closeted because you just get tired of lying to them. You get tired of being in an uncomfortable situation, so you don't do as much with them."

The same concerns ultimately prompted George to come out at work. He had tried being discreet, but felt that he was "living a lie." As he grew closer to his boss, a woman in her forties, George found it easier to change strategies than to live with an unclear conscience. "I respected her so much and she was so valuable to me, the thought of *not* acknowledging it was anathema to me. It would have been so false, our relationship. So we went out to dinner and I had four martinis before she got there, and then I just blurted it out. She was so wonderful about it." Years later George feels his consicence is clear. "You're free and you can eliminate that one area of lying that so many of us grew up with or evolved at some point."

Because they often anticipate coming-out scenes like this, gay men are sometimes careful not to do anything in the present for which they may be held accountable in the future. When asked what would happen if he came out at work, for example Ralph is troubled. He thinks that Perry, a coworker about his age, "probably won't want to play tennis with me anymore." He also worries about the reaction of a former unwitting accomplice. "I dated one of these girls at work, so she would feel kind of weird. She'd probably sit there and worry that she has AIDS or something." But more than that, she will know that Ralph lied to her and everyone else in the office. "The 'straight thing' has been part of me at work, and people might lose trust in me. I mean, you've lied to people. They'll know you've lied to them."

As he contemplates his own coming out, Miguel wonders if his relationship with "Kathy" will return to haunt him. "My coworkers, with whom I have a great relationship, will feel hurt because I was never honest with them. And the last thing I want to do is hurt their feelings, though I admit that I may have done something wrong." Today he no longer talks about "Kathy" and avoids situations in which he'll be pressed to lie. When other residents make a comment about a sexy nurse, Miguel's response is oblique. "Before, I used to make a comment also. Now I make a comment that won't compromise me if they find out I'm gay. I used to say, 'Yeah, I'd fuck her.' But now I won't say that, because I don't want to do it. So I'll say, 'Yeah, she has big tits.' " For Miguel the distinction is an important one. The net effect may be the same for the receiver, the one who is deceived, but Miguel feels he is morally prohibited only from making direct, intentional misstatements. "Somewhere down the line, when they find out, they can't blame me for anything. I was honest with them—I just didn't tell them everything. But I didn't lie."

Even when they acknowledge that they have been dishonest, however, not all gay men are bothered by the moral implications of their behavior. Even when they view a counterfeit identity as a *lie,* gay men are often quick to argue that the deception is justified by the circumstances. Coworkers will understand, they say. Under the same circumstances, any reasonable person would do likewise. "I think it would be more of a concern that I'm gay than dishonest," says Ralph. "If people really thought about it, they'd realize I didn't have any choice."

In fact, we often condone lying when it is part of an effort to survive, to avoid harm, or to avert crisis.[17] "Lying to the enemy" is usually permitted, for example, when one is in some kind of physical peril. I am permitted to deceive a would-be mugger by boasting (falsely) that I have a black belt in karate, by denying that I have any money, or by threatening that the police are already on their way. Likewise, we condone deception in the pursuit of national security, mounting disinformation campaigns to mislead or defeat those who threaten our lives, principles, or property. In either instance the deception can be justified on the grounds of self-defense. When telling the truth would endanger the teller, he is usually permitted to protect himself. He may lie to distract his enemies (by bluffing a counterthreat), to disguise himself (by posing as one of them), or to defeat them in some more indirect way (by leading them into danger).

Gay men often invoke some version of this argument to justify a counterfeit identity, arguing that the other person, the one deceived, is an enemy. They talk about homophobic coworkers and bosses who "wouldn't understand" and thus forfeit their right to honesty. Steve struggles with the issue while trying to decide if he should come out to Tamara, a woman in his department. "Four months ago I had a strong urge to tell Tamara," he says. "I went on this honesty binge. I wanted to tell everybody; I wanted to buy a neon sign." He and Tamara had become close, and she often spoke to Steve about her own romantic involvements. Over time, Steve had begun to think of Tamara as one of his closest friends, and as his birthday approached, he thought: "You're twenty-four, what are you doing with your life? Living this big lie in front of everyone?"

He stopped short, however, after telling his mother. "I recently came out to my mother, who is not handling it well at all. I came out to a few friends, and they handled it great; our relationship just grew and blossomed. So for a while I thought, 'Okay, everyone is going to react like that.' But then it occurred to me: They might react like my mom." Realizing that he couldn't count on a positive response from Tamara, Steve quickly lost his nerve. His desire for honesty was outweighed by his fear of its consequences. He couldn't be sure that Tamara would turn out to be an ally. "So the honesty binge went bad," Steve says. "Let's not do this honesty thing too much."

Eric was quick to see his boss as a hostile party. "I feel bad, because I'm really lying to myself and everybody else," he says. "But I still don't think being gay in today's world is as acceptable as it should be. My boss is so ultra—so supermacho—and hates anybody gay. I mean he just has a *hatred* for gays, absolute hatred. His son had to play every sport, that type of person. He has definite prejudices about a lot of things." Eric's solution is to counterfeit an identity, using his wife, his womanizing manner, and his frequent sexual innuendos as a disguise. All of this is justifiable, he explains, because his boss is so unreasonable. "I really have to play up to him. I have to be very careful to be sure that my image is not ruined. If he found out he'd fire me on the spot."

Geoff has a similar opinion of his employer, the Catholic church. As a construction manager he supervises building projects at a small college in northern California, a working environment that he describes as "incredibly homophobic." When speaking of the Brothers who supervise his work, for example, Geoff is filled with contempt and expresses no remorse about the numerous ways in which he has misled them about his sexuality. In fact, Geoff suspects that if he were to come out, the church would have more trouble with his sexuality than with his many patent falsehoods. "They would be upset that I'm gay, not dishonest. They'd say, 'I understand it was hard to come out, so I understand why you've been doing what you've been doing.' "

Although few gay men will ever be taken to task for their deceptions, most have given the possibility some thought and have already pondered how they would defend themselves. Whatever ethical framework they employ, the men usually reject the notion that they are morally at fault.[18] Some feel that while they are misleading their coworkers, they can't be accused of lying per se. Others justify their lies in the short term, explaining that they eventually plan to change strategies. Still others shift the moral culpability to coworkers, whose homophobia they feel has made honesty impossible. The greater evil, they say, lies in the treatment gay people receive at work, and therein lies their defense.

Social Invalidation

A man's sense of himself is shaped, to a significant degree, through contact with others. He looks to "social reality" to obtain feedback, to test and rehearse his beliefs and values. He consults those around him as he learns how to behave and what to think. Seeking social validation, he reveals something of himself to others.[19] His self-concept is thus the result of a complex, ongoing negotiation with his environment.

But what happens when a man's internal, psychic world isn't reflected back at him? What are the consequences when others respond not to him but to some fictional creation who stands in his stead? Under these circumstances it becomes difficult for a man to feel affirmed or responded to in any meaningful way. For men who counterfeit an identity, there is the recurrent sense that the social world has become unreal. The more effectively he presents a facade, the greater a man's difficulty in experiencing the reality of his everyday life.[20] Indeed, lesbians and gay men often complain that being in the closet places "distance" between themselves and their families, friends, and coworkers. Interpersonal distance is cited by many as the chief drawback of being in the closet.[21] A study of gay fathers found, for example, that the desire for closeness and intimacy was the consideration that most often motivated these men to reveal their homosexuality to sons and daughter. "The gay father discloses to his children (and to others) primarily in order to explain to them his social and personal world."[22]

One can speculate, however, that it is not the distance that troubles these men, but the artificiality of the closeness. This, at least, was what troubled Tip, who maintains active social relationships with several of the men and women at the hospital. He chats with coworkers about his romantic escapades, both real and imaginary, and has taken several of the women out for a night on the town. One of the residents, Fred, has been especially friendly. "He's probably the wildest person at the hospital," Tip explains, "and somehow he saw this in me, and we partied together. We've done drugs together. We run across to the bar and drink together, and then he smokes cigarettes. He thinks that's a big sin, so he doesn't want me to let it out." Last year Tip took a trip to the Jersey shore with Fred and some of the other residents. "I drove down there, and we had fun, but in a straight way." The group baked lobster, went bike riding, and danced at some of the straight clubs. "We did what straight guys do in bars, talked pussy, and all that."

Looking back, Tip describes the trip as "a gay person's nightmare." Because he counterfeits an identity with most of his coworkers, Tip couldn't be himself. "It's fun up to a point, but it gets boring for me. That's a shame, because I really like them. Our relationship is casual and supportive, as straight friends go. But see, they don't really know who I am." Tip's sense of social detachment peaked when he attended a recent meeting of lesbian and gay medical students. Most of the members were younger than Tip, some of them just beginning medical school. "It was fun," he says, "and I longed to have what they had. They're students, and they're out. The guys had their boyfriends there. Everyone knew the volleyball players, the theatrical group; everyone was screaming *Mary!* and *Go girl!* all over the place. And I was jealous. It pissed me off. I kept thinking, Shit!" Tip doesn't complain about being socially withdrawn at work because he isn't. On the contrary, he is fully integrated into the social network of the hospital and participates in

many of the staff's extracurricular activities. But because his participation is predicated on a counterfeit identity, he complains that
others "don't really know who I am." He finds himself confined to
the sidelines, simultaneously anxious and bored, required to feign
enthusiasm and experience in areas where he has none.

As a man's social and psychic worlds fall out of alignment, the
results can become absurd. "I had this patient who was married
and was part of a group," recalls Ron, a psychiatrist with a practice
in suburban Maryland. "He said he needed to talk to me individually—there was something he had to talk about—so we set up a
time. So he tells me all about this terrible conflict he has because of
his sexual attraction to men, and how it's something he can't act on
because of his marriage—though, actually, he *has* acted on it a couple of times. He's just so tired of having to be one way on the outside and another way on the inside, and he goes on and on, and
then he looks me right in the eye and he says, 'I just want to be like
you! I don't want to be conflicted about this stuff!' And I thought,
'Great, if he only knew.' "

The resulting situation can also have consequences for a man's
career. Denied validation for traits he in fact possesses, the man
who counterfeits an identity may find it difficult to navigate his organization. His professional and emotional needs have been mis-
represented, affording him only distorted feedback from others.
The lack of social validation is most conspicuous in organizations
that place the heaviest social demands on its members. Martin says
that this is one of the major drawbacks of hiding his sexuality.
"Eventually I'll have to come out," he says, "because there are so
many social demands placed on people in this business. I can't get
away with it for more than another year or two." Yet he was unsure
about the impact this would have on his career. "It's hard to know
how I'll handle it. I mean, should I get out of this business now?
Or will it be fine? When you're in the closet, you're never sure how
people will react to *you*. They've never really met you."

Some men try to alleviate the problem by seeking social validation in other ways. Their masks still tightly affixed, they reveal
themselves in oblique ways. They talk about "a friend" who is gay

and initiate conversations about sex, civil rights, or AIDS without identifying the true nature of their interest in these subjects. They cultivate alternative identities—as liberals, feminists, or worldly urbanites—that allow principled stand-taking without inviting suspicion. "I've discussed homosexuality with other people in the office," says Chuck, a Wall Street trader. "I've never said I'm a homosexual, but I did say lots of my friends are. It was my way of giving my side of the story."

Sometimes the veiled disclosures yield the desired response. Joel uses this approach to air his personal convictions about civil rights, a subject that has great personal meaning for him. Over the years he has been involved with the Lutheran church and a number of activist organizations, and cites as an example a recent seminar on race, class, and sex that he led at a local church. "I feel very comfortable talking about these issues, and do so frequently," he says. Another time he wrote a letter to the bishop in San Francisco about the ordination of gay priests, and his business partner knows that he gives money to AIDS organizations. "I've been a traditional fighter against discrimination," he says, "whether it's against gays or blacks." At work he makes no secret of this. Yet Joel is scrupulous in avoiding discussion of his own sexuality, and doesn't know what his coworkers suppose it to be. "I don't know what they'd say about my sexuality," he says, but "it's important they know where I stand on civil rights."

Often a man may want to share no more than an emotion or personal experience. Martin recalled a painful situation. "A friend died after a long fight with AIDS, and I was a total wreck. I was really busy at work, but I kept falling apart, forgetting things, running to the bathroom to splash water in my face. I thought about telling everyone I was under a lot of pressure or something, but that sounded stupid. So I finally told them I had a sick relative— 'My uncle's dying of cancer,' or something like that. Next thing I knew, I was bawling in the office, and my secretary's bringing me coffee, telling me it's okay, that she understands. And, of course, she really didn't understand. But in another way, in the way that probably matters, she did."

Disclosures like these can inject a dose of reality into an otherwise artificial situation, lessening a man's sense of isolation. By putting clear limits on such moments of authenticity—by framing his disclosure in generic political terms, as something that happened to "a friend," or as an emotion that sprang from another source—he finds it possible to reveal something of himself to those around them. But despite these attempts, men who counterfeit an identity place an unbridgeable gulf between themselves and their coworkers. They experience their professional relationships as being desiccated and contrived. When speaking of their contact with bosses and peers, they admit that they often feel bored, invisible, and insulted—the lament of those who go unnoticed or find themselves treated as if they were someone else.

Like other efforts to pass, a counterfeit identity promises a "deal."[23] The professional world holds out the lure of success, power, or wealth—but only for a certain category of persons. The gay professional, hiding his status as a member of the underclass, accepts the offer. Like a forged passport, a counterfeit identity permits him to travel freely through the heterosexual spaces of the professional world. In this sense gay men are different from women, nonwhites, and others who routinely find themselves marginalized in the workplace. With the right disguise, gay men can pass. They are invited to take part in the male rituals that cement relationships and launch careers. They look the part of the aspiring executive. They imagine that they are members of the club.

But to do so they must enter a Faustian bargain. Well aware that there are severe penalties for coming out, some men wonder why anyone would give up the security of the closet, especially if he has no difficulty passing as a heterosexual. What is often ignored, however, is the less obvious fact that passing also has its costs.[24] The closet, in any of its forms, creates as many problems as it is sometimes thought to solve. A substantial psychological literature emphasizes that significant and continuous self-disclosure is required to maintain a healthy personality; when salient personal characteristics are withheld from others, the frequent result is stress, anxiety, and depression. Secrets can become pathogenic.[25] Like cancers they consume an ever-growing share of an individual's resources as deception is built upon deception. Except for the rare individual who guards a terrible secret—a debilitating but hidden affliction or, in earlier times, an illegitimate birthright—such "pathogenic secrets" are essentially unknown in the heterosexual world.

When asked if there are "any penalties to being in the closet," some men are clearly afraid even to contemplate the question. Quite often there is little evidence that the men have given their choices any conscious thought at all. Some say that there is no point in thinking about a situation they have no power to change. Others find the subject too painful, something better left alone. For these men the choice of strategy may be a function of inertia more than any conscious intent. Toward the end of each interview, I asked each man to imagine a hypothetical situation in which all lesbians and gay men had suddenly been "outed"—by turning green. My purpose was to disentangle the men's feelings about *coming* out from their concerns about *being* out. There would be no painful coming out scene, I told them, and no nervous conversation. They would simply be exposed. The so-called green question drew some startled replies. Consider the following exchange:

JIM: Let's say that one day all of the gay people turned green. Suddenly you would be visible, so that your coworkers would have no choice but to recognize that you are gay. What do you think would happen at work?

DEREK: [Long pause] I'm not sure . . . I might be compelled to say something to a few people.

JIM: Like what?

DEREK: That's a little uncomfortable.

JIM: Okay.

DEREK: This is real uncomfortable for me, I just . . . so I think I'll have to bypass that one. It's uncomfortable because I don't know the answer . . . I don't think I'd be uncomfortable telling you if I did, but I haven't worked that one out yet. The thing that would really piss me off is if everyone said, "Christ, we've known that for years." And I'd be thinking, "Why have I been doing all these gymnastics?"

Other men confessed that they had never thought about the possibility of being out. "I'm probably going to have a nightmare about turning green," one man told us. "I'll have to give it some thought."[26]

For these men, the "choice" of strategy amounts to little more than what involves the least risk. The constraints of the closet may be uncomfortable, but they are familiar, known—they are manageable. Like chronic pain the closet is endured without thinking, acknowledged only tacitly. Perhaps this is why many gay men seem reluctant to trade the certainty of these habits, the familiar grooves they've worn in their relationships, for the uncertain promise of being out. Some even protest that they have grown to love the closet, that they are accustomed to its contours. "I was good at it," says Rodney, looking back on his Wall Street career. "It worked well for me then." Chuck agrees: "The reason I didn't tell my mom until very recently isn't because I didn't see any reason to. I didn't have a problem with her knowing, and I didn't think it would be hard for her to accept. It's just that I was perfectly comfortable in the closet."

5

Maintaining Boundaries

As HE SHUTTLES between home and office, between his social and professional worlds, Eric undergoes a dramatic transformation. With gay friends he feels comfortable and authentic. He speaks candidly about the man he is dating, about gay political issues, and about this frustrations at home. Then, from nine to five, he becomes the office "superstud." Like the other men in his office, he swaggers and flirts, teasing the receptionist about her shapely figure, asking when it's "his turn" for a date. At home, later, Eric avoids the issue altogether. He initiates sex with his wife on a regular basis, at least once every few weeks, "so that she won't get suspicious." He hopes that she has forgotten about the incriminating phone call she overheard several years ago. "I think she suspects," he says. "I mean, she's not stupid. She was having empty nest problems a few years ago, after our youngest daughter left for college, and she said, 'Maybe you'd prefer to go live with another man.'" At the time Eric insisted that this was not what he wanted. "I always deny it, and I always say, 'I'll never leave you.' That type of thing. She first had suspicions back when I was twenty-two or

109

twenty-three, but we still stayed married all these years." To which he adds, "But it's been hell."

The bank in which Eric works is headquartered in Wilmington, sixty-five miles from his home in suburban New Jersey, requiring a lengthy morning and evening commute. Clients are scattered up and down the East Coast, requiring frequent overnight trips to other cities. The constant travel, over many years, has allowed Eric to build an extensive network of gay acquaintances. "I have friends in New York that I've known for a long time," he says. "I also have gay friends in Washington, Philadelphia, and Harrisburg, where I go quite frequently." One of these men responded to an ad that Eric placed in the *Philadelphia Gay News* back in 1984. "We still talk to each other every day on the phone," Eric says. "We became really close, like brothers. We talk about our problems, being married and stuff like that."

To keep the halves of his world from colliding, Eric bars all contact between gay friends and the people in his office, neighborhood, and family. Eric's wife has never met any of these friends—she has never even heard their names. To keep in touch with them, Eric keeps a post office box in Wilmington. He has a credit card through that address and uses it to place long-distance calls that won't appear on his home telephone bill. At work he has a secure telephone line, which prevents coworkers from spying on his conversations. He asks that gay friends either phone him at work or wait until Tuesday evenings between six and eight, when his wife plays bridge. Although he occasionally visits a gay bar twenty-five miles from home, Eric prefers to maintain stricter boundaries. "I'm very careful," he explains. "There's a definite geographic distance between my home life and my gay social life, so it's a comfortable feeling for me. Basically I don't go looking for people in the area where I live."

For almost thirty years, Eric has used these geographic and temporal barriers to segregate his professional, family, and gay relationships. In the fall of 1990, he was offered a job with a company located closer to home but worried that the move would breach these precarious boundaries. "I have a selfish reason for wanting to stay where I am," he explains, "because I'm able to travel to

Washington and New York, and get out of the house. The new job would be local, just southern Jersey. It would limit my travel. I'd be confined, and I don't know if I'd be happy with that." After thinking it over, Eric turned the job down.

Dividing the World

Like many gay men, Eric responds to a hostile world by dividing it up. He knows that his wife would be unsympathetic to the truth about his sexuality. (When she overheard the incriminating phone call, several years ago, she suggested that Eric "see a psychiatrist to deal with the problem." When they argue today, she sometimes reminds him of that embarrassing episode.) Male coworkers seem no less intolerant, embellishing their conversation with homophobic remarks. Eric's response to all these individuals is to isolate and contain them, to divide his social life into zones. He thinks in terms of distinct in-groups and out-groups and cultivates categorically different relationships with the individuals assigned to each. By erecting temporal and spatial barriers, he minimizes the opportunities for the groups to come into contact.[1] If Eric's tactics are somewhat extreme, most gay professionals have used some version of them at one point or another. Virtually all have learned to live with the kind of social distinctions and transitions that Eric describes.

Geographic boundaries are one way for a man to segregate his social activities. Jason divides his time between New York City and his company's headquarters in suburban New Jersey. "I end up with a schizophrenic life because I meet or associate with my gay friends on a separate basis," he explains. "The two worlds are distinct." Brent commutes from his home in downtown Houston to a clinic in a small town, thirty miles to the west. "It helps me keep things separate," he explains. Geoff has a similar arrangement. In San Francisco he maintains a large group of gay friends. Forty miles to the north, he works as the construction manager at a small Catholic college. His home is located in between. "You're always walking a tightrope between the two worlds," he explains, "hoping they won't collide at some point."

Rodney's scheme didn't collapse until he was diagnosed with AIDS several years ago. He had been working on Wall Street less than a year when he met a man from Holland during a vacation. The two fell in love, and after several months Rodney requested a transfer to the company's office in Amsterdam. He let it be known at work that he and "Tracy" were planning to marry and began to spend many of his weekends in Holland. Shortly before he was scheduled to relocate, however, Rodney ended the relationship and informed his employer that he planned to stay in New York. The news spread like wildfire. "You should have heard them in the office: 'Tracy, that lovely woman Tracy. What he did to Tracy.' "

The story unraveled several years later, when Rodney was diagnosed. "Everybody at work figured it out real quick," he says. "I remember having a conversation, about a month after I went on disability, with the head of the arbitrage desk. He said, 'So, Rodney, just a question here. That girl in Amsterdam, it was a man, wasn't it?' Yeah, yeah, it was a man. It all began to fall into place. 'Boy, you put on quite a show, you had us fooled.' " The story had been relatively easy to construct, Rodney recalls, because the details were essentially accurate. "All I had to do was switch genders, which was no big deal; it became second nature after awhile." Because "Tracy" was almost four thousand miles away, there was little risk that the key biographical detail, Tracy's gender, would find its way to New York.

Because it diminishes the likelihood that social circles will overlap, a diverse urban setting can also be useful to men who compartmentalize their lives in this way. In addition to greater tolerance of diversity, cities often promise a large and transient population. "I don't worry too much about the worlds colliding because I live in a city of ten million people," says Martin. "The world is small, but it's not that small." In rural or suburban settings, on the other hand, there may be no naturally occurring spatial or interpersonal boundaries. Bill, a ranger with the California Park Service, says that in his line of work it's often difficult to separate one's personal and professional worlds. He is currently stationed at a park near San Francisco, which allows him to be part of the Bay Area's gay community. This may no longer be possible, however, if he is transferred to another park. "You're living in Yellowstone or one of these places where the park service is the whole community, and there's no screening of your private life anymore. Everyone knows what everyone else is doing."

For most gay men, however, crossover friendships are a source of far greater concern. When a friend inhabits both one's social and professional worlds, he or she raises the spectre of exposure. "Basically I don't have any crossover friends," says Geoff. "I have two completely separate groups of friends, and I don't tell them anything about each other." He never mentions gay friends in the company of coworkers, not even their names. Only once did a "crossover friendship" pose a problem. Several years ago a former boyfriend became friendly with a woman who worked in Geoff's office. For Geoff this spelled trouble. He remembers thinking, "Well, this is the way the worlds will collide," and took several pre-emptive steps. He avoided the woman at work and turned down social invitations from the former boyfriend. Although it apparently worked, Geoff anticipates that this was not the last time he will run into a situation like this. He worries that his scheme will eventually collapse, that someone at work will ask a pointed question about a mutual gay friend. "I know I'll turn bright red when it happens, and I'll start stuttering, and soup will spill out all over my socks. 'Excuse me, *what?* But until then . . .'"

Even when a man lives in a diverse urban setting and is careful to segregate his social activities, certain individuals may inadvertently cross the boundaries. A single point of overlap between the groups—a coworker who stumbles onto a man's gay life, or a gay friend who intrudes on a professional situation—can threaten the entire scheme. One of Martin's college roommates briefly dated a woman in Martin's office, a situation that he feared might lead to his exposure. "She was always asking him about my private life," he recalls. "She would say things like, 'So, did Martin have girlfriends in college?' 'Why isn't he dating anyone now?' It really put him in an awkward situation, because he didn't want to lie to her. We finally agreed that he would just say something like, 'Hmm, that's an interesting question. I'll tell Martin you asked.'"

The risk of contact between the groups is also increased when a man socializes with the people in his office. Ralph frequently joins his coworkers for meals, concerts, and sporting events and worries that some evening, during one of these outings, the group will run into some of his gay friends. Segregating the groups is further complicated by the fact that Ralph's lover, Jack, is openly gay. "Jack has a lot of straight friends who know that he's gay," Ralph says, "which is dangerous if you want to keep it quiet, because if you meet someone that doesn't have any connection with you, who doesn't feel any loyalty to you, you can't trust them." More to the point, Ralph is uncomfortable with the fact that he and Jack use different strategies at work; as a couple they send somewhat mixed signals about the importance of secrecy. He worries that if Jack's coworkers ever encounter any of the people in his own office, they may inadvertently say the wrong thing. "They might assume that since Jack's openly gay, I must be, too. They don't realize that I'm in a totally different situation." To minimize the risk of such a collision, Ralph has never introduced Jack to any of the people in his office. He says as little as possible about Jack at work and avoids situations in which his coworkers might encounter them as a couple.

Even so, Ralph has already had several close calls. Leaving the grocery store with Jack one evening, he ran into a man from work. "Jack and I had all these grocery bags in our hands, and that always kind of looks—maybe I'm just being paranoid—but when two guys walk out of the grocery store carrying bags . . . I mean they *may* go shopping together, but let's face it . . ." Ralph thought quickly. "We went up to the guy and talked, and I said something really stupid, like we were cooking steaks for these two girls tonight or something like that."

Another time the worlds collided when Ralph and Jack attended a cocktail party together. One of Jack's college friends was getting married and had a small gathering for friends a few days before the wedding. There Ralph encountered a woman from his office, a secretary who asked if he was a friend of the bride or the groom. Ralph explained that he had met the bride through Jack, to which she replied, "Oh, and how do you know Jack?" Ralph wasn't sure how to respond. "Well, Jack's from Nebraska, five years older than I am. He works in the adolescent psychiatric unit of a hospital—I mean, how *do* I know someone like this? So I told her that we had met through a friend, this other guy, Scott, and she seemed to believe it. But then I find out that she also talked to Jack, and that she asked him, 'So, how do you two know each other?' And he made up something completely different. So, if she remembers what I told her, she knows that one of us was lying." Because he never intended for Jack to meet anyone in his office, Ralph had never bothered to coordinate a cover story that would explain their relationship.

Stories like these figure prominently in gay folklore. Like all cautionary tales, they illustrate the possible consequences of failing to take certain precautions, of failing to perform the necessary closet maintenance. From gay men one hears horror stories about deceptions that were unconvincing, evasions that were ineffective, or cover stories that became inconsistent. One often hears about "oops" experiences, in which a man inadvertently said or did something that blew his cover. Miguel remembers a fateful outing in which he ran into one of the chief residents, a woman who worked in his same unit of the hospital. He and his boyfriend were spending a day at the zoo when Miguel spotted her. Looking back, he realizes that he panicked. "I think I handled the situation really poorly," he says, "because I didn't introduce my boyfriend to her. I made a mess. And then we were laughing at how badly I handled the situation. It was just the first time I had seen someone, one of my bosses, outside the hospital. I got nervous, and I didn't know what to do. I was really rude."

The moral of the story, according to Miguel, is not to panic when gay and straight worlds unexpectedly come together. A few weeks later he was leaving a local gay disco with several of his friends and ran into some of the other residents. This time, he thought more quickly. "There were five of us, all guys. And I said, 'Oh, I just came from a party—a bachelor party.' " A few days later, at the hospital, "they asked me, 'How was the wedding?' And I said, 'Oh, it was good.' "

To preempt encounters like these, gay men are often wary of social situations in which they might be "spotted" by someone from work. Dan finds that even inconspicuous dinner dates make him uncomfortable, given the frequency with which he seems to run into clients. "I'm out on a date or something, and all of a sudden a former client or somebody from the clinic comes up," he says. "It happens all the time; I can't go out and eat anymore. Just a couple of weeks ago, someone tapped on my shoulder. It was a couple of former clients, a mother and father. She gave me a hug, and I shook the husband's hand. We talked a little bit, you know." Dan worries that the encounter may have exposed him. "It's really stupid, I know it's stupid," he says. "I mean, *I* know why I'm there, but *they* don't necessarily know. The other guy could just be a friend. It's really interesting though: If I'm out on a date, I'm paranoid. Even if I'm just with a friend, it doesn't make any difference."

Even more stress provoking would be an excursion, with coworkers, into a gay social situation. Scott found himself in this predicament when several of the people in his office decided, for a lark, to go to a gay bar. "One of the women thought it would be fun" to take the staff out for dinner and dancing. "But of all places," Scott recalls, "she wanted to go to the Raven for dinner. I've never been to the Raven, but I've heard of it, and I thought, 'There is no way I'm going to go. Someone will see me there.' " Scott knew that the Raven was a gay bar in New Hope, and worried that he might know some of the other patrons. "At first I didn't know if the Raven she was talking about was the same Raven I was thinking about, but it turned out to be the same." Fortunately for Scott, fate intervened. "There is a God," he says. "It was the worst weather that night, raining hard, and New Hope is a long drive. It was the perfect excuse." For Scott, missing the party was far less upsetting than the prospect of being caught in a compromising situation.

Inviting coworkers into one's home is also viewed by many as a way of courting disaster. Some men speak of having to "de-gay" their homes before holding a cocktail party or dinner for people from the office. Magazines, books, posters, mail, and datebooks are hidden. Photographs are removed from shelves, and in some cases medicine cabinets are cleared. One man remembers turning his answering machine off before his guests arrived "to make sure that no one called during the party and left a message about something gay."

For others entertaining coworkers at home is considered too risky, permitting too close a brush between worlds that they intend to keep apart. "A lot of times when I have dinners or parties, I'd love to invite people from work," says Tom. "But you can't because you don't know what their reaction is going to be. Even if you invite them over for dinner, suppose some friends stop by? It's a sticky situation." Matt faces a similar dilemma. He lives near several of the men who work in his office, making it risky for him to have gay friends over for dinner. "I have to lead a very discreet life," he says. "Because I'm single some of the men in the office, especially the younger ones, will drop by unannounced to have a beer or something like that." Although he enjoys the camaraderie, Matt says that the situation imposes "extreme discretion." He rarely socializes with gay friends and is careful to avoid those he considers effeminate or "obviously gay." Nor does he usually patronize gay establishments. "I'm not a bar hopper," he says, "and I don't spend very much time in those places anyway. I'm afraid of somebody seeing my car out front."

Yet even when they avoid situations that are obviously risky, men sometimes find themselves in compromising positions. Carter recalls a vacation that he took with Terry, during which there was an unexpected collision. While Carter is openly gay at work, Terry remains in the closet. "Terry is known by all these lawyers everywhere," says Carter. "Everywhere he goes he sees somebody he knows. We were coming back from Puerto Vallarta and we get on the plane, and right behind us sits a good friend of his, a big lawyer, and his wife. And there we were, four guys. Terry has such a hard time at work. His firm is really conservative. So he leaned over and said, 'I know this guy, so let's butch it up.'" Carter did what he could. "So I said, 'Hey, how 'bout those Astros, aren't they playing today?' And the other guy says, 'Yeah, aren't they playing the Oilers?'" Though fuzzy on their sports trivia, the men helped Terry through a potentially awkward situation. "Terry's working under pretty stressful circumstances," says Carter. "That's why he's got all those gray hairs."

Choosing Allies

As they patrol the border between their personal and professional worlds, gay men often rely on the assistance of others. They turn to allies for support, for help in managing a particular situation or corroborating a fiction. Like Terry, they may ask friends to help them avert a crisis when groups unexpectedly come into contract. At times they may even turn to strangers who are asked to keep their secrets or to participate, as extras, in a performance. Because a gay man's strategy is quite often the result of a collaboration, he may be unable to carry it out without the help of others.

Allies play a number of crucial roles. Many of the situations and appearances a man must engineer to disguise himself require the participation of others. Among men who engage in strategic dating, for example, sympathetic women are often favored as allies. Sometimes the woman is a friend, a "beard" in gay parlance, who is pressed into service for an occasional evening. "Usually we have a little prep session," says Mitch, who frequently escorts women to company events. "One time I went with this girl I barely knew, a friend's secretary. If anybody had asked questions about us, she wouldn't have had any idea how to answer. So we had a little session where we sat down and said, 'Okay, this is where I went to college, and this is where I went to law school. Let's make up a story about how we met in case anybody asks.' "

The woman may be a lesbian counterfeiter who expects the man to return the favor, and long-standing arrangements between lesbians and gay men are not uncommon.[2] "There are quite a few attractive lesbians in Houston who are happy to do things like that," says Terry. "They need to take people to things, too, so it's a trade-off." Martin frequently escorts a female friend, a lesbian who runs her own design firm, to openings at galleries and restaurants. Matt refers to his arrangement with a lesbian friend as their "dial-a-dyke service."

Allies also play a less dramatic but no less important role in helping a gay man conceal information that would discredit him. Observing a man as he fabricates a story for the benefit of some third party, for example, they know not to interrupt the ruse. They understand the game that is being played when they overhear him utter a patent falsehood, in homophobic company, about his (hetero)sexual life. They know to avoid sensitive subjects in conversation until they are certain that everyone present is privy to certain key information. Likewise, they know to abandon sexual topics when someone new enters a conversation and have learned to play along when a conversation abruptly shifts into an alternative, fictional reality. Even when they seem spontaneous and automatic, these subtle alliances may be crucial to the execution of a man's strategy.

But who makes a suitable ally? By enlisting someone else in his performance, a gay man places himself in a vulnerable position. Knowing that he is gay, his allies have the capacity to expose him. They have the power to discredit a counterfeit identity by bringing contrary evidence to light. They can destabilize his efforts to avoid the subject altogether by forcing him to address sexual topics, asking the wrong questions, and so forth. For this reason men who counterfeit an identity must be cautious in their selection of allies. Questions of trust and loyalty are of paramount concern.

Historically gay men have resolved the problem by limiting their self-disclosure to other lesbians and gay men.[3] Eric, for example, is most comfortable in gay company. He is surrounded by an extended family, a neighborhood of friends, and a church community in which he is active—yet considers the gay personal ads a more reliable and trustworthy source of companionship. "Not that I'm uncomfortable in a straight situation," he says. "But I feel I can talk about things better with a gay person, especially one who is married. A straight person just can't understand what I'm going through." Eric doesn't hesitate to give out his phone number to the men he meets at gay parties or bars. Even with new acquaintances, he shares personal information that, carelessly repeated, could destory his marriage or threaten his career. "I respect the gay community a lot," he says. "I haven't had any problems. Most of my friends can call me at work, because I trust that they will act as true professionals." When invited to take part in this study, for example, Eric showed no hesitation, eagerly divulging the things he would never tell his wife, children, or employer. "I trust you guys," he told us.

Historically the convention that gay people keep one another's secrets has been a defining feature of gay social life. As philosopher Richard Mohr has observed, "Any field anthropologist examining the folkways of the gay community would easily notice that among all the variety in the gay community—just for starters divisions of life-styles between lesbians and gay men—The Secret is *the* social convention that most centrally defines the community."[4]

The convention is not an agreement in the usual sense, of course. One makes no explicit contract or promise when he enters a gay environment or trades information with a gay confidant. He is given no opportunity to think it over, to accept or refuse. Nor is the code presented as a formal condition of membership to something called "the community." Yet the code of secrecy is a powerful unwritten rule that all have learned, and most observe. Without having formally agreed to do so, gays are often committed to the protection of one another's closets.[5]

Secrecy has long been a necessity for homosexual men and women, and in this country its roots as a formal convention can be found in the earliest gay communities, in the fledgling gay enclaves that grew up in San Francisco, New York, and other cities after World War II. In a world that viewed them as criminals and perverts, these men sought safe spaces in which to meet. Its key institutions were taverns, baths, and nightclubs that were largely invisible to those outside the community.[6] There were rules about discretion, coded ways of speaking, even procedures for identifying, and identifying oneself to, sympathetic others.[7] The political rhetoric of the day, limited as it was to a handful of underground newsletters, lacked the present-day emphasis on coming out.[8] Indeed, the Mattachine Society, which in 1950 became the first national gay group in the country, stressed the importance of discretion and the ultimate assimilation of its members into society at large. Even the cryptic name of the organization, which refers to medieval court jesters who told the truth to kings while hiding behind masks, reflects its clandestine nature.

Like any secret society, the nascent lesbian and gay community developed coded ways of identifying its members and of talking amongst itself, especially in the presence of outsiders. Words like "sensitive" and "gay" became euphemisms for "homosexual," making it possible to inquire about a man's sexual proclivities while maintaining a measure of ambiguity, and thus deniability.[9] Other members were referred to as "family," "friends of Dorothy's," or men who were "in the life." Even today in professional circles there are coded ways of talking about fellow community members. Although the terms are now typically used in jest, they can at times be a useful way of eluding others who might be within earshot. While recruiting participants for the study, for example, I was told about "a fellow European" who might be a good candidate, and later about "some vegetarian friends" who might take part. Other men referred to gay friends as "sisters" or as members of the "club," "fraternity," or "congregation." When asked if she could recommend anyone, a woman in Dallas talked about the "junior varsity," naming several men who "play on the small team." A Philadelphia man repeatedly used the term "motefs" to refer to gay friends. When asked what a "motef" was, he laughed. "Oh, a motef is a 'member of the enchanted forest.' That's what we call them here at work."

As the community has become more visible (and its borders more permeable) in recent years, The Secret has remained its defining convention. Even when lesbians and gay men abandon their own closets, they tend to insist on the sanctity of others'. Coming out has become the central strategy of gay liberation, and there is now considerable pressure within the community to come out. Yet to expose someone against his or her will is still seen by most as an act of betrayal. It is considered disloyal to allow information about fellow gays and lesbians to slip into the hands of potentially hostile third parties, whether they are coworkers, family members, friends, or strangers. Several years after the "outing" controversy first made headlines, the consensus of opinion is that except in cases of blatant hypocrisy (such as a gay politician who votes against lesbian and gay causes), there is no justification to "out" other lesbians and gay men. Even if I reveal my own secret, the reasoning goes, I am obliged to keep yours.[10]

Beneath this convention lies the tacit assumption that with access (to the community and its secrets) come certain responsibilities. As Erving Goffman would say, once a man has been permitted "backstage," he must behave as a guest.[11] Audiences see only the performance, but those backstage see the mask come off, the props laid to rest. Having seen a man out of disguise, I know something his audience does not. Perhaps he and I will now engage in backstage talk about the stress of the performance (the hassle of inventing the story, the risk of forgetting who has been told what). We can rehearse together or share tips on technique (dodges and deceptions that were effective, disguises that failed). Perhaps we will also discuss another performer, concluding that his act is or isn't especially convincing ("Everybody knows he's gay. Who does he think he's fooling?"). In short, my fellow performer and I have acknowledged one another *as performers*. I now have a responsibility not to disrupt his performance.

When there are other lesbians or gay men in his office, a man may find that he has been admitted, automatically, to their backstage regions. Indeed, gays and lesbians usually take reciprocal access for granted. It is usually deemed quite acceptable, for example, for a gay man to reveal other lesbians and gays to their peers *within* the community, others who would presumably be welcome backstage. A man who would jealously guard a gay friend's backstage region in other settings, in the presence of strangers or potentially hostile outsiders, usually feels little need to do so in the company of other lesbians and gay men. No betrayal is intended when I inform a gay friend that a certain mutual acquaintance is gay, and the exchange of such information along extended gossip networks is rarely viewed as disloyalty.[12]

In part this is a function of the mechanics of self-disguise. Most gay men assume that their sexuality, however they (mis)represent it to others, will be apparent to lesbian and gay peers.[13] The disguises or dodges that work for straight audiences are often transparent to those who have used the same tactics themselves. As Barbara Ponse noted in her study of secrecy in the lesbian community, "A gay woman would be more likely than others to spot someone who, like herself, is passing for straight, as she would be aware of the nuances of passing. People who pass are alive to the cues given off by others who are passing. Among these cues is the recogniton of others' passing techniques and strategies."[14] The failure to say or do certain things, for example, can start the speculative ball rolling. Lesbians and gay men tend to notice when a coworker is vague about the gender of a frequent companion, when he is secretive about his personal life, or when he remains single and shows no sign of doing anything about it. "It takes one to know one," as the saying goes.

Gay lore has its own terms for this marked but difficult-to-define skill. Some call it "gaydar." Others joke that they can identify other gay men by looking them up in "the directory." Sean says that he knew one of his coworkers was gay "from the guy's persistence, and just from my intuitive sense." As he explains, "The guy wasn't looking at me as a buddy; he was looking at me for more than that. There are subtle mannerisms that one picks up as a homosexual, the certain smile, the picosecond-length longer in eye contact."

Todd remembers how he and Gary, both of whom work for Bell Atlantic, identified each other. "I was just moving into this condominium, and I had a lot of hassle getting this place ready," Todd recalls. "I had to make a lot of phone calls at work. Gary walked by my office one day—he told me this later on—and I had a floor plan of where the furniture was going. That was his tip-off that I was 'high-potential.' I didn't know if he was gay or not, but he kept wondering about me, asking questions like, 'What do you do on the weekend?' And I would say, 'I go to the beach.' 'What beach?' He got so inquisitive, I sort of caught on that he was gay and was trying to figure out if I was gay or not by how I answered these questions."

It wasn't until later that the questions gave way to an explicit conversation. "It took several months," Todd recalls. "Gary kept talking about Rehoboth, and then he talked about a particular guesthouse in Rehoboth. I knew that the guesthouse was gay. At that point I gave up the charade. Whenever Gary would ask something, I would tell him the truth. I don't remember quite *how* we ever talked about it, but I guess we must have. It just became real normal and natural. We got to be pretty decent friends."

Gay professionals also identify their peers by socializing and networking with them. Given the extended social circles in which gay men often travel, there has developed an elaborate web of interconnected gay friends and acquaintances, a national network that one man refers to as the "gay mafia." Glen remembers a not-too-unusual scenario. "My last year in the military, I was captain of a basic training company in Fort Bliss, and I dated this guy named Bruce Johnston, who had just graduated from Yale. Bruce later went off to Vietnam and then to Stanford Law School. Six or seven years ago, we were interviewing for a new position. They had identified this guy Jim they thought would be ideal. He was with a firm in San Francisco, so I flew him in and we all met at the Houston Club. There were about seven people there. Jim was a Stanford graduate, and during lunch I said, 'Jim, I'm not sure when my friend went to Stanford, but you might know him: Bruce Johnston?' Jim literally dropped his fork, and said, 'Very much so, we were in class together.' Well, I presumed Jim was gay, but I didn't know for sure, and it really didn't make any difference. It certainly wasn't the reason he was being considered; he was very qualified. So I put in a call to Bruce, and he called me back the next morning. It turns out that Jim had already called him about me. Bruce came on the line and said, 'The answer to all questions is yes. He's qualified, *and* he's gay.' Well, it turns out they were lovers."

Believing that they can usually spot a gay peer—and knowing that the world is often quite small—gay professionals typically make little effort to deceive one another. They presume backstage access and grant it freely to other members of the community. They also speak with confidence about the presence or absence of other gay people at work. "There are no other gays in my office," says Matt. "I would know it if there were." Others describe coworkers they "know" are gay, although they frequently base this conclusion on subtle behavioral clues. A recent survey of professional journalists, conducted by the American Society of News Editors, found that gays in the newsroom are almost universally aware of one another. Some 90 percent of the 205 respondents assumed that their fellow gay staffers knew about their sexuality, whether or not they had actually spoken about it.[15] A 1992 survey of *Out/Look* readers found that virtually all knew of other gay people at work—though many of these coworkers were ostensibly in the closet.[16]

Access to a man's backstage region is rarely limited, however, to fellow lesbians and gay men. Indeed, while gay peers tend to receive such access automatically, any number of people may populate a man's backstage region. It may include sympathetic friends who have been granted token membership in the clan, as well as people who have stumbled onto a man's secret through some other means.[17] It may even include people (like the company nurse) whose formal roles give them access to information about a man's sexual life. Of the men we interviewed, all but one included a heterosexual friend in their circle of confidantes. Likewise, my survey of *Out/Look* readers found that while 93 percent of respondents had come out to one or more of their coworkers, only 5 percent had limited their disclosures to other lesbians and gay men.[18]

Not all these people make effective allies, of course. Allies must have the requisite skills and motivation to assist in the performance. To be effective they must share a man's awareness of the situation and coordinate their own moves and countermoves to support his. They must also share his sense of urgency, his fear that there will be consequences should the performance fail to be convincing. For this reason lesbians and gay men are often cited as the best supporting players. They tend to have firsthand experience. They are also more likely to understand and abide by the community's unwritten rules about secrecy, to be socialized into its customs.[19]

But whether they are gay or straight, when allies fail they may place the entire performance at risk. Derek describes a woman in his office, June, who proved a poor ally. "There was this new kid in the office, a real cute little blond, quite the yuppie, quite the chase around women. All the women were crazy about him, and he was playing the game to the hilt. We were all dining one night in some nondescript place in Atlanta, and he said, 'Oh, I really like going to the Pleasant Peasant,' which is a chain in Atlanta. And the other guy said, 'Oh, God, I wouldn't go there, you know they're gay.' And the blond kid said, 'What the fuck do I care if they're gay or not? They're not screwing in my soup.' " Derek didn't know how to respond. "It took me aback," he says, "and I just got real quiet." Then he looked over at June, who was clearly upset. "June died a thousand deaths for me," Derek recalls, "and I was more upset by her reaction than the statement against being gay—I mean, you get used to that."

Apparently the others noticed June's reaction. "Afterwards this kid came up to June and said, 'My God, did I say something wrong? Is he gay?'" June tried to cover for Derek, saying, "'Oh, no, no, no. It's just that Derek has gay friends and might be offended.'" For Derek this set off a chain of complications. "This kid flipped backwards over me for a year, trying to make up, apologizing to the point that I finally said, 'What the hell are you talking about?' Because if I acknowledged it, that would be the same as saying, 'Yes, I'm gay.' He would call patronizingly, and when I went to Atlanta he made a point of taking me to the Pleasant Peasant." Looking back on the incident, Derek is critical of June. "You know, you don't need that kind of an ally," he says. "That's where the vulnerability lies—the ones who want to protect you but don't know how."

Breaking the Rules

Like any social convention, The Secret exists only to the extent that lesbians and gay men observe it. Unenforced it would cease to be a rule. Whatever its history it must be continuously defended if it is to remain binding. New members must be taught its significance. Indeed, even when they have independently drawn conclusions about the need for secrecy—from their own childhood experiences with homophobia, for example—new members learn its particular social forms through experience. Their specific ideas about exposure and disclosure are shaped by contact with other lesbians and gay men.

Within lesbian and gay circles one often witnesses what must be seen as rites of initiation or enforcement. Derek recalls a conversation he had with another gay man in his office. On several occasions Derek had overheard the man speak publicly and disparagingly about other gay people at work, and his response, ultimately, was to remind the man of the rules. "One day I went into his office—he was dropping all these little innuendos about gay people, little negative comments. I walked in and slammed the door shut, and said, 'Look, I know you're queer, so just cut the bullshit. I know you are, you know I am, so stop the games, stop the gay bashing. It's telling everybody in the world that you're gay.' The guy turned white, passed out, and wasn't able to see me for about a week in absolute terror that I might do something to him. Then he was great."

The conversation took the form of a lesson. In taking a scolding tone with someone he barely knew, Derek imagined himself a community elder, an agent of enforcement for a group to which both men presumably belong. He relied on the unspoken bonds of gay connectedness, the presumption that their mutual vulnerability made necessary a united defense. Teh other man had little choice but to oblige, especially given that Derek was also the more senior employee. Dan finds himself in a similar situation with Paul, a nurse in his clinic who is quite open about his sexuality. "It doesn't bother me that Paul has told people on staff that he's gay," Dan says. "If people want to know and he feels comfortable telling them, that's fine. But if there is somebody around, like one of our referring psychiatrists or psychologists, we have to put some limits on that." Nowhere is this more true than during lunch. "People come in and out of the lunchroom," says Dan. "Paul is very outgoing, very talkative. At the lunch table I've had to redirect the conversation just to cut down the risk. He knows that when I do that, it's because he's going a little bit too far, becoming a little too obvious, and he's okay with that."

Especially when a man's behavior threatens to expose his gay peers, they often consider it their right to step in and police the situation. Brent felt he had no choice but to do this with Keith, another gay man in his department. As Brent explains the situation, Keith is just a bit too "flamboyant." "Keith does more than he thinks he does," says Brent. "There are some minor things that I don't think he realizes, certain gay gestures and expressions." To protect himself Brent effects a studied dissociation from Keith while at work. He avoids Keith around lunchtime and steers clear of anything that might be seen as a personal conversation. "Maybe I'm just paranoid," he says.

Keith, meanwhile, thinks that Brent is the flamboyant one.

Several years ago, after a vacation, Brent came to work wearing an unevenly applied facial bronzer, which Keith considered "painfully obvious." Brent's boyfriend has an English accent, "which is pretty hard to disguise in Texas," and his telephone calls attract special notice among the office staff. "Brent comes to work in his Hugo Boss suits and Armani ties, decked out," according to Keith. "They've got him pinpointed." Like Brent, Keith assured me that it is not he but his coworker who is more obvious, more effeminate, more recognizable as a gay person. Each is self-conscious in the presence of the other, fearing that his own disguise is threatened by the presence of a less discreet peer.

Brent ultimately raised the issue with Keith. "Keith knew I was gay, and I knew he was gay, but we had never discussed it," says Brent. "One day he asked me to read a paper that he was very proud of, and it happened to be about homosexuality. That was the first time there was confirmation that 'I'm gay, you're gay, and we both know it.' After that happened I felt an obligation to discuss the situation. Basically I said, 'What you do in your own time is your business, but between eight and five it's my business, and we keep that separate. We work for a very redneck company, and don't think otherwise.' We just discussed the reality of our situation, that we work for a conservative company and some things are just not appropriate, whether that's personally objectionable to us or not. We're not on our own turf, we're on somebody else's turf.' " Since that time Brent feels that Keith has been compliant. He hasn't tried to "flaunt" his sexuality or "confirm things" to others in the department. "He understood the seriousness of the situation," says Brent, who now regards Keith as an ally.

Despite these efforts at enforcement, one cannot always take the loyalty of others for granted. Those backstage sometimes abandon the performer, no longer willing to participate in his act. Jack remembers the day his scheme collapsed. At forty-nine, with the help of a therapist, he had concluded that it was time to come out to his family. "I immediately told my wife, and as I anticipated, she immediately told me that I was leaving. She was working in another division of the company at the time. I was in a management job; she was in a marketing job. I had no choice but to let my friends know, because I knew they would eventually find out about my sexuality through the office grapevine. It was very painful to me at the time."

Phil recalls a similar situation in which a former ally turned sides. "Someone I dated in Raleigh was friendly with a straight guy in my office," he says. At some point the former boyfriend must have spilled the beans. Word eventually reached one of Phil's close friends, and she called him a few days later. "She called and said, 'Well, I hear you've been through some major changes.' And I said, 'Yeah, I got a divorce.' And she said, 'No, I heard more than that. I heard you were changing your sexual preference.' That was pretty early in the game, and I thought, 'Holy shit.' At the time I just said, 'Oh, really?' Since then we've had conversations, and I think she knows the truth, but my initial response to her was, 'That's bullshit. This guy is lying.' " Looking back, Phil describes the former boyfriend as a "bitchy queen" who was vindictive that he had been rejected. The gossip ultimately ceased, but even so, Phil thinks there is now little chance of reclaiming his former disguise. "It was one of those things that people thought was a joke at first," he says. "But after awhile they started to take it seriously."

Catastrophic failures like this are especially likely when a man confides in some, but not all, of his coworkers. By permitting them backstage on a selective basis, he eliminates the most important temporal and spatial barriers to the spread of his secret. Those in possession of the information are now in direct physical contact with those denied it. They may share office space, have lunch together, or play tennis after work. Only their loyalty stands in the way of a man's exposure. "We had to fire an attorney, Dana, who knew that I was gay," says Roger, an attorney with the Department of Labor. "As a supervisor it was my job to let her go. But first I felt I had to tell Maria, who was my boss, that there might be some repercussions or some threats against me after the firing. I was vulnerable. Dana could have started calling me a fag or something like that, and I didn't want Maria to be broadsided with something unforeseen. So I came out to her."

In part to avoid compromising situations like this, gay men rarely solicit their coworkers as potential sexual partners. While they often come out to others at work, they rarely come on to them. Of the men we interviewed, most knew of at least one other gay man in the office, but not one admitted to an intraoffice affair with him (suggesting either that such liaisons are highly uncommon or that gay men consider them too shameful to admit). Even when heterosexual coworkers engage in conspicuous romantic liaisons, gay men are usually loath to think of coworkers as potential sexual partners, at times holding themselves to a higher standard of professionalism than they observe in heterosexual peers. Others express their concern in more practical terms. A spurned lover could too easily become an enemy, they point out. "That would be unbelievably risky," says Martin. "Things might not work out, and then you would be stuck with that person in the office. There's no one in my office who's worth it."

Even when he avoids romantic entanglements at work, a man may find himself in a compromising position. "I was called in to take over this theater company in Washington," recalls Chris. "They were ninety days from bankruptcy and in terrible shape. As it turned out, an old 'trick' of mine worked there. He was very low in the hierarchy, and I think he was as shocked to see me introduced as the new president as I was to see him. It turned out that within a couple of months I had to fire almost the whole department, including him. He just went apeshit: 'I know about you! I'll tell!' It was really nasty. I told him, 'Go right ahead.' And he actually did try to get an appointment with the chairman of the board, who refused to see him." By this point, however, Chris had already changed strategies. He called the chairman and warned him that a disgruntled employee might be calling. "I told him that he was going to get a phone call and told him what it would be about. He thanked me for telling him and said that he would take care of it."

To avoid the opportunity for such betrayals, some men try to close off their backstage regions at work, to prevent access altogether.[20] They adopt a blanket policy of deceiving coworkers, withholding their secret even from the most trustworthy among them. They may also try to deceive gay coworkers, sometimes going out of their way to avoid them. Mark remembers being upset at first when another gay man at work gave him the cold shoulder. "The senior people are trying to stay closeted," he says. "They'll acknowledge me in the hallways, with 'Hi, how are you' kind of stuff, but they aren't terribly friendly. I used to have lunch with a senior vice president who's gay, but he would always call me to meet him in the lobby in ten minutes, or stuff like that." When Steve ran into a coworker at a local gay bar, the other man was obviously stricken. "At first I thought, 'Ohmigod, ohmigod,' but then I thought, 'What the hell,' and went up to him and said, 'Aren't you an auditor at United Savings?' And he said, 'Yeah,' and I said, 'I thought I'd seen you up there.' He was kind of cold and he backed off, so I didn't pursue it at all. I've seen him twice in the office since then and he's ignored me. I can deal with that."

John recalls the anxiety he caused when he ran into a gay parishioner at a local gay restaurant. "The first week I was here," he remembers, "I went up to the Venture Inn for dinner. Two members of the parish were there, and one of them said to me, 'I don't think it's a good idea for you to be here.' I said, 'Why, is the food that bad?' I remember going home and calling one of my friends and saying, 'This may be a real mistake.' " Even more hostile is the response John sometimes gets from other gay clergy. As he has become increasingly public about his own sexuality, John finds that they often avoid him at conferences. He's also excluded from Philadelphia's cocktail-party circuit of gay clergy. "I don't want to divide my life up the way those men do," he says. "It's hard to describe the feeling one has in a room of gay men, all breathless, all intent on not being out anywhere else."

A more extreme solution, of course, is simply to keep other gay men out of the office. Rather than guard his backstage region by avoiding contact with gay peers, a man can see to it that he has none. "It raises some concerns, especially when a guy is 'out,' " says Terry, who handles recruiting for his law firm. "It's hard to tell, during the interview process, if a person would be a bitchy mean queen if it doesn't work out. Let's say I hired somebody as an associate, he knew about me, and professionally it didn't work out. If I had to let him go, would he feel compelled to get back at me? His way of getting back might be to tell everybody about me." Clay says that this was the reason he blocked the hiring of another gay

secretary at his firm. Clay's boss was looking for a temporary secretary, and the top candidate was a man that Clay recognized from
the local gay bar. "I know him, and he's seen me out," Clay says.
"So I put the hook on him: 'Anthony, we don't want Anthony.' I
said something like, 'I hear Anthony comes in late, and lies a lot on
the job.' My boss went along." In fact Clay knew almost nothing
about Anthony and had no reason to question his work habits. He
knew only that Anthony is gay. "I just didn't want him around,"
Clay explains. "It would make me uncomfortable. I just didn't like
him. I don't care how good he is, I didn't like him, especially since
he was gay. I mean, I know there are gay guys here. There are
lawyers who are gay. I *know* they're gay, but I stay away from them
at work, too."

Matt used a similar maneuver to keep a gay manager out of
his district. "There was a trainee in Ford's regional office that
they were thinking about moving to Houston. I'd never met the
guy." Matt had heard through others, however, that the man is
gay. "He had gone through a training program with a bunch of
people who work for me, and he had publicly told them he's
gay. A couple of them warned me when they heard he was coming to Houston. Whether it's true or not I don't know, but I
stopped him and got somebody else. If he was indeed gay and
came to work for us, regardless of how good of a performer he
was, the boss would have just absolutely destroyed him." Matt
further confessed that the prospect of having another gay man in
the office made him uncomfortable, especially a man who
seemed to make no secret of it.

There is evidence that these concerns about loyalty are a function of increasing fragmentation within the gay community itself.
As a number of observers have pointed out, the code of secrecy is
breaking down. The rhetoric of gay liberation today endorses visibility as its chief strategy (whether achieved through the disclosure
of one's own sexuality, or at times, through the exposure of someone else's). Lesbians and gay men are also more visible than ever before, and with visibility has come the recognition that they are a
diverse, widely scattered group of people in disagreement about
who their enemies really are.[21] Community infighting, over every-

thing from AIDS to "outing" to the use of the term *queer,* has found its way into the mainstream press.[22] Only the most naive observer would now argue that homosexuals are a coherent community, defined in opposition to a single, readily identifiable foe.

The erosion of solidarity may explain the nostalgia older gay men sometimes feel for an earlier time. Jack, who is in his fifties, says that "as we become more and more visible and more and more open, I sometimes have a little sense of nostalgia, missing that secret society element that ran through the gay world more in the past than today. The more we demonstrate to the world that we're professional people and come from all walks of life, just like straight people, the better off we'll be. But there's part of me that likes the secret society we had ten or fifteen years ago."[23]

The result, as the secret society is displaced by a visible subculture that more closely resembles ethnic minority communities, is uncertainty about the rules. The responsibilities that once came with backstage access are now less clearly defined, and allies can no longer be taken for granted.[24] "I had this friend, Jim, who worked at Rohm & Haas," recalls Dave. "One time this guy from Jim's office saw him at Woody's [a local gay bar], and that Monday he called Jim into his office. He said, 'Jim, I want to introduce you to some people.' Then he got on the phone and called five or six gay men into his office. Jim was embarrassed, because it was pretty obvious that some of these guys were gay." In recounting the story, Dave expresses surprise that other gay men would be so careless with Jim's secret. "The office had glass walls, so Jim felt really exposed." Men that Jim regarded as potential allies had subverted his choice of strategy.

As norms about secrecy continue to change, such disagreements, misunderstandings, and outright betrayals will become increasingly common. There is less and less consensus in gay circles about the value of secrecy. For a growing number of men, visibility has become a personal as well as a political goal, making the closet—anyone's closet—seem like so many other quaint remnants of an increasingly distant, more oppressive time. Especially for men who came of age in the seventies and eighties, strict boundaries between gay and straight social worlds often make no sense. To some it is secrecy, not exposure, that constitutes the true betrayal of the gay community.[25]

Whatever position he takes in the debate about secrecy, a man can no longer take his allies for granted. If reflexive, unbounded loyalty was ever the norm in the gay community, it has now largely given way to more partial and conditional alliances. On all sides there is growing mistrust. Men who are closeted now complain that indiscreet peers threaten them with exposure. Those who are open, meanwhile, accuse those who are closeted of shirking a responsibility. "I have a lot of problems with closeted gay workers," says Chris, "because *they* have a lot of problems with openly gay men in the work environment. They're very standoffish, like, 'I don't want to associate with you because somehow by my proximity you'll give me away.' The worst experience that I had was with a fellow partner at Peat Marwick who was gay. We had mutual friends in common, and he ran for the hills any time I came around, just out of sheer terror that we would be associated."

In particular, from men at either end of the strategy continuum, one hears the accusation that those at the other end are cowards or traitors.[26] "I have to catch myself up short," Jack says, "feeling anger and frustration at people who are closeted." Indeed, the lingering notion that gay people are a *community*, bound by shared customs, makes it impossible to dismiss the behavior of those regarded as peers. The concern reflects more than a debate about abstract principles. Because he often relies on their support to execute his own strategy, a gay man may have a direct, personal interest in the strategy choices of his peers.

Men who counterfeit an identity, in particular, speak as if they've been betrayed by those who are more open. There is often scorn for "those activists," whom they imagine to have started "all that 'outing' business." When asked at the end of the interviewe if he had any further questions about the study, for example, Clay alluded to these frustrations. "If you're trying to make me come out at work, you're not gonna get it," he told us. When asked if he perceived that to be the purpose of the study, he replied: "That's how I felt during the interview. I think you would like for me to be 'out' at work." Another man asked, after our interview, if *The Corporate*

Closet would be published under a pseudonym. When we answered that it would not, he seemed annoyed. "I've never understood people who make sexuality their whole lives."

For men who counterfeit their sexual identities, an openly gay coworker is a concern for yet another reason By coming out a gay man changes the sexual culture of his workplace. Even if he doesn't directly implicate gay peers (or through association, draw attention to them), he creates an environment in which heterosexuality can no longer be taken for granted. Perhaps gay news items will now filter into discussion. Information on gay life-styles will become part of the office lore, and coworkers may now think to seek the "gay angle" on a political or moral question. Other gay people, his friends or lovers, will gradually become part of the social landscape. As this happens the presumption of heterosexuality will be shattered. A man who remains in the closet may face increased pressure to come out or increased difficulty in remaining closeted.

Carter suspects that this is why a particular coworker has always been hostile towards him. The reservations manager at the hotel, a man in his fifties, has always seemed distant and unfriendly. Carter thinks that this is because he "resents me for being happy and gay, decent looking, running around the world having fun. I think he's resentful that he can't be more open about it. I'm having fun with it and he's not." Even so, Carter observes the unwritten rule. When asked by other people if the reservations manager is gay, Carter tells them, 'You'd have to ask him.' It's just my standard answer for anybody. It's too fresh in my memory, being afraid that people would find out about me. So I'm not going to burn anybody."

By dividing his social world into distinct groups, a gay man forces on himself a series of difficult transitions. With each of his audiences, he must develop a distinct repertoire of behavior, shifting from one behavioral set to the next as the occasion demands. Even when the transition has become automatic, it is more than a matter of adjusting outward appearances. Not only can a man say and do things with one group that are forbidden with another, he may *feel* differently about himself in each of these settings. The transition inevitably produces a moment of psychic disequilibrium.

The transition is most jarring when the difference in roles is greatest.[27] As his work with ACT-UP became more consuming, Rodney felt increasingly disoriented, anxious, even disloyal as he returned to Wall Street each morning. "The other traders went out with brokers all the time; their whole social life was with other traders, and their friends were other traders. They would spend weekends together and go on extravagant trips—taking seaplanes to some lake to go fishing, or some shit like that. I was different in that respect. I kept my social life separate. I was gay on the weekends and a trader by week, so they had no idea. I didn't even join their gyms." The double life ultimately took its toll on Rodney, however. "Every minute off the trading floor I was doing ACT-UP stuff, going to meetings every night. It was just insane. I saw a shrink for six months about the fact that I was going crazy trading by day and being an ACT-UP activist by night." Even as Rodney embraced ACT-UP's famous slogan—Silence Equals Death—he continued to disguise himself at work. The hypocrisy ultimately became intolerable.

For other men, the transition becomes symbolic of the rejection they feel at work. As they repeatedly force themselves in and out of disguise, they internalize negative feelings about themselves. Mitch remembers a situation that left him feeling particularly degraded and foolish. "When Jay and I were together, we used to wear gold wedding bands," he recalls. "They were unmistakable. In fact, a lot of times it made me uncomfortable, because people would see the ring and assume that I was married and then start asking questions. So I got in the habit of taking the ring off at work, especially when seeing new clients or other people who knew I wasn't married."

Mitch had come out to some of his coworkers, but with others he continued to counterfeit an identity. Moving from one situation to the next, he shifted gears and adjusted his ring. "One time it really backfired on me. I went to see a client, a liberal young couple. He's a psychiatrist, she's a teacher. But I had met them socially, and they knew I wasn't married. I showed up for the meeting, and then I realized that I had my wedding band on. So I excused myself and went to the bathroom to take it off. I came back, and we finished whatever business we had to do that day. Then, as I'm leaving the apartment—the husband is walking me out—he says, 'Can I ask you a question?' And I said, 'Uh, yes.' And he said, 'When you came in you were wearing a gold wedding band, and at one point during the morning you took it off. Why did you do that?' "

Mitch was stung by the question. "I turned purple and said, 'Well, I'm involved in a relationship with somebody, and we exchanged rings, but we're not married. Sometimes I take the ring off.' And then I felt like a total jerk for even thinking that this would bother him." Eventually Mitch hopes that by coming out to all his coworkers, he can avoid awkward situations like this. "It's just too traumatic to keep shifting gears," he says. "It would be nice to be the same person, myself, all the time."

6

Dodging the Issue

WHEN A MAN is unwilling to remain in the closet but mindful of the dangers that lie outside its protective walls, he may try to find middle ground. Between the extremes of deception and disclosure, between counterfeiting and coming out, he seeks an alternative. He wants a way of protecting himself that doesn't require an elaborate, tiresome fiction. More than anything, he wants the issue to go away. Professional culture—demanding that he be asexual while presuming him to be heterosexual—encourages him to believe that this is possible.

Justin faced this dilemma when he accepted a teaching job in the Washington area. "When I started at the university, I made a conscious decision about how I wanted to act," he says. "I had just moved here, and had decided to separate from my wife. I planned to get more involved in the gay community." It wasn't that the university, a private liberal arts institution just outside the city, seemed inhospitable. Indeed, one of the reasons Justin had taken the Washington job was that the city seemed a tolerant place for gay people. Still, he worried that being gay would be a liability at work. He had heard that the administration was conservative and knew other gay faculty members who had paid for their candor. "I decided that coming out on the job could hurt me for tenure," he recalls.

Justin's response was to dodge the issue altogether. "I made a decision that at least until tenure came around I was going to be really quiet," he says. "I'd do my work, do my teaching, work on my alcoholism, get involved in some gay organizations, but have as little involvement in the job as possible." The idea, he says, was to avoid deception without putting himself at risk. "I thought that would protect me," he says. "If nobody knew, they couldn't hold it against me. So that was my approach—to deliberately not make friends, to deliberately not get to know anybody too well, to just do my work and teaching and research."

Justin adopted a busy, professional manner and avoided social activities with colleagues. "I always kept the boundaries there," he explains. "We'd go out to lunch, for example, but I'd have to be in class *promptly at one*. I always made sure there were conditions to cut it off." He also established spatial barriers that limited his contact with others. "I even requested an office that was out of the way," he says. "Office space is very tight at the university; it's such a small campus that everybody has to share offices. Well, they had this one office way down in the basement, two floors below ground. I asked for that one because I could be all by myself. I isolated myself that way, and that's the way I kept it."

The result was a series of one-sided relationships with colleagues and students. "When I say I cut people off, I really *cut people off,*" says Justin. If the conversation was going even remotely in any direction about me, I'd steer it elsewhere. I'd just put it back on them. So if they were talking about a party or get-together, I'd just ask, 'Was so-and-so there?' Or I'd follow up on something else they said. I'd let it go for a few minutes, then I'd say, 'Well, I've got to get to work.' They'd be willing to talk for an hour, but I'd take off." As a result, although Justin's coworkers seemed to like him and seemed eager to spend more time with him, they knew little about him. "It was fairly extreme," he says. "I would avoid all social invitations. I wouldn't even get into conversations in the hall with people, because I didn't want someone to say, 'Oh, how was your weekend? What did you do?' I didn't even want those things to come up, because I didn't want to lie either, I didn't want to get into lying. I was trying to avoid the double life that lots of people have."

Justin ultimately paid a price for his choice of strategy. He had known since 1987 that he was HIV-positive. In the winter of 1989, fatigued and afraid that he wouldn't be able to carry his spring teaching load, he decided to go on disability. The formal procedure was quick and painless, but it left Justin feeling isolated and alone. From the other faculty, whom he had carefully avoided for years, there was scarcely a word. "That's probably when the isolation hurt me most," he says. "Looking back on it, I think that if I'd been friendlier with people, none of that could have hurt—the bonding and contacts with people, feeling more involved."

Since leaving the university, Justin has worked out of his home. "I still go over to school now and then," he says, recalling his last trip to the campus. "Just as finals were going on last semester, I ran into one of the other faculty, and he asked me, 'Oh, how's your grading going on finals?' " Justin pauses while telling his story and shrugs his shoulders. "That was probably—in all the years I was there—the toughest question I ever had. It put me on the spot, since I would have to acknowledge my situation. I made one of my usual, neutral comments: 'Well, this *is* a busy time of the year— how are *yours* going?' He didn't even know I was on disability. It's a full year I've been gone—that's how invisible I was. He hadn't seen me for a year, and he didn't realize it."

Avoidance tactics like this are enormously common among gay professionals. Among the men we interviewed, more than half were currently using one or more of them.[1] Rather than fabricate a sexual identity, they try to elude one altogether. They provide coworkers with as little evidence of their sexuality as possible, encouraging them to reach for alternative, nonsexual interpretations of whatever evidence does exist. They sustain the presumption of heterosexuality, withholding evidence that might shatter it. Sexuality becomes no less managed a status in these cases, but the management now has a different aim.[2] Rather than reveal misinformation about his sexuality, a man reveals nothing. He tries to appear asexual.

Dodging the Issue

Many explicit sexual disclosures can, in fact, be avoided. For every situation or behavior that communicates something about sexuality, we can identify a corresponding dodge.

The most common of these are verbal dodges, attempts to withhold the sexual information that is routinely exchanged in conversation. "When people ask questions about my personal life, I behave like a politician," says Stuart. "I try not to answer, but not to have people *realize* that I'm not answering." Dave uses the same tactic with people in his office. "The worst times are Monday mornings," he explains, "when people start talking about what they did over the weekend. They did this or that with their girlfriend or wife, and they ask me what I did. I just keep things as general, as generic as possible, not mentioning any names. I try not to use 'we.' It's easy to do, but I think that's the most stressful time."

All of us, at one time or another, have used conversational gambits like these. We avoid touchy subjects or sidestep unwanted questions. We draw attention away from ourselves and steer the conversation in the direction of the other party. Dave remembers a typical conversation with Audrey, a woman from personnel. "She had a friend who was gay, very blatantly and openly gay, and I know him. One day Audrey came over and says, 'Oh, I didn't know you knew Victor.' Then she says, '*How* do you know Victor?' Luckily Victor and I lived in the same apartment building at the time, so I said, 'We live in the same apartment building and there are social functions; that's how I met him.' "

The initial dodge seemed to satsify Audrey's curiosity, but before long she raised the issue again, this time with a question about Dave's roommate (and lover), Kyle. "I guess Audrey put more and more together," Dave says, "I don't know *how* she found out, but last fall we were walking through the Reading Terminal Market and she asked if I was going to my parents' house or to Kyle's parents' house for Thanksgiving. And I said, 'Well, my parents invited Kyle, but we're going to his parents' house.' As the conversation continued, Dave grew uncomfortable. Finally, when Audrey asked how long he and Kyle had "been together," Dave responded with an explicit dodge. "She started talking about how long she'd been with *her* boyfriend, so I finally said, 'Audrey, I'm not going to discuss relationships with you.' I just changed the subject." Tom used a similar dodge when a fellow teacher, a woman named Alice, made a string of suggestive remarks. "One day, in front of everybody, Alice says, 'I'm practically throwing myself at you and you're not reacting. Are you gay?' I said, 'Alice, what the hell makes you think you're so fucking desirable? I've kicked better out of my bed.' She was the only person that's ever come out and asked something like that. And that was that."

Some men use more subtle maneuvers, turning personal questions into generic ones, answering them in impersonal ways. "Everyone at work knows I live in a brownstone," says Clay, "and they ask, 'Well, do you have a roommate?' And I say, 'Yes, I have a roommate, and we live in a brownstone, *thank you very much*. Do *you?* Or 'Yes, I do live in a brownstone—aren't they wonderful?' I get off the subject of my roommate right away." When a secretary asked Martin if he thought lesbians and gays should be allowed to serve in the military, he joked that he was "on the side of world peace. 'You know me, I'm a leftover hippie. We don't need an army.' " Tony uses this approach with his father. "One time, I was talking about buying a house, and my father insisted on telling me about these two men—one of them was a salesman at his company—who bought and rehabilitated a house together in Society Hill. He wanted to know what I thought about that. Now, I *knew* what my father really wanted to talk about—these weren't the only men to buy a town house in Society Hill." Tony tried to steer the conversation back to his own questions about real estate. "My reaction was, 'That's interesting, Dad, but I want to talk about buying my own house.' I didn't want to talk about being gay right then."

Even in contexts that seem to encourage sexual candor, men can avoid self-disclosure with calculated evasions. Joel runs a weekly church discussion group that focuses on minority issues. The group is small, he says, and the conversation is often intimate. Yet Joel has never revealed his own sexuality to anyone in it. "If I were asked directly, I might just say, 'Well, we're really not talking about our own orientations here.' That's one possible response. Another response might be, 'I'm black, I'm a woman, I'm a Muslim, I'm gay, I'm very poor, I am *all* those things that are discriminated against.' That's another way to cut the cloth." Both of Joel's replies take the form of verbal dodges. The first is a nonanswer, an explicit refusal to supply the information requested, while the second answers the question in metaphorical, nonsexual terms—clearly not the spirit in which it was asked. For the time being, however, no one in the group has asked Joel a direct question about his sexual orientation.

Darren tries to temper his evasions with humor. In his dental clinic, several of the hygienists are young women who enjoy teasing him; the clinic administrator, a woman named Regina, is especially fond of sexual jokes. "She embarrassed me terribly one day," Darren remembers. "We're in the lounge at lunchtime, and a lot of people were around, and she said, 'Oh, Darren, I hope you don't mind, I used your name.' I said, 'What do you mean?' She said, 'I entered you in the wet Jockey shorts contest at Gatsby's [a local gay bar],' because they were having a bikini contest or buns contest or something like that. 'I think you'll win.' It just embarrassed me tremendously. There were fifteen people around. I said, 'Regina, I don't know—I'm about ten years past my prime. I don't think I'll be going.' Then I said, 'Oh, *look at the time!* I gotta go.' Got out of that room real fast. I try to avoid those homosexual conversations." Rather than confirm or deny what Regina had insinuated about his sexuality, Darren called attention to his age.

Darren routinely deflects personal questions with this sort of dodge. "I'm really unfair in that respect," he says. "I ask these women about their personal lives because I care about them so much—I really *do* care about them and want to know that they're happy and that type of thing." Yet when asked an explicit question about his own life, Darren makes a joke. "I simply deny that I have a relationship. I tell them that I'm celibate. That's how I handle it. 'I just don't date. I'm fickle, and no one would date me.' If pushed, I'd say, 'Well, I just never found the right person. No time to date. Work too much. Can't afford it.' "

Rather than improvise a verbal dodge, it's often easier (and less stressful) to steer clear of situations in which a dodge might be needed. One can often avoid intrusive questions altogether by using situational dodges to avoid casual lunches, cocktail parties, company softball games, and other settings in which sexual communciation is expected. Clay says that this is the reason he doesn't invite coworkers into his home. Though he's a superb cook and enjoys playing host, he worries that the intimate setting would invite questions about his private life. Other men avoid company parties and outings, especially those at which dates and spouses—and thus the subject of dating and marriage—might be part of the evening.

Todd finds that situational dodges have become second nature. Circumstances constantly arise that require him to decline a social invitation, withdraw from an activity, or protest that he has another obligation. Because he lives in Manhattan, Todd usually finds it easy to avoid after-hours socializing with coworkers, most of whom live in suburban New Jersey. When they travel together, he simply excuses himself from evenings out with "the guys." "On business trips they like to go to go-go bars," he says. "I make a statement like, 'That sounds like fun,' but I conveniently arrange that I can't go. Or I say, 'I have to work on this,' or I say, 'No, I'm going to work out and I'll meet you for dinner or something.' I try to make it a nonissue."

For Todd these tactics have coalesced into an entire attitude, a disposition toward his professional peers. He neither extends nor accepts social invitations, a habit that over time has put miles between himself and the other staff members. "It's not really conscious," he says. "It's just so natural at this point. I don't make up any stories; I just avoid having to. My secretary is having a dinner party next weekend, and her boyfriend works at the company. I overheard her making these dinner plans, inviting some people that I'm friends with. My first thought was, 'Oh God, I hope I'm not invited.'" To his relief he wasn't.

As he settles into this pattern, Todd imagines the road ahead. "I know this one guy who is much older, who's in a real senior-level position. He's rumored to be gay, and I'm sure he *is* gay. But I don't think he's ever let on." The man is rarely seen socializing after work, and is perceived as something of an enigma. "Maybe someday I'm going to be in the same position: fifty years old, never married, and there'll be plenty of speculation that I'm gay. But I won't ever acknowledge it."

Sensitizing the Subject

Some men withhold sexual information without actually avoiding social contact. Verbal and situational dodges permit a man to withdraw from intrusive situations, but it is often preferable to change the situation itself, to make it less intrusive without abandoning it altogether. He can make sexual inquiries per se seem rude, inappropriate, or unwelcome. In many cases, a man can project the image of an aloof, intensely private, or doggedly professional man—a guy who is "strictly business." Rather than rely on specific verbal or situational dodges, he can create an environment in which they are unnecessary.

William, a psychiatrist with a large practice in suburban Maryland, uses this tactic with the men and women who share his office. In his four years at the clinic, not one of his coworkers has shown the slightest interest in William's personal life. When asked how that situation evolved, William says he isn't sure. "They don't ask, and I'm not sure how I do this exactly, but I've always managed to project that I don't want to hear those questions. And I don't." Several years ago, he ran into a former coworker in a gay bookstore, and the conversation turned to work. "At the hospital, people were forever asking this guy about what he does, who he does it with, and what his personal life is like. I told him that no one *ever* asks me those kinds of questions. And he said, 'You have a completely different aura about you. You were there to work, and that's it. People talked to you about work, and they felt you were very open about it. But there was never any question of talking about anything else.' " Indeed, William admits that he is shy, someone who is most comfortable in the role of therapist, listening rather than talking. He appears testy when asked direct personal questions. "I don't know exactly how I avoid those questions at work," he says, "but I do."

Where William is reserved, other men forestall personal inquiries by being aggressive. Grey makes them seem rude and old-fashioned. His demeanor is aristocratic, and he recognizes that coworkers sometimes resent his pretentious manner. When asked if his sexual life is ever discussed at work, he seems ruffled. "Oh God, no, no! That's just not appropriate," he says. "I mean, we *never* talk about that. No one has ever asked me, in six years, 'Do you have a girlfriend?' That's such an old way of thinking; people just *don't* any more." Around Grey one can imagine feeling that personal inquiries are impolite; his huffy evasions seem to forestall them.

When people complain that he is being evasive, Scott simply stands his ground. "People tell you you're antisocial," he explains. "I just say, 'Yeah, so?' I think they're unprepared for that." At least once someone teased Scott for being so aloof. "Scott, you're not on this earth," a coworker told him. "You hover." Tom struck a similar pose when a fellow teacher began to meddle in his affairs. "She was a busybody," he says. "She said, 'You're thirty-seven or thirty-eight years old, and you're still not married.' And she said, 'I know a girl.' So I told her, 'If I want to find somebody, I'll find them myself. I really don't need your help.' And that put an end to that."

Such rebuffs are tolerated because cultural norms set ceilings on the amount of disclosure that is considered appropriate in relationships with coworkers, friends, and complete strangers. By emphasizing the boundary aspects of a relationship, a man can withhold information or exercise "reserve," making it clear that further disclosure is inappropriate.[3] When a woman in his clinic posed a direct question, Darren reminded her of the rules. "She had been there two or three weeks," he recalls. "I had just gotten to work. She walked back and stood at the door of my office with her hands on her hips, and said, 'Are you gay?' " Darren replied that it was none of her business. "I think you're rude for bringing it up," he said.

For the tactic to work, however, a man must limit his own curiosity about the lives of others. If questions about sexuality are to seem "rude," he must himself refrain from asking them. By showing an interest in the personal lives of his peers, he invites reciprocal inquiries, and this so-called "reciprocity effect" tends to draw him into the exchange.[4] Nick, a middle manager with a data management company in New York, explains that he knows "who's married and who's not, but I don't ask about other relationships, I guess because I don't want them to turn around with the same question for me." Another gay man in Nick's office takes this approach to an extreme. "He keeps his distance from most people. He won't eat lunch with anyone and won't go out with anyone after work. He arranges these very formal Christmas dinners, and they're only for the people at work. They can't bring their spouses or boyfriends or girlfriends." In the office no one asks questions about the man's personal life. "He is so uptight about his extracurricular activities, they wouldn't dare."

Roy, who works for a division of Time-Warner in New York, says that no one at work ever asks the "tough questions" about his life. "It has to do with how often you ask *other* people questions," he says. "I never volunteer any information, and I certainly don't lead conversations in that direction." Although he did not consciously arrange it, Roy recognizes how the situation evolved. "I think it's part of a protective thing that a lot of gay people do. You don't go out of your way to inquire about other people's personal lives because that invites questions about your own. It becomes a little habitual in terms of keeping to yourself and going out of your way not to mix business and private."

Organizations vary widely in the degree to which they permit or encourage such segregations. All set up some kind of boundary between work and nonwork, business and leisure, the personal and the professional. In some, work relationships extend well beyond the office to dinners with clients, opera nights with the boss and his wife, or ski trips with others in the department. Social activities flow seamlessly into work activities as spouses, roommates, and girlfriends are drawn into the company's extended family. In others the boundaries are more strict. Interpersonal contact may be limited by work that requires men to spend most of their time on the road, with clients, or alone. After-hours socializing may be rare. Personal conversations may be limited. Sexuality is implied more often than discussed, presumed rather than explicitly displayed.

An organization's "social intrusiveness" has implications for a gay man's choice of strategy. Avoidance tactics are easier to use when personal questions are rare or when social obligations are limited. "I think the law is one of the more fortunate, white-glovey professions in that respect," says Arthur. "If it were necessary for me to do a whole lot of socializing—like playing golf or bridge with the "old man" and his wife—if I were in that kind of place, if I were always required to have a perky little Buffy by my side, it would be harder. In the early days I had to do that, but I'm speaking from a position where I'm older. I can call my own shots now."

Organizations that emphasize social activities, whether they are company parties or client dinners, tend to be more intrusive. "That's one of the things that's good about working for the federal government, as a gay person," says Roger. "It's much easier to keep the worlds apart." The men and women in Roger's department spend little time together outside work. Although he knows that some are married, he has never met their wives or husbands. The department has a softball team and an annual holiday party, but there is little pressure to take part in either. "You don't have to belong to the social clubs or bring in clients. You don't have to expose your private life to members of the firm on a social basis in order to succeed at the organization. People in the government don't have to socialize one bit. And they usually don't."

John, an Episcopalian priest, says that his choice of profession was influenced by these same considerations. He recognized, as a young man, that the priesthood set limits on the disclosures that would be required of him. "Part of what appeals to people—why they go into the ministry—is that it allows you to be very, very close to people without having them ask *you* any questions. So there's a sort of voyeuristic part of the ministry, and I think that's why it appeals to gay people to some degree, because I think most gay people are really good at viewing other people's lives, kind of like spies. You've been planted in this heterosexual world, and we're always outsiders to a degree. And ministry's exactly the same kind of thing. It's very much like being gay in general, only raising it to another level."

Like doctors, lawyers, therapists, and other professionals who are paid to ask questions, John finds it easy to keep the relationship one sided; the usual rules about reciprocal curiosity do not apply. "I can go into any situation and ask embarrassing personal questions, really participate in people's lives in a way that no other person can as an outsider, as a nonfamily member, and yet I can be confident they're not going to ask a single thing about me unless I offer it or give them permission." The nature of John's job, and the relationship it prescribes with his congregation, ensures that he can avoid unwanted probes into his personal life.

Other structural characteristics, like the organization's size, can erect boundaries to disclosure. Larger organizations ensure a degree of anonymity and mobility that tend to discourage intimate social ties. At the same time they offer a larger pool of potential friends and lower the relative importance of any one relationship that has become a source of trouble.[5] This was one of the first things Barry noticed when he moved from a small firm to a much larger one. "One of the reasons I changed companies was because I had too many people that I was extremely close to. I wanted to go to a more anonymous type of firm, a bigger firm, where people are friendly but there aren't the same kind of heated relationships that there were in the other firm. There's a big difference between a law firm that has three hundred people in it and one that has seventy, eighty, ninety people in it. At the old firm I knew every single solitary person including the people in the mail room, and they all knew me. Here I don't even know all the laywers down the hall from me."

Even the physical design of the workplace can discourage coworkers from being intrusive. Some offices are designed to be open and communal, with rooms that have no doors and desks that are not separated by walls or partitions. In Carl's company, a real estate firm in San Francisco, some fifty people share a large room with long rows of desks, bordered by some smaller offices with glass walls. "This isn't a place where you can easily keep secrets," he explains, pointing to the telephones on each desk. Traders and stockbrokers also describe large, unpartitioned work spaces that facilitate constant interaction. "You hear everyone else's phone calls," according to Rodney, "and you don't have much privacy." From surgeons one hears about the long hours and confined space of the operating room. According to Kirk, "People who work together in a constant workplace, a confined environment like an office, it's second nature for them to talk about their private lives, to know about each other's private lives. I think sexuality enters into that if someone wants to be included in the general give and take around the water cooler. I think that eventually it becomes unavoidable."

Organizations that observe weak boundaries between personal and professional matters tend to discourage the use of avoidance tactics. Of the men we interviewed, almost half (49 percent) said that coworkers frequently talk or joke about sex. Thirty percent said that social obligations were common at work, whether they were formal parties, client events, or informal social get-togethers. Another 34 percent said that socializing with coworkers was at least sometimes a necessity. Under these circumstances avoidance strategies may be unavailable. When he spends a good deal of social time with people from work, a man may be forced to reveal *something* about his sexual life. He responds either by inventing one (counterfeiting), or by revealing something authentic (integrating). "I try to be as vague as possible," says Glen, "but if I need to lie, I'll lie."

Milton feels his choice of strategy was forced by an inquisitive superior. "Several years ago, my boss came into my office," he remembers. "It was late at night, and as he turned to walk away, he said, 'Oh, by the way, *get married.*' Now, I knew what that meant. Earlier in my career I had worked in the U.S. Senate, and I was sitting in the back of a limousine with a senator, the chairman of the committee for which I worked. He was clearly trying to get at what my sexuality was. He said, 'Are you married? Have you ever been married? Is there anyone special in your life?' It scared the dickens out of me, first because I thought he was coming on to me, and secondly because I just wasn't prepared for it. So I lied. I said, 'I'm not married, never have been, but yes, there is someone special in my life—and she's wonderful.' "

Pressed in this way, other men shift in the opposite direction. Several years ago, when asked if he was gay, Carter decided it was time to come out. "This woman came into my office and shut the door and she said, 'I just thought I'd ask you, are you gay?' And I turned beet red and everything, because I had never really discussed it with peers before, and I said, 'Yeah.' And she said, 'Well, I just don't believe it. I heard the rumors, but I can't believe you're gay. You don't act like it, blah blah blah. So she and I started talking about it openly, then another person would get brought in, and finally it was just all out."

Until he finds himself in this situation, however, a gay man may not know which way he will jump. Some say they would prefer to come out, but admit that it will depend on the circumstances. "I've often thought what I'd say if someone asked me," says Nick, "but no one ever has. I'd like to think I'd be honest, but I doubt I would be. It would depend on how I was asked. If they asked in a degrading way—'Are you gay *or what?*—I'd probably tend to say no. But if they asked in a more positive way, I'd probably say, 'Yeah, why do you ask?' or something like that." Howard, a labor relations executive at Pacific Bell in San Francisco, says that, "My general rule is that if I don't really know who you are, and don't really know where you're coming from, I keep the conversation fairly oblique."

In other organizations, when such questions go unasked, avoidance strategies become the obvious choice. "I wouldn't mind being out to a handful of people, including my boss," says Tony. "But even if I *were* out, my boss wouldn't ask me about my personal life. That's the thing about him. He keeps a hands-off attitude with the staff and doesn't like to socialize with them." For Tony this seems almost to force an avoidance strategy. Jeff says the same thing about his boss, Skip. "Skip's whole attitude toward work is that he really keeps his private life private, to a greater extent than most people I've worked with. So I don't see the point in coming out." In the long run, if he stays with the firm, Jeff plans to raise the issue. "But it's not like previous jobs, where I had annual office dinner dances where everybody was expected to bring a date and everything. I don't run into those situations. If I go to work for another company where there is a lot more social activity, then it might make sense. There may eventually come a time when I need to say, 'Look, you guys go out and do all these things with your wives or dates, and here's the reason I don't.' "

But until someone forces the issue, these men find it easiest to accommodate the prevailing climate of professional indifference. Several of Randy's coworkers know that he is gay, and he admits that "it would be nice" to speak more openly on the subject. But in his environment, a large Wall Street firm, there is little incentive. "Even when I've been out with guys who know I'm gay, they don't ask anything about who I'm seeing. It would be nice to have people ask about your relationships, 'Are you happy?' and all of that." But, given his environment, Randy doesn't consider this likely. "People don't talk like that anyway," he explains. "Even the straight guys, among themselves, they never ask, 'Gee, how's it *really* going with Joe and the new kid? Are you guys *really* happy? It's *really* tough, isn't it?' People just don't have conversations like that. This is a business of strength, and it's just not part of our personality to be so nurturing." For the time being, Randy uses an avoidance strategy. "I chalk it up to the fact that work relationships aren't like that anyway, whether you're straight, gay, whatever. That's just professional environments in general."

Distracting the Audience

A man can also avoid a (homo)sexual identity by encouraging coworkers to draw alternative, non-sexual conclusions about his behavior. Rather than dodge or preempt a specific disclosure, he can supply an asexual interpretation of whatever *is* revealed. Rather than disguise traits that might otherwise be coded as "gay," he interferes with his coworkers' construction of the evidence.[6]

Often this means that signs of nonconformity, sexual or otherwise, are given "cover stories" that explain them away. Traits that might lead others to conclude that a man is gay (effeminate manners, natty clothing, or a disinterest in traditional male pursuits such as sports) are comfortably assimilated into an alternative, nonsexual identity (as an oddball, eccentric, or intellectual). Unconventional behavior is thus assigned a nonsexual label, dismissed as evidence of an unconventional personality, not sexuality. Tip, for example, uses his southern background to explain the fact that he is "different." The other residents have at times teased him for being mysterious about his social life; they also joke about his accent, a gentle Louisiana drawl. Tip hopes that they interpret these traits as regionalisms, a sign of his upbringing. "I'm from the South," he says, "and maybe I'm a little different anyway." Chuck, likewise, hopes that he is simply perceived to be a different kind of person. "I'm somebody who doesn't like sports, for instance, which is very unusual on the trading floor; *everybody* likes sports. I tell people that I don't even read the sports page. I have a different sense of humor—that kind of different."

Al suspects that his coworkers see him as someone whose temperament sets him apart from the other men and women at work. "There are single people who break the curve," he explains, "and I think that's the category they probably put me in—you know, eccentric. The model is: Men take wives and have children. But maybe the model is also that some men just can't get along with women or want to live alone—which is really odd, because while I live alone I wouldn't describe myself as being a loner or alone. But I think they have that impression of me. I think they just say, 'Well, maybe he's just one of those people who isn't going to settle down until late in his life.'"

One can "break the curve" in other ways. Al described a gay coworker, Brian, whose sense of humor sets him apart. Although he is effeminate and fits the stereotype most people have of gay men, others do not seem to interpret these traits as a sign of Brian's sexual orientation. "I doubt that they know Brian's gay," says Al. "They probably put him more in the category of being 'eccentric.'" The evidence that Brian is gay—single, effeminate, odd—is assimilated into his role as the office practical joker. Coworkers explain his differentness as a function of his personality, not his sexuality.

Men find this tactic difficult to use, however, when they are otherwise perceived to be "normal." Steve recalls a conversation in which one of his coworkers, Tamara, seemed puzzled that he never semed to have a girlfriend. Several of the young people in the office are single, and Steve had often complained that he just "hadn't found the right girl yet." But after a while the excuse began to wear thin. "Some people are reserved," Steve says, "but I'm very outgoing. So it's harder for them to see me being this way and not dating. I'm friendly. I meet people. But why don't I *date?* So something doesn't add up right there. Some of the other guys at work are quiet, and they might have a problem, theoretically, meeting girls. But that explanation doesn't work for me."

Rather than point to a personality trait like shyness, some men use more concrete identities to forestall sexual interpretations of their nonconformity. Miguel uses his status as a medical student and temporary U.S. resident to mollify his family. "When I went to medical school [in Puerto Rico], it gave me four years more to have an excuse not to have a girlfriend. Then I moved here [to Philadelphia], which gives me another excuse, because my mother doesn't want me to get married here. She thinks I'm going back to Puerto Rico." Similarly, Russ uses his transitional status as a cover story. "It's very easy to explain my lack of a spouse because I'm in law school; everybody knows that. And so I just don't have time. That's what I say, and that's what they assume." When pressured to participate in after-hours socializing, Russ explains his reluctance as a function of his personality. "I'm a very conservative person. If I were straight I probably wouldn't go to a bar anyway. So it's easy to explain that away, too."

Other men cultivate a conspicuous political reputation, as a liberal or feminist, to avoid the more damning reputation of homosexual. Our model of "professional" behavior easily accommodates political and ethical stand-taking, and it is no breach of office etiquette to make one's views known in the context of office small talk. When asked why he cared so much about gay issues, for example, Scott told a coworker that, "I live downtown, and I see homophobia all the time. I'm with it. I want to combat it." With this move Scott claimed an identity as a liberal or urbanite, sidestepping an identity as gay man. He implied that his interest in gay politics was a function of his ethical convictions, not his sexuality.

Whether the alternate identity is temporary or lasting, formal or informal—as a law student or liberal, foreign resident or feminist—it supplies a nominally asexual cover.[7] As Martin explains, "My views about abortion, civil rights, and homophobia are all well known. I haven't made a secret about any of them. What *is* a secret, though, is the reason I probably hold those views. When push comes to shove, I'd insist that I'm an educated liberal, not a queer."

On balance, can we say that avoidance strategies are effective? Have these men made their sexuality seem irrelevant and unimportant to their work? Do others think of them in asexual terms? Or do coworkers know that they are gay, even as they politely dance around the subject?

The answers are less important than the fact that the questions typically go unasked. Men who use avoidance tactics are often perfectly comfortable with the idea that coworkers *might* be aware of their sexuality. What matters is that they have not been forced explicitly, unambiguously to address the issue. The success of the strategy lies not in the conclusions their peers may or may not draw, but in the freedom it gives a man from dwelling on the subject. When he uses avoidance tactics, a man does not in fact escape a sexual identity; there is no way of avoiding one altogether. Rather, he abstains from supplying active input, thus assuming a passive role in the construction of an identity, to be assigned by others. As the audience draws whatever conclusions it will in an informational vacuum, assumptions and guesses fill the gap left by his silence.

The result is a spiral of silence on the subject of homosexuality.[8] In most professional settings there is no regular forum for the discussion of gay lives or individuals, no context in which such topics routinely come up. The resulting silence on the subject only reinforces its forbidden status. When asked if coworkers ever discuss homosexuality, gay men sometimes recall a conversation about a celebrity or politician rumored to be gay, or about AIDS. More recently, they recall debates about the U.S. military's ban on homosexuals. But few recall conversations about anything as mundane as the house payments, career decisions, or domestic squabbles of people known to be gay. The silence, in turn, begets more silence. When asked why he thinks his coworkers have "no idea" that he is gay, Gary, a tax administrator at Bell Atlantic, offered this explanation: "I think that they would feel uncomfortable if they knew. I don't sense that discomfort, so I assume they don't know." The circularity of Gary's illogic would be evident—if not for the fact that no one in his office actually talks about the issue.

It is much easier to capitulate to the spiral than to break it. Russ finds himself in a typical situation. When asked what his coworkers think about homosexuality, he admits that he isn't sure. "Maybe I'm not giving these people a lot of credit," he says. "I just assume that they don't have any contact with the gay world—but then one of them had a stepbrother die of AIDS. I mean, they *may* all have sons or daughters who are gay; I just don't know." Because he uses an avoidance strategy, Russ may never know his own coworkers' opinions about the subject. As the silence becomes more conspicuous, the spiral perpetuates itself. The penalties for breaking it seem only to increase. "My perception is that they don't have any contact at all with the gay community, that they don't even think about it. So I'm not about to bring it up."

Social Ambiguity

When a man avoids the subject of his sexuality, it's difficult to know what conclusions others have drawn about it. Men who carefully avoid direct references to their own sexual orientation often find themselves stuck in ambiguous situations, wondering—but never knowing for sure—if others realize that they are gay. "I know the scoop on most everyone at work," says Jim. "So you might think that they know the scoop on me. But one's not sure. They may know that I'm not in a relationship with a woman, but I don't talk about it at work. Maybe they ask other people, 'Oh, what's Jim doing?' But I don't know that for sure."

Even when he considers his sexuality utterly apparent, a man who uses an avoidance strategy has no opportunity to confirm his own understanding of the situation. It may seem inconceivable that coworkers haven't figured him out; it's so *obvious,* he insists. Yet coworkers do nothing to verify that they've properly construed the evidence, that they've read between the lines. When asked what coworkers know about his sexuality, a gay professional may have no idea. "I'm *certain* that they all know I'm gay," says Grey. "They've got to be really dumb if they don't. I'm certain my brother and sister know because they have friends—I lived in Dallas for twenty-five years. I knew everyone in the entire city, and people just talk, people blab. So if you lead an open life-style, word gets back. We all have a lot of mutual friends. They've never been bothered by it enough to ask me about it, so apparently it's no big deal. I've never said, 'Hey, we need to talk.' But I would think . . . I would *hope* that they have figured it out."

Tom has a similar relationship with the other teachers in his school. "I would assume they know," he says. "But it's strange. I've been with my lover now for twelve years, and people just accept the fact that he's a roommate. No one has ever questioned it. My principal calls the house, and he'll answer the phone. And they just don't react to it. So my feeling is that they have to know. You can't be forty years old and not married and still be straight. But it's never been talked about. Nothing's ever—nothing's in the open."

Quite often these situations resemble what Barbara Ponse has called "counterfeit secrecy," an arrangement in which others know that an individual is gay, but collude in the mutual pretense that they do not. In these situations, both parties to an interaction know a secret but maintain the outward appearance that they are unaware of it. "Both audience and gay actor cooperate to maintain a particular definition of the situation and both parties tacitly agree not to make what is implicit, explicit by direct reference to it."[9] Counterfeit secrecy thus allows individuals to smooth over a potentially disruptive breach of social expectations by behaving as if they have not noticed it. When presented with an individual they know to be gay, for example, they can pretend that "nothing unusual is happening," so long as no one calls attention to his sexuality. They play along as he talks about a "girlfriend," ignoring the (perhaps blatant) evidence that he is gay. "Making the violation obvious, by naming it or pointing it out, would of course force acknowledgment of the pretense."[10]

This seems to be the situation in which Chuck finds himself with the other traders at his firm. "They all know I'm gay," he says. "They've known for a long time." But when asked to describe a particular conversation in which this understanding was made explicit, Chuck thinks for a moment. "It's more subtle than that," he says. "There's a good friend of mine there, and whenever the subject of dating girls comes up—he's always talking about the girls he's after—there are just knowing nods, knowing looks. It's just generally understood, and it's not a problem. As far as them knowing for sure, that's different. I guess if I went in and said, 'I definitely am gay, just wanted you all to know that,' perhaps the feeling would be different."

The problem is that these men cannot be sure. They have no way of knowing that coworkers have assembled and made sense of the clues, even when the clues are abundant. Joel is renowned in his office for his activism on behalf of gays and people with AIDS. But he has little idea what coworkers know or assume about his sexuality. "I don't know what they think," Joel says. "They might say, 'We don't know, but he does support all these gay causes.' And they might say, 'I notice that he has his friendliest conversations with men, as opposed to women.' " Joel also assumes that they remember a lengthy letter he wrote to the bishop in San Francisco, supporting the ordination of lesbian and gay priests. Still, he has no way of knowing if they recall or have noticed any of these things.

These ambiguities sometimes lead to moments of misunderstanding or paranoid confusion. The numerous unspoken assumptions can make it difficult for a gay professional to navigate certain characteristic situations. Dave remembers stumbling into a conversation that puzzled him. "One of the guys in my company was getting married," he remembers. "I'm single and so is one other guy, but everyone else is married. So I overheard one of the vice presidents say, 'Well, Mike, it looks like you're the only one who's single now.' I was outside the office when I heard this, and Mike said, 'No, Dave is.' Then somebody said something and everyone laughed. I didn't hear what was said; I'm kind of glad I didn't. I walked into the room two minutes later." Darren recalls a similar situation. "After a couple of years in this job, people assumed I was gay because my lover called me every day. I never dated women; you know, all the signs were there. I even had a couple of people ask me if I was gay. So I think they knew. But then I showed up at a company party with this woman. Everyone seemed shocked. I don't know if their looks implied, 'We know you're gay, why are you bothering with this?' or 'We thought we had you all figured out, and now we're not sure what your preference is.' I just felt it was uncomfortable, so I stopped it. I wasn't sure."

Grey recalls an even more elaborate misunderstanding. Several years ago the mall was in the process of redesigning its logo. "We had this sample *G*, a big *G* for the ice rink. It was just a sign, a prototype of the letter, and so I took it and put on my door. This girl I know just walked by and said, 'What does the *G* stand for? Oh, *Grey?* And later that day, that same day—I had just put it up—my friend Scott, who's a graphic designer, had an appointment with me. And he said, 'God, what's that *G* on your door?' And I said, 'Well, it's for Grey.' And he says, 'God, that's so funny—I couldn't figure out what it was for. I thought maybe . . . you know what some people might think.' And I thought, 'Oh my God! Don't you know they're all walking by thinking the *G* stands for gay." Given that his own sexual identity is ambiguous at work, Grey has no idea what others were in fact thinking.

The ambiguity becomes most acute when homosexuality is, or seems to be, the subject of conversation. When gay issues are discussed, for example, men who use avoidance strategies often wonder if the discussion has been staged for their benefit or if it is being censored to protect them. Dan recalls a puzzling incident in which a local school administrator asked him for help. The woman called Dan aside and told him, "off the record," that she had a friend who was infected with HIV. She wanted to be sure that her friend was cared for, and asked Dan to recommend a good doctor. Dan's response was to wonder, " 'Why is she asking *me* all this?' I was getting real paranoid but I kept cool and said, 'Well, this is not my area, but I'll find out for you.' I honestly didn't know much about the subject, but I thought this would be a good opportunity for me to find out." Looking back Dan isn't sure what to make of the incident. "I think she was trying to tell me something about herself. You know, 'Hey, we're all in this together, even though we're not talking about it.' "

But Dan cannot be sure of this interpretation. Although gay men often point to conversations they presume convey a coworker's understanding or support, they recognize that their conclusion may be unwarranted. "About a year ago, we were having sort of a summit meeting, and there were four or five of us in the president's office," recalls Glen. "We had all these New York investment bankers on the phone, and something was said about 'gay.' The president said something like, 'Well of course that has a different meaning now than it did then.' I don't even remember how the word came up. But there was just the slightest hesitation or embarrassment on his part. I just sensed something in the room; it may have been coming from me. But I sensed the recognition and recovery from it, the sense that maybe someone shouldn't have said that." The incident itself was unimportant, Glen says, but it underscored his uncertainty about his own reputation at work.

Jeff recalls a similar incident involving his boss Skip. "Shortly after I started work here, Skip tried to set me up with his sister-in-law, and I expressed no interest whatsoever. A few months later Kevin and I were talking with Skip, and they talked about somebody Kevin had hired who didn't work out. And Kevin said, 'Yeah, he and the two homosexuals are the only ones who didn't work.' And Skip said, 'Well, the problem wasn't that they were homosexual—that's okay—the problem was that they were stupid.' " Given that he has never discussed his sexuality with Skip in any direct way, Jeff wasn't sure if he should take the comment as a sign of acknowledgment.

In situations like these, the silence on personal and sexual topics can make it difficult for a man to plan his career. Kirk ran into this dilemma while interviewing for a teaching position at a hospital in Seattle. He was optimistic that his sexuality would not be a problem at the hospital, which had a liberal reputation, but was reluctant to seek a more definitive answer. "I certainly wouldn't have been coy about it, had they asked me," he says. "I just felt uncomfortable bringing it up in an interview with people I was meeting for the first time." Kirk knew that he would be invited to social functions with the staff and wanted to assess how comfortable he would be bringing his lover, Jeffrey, along. He would be working long hours with a small group of people and wanted to know how they would handle information about his personal life. He had several competing offers and wanted to weigh the level of comfort he could expect at each. But he felt hamstrung during his interviews, limiting himself to vague remarks about his "significant other." "It wasn't the sort of thing I brought up in job interviews, though I wanted to get a handle on what their attitude would be." Kirk ultimately took a job in Philadelphia, and before long he came out at work.

The inability to gather information has become a more serious problem for Bill, a California Park Ranger. At thirty-one Bill is handsome and athletic, and lives about an hour north of the Golden Gate Bridge. As the district naturalist, he hosts guests through the park, conducts nature walks and educational programs, and runs the visitors' center. Although he works with a small, close-knit group of park employees, he manages to avoid the subject of his own sexuality. "I'm sure it's crossed all of their minds," he says, "but I really don't have a good handle on how other people think in that regard, whether they've formed concrete conclusions, or whether they just leave it unresolved. I can't think of anything I've done to give them irrefutable evidence that I'm gay. Or that I'm not."

As a result, Bill often finds it difficult to make sense of his interactions with peers. "Some of the women joke with me and flirt," he explains. "They go further with me than they would with other men, because they know that it's not serious. That's the impression I get." When asked about his boss, Bill is more certain. "I'm sure there's no doubt in his mind that I'm gay, based on what he says about other people. He speculates about other people's personal lives and even talks to me about them. But he's almost surgically careful not to bring up anything about me personally—which is kind of interesting. I'm sure he avoids that because he's sensitive to the fact that I'm gay." Based on this scant evidence, Bill concludes that his sexuality is "not a problem" at work.

Even so, Bill recognizes that by encouraging silence on the subject of his sexuality, he may be thwarting his own career. He knows that in the long run, if he continues to work for the park service, it will be impossible to use an avoidance strategy. "The biggest dilemma for me is that most national parks are in remote areas that I wouldn't want to work in. My boyfriend sells real estate in Marin County, grew up there; his whole family and all his business connections are there. So I don't know what's going to happen when I get to the point where I can't go any further in my career advancement. He's not going to want to follow me to Montana or something." Under the circumstances, however, Bill finds it difficult even to gather the information that might help him make the right decision. "I suppose if I were out, I could better judge the long-term effects that being gay might have on my career. I could discuss it openly with anybody who I thought could help, like my boss. You know, 'What's it going to be like for me in the park service, being gay and being open about it?' "

Social Withdrawal

Men who counterfeit a sexual identity often complain that their social lives do not reflect their psychic realities, that they are treated as if they were "someone else." Avoidance tactics, on the other hand, can rob them of *all* contact. A man's dodges and evasions can leave him feeling isolated and detached, denied even the distorted social feedback that would be possible if he were willing to don a heterosexual mask.

When asked to describe the biggest disadvantage of refusing to talk about sexuality at work, gay men say that it severely limits their social involvement with peers. "I have to exclude certain people from my life," says Terry. "I might be more social. I would encourage people to have drinks with me, except that I don't want to get too close to them. You miss out on some things." Miguel voices a similar frustration. "There are so many people in the hospital who are really, really nice," he says. "And I'm sure if I didn't have this concern about being gay, I would have excellent relationships with them. So that's something that's getting lost."

In particular, these men are often deprived of the sense that others understand or appreciate their lives. Milton, a Washington attorney known for his pro bono efforts on behalf of African Americans and people with AIDS, finds that this is the most distressing aspect of his situation. "I would like to maintain some level of privacy," he says. "Still, there are times when I wish people would come to me and say, 'How are you doing?' and, 'How does it feel to lose so many friends to AIDS at such a young age?' 'How has all this affected you on a personal level?' And people never do. I

wish they would ask me, sometimes, 'What is it like to be a successful gay black man? What are the challenges, what are the diffi-
culties, what are the rewards?' I wish they would, but they don't."
Like everyone else Milton wants to be noticed and cared about.
His social withdrawal discourages such caring.

"It's a little numbing," says Derek, to forgo contact in this way.
"It's no big deal because I've always had to do it," he explains. "I
can't imagine what it would be like to be able to show affection, or
to allow anybody to think that you're even *capable* of feeling affection as they do: a wife stopping by, and everybody wanting to meet
her; a discussion about what your family did the night before; admitting that you had a fight and having people care or offer their
token advice. Imagine the thrill of being able to show public affection the way other people do, to let somebody know that you're sitting next to somebody you happen to love, not somebody that you
happened to watch the football game with that afternoon. It must
be *bliss;* I can't comprehend it. To me it's only a concept."

Derek recalls a situation in which his own silence became almost
unbearable. An employee in New York, a man named Charlie, told
Derek that he had been diagnosed with AIDS. A few days later,
suring a meeting, Derek realized that Charlie's condition might
put him in a compromising position. His response was to feign ignorance:

> I'm so ashamed . . . that when Charlie called me, when I heard this,
> the first thing I thought about was not that this very charming,
> lovely, adorable, almost little brother-son to me, had this disease.
> The first thing I thought about was *me*. Not that I was ill, but that
> my career might suffer. And I was so ashamed . . . for an entire day
> I was calculating how I would deal with this. It's demeaning when
> I'm sitting in the room, and we talk about medical expenses going
> up, not the fact that we've got this kid with AIDS: "We've got to be
> more careful about the way we hire. . . . We've got to be sure that
> we're not going to be hiring any homosexuals in here."

In these meetings Derek felt muzzled and paralyzed, as if his voice
had suddenly been stolen. He was unable to explain the situation
or acknowledge his feelings about it, because to do so might im-

pede his own efforts to avoid exposure. Derek recognizes that he has some tough choices to make in the coming months. "People will be asking, 'Wasn't this your friend, Derek?' It's going to be very tough."

In fact, personal problems or crises are often cited as experiences that gay men would most like to share with coworkers. "Heterosexuals who are having family problems or kid problems or money problems or *anything* can pretty much talk to someone about it," says Glen. "They can just say, 'I'm having a shitty day.' Just saying that much is enough." Chip explains, "I don't get to share my personal life in the same way that heterosexual workers do, all the little day-to-day things. You know, 'I went on a date with my girlfriend,' or 'I've been dating the same person for two years, and she's important to me,' or 'I've had a fight with Frank, and today's a bitchy day for me.' "

The invisibility of their lovers and friends is a source of particular frustration. Because these most meaningful relationships go unacknowledged at work, gay men are denied the support and affirmation of peers. In a survey by *Out/Look,* 29 percent of lesbians and gay men who had come out at work said that they did so in order to "improve relationships with a boss or coworker," while 25 percent said they wanted to "include a spouse" in social activities with people at work.[11] Larry, the managing partner in a small Washington law firm, recalls the end of his relationship with a lover of ten years. "In the office I toughed it out," he says. "I don't think I ever said to anyone, 'My most important relationship has broken up, by the way.' So I did the usual thing I do in those kinds of situations: bifurcate it, split it up, get my support outside the office where I knew I was safe, and pretend that everything was fine at work. I look back now at how awful it was not to have the kind of support anyone else would have gotten in the workplace."

Chris suffered an equally painful "divorce" from his lover of many years. Both men worked for the same firm but had carefully concealed their relationship at work. "Here's one of the most traumatic things that can happen to you—the end of a relationship," says Chris. "I think if I had been straight I would have gone to my employer and said, 'My wife and I are getting a divorce, and it's a tough time for me.' But I didn't do that." Years later Chris looks back at that time with great sadness. "Divorces among straight people are so public," he says. "Gays don't have that."

Even when their personal lives are stable, gay professionals find that they miss out on the friendships that often develop in work situations. Tip still has regrets about a friendship that ultimately fell apart when he found himself unable, after months of indecision, to reveal that he is gay. He and Fred were both surgical residents and had become close over the years in school. "Fred was one of my best friends," Tip says. "Actually, I took him hunting with me a few times, and he met my family." The problems began when Fred and his wife tried to arrange a date for Tip:

> He and his wife kept trying to set me up. The last time we spoke was about six months ago on the phone. Actually, we had a direct confrontation. He came out and said, "Tip, what's going on? I've been trying to set you up with this girl that works with my wife." I said, "No, Fred, I don't like being set up. If I don't like her, then it's going to hurt your wife's feelings." I had used that excuse before, and he wouldn't let it go this time. He said, "Tip, I'm doing you a favor. All you have to do is show up and drop your pants. That's all you've got to do." And I'm thinking that's exactly what I *don't* want to do. And he says, "What is this, are you gay or something?" That's what he asked me. I said, "Fred, forget it. Look, the girl's already pissed. She's already asked your wife why I wouldn't want to go out with her, so it's already doomed and I haven't even met her."

After this confrontation Tip and Fred quickly drifted apart. Tip remained unwilling to come out, worried that he would be too vulnerable at work. Still, he acknowledges, "The way I'm doing this is costly. It's caused me to lose two friends because I didn't socialize with them. I didn't produce a date; I avoided the whole situation. It caused me to lose a friend, and Fred was a good friend."

Even so, Tip feels that these friendships must be sacrificed if he is to protect his job. "People aren't happy knowing you without knowing something about your social life. If I had it to do over again I probably wouldn't say a word. I'd rather not know a lot of the people that I know now, because it's like starting a friendship and only being able to carry it out halfway. It would have been better if I had just done my work and gone to the library or something."

Not all gay professionals mourn the loss of social opportunities at work, however. Some have little interest in spending more time with coworkers they consider dull or with whom they have little in common. Some consider themselves antisocial or private "by nature." Still others feel it is sufficient to build a small, intimate network of contacts, keeping the rest of the office at arm's length. There are certain advantages, they point out, to social withdrawal.

Mitch prefers to focus his attention on a small number of coworkers with whom he is especially close. "There's a core group of people with whom I feel I can discuss what's going on in my life," he says. "The people with whom I deal most frequently, including my secretary and the other people in my department—they know what my social situation is. So if something is going on in my life that's impacting the way I'm working, then it's fine." Consequently, while Mitch has told a select group of associates that he is gay, he avoids the issue with others. "If I felt there was nobody at work that I could walk into their office and talk to, that would be a problem. But that's not the case."

Some men feel that it is simply their nature to be reserved, and have little tolerance for what they perceive are intrusions from coworkers. "It doesn't bother me that people don't know that I'm gay," says Nick, who avoids after-hours socializing with coworkers. "There's no elaborate company event that I want to take my boyfriend to. I don't want to go to the football games myself." "As a human matter, I think you need just a certain amount of intimacy, a certain number of friends," says Roger. "I have to make a certain amount of contact in order to feel like I'm human, to feel that I'm connecting up with the rest of the race. But my experience is that most people have maybe five or six very close friends, no more. A lot of people *know* a lot of people, but there's only so much intimacy that you need or can develop in the world."

In most organizations, however, it is virtually impossible to distinguish work performance from participation in the social life of the office. Managerial jobs, in particular, require a man to operate a network of relationships—with clients, peers, bosses, suppliers, and support staff—and place a premium on his social competence. If he withdraws from others, he may be unable to do his job. Especially when the relevant tasks require teamwork, avoidance strategies sometimes leave a man little elbow room. Geoff describes his office as a small, "family-oriented" place, in which he has been reluctant to reveal very much about this personal life. "I think that's something that probably bothers the others. I'm not a warm, friendly, slap-each-other-on-the-back, go-out-for-a-couple-of-beers kind of guy. I ask a question, get an answer, and go on and do my job. Get in, get out. So I'm not real warm and friendly around them, which I think bothers them."

Some will eventually bump into a "glass ceiling" imposed by their social isolation. Greg feels that his social withdrawal helps explain his inability to "fit in" with the other men and women at his former employer. Although his coworkers were a tight-knit group, Greg was careful to reveal almost nothing about himself. "I think that's the problem when you withhold these kinds of personal feelings in your relationships with people. It's a great handicap, I think. People tend to think that you're uninteresting, that you don't have a personal life." Greg admits that he also found his coworkers somewhat dull, further discouraging him from taking part in the social life of the office. Still, he wonders if his aloofness, his reluctance to discuss even the most mundane aspects of his life outside the office, is one of the reasons he was recently fired. "I didn't associate with these people very much, except at the office," he says. "I was kind of a loner there."

Stuart received a similarly harsh lesson in the importance of being social at work. Five years out of law school he knew that he was considered something of an enigma at work. "I never held casual conversations with the other attorneys," he recalls. "I didn't stop by to chat with people unless I felt I absolutely had to. I kept the door to my office closed a lot of the time, especially when I took personal calls at work, because I didn't want my conversations to be monitored. Other people didn't do that. I also knew that I wasn't everyone's favorite luncheon companion. I would see other groups of people going to lunch, and there was an inner clique of people who ate together at least once a week. They would have lunch for two or three hours, drinking and socializing. I was only invited when I ran into them in the elevator or in the hallways, so that they were embarrassed and had to ask me along."

It wasn't that Stuart disliked the other attorneys or considered himself an especially shy or unfriendly person. "It's just that those sorts of encounters are painful for me," he says, "because they force me to play-act. The other attorneys talk about choosing a stroller, getting their kids into the right kindergarten, raising a family. I never feel that I fit in, since almost everyone else in the firm can be categorized as 'young and married.' " The same is true of company sporting events. "I never took part in the softball team, because the prospect of spending several hours with people from my office, playing sports—it guaranteed that I would feel like an outsider. But it was a big deal for them. Even the women in the department adopted masculine tastes in sports. There was a betting pool, and it was highly publicized. Every day during the summer I would get a memo about the games coming up, the current bets, and who had participated. It was a big self-promotional vehicle for the people who took part in it. But for me softball would have been a dangerous game. I wasn't scared of being hit by the ball; I was scared of being asked questions about my social life, questions that would just naturally come up in that context."

By this time Stuart's social isolation had also begun to affect his work. "Because I wasn't interacting with everyone socially, I wasn't getting work the way other people were. Projects are supposed to be doled out by an assigning partner on the basis of who is busy, who has experience in a particular area, and so forth. But in practice, whenever a project came up, whoever happened to be friendly with a particular partner at a particular time would get the job. Hanging out in someone else's office, talking about nothing, meant that you got work. I would always hear about projects for which I was ideally suited that had been assigned to somebody else. Sometimes it made me really angry. In order to make partner, I knew I had to work for as many people as possible, to demonstrate my skills to as many people as possible. And that simply wasn't happening. Most of the partners simply weren't thinking of me because I never talked to them."

At the end of his fifth year with the firm, Stuart was called in for his annual performance review. Two of the partners in the department discussed his work over the past year, emphasizing how pleased clients were. "During the first part of the review, they talked about how excellent my work was. One of them said that I wrote and thought clearly and professionally, skills that he said couldn't be taught. They praised me for the responsibility I had shown on several key projects. But then they said that there was a problem. They said that I didn't talk to them often enough. They said that while they didn't expect me to go out drinking with them—they could see I wasn't a back-slapper—they did expect me to spend more of my social time with them. Then they warned me, quite explicitly, that this was going to be a problem for me in making partner. They made it clear that there was no problem with my work, that they didn't expect me to socialize with them on a grand scale. But they did expect me to schmooze with them, to hang out and be casual with them." Hearing this, Stuart knew where the conversation was headed. "It was suggested," he recalls, "that I start planning a career elsewhere, somewhere that was a better fit for me."

7

Coming Out, Moving On

LONG BEFORE STUART learned that he would not make partner, he had begun to contemplate a change in strategy. "Everything seemed to hinge on my coming out," he recalls. "I was feeling more and more pressure to be social at work, and was increasingly convinced that that would be impossible until I came out. Being in the closet seemed to be the primary barrier." As the pressure mounted, Stuart considered his various options. "I was terrified, but I told myself that if I could get through the conversation itself, I would be fine. Everything else would fall into place if I could get my big, terrible secret out in the open."

These concerns were foremost in Stuart's mind as he sat through his performance review. "When the partners told me that I needed to be more social at work, I just let them talk. My assumption was that if we could identify the particular problem I faced in making partner, then I could do something about it. So when they said I should make more of an effort to socialize and chitchat with the other attorneys, I decided to address the issue head on." Stuart paused and uttered the words he thought would be so hard to say. "I explained that there was a good reason I wasn't hanging out with the other attorneys. I said

that I was glad we were being clear about the problem—that the criticisms were of my social performance, not my work. If that's the case, I
told them, I can identify the reason for it: I'm gay."

As Stuart made his announcement, the partners shifted in their
seats. One of them took a quick puff on his cigar. "I realized that I
had made both of them extremely nervous," Stuart says. "First
there was this stunned silence. Then they both jumped in to assure
me that they didn't care one way or another if I was gay. They said
that their criticisms had nothing to do with my being gay or
straight, and they insisted that it had never been a problem at the
firm. To illustrate the point, one of them told a peculiar story. He
said that homosexuality had never even been mentioned in the
partnership meetings, except when they were discussing another associate who was 'openly gay'—by which I assume he meant flamboyant or effeminate. One of the senior partners had made a
negative comment about the associate, but that partner had since
left the firm."

Leaving the room, Stuart realized that he had just confronted
one of his most long-standing fears. "It was as if the floor dropped
out from beneath me," he says. "I knew that for the next several
months—perhaps for the rest of my career—everything would be
different. I had opened Pandora's box. What I didn't realize, before
I came out, was just how different it would be. My intention at the
time was just to get through that conversation. I didn't think much
beyond that."

Like Stuart, gay men often speak of coming out as if it were the
final frontier, the destination of a long and arduous journey. Yet in
many ways coming out is less an arrival than a change in direction,
the first step down a different but no less arduous road. There are
at least as many ways of shaping a gay identity as there are of trying
to evade one, and while the man who reveals his homosexuality no
longer finds it necessary to hide, his change in strategy brings with
it a new set of obligations. Where he was previously concerned
with the maintenance of secrecy, he now faces decisions about
where, when, and how often his sexuality is to be displayed. His re-

sponsibilities shift from the suppression of information to the mechanics of its disclosure: How should others be informed? How much should they know? And what will be the consequences of these choices? By coming out, a man trades one set of managerial tasks for another.[1]

Integration strategies, which are characterized by the authentic expression of a man's sexuality, are increasingly common among gay professionals. Of the men we interviewed almost half had revealed themselves to one or more of their coworkers.[2] Likewise, a 1992 survey of *Out/Look* readers found that 93 percent of lesbians and gay men had revealed themselves to one or more coworkers. Sixty-eight percent had discussed a same-sex lover with someone at work; 30 percent had displayed a photograph, ring, or some other symbol of the relationship; and 74 percent had been vocal about their beliefs on lesbian and gay political issues.[3] In the gay press (as well as in many mainstream publications) stories now abound about lesbian and gay professionals who are openly gay at work.

The first step in using such a strategy is to come out. Except in those rare organizations that do not take heterosexuality for granted, a man must usually say or do something explicit to let others know that he is homosexual; silence on the subject constitutes an implicit claim to be heterosexual. A man's coming out is thus a crucial turning point in any relationship, marking a transition from the use of one strategy to another. It is also one of the quintessential gay experiences, a rite of passage familiar to all within the community. Dozens of books have been written on the proper ways to come out to parents and friends. Gay support groups, public meetings, and cocktail parties are often sites at which tips on coming out are freely sought and provided. Before the arrival of AIDS no subject was burdened with greater significance or prompted more advice, nervous laughter, or abject terror within gay circles.

The net effect has been a tendency, especially among those who remain in the closet, to focus their attention on the transition itself. In retrospect a man can usually pinpoint the precise encounter, telephone call, or letter in which he came out to a boss or coworker. He remembers laying the groundwork for his disclosure, giving his listener some kind of explanatory context. Sometimes he can recall the exact words that were used—and he rarely forgets the response. "You spend so much time worrying about the best way to come out," says Stuart, "that your attention is really focused on the coming out itself, not on what follows it."

The particular form of the disclosure is crucial, given that the initial revelation serves to "frame" a man's sexual identity for a specific audience. It supplies a context for it, establishing the terms of the discourse. The information itself may be conveyed in a gesture of friendship ("I'm telling you this because I want us to be closer"), a political demand ("This policy discriminates against lesbians and gay men, myself included"), even an expression of sexual interest ("Can I buy you a drink?"). Some men introduce their disclosures with talk about honesty, framing them as a matter of integrity ("I can't lie to you"). Still others, sadly, must reveal themselves during conversations about HIV illness, as part of an appeal for compassion or financial assistance.

Whichever frame is used, it has consequences for the way a man's sexuality will be interpreted by others. Indeed, without such a frame, his coming out will strike them as puzzling. It will seem unmotivated, irrelevant; they will see no reason for it. As Kath Weston observed in *Families We Choose,* "The idea of going up to someone and bluntly stating, 'Hi, I'm gay,' without further elaboration elicits laughter from a lesbian or gay audience."[4] As Milton explains, "You can't just *say it.* There has to be a reason for it, or it will seem ridiculous. People will think, 'Why is he telling me this?' "[5]

Gay men often struggle to establish the appropriate frame, the right context for their disclosures. Indeed, they often complain that their inability to find the proper frame prevents them from coming out altogether. "Having everyone know is one thing," says Glen. "But *how* they find out adds another whole dimension." Glen worries that a formal announcement would seem too "political" or "aggressive." He doesn't want people to view his disclosure as "a conversation about sex. . . . If they just learned that I was gay because their brother-in-law told them or something, I don't think there would be any problem. They'd say, 'Oh yeah, we knew that already,' or 'He's kind of an aloof jerk anyway, so it doesn't make any difference.' But if I *told* them, I think the emphasis would be more on my reason for coming out than on the essence of the message." Finding no such reason, Glen has never formally come out at work.

When Carter comes out to clients, he wants them to view his disclosure as a sign of their growing rapport, a token of trust between business partners. He tries to frame it accordingly. Only after a successful deal or two, after he's fully established his credentials with a client, does he mention the fact that he is gay. Until then he avoids sexual small talk altogether. Because he considers the particular form of the disclosure crucial, Carter was upset recently when a coworker preempted his handling of it. A new client let it be known that she was attracted to Carter but was told by one of his associates "not to waste [her] time. Carter's gay." Carter wasn't upset that his secret had been revealed but was furious that he had not been permitted to handle the matter himself. "I get mad about that sometimes," he says. "I mean, *I* should be the one to tell them. Other people in the office know I'm real open about it, so they don't think there's a problem with saying something. It's hard for me to make them understand that I'd like to be in control." Rather than learn about Carter's sexuality in a professional context (a company party, a business lunch), his client made the discovery when a third party discouraged her from making a romantic overture.

As he chooses the particular way in which to reveal his sexuality—and then manages its ongoing visibility—a man may be guided by one of several aims. Sometimes his goal is to accommodate, to put others at ease as they grapple with new and potentially discomfiting information. Like Carter, a man may have no interest in creating a stir. Others hope to educate and enlighten, to create change, even to provoke. As with other strategies, there are a number of tactics at one's disposal.

Minimizing Visibility

Some men want others to be aware of their sexuality, but take steps to ensure that it will be as unobtrusive as possible. They strike a low profile, expressing their sexuality only in limited ways. They favor tacit acknowledgment of it to direct references or discussions.

While their sexuality is no longer a secret, neither is it especially visible.[6]

The "minimizing" approach is often used by stigmatized individuals who try to lessen their vulnerability by limiting their visibility. They fear that if they become too conspicuous or appear too numerous, they will invite retaliation. At Yale in the 1940s and 1950s, Jews tried to downplay their significant presence on campus, wary of provoking a backlash.[7] Likewise, Rosabeth Kanter has observed that professional women sometimes try to become "socially invisible" when working in male-dominated environments. In order to blend into the predominant male culture, they try "to minimize their sexual attributes." Some adopt "mannish dress" or speech patterns. Others avoid public events and occasions for performance, staying away from meetings, working at home rather than in the office, keeping silent at meetings. Unlike male peers who seize every opportunity to make themselves noticed, these women try to blend.[8] Like gay men who use a minimizing strategy, they are not trying to disguise their gender per se. Rather, they are trying to play down its visibility and the conspicuous status it bestows on them in male-dominated environments.

By coming out in indirect or unobtrusive ways, gay men hope to downplay the significance of their revelation. Some invite speculation by making suggestive remarks, encouraging their peers to read between the lines. Others allow coworkers to stumble across evidence (a photograph of a lover, a gay magazine) or to decode some subtlety in a conversation (the mention of what "we" plan to do for Christmas) while denying them more explicit verbal cues. "I assume my secretary knows 'my deal' because of the demography of my phone calls," says Arthur. "So overwhelmingly male, so overwhelmingly cute and perky and *that age,* all with weird names, as she puts it, like Trevor and Thad and Biff. She says, 'Don't you have any friends with real names?' " Al seems to have reached a similar understanding with his secretary. "She knows I'm gay, because she takes phone calls from all my male friends. She chats to them and actually *knows* some of them because they have business relationships with the company. We talk about restaurants—I'm her 'cultural coordinator.' We also talk about the occurrence of

AIDS among professional men." Some men say that their sexual identity is conveyed by their mere status as middle-aged bachelors. "Anyone who's a forty-one-year-old man, who's never been married, and who's never talked about a social life with women, has got to be an anomaly," says Burt. "The only explanation is that he's gay. Or that he has an old war wound."

Allusions and oblique signs of ackowledgment thus take the place of explicit conversation. Mitch feels that he has this sort of relationship with Neil, one of the other associates in his firm. The two men travel together and have worked closely on a number of important cases. Mitch feels certain that Neil "has me figured out." But until last summer he didn't give it much thought. "Neil wanted to rent a place in the Hamptons for his wife and daughter," Mitch recalls, "and I said, 'Well, if you want to rent my house for a week and a half, I'll rent it to you.' The only problem was that the house was full of photos of me and Jay [his lover]—there was no way you could stay in this house and *not* understand that this person was gay and lived here with his lover. Neil went out the next day and spent ten days in the house, and when he came back, he couldn't have been more cordial." Still, the men's shared understanding was never formally acknowledged until Jay and Mitch broke up. At this point it became obvious that Mitch was upset due to "relationship problems." When he finally confided in Neil that this relationship with Jay had ended, Neil tried to be supportive, asked questions, expressed sympathy.

Quite often, the men's reticence is encouraged by the fear that to go further, to be more explicit, would be to overstep the limits of their coworkers' tolerance. For seven years Les has worked in the same office, and feels certain that the other staff members perceive Brad, the man with whom he lives, to be his lover. "I'm sure the boss knows where I'm at with Brad. The first time you go on a vacation with your roommate, fine. But I go someplace with my roommate every year. And I talk too much. If my roommate were sixty there might not be much thought about it. But when your roommate's thirty-six—I'm sure that my boss knows." Les says that he'd like to be more up-front about his relationship with Brad. "I'd love to shout it from the treetops. It's really irritating that I have to be careful," he says. "But in a way I suppose I already have. If I didn't have Brad, I'd probably be more frustrated than I already am because no one would know where I'm at. By having a lover and doing things with him, I've already stated where I'm at."

Chuck confronted these same boundaries several years ago when his boss asked him to dinner, encouraging him to "bring a date." Although his coworkers know he is gay, Chuck was reluctant to invite his lover, John. "I guess if I felt completely comfortable that everybody knew and didn't have a problem with it, then it would be easier," he explains. "I just didn't know how well that would mix and go over." Craig, a VP of finance at American Express, says that while coworkers know about his sexuality, they may not be ready for an explicit display of it. "I've never spoken to anyone about sexuality, but I assume they all know," he says. "Craig's lover, Roland, frequently calls at work, and everyone knows that they live together. "There are people who've called me on the weekends or at seven in the morning and gotten Roland. I assume they at least *suspect*." When asked to imagine a hypothetical situation in which he and Roland were publicly identified as a couple, Craig shrugs. "I think many people are accepting as long as they're not confronted with it. It's easier for them that way."

There is a big difference, these men point out, between knowing about and actually facing a gay man's sexuality. Even men who are clearly identified with gay causes or activities are often reluctant to participate in personal conversations on the subject. Don cofounded the lesbian and gay employee association at Levi Strauss & Co. in San Francisco, and is known for his work on its behalf. His name and photograph have appeared in magazines and company newsletters. Yet despite his public role as an advocate, he is wary of drawing attention to his own personal life. "One thing about the company is that while I feel everybody is pretty accepting overall of working with a gay or lesbian person, they don't want to hear anything more about it. It's a more subtle form of discrimination. It's okay to be gay, but don't bring your partner to me and introduce him to my wife and have me confront that in my personal life." Although the company has an explicit nondiscrimination policy and is subject to city ordinances that protect lesbian and gay workers, the social barriers remain. "Nobody's going to come up and point to the photograph of a man on my bulletin board, and ask, 'Who's that?' They'll only ask the people who have children and families and a conventional relationship."

Even when coworkers seem interested and supportive, even when there is no immediate threat of discrimination, gay men are often wary of making explicit, unambiguous mention of their sexuality. Most feel safer behind veiled comments and insinuations. George has a flamboyant personal manner and recognizes that "my voice and walk give me away." He has even learned, through his boss, that his sexuality was discussed long ago by the committee that hired him. Nor are his romantic activities much of a secret in the office. Yet George remains reserved when speaking about his personal life. "Somebody I had a crush on called the office the other day," he recalls. "The secretary walked up with a message while I was talking to Rose and Jean, and they were both teasing me. It was a male name, obviously. Those two know I'm gay, though we've never actually used the word."

These signs of acceptance notwithstanding, George is afraid to push the envelope. "The acknowledgement issue is a big step for me," he says. "It's one thing for it to be understood, but it's another to go into open dialogue." In particular George decided not to invite a guest to the company's Christmas party and doesn't plan to take anyone next year. "I'm not real comfortable having people experience that interaction. It's probably a little bit of self-consciousness when it comes to the work environment." When asked how he would respond if someone else used 'the word,' explicitly asking him about his sexuality, George shudders. "It would be difficult to answer a direct question," he says. "I would never say no, because I think it's obvious that I'm gay." Yet George doesn't think he will hear a direct question until his coworkers are ready to take the next step. "I'd love to feel so comfortable that I could say it to anybody, but I don't think that will ever happen. I'm really responding to my coworkers' fears. Until that changes I'll have to position it a certain way to be socially acceptable."

Whether the boundary is the product of internalized fears or the discomfort of a man's peers, it limits expression of his sexuality. At thirty-eight, Roy has begun to find these boundaries restrictive. "I think virtually everyone has me figured out by now," he says. "My approach has been to gently send out signals over time. I wasn't terribly outgoing on this issue at first, but as I've felt more comfortable and safe, professionally, I've sent out more and more signals that I'm gay. My colleagues know that I went to Key West a couple of Christmases in a row. I have a share in Fire Island. I vacation in Provincetown. We're all in a small group of offices together, and if you hear my phone calls you know that there are a lot of men calling. Some of them call quite regularly. Last week I probably did my most 'outish' thing yet. I was invited to a screening of the new Quincy Jones movie, and I brought a guy that I've been seeing. It wasn't a major social function, but a lot of my business colleagues were there, and they saw me there with a guy whose name they may have recognized from my phone messages."

Roy hopes that these signals will facilitate his transition to full disclosure. "I'm looking for an opportunity to make a comment that explicitly puts on record the fact that I'm gay, so that everyone will understand that it's perfectly okay to talk about it. There have been a few occasions, not many, where we would be in a meeting and someone from outside would make some comment, and I would notice one of my colleagues artfully trying to move the conversation, trying to avoid an embarrassing train of thought. I would prefer that everyone be comfortable."

As his own comfort level grows, Roy wants to be more open, to dispense with caution and restraint. At the moment he fears that his sexuality is a "sensitive" issue at work, and he wants to desensitize it, to make it more of an everyday matter. He wants, in other words, to normalize his identity.

Normalizing the Abnormal

It's hard to be inconspicuous when others consider you extraordinary in some way. Men and women who are "abnormal"—whether the norm relates to sexuality, national origin, race, or job performance—receive special attention and scrutiny. They become the *gay* engineer, the *foreign* boss, the *black* accountant, the *top-ranked* salesman. Their difference, whether valued or devalued, sets them apart. "Everyone gets hung up about the fact that you're gay," says Barry. "It's hard to be just one of the gang."

To normalize his sexual identity, a gay man must make it seem mundane and familiar; he must assimilate it to the norm. He does this by downplaying differences between gay and straight lives, highlighting instead their many commonalities. He presents information about an unfamiliar sexuality in familiar, heterosexual terms. With his initial disclosure, in particular, he tries to establish common ground.

"Lovers" and "boyfriends" are the categories most often invoked by men who wish to normalize their identities in this way. Kirk has lived with his lover, Bruce, for a number of years. He was initially secretive at work about his life with Bruce but soon grew dissatisfied with the resulting sense of detachment. He wanted to share more of his personal life with the staff, and needed a way to broach the subject. An opportunity finally came in the form of the hospital's Christmas party. "I spoke to the divisional chairman, and told him that I was going to bring someone," Kirk recalls. "He said, 'That's fine. I'd be more worried if you didn't bring someone.' "

The groundwork laid, Kirk invited Bruce to the party. He then spoke to the department chairman's wife and told her that he would be bringing Bruce. "It was the first time I'd actually mentioned Bruce to anybody," he recalls. "I asked if she thought her husband was going to be too nervous about it. She said, 'Don't worry, he lived in San Francisco. He can deal with it.' " As it turned out, Bruce was warmly received. He was introduced as Kirk's "spouse" and was accepted as such by the other doctors and nurses. "Although I hate myself for saying it," Kirk adds, "it helped that Bruce doesn't fit any of the stereotypes about gay people. If it came to that, it wouldn't have made any difference, but it just wasn't an issue." Several years later Kirk and Bruce are known as an established couple, an identity that supplies a "normal" interpretation of Kirk's sexuality. As plans were made for last year's Christmas party, the chairman asked if Kirk would be bringing Bruce again.

"Bruce couldn't come because he was on call at the hospital, but the chairman said, 'Well, tell him we're sorry he couldn't make it.' "

Rob, a music instructor at a private school in the Philadelphia suburbs, reveals his sexuality in a similar fashion. For forty years Rob has lived with his lover, Albert, and frequently brings him to performances and recitals. "They've all known Albert for so many years," Rob says. "They always knew him, because I always brought him to everything." For Rob revealing his sexuality amounts to revealing his "marital" status. "Everyone knows, without me having a badge on my chest, that I'm gay. They know that I live with another man and have for forty years."

As friendships develop at work, Rob eventually mentions his relationship with Albert. "Last year, there was a young woman, Sarah, who taught violin. We wanted to do a performance of the Ravel Trio. It was obvious to me that she was a lesbian. (I mean, *good Lord!*) We started to work on the piece, and Sarah said to me, 'You'll have to come out to my house. Kathy and I would love to have you.' And I said, 'Well, you'll have to come out to our house. Albert and I would love to have you.' So it was that kind of mutual thing." Rob and Sarah both divulged their sexuality in the familiar and expected context of a conversation about their respective domestic relationships. "If a teacher came up to me and asked if I was gay, I'd say, 'Yes, of course'," Rob says. "But it has never come up that way."

Domestic events can also be arranged to demonstrate normalcy, to make gay households seem ordinary to coworkers. Russ recalls a dinner party he threw, in part because he wanted to put his home life on display. He invited four of his coworkers to the apartment he shares with his lover, Ed. He gave them a tour of the house, the shared bedroom, and the shared automobile. "Ed and I bought a Jeep, and I used to talk about the fact that it was his idea, that it was too expensive and we can't afford it, and that kind of stuff." His peers apparently got the message and are now comfortable talking about Ed. Sometimes they even joke about it. "Ed's a plumber, and maybe they'll say, 'Well, you gonna get your pipes cleaned out tonight?' Something like that."

For others the end of a romance supplies common ground, an opportunity for gay men to share a familiar experience with nongay peers. "Jay was a major part of my life," says Sean of his former lover. "Whenever I talked about weekend plans, Jay's name automatically cropped up. If I hadn't been dating someone, they probably wouldn't have known that I'm gay." When Sean and Jay ultimately broke up, Sean's coworkers were supportive. They expressed concern and told him of their own disappointments. It was a bonding experience, Sean recalls, and it gave him a chance to talk about things that usually went unsaid. Peers who might otherwise have avoided the subject were comfortable using the language and gestures of sympathy.

Gay men also emphasize the normalcy of their lives by stressing beliefs or interests they share with straight colleagues despite the differences in their sexual orientation. Indeed, some find it easiest to come out in the course of a discussion about political beliefs and civil rights. By raising the subject of homosexuality in these contexts they depersonalize it, even as they reveal their own particular relationship to the subject at hand. Al unintentionally revealed himself when his boss spied him mailing a letter to a gay organization. "I put an envelope with a dues check in my out bin, to Philadelphia Attorneys for Human Rights. PAHR is the gay attorneys group, and my boss noticed it. He's liberal, and was involved in other human rights organizations. He said, 'Tell me about this organization. What do they do?' I wasn't going to lie and tell him it was something else. So we talked about it." The ensuing conversation was framed as a dialogue about civil rights and the role attorneys play in their defense.

In recent years AIDS activism has become another route through which many gay men reveal their sexuality. "Everyone knows that I work for Action AIDS," according to Rob, "and while that's not really a gay organization, in the eyes of most people it is. Like it or not, AIDS is a gay men's disease for many, many people. You work with a gay organization, you're a gay man." Jerry's activism became public news when he cosponsored the first AIDS Walk in New York. "My name ends up getting plastered all over the city," he says, "because the posters for the AIDS Walk have the names of the major sponsors. A lot of the other traders came up to me and said, 'I saw your name in the press.' " Glen expressed his concern in more personal terms. "I identified myself as being part of a vulnerable minority," he says, recalling a conversation with the CEO of his company. "We were talking about AIDS in another context. I admitted that it was a personal concern because I considered myself more susceptible than the average person, because I belong to an affected minority." In doing so Glen emphasized the civil rights and public health implications of his sexuality, concerns he knew his boss, as an attorney, would feel comfortable discussing.

In their efforts to make the unusual seem usual, gay men often find that they have assumed the role of instructor, educating or enlightening their peers on the subject of homosexuality. To normalize their own identities, they set themselves up as authorities. They encourage others to use them as a resource. They also try to debunk some of the more absurd myths they encounter about gay people. Patrick recalls a question he got from a coworker. "My administrative assistant, Diane, asked me, 'Who's the girl?' She didn't ask the question directly. She said, 'Patrick, I've been meaning to ask you . . .' We were talking about my ex-boyfriend, and I said, 'You want to know who's the girl, John or me, right?' And she said, 'Yeah, how'd you know?' And I said, 'I get asked that occasionally.'" The question led to a conversation in which Patrick tried to fill a few gaps in Diane's understanding. "She had decided, at first, that I was the girl. Then she decided he was the girl because he's much more nurturing. I tried to explain that things don't work that way."

Barry is especially fond of enlightening his coworkers with carefully placed comments and rebukes. Shortly after joining a large Manhattan firm, Barry began dating a man named Leonard. When talking about Len at work, he routinely found that his associates assumed he was dating a woman named Lynn. One time, he recalls, "one of the summer associates said, 'Well, what's she like?' I replied, 'You mean, what's *he* like?'" After a quick "Oops," the associate recovered and the conversation moved on. On other occasions, when coworkers ask about his marital status, Barry offers a quick rectification. "I'd say, 'We've got to get some things straight here.' And they'd say, 'What?' And I'd say, 'Well, I'm not married, but if you know a nice guy, I'd like to be.' Something like that."

With these pointed "corrections," Barry hopes to make his sexuality seem mundane, unextraordinary. During recruiting lunches, for example, he raises the issue in a casual way. "I take the summer associates out to lunch, and we go to Lutèce. It's a big deal, a three-hour lunch, and they always get smashola drunk. And they always ask me about being gay, with maybe three exceptions out of a hundred candidates that I took there. They say, 'You know, you're the first gay person I've ever known.' And I say, 'No, I'm not, I'm just the first one you know about.'" Even when these lessons get out of hand, Barry tries to normalize the situation. "Some guys try to be smart," he says. "They try to say things that will make me say, 'That's none of your business.' And I would never do that. So they ask, 'Well, how many people have you slept with?' And I just tell them. Anything they ask, I answer straight out, in a totally matter-of-fact way. That shuts them up after awhile."

Other men joke with their peers as a way of desensitizing the subject. Keith uses this tactic with one of his coworkers. "She found out that I'm gay, and I knew that she was having trouble with it. So I told her a joke. I said, 'Do you know what's worse than a guy with a switchblade?' And she said, 'I don't know.' So I said, 'A fag with a chipped tooth.' She kind of stood there for a second; she didn't know what to say. Then she started to laugh. Later she told me, 'Keith, you just took me aback; I didn't know what to think then.' Then after we started talking and stuff, she told me, 'I used to think that all gays were sick, that they were perverts. I'm really glad I got to meet you, because you've helped change my opinion of that. I realize now that when I was growing up and started liking little boys, that you did, too.'"

Especially when this sort of sexual banter is part of the daily routine, it can be an effective way of making others comfortable with a potentially troubling issue. "Sometimes we just sit around the lunch table and dish," says Peter, a Philadelphia realtor. "A lot of rude jokes go back and forth, which is par for the course." Some of these jokes are about gay people, which Peter hopes will make the subject "less of a big deal." Sean is also fond of jokes and says they help make his sexuality "more run of the mill. When they see that it's not an issue with me, that I don't have a problem with it, hopefully they won't have a problem with it, and it becomes more of an everyday situation for them. They can joke about it and make little asides, jests. I like that because it means that I'm getting somewhere with them, and they're able to see things in a different way than before. Hopefully when they have children, that will be passed on."

Carter, likewise, finds that his sense of humor is often the best way of putting coworkers at ease. His office is populated largely by women, and they often meet after work for a meal or cocktail together. "We just have a blast," says Carter, describing a typical lunch hour. "I show them pictures from a trip, with all guys, and they critique the different guys. Whoever I'm seeing will come to the office, and I'll introduce him around, stuff like that. We go cruise at the mall, and they'll go, 'Do you think *he* is?' and I'll go 'yeah' or 'no.' Then they'll say, 'Do you think he likes me or you?' Stuff like that. It's just a real open thing." By making his sexuality a casual subject—a matter of flirtations, vacations, and fleeting attractions—Carter has tried to normalize it for his coworkers.

Quite often other gay people are the subject of Carter's jokes. "I make fun of being gay sometimes," he says. "I'll say, 'Look at those faggots' or something like that, to get it out in the open." In June the office staff watched part of Houston's gay pride parade on television. "Some of our people, some office people, were on TV dressed up like girls, and the other people in the office thought that was kind of revolting. Laura was saying, 'Did you see them dressed up like girls? Wasn't that disgusting?'" Carter played along. "I can't get too nellie around them," he says, "and I think 90 percent of the negative comments involve somebody acting like a girl or being effeminate." Rather than question these stereotypes about gender-appropriate behavior, Carter joins the chorus of criticism. By playing to his coworkers' stereotypes about homosexuality he hopes to put them at ease. He makes fun of "effeminate" men and "dykey" women. He is careful not to seem "faggy" at work. At one point he got rid of a bathing suit that a woman at work told him was "really queer."

Whatever one thinks of Carter's tactics, his goal is to normalize his identity, to make homosexuality the functional equivalent of heterosexuality. Indeed, the chief aim of all normalizing strategies is the attainment of equality. Men who use them often say that they want only what their straight coworkers already have. They want the same privileges when it comes to talking about their sexuality. To achieve this, they become attentive, in their interactions with peers, to matters of balance and fairness. Jack explains, "After putting up with the frustration, for years, of having my male drinking buddies talk so openly about what was going on sexually—by God, now that I'm open, I'm going to discuss my life as openly as they discuss theirs." When the conversation turns to personal topics, Jack tries to balance his own revelations against those made by others. "Sometimes drawing that line is very hazy, and I have to be careful to stop short of deliberately rubbing people's noses in my sexuality when I don't have to. It's not an easy line to walk."

To draw this line some men look for analogues in the behavior of their peers. When a coworker reveals something about *his* sexual life, the remark is often taken as an invitation. "Once I know people fairly well, I'll say, 'So-and-so and I spent the weekend together' or something like that" says Chris. "They know I have a house in Virginia, and I take friends there. It becomes a part of conversation just like they talk about their own husbands or wives."[9] Patrick simply monitors the ebb and flow of information between his coworkers, matching his own disclosures to those made by peers. "People talk about their families and their kids constantly," he says, "so I chime in with, 'We did this' and 'That's *my* family.' Or I'll mention gay friends who want to adopt, if we're talking about kids."

The result, for Patrick, is the sense that he is treated much like everyone else. "I think my relationship with people at work is probably much the same as a straight person's. Where I'm reserved, a lot of people are reserved. I don't really care that much who Diane's date was with, so I don't go into details about mine and say, 'He's really cute and his name is Mark, and he's five foot eleven inches.' I don't do that. But if Diane says something about her dates, I counter with something about mine. Sometimes when people are telling me a lot about their lives, I think, 'Well, it's my turn to talk now.' "

By educating their peers, and by highlighting the familiar aspects of an unfamiliar identity, gay men attempt to transform the unusual into the commonplace and acceptable. They situate self-disclosure in everyday narrative contexts—family, romance, civil rights—showing the connections between gay and straight lives. They remind straight peers that they share many of the same concerns—finding a date, making house payments, dealing with in-laws—thus supplying them a framework for thinking about gay relationships. With the parallels made evident, they encourage others to treat them as equals.

Dignifying Difference

An exclusive normalization strategy strikes some men as absurd. "Of *course* I'm different," says Sean. "My life has been shaped, in a profound way, by my sexuality." The real issue, he says, isn't the mere fact of his difference, but the particular use he has made of it. "My sexuality is more positive than negative, because that's how I've used it. I can see how it would easily be a negative, if you let it be. I personally don't let anything become a negative. Give me lemons, and I'll make lemonade."

Dignifying strategies assert control over the terms in which homosexuality is understood at work. Rather than emphasize how normal homosexuality is, assimilating it to the mainstream, these tactics *preserve* its marginality. Differences are transformed into assets. Instead of highlighting the many things gay men have in common with their hetereosexual peers, these men draw favorable attention to the differences that do in fact exist.[10]

Some men find themselves in work situations that require knowledge of the lesbian and gay community, and this becomes the basis for their choice of strategy. A man's employer may have a product it wants to market to gay consumers; others recognize that a large segment of their clientele is gay and thus has particular needs or concerns. In these situations, gay men have special access or insight that can be of use to their employers. While working on a marketing project involving a new AIDS medication, for example, Sean encouraged coworkers to take advantage of his familiarity with the community. "I was always deferred to in those situations," he recalls. "My opinion was always sought, and they pretty well took what I said as gospel." As far as Sean's boss was concerned, "My being gay was a boon for the company, because I knew how to deal with situations that came up on the AIDS drug we were working on, and was able to explain a lot of things they didn't understand. I thought of problems that there was absolutely no way a person who wasn't gay could possibly conceive of, like the ways we might be slighting certain subgroups."

Peter identified his connections to the gay community in his first interview with his current employer, a Philadelphia real estate firm. "When I interviewed with my boss, I told her that I wanted to advertise in the *Philadelphia Gay News*. She was completely open to it. I'd sold to several gay men before, and I suggested that I do an ad just for me, promoting myself as a realtor. There's a market out there for me, I told her. I just have to tap into it." Since that time she has encouraged Peter to handle the firm's advertising and public relations to the gay community. The other realtors, most of whom are hetereosexual, seek his advice: What special living needs do gay clients have? How can I best reach gay customers?

Peter thinks that being gay can also be an asset in more indirect ways. As a marginal person, he has cultivated other, transferable talents that he now brings to the workplace. He says that he is a highly individualistic, creative person, traits that are useful in his line of work. "There are a lot of gay people in real estate, especially in residential real estate," he says. "I guess it's because in homosexuality there tends to be a lot of individuality, and this is a very individualized business." Michael says that gay people also have an edge in his line of work, a branch of consulting best known by the euphemism "competitive intelligence." Michael's job often requires him to work under cover, posing as a college student or researcher, to dig up information on companies that compete with his clients. "I think that for what we do, being gay is an advantage," he says. "I genuinely believe that in corporate spying—whether it's called competitive intelligence or whatever—being sensitive to context, to what is said and how it's being said, is a really important part of the business. Being gay, in this culture, means being sensitive to context." When hiring junior associates, Michael favors other gay people.

John says that his sexuality is crucial to the work he does. Although he does not consider himself "corporate" in the usual sense, he faces the same pressures from his boss (the bishop) and his peers in other congregations. John began his career as the associate pastor at a large, fashionable congregation in the Philadelphia suburbs. Most of his parishioners were married, and John felt that this limited his effectiveness. Upon his retirement, the head pastor told John that the church needed a replacement who would understand these people's lives. " 'I can't give you the job because we really need a married man in that job,' he told me. That's as close as he came to saying that he would have been embarrassed to have a gay man. He used the word *single*. He wouldn't use the word *gay*."

Several years later John was invited to interview for a position with a congregation in downtown Philadelphia. He met with the vestry, who told him that the congregation was a diverse group of single, elderly, and gay people. They were worried that the church had not managed to attract many married couples, and wanted to know how John would tackle that problem. John encouraged them to see that "the common theme in the congregation is 'singleness.' " He urged them not to worry about courting married people, to take pride in the fact that they made single people feel at home.

As a single gay man, he told them that he could "model singleness" for the congregation. His marital status, which had been a handicap in the suburbs, became an asset in his new congregation; rather than hide or downplay his experiences as a marginal person, John made them a selling point. "In the interview, I said that in many ways, being gay saved my life. I've always been very positive about being gay once I came out, because I really think it's the best thing that ever could have happened to me. I'm looking at all these faces in the interview, and I said, 'I'm like you. I'm an upper-middle-class white kid from the suburbs. I'm male, and there's nothing in my background that would have enabled me to make a connection with the oppression of other people if I weren't gay.' Being gay helped me make sense of the world, to some degree—the way the world really is."

Unfortunately no more than a handful of gay professionals manage to turn their sexuality into an asset in the eyes of their peers. They often point out that their sexuality *is* an asset in one way or another. They recount experiences and insights that would have eluded them had they lived more conventional lives. They describe risks taken and opportunities pursued, and explain these as a function of an avant-garde sensibility, freedom from marital responsibilities, or a deep-seated insecurity that drives them to work—traits that are tapped in subtle, often unrecognized, ways. Yet rarely do they feel that coworkers recognize the role their sexuality has played in the kind of professionals they have become. While employers are only too happy to exploit a gay man's unique or special qualifications, they usually do not want to know about the personal struggles in which he acquired them.

Politicizing Marginality

When coworkers are openly homophobic, there may be little point in proposing that a gay man's sexuality is an asset to the company. Dignifying strategies are available only when coworkers are receptive to the idea that sexual diversity is something to be valued. Faced with open hostility, but unwilling to remain silent, a man has little choice but to turn confrontational.

Barry says that he never intended to be political about his sexuality. For several years he worked for a prestigious New York firm at which he was openly gay. "It became self-perpetuating," he recalls, "because people knew I didn't care if anybody knew. They'd take new people around and say, 'This is the xerox room. This is the mail room. And by the way, Barry's gay.' " Barry tried to normalize the situation by being frank with the other attorneys. He answered their questions and volunteered information about his personal life. Most of them handled the information well.

"Unfortunately," Barry admits, "this did not go well with the macho standards of the litigators. The guy who gave me the job is a really nice man, but he's a friend of Jesse Helms. He's a friend of Strom Thurmond. He backs groups that try to prove that black people are inherently inferior, that kind of stuff." When word got out that Barry was gay, "they despised me, sight unseen. They despised me for being gay." The result, for Barry, was a series of painful episodes.

The conflict first surfaced over Barry's handling of the recruitment program for summer associates. As head of the program, Barry arranged picnics in the park, trips to the ballet, individual dinners with candidates, and other social events, all of which made him highly visible within the firm. The response, from the litigators, were homophobic jokes and comments. "For instance, when I was running the summer program, one of the partners circulated a note about the 'Turkish Bath Outing' that suggested we were all going to dress up in high heels. The first prize was going to be a night with a big hunk. They called it a 'weenie roast,' that kind of thing. Of course, the subtext was that we were hiring 'a bunch of fags'—which we weren't, as a matter of fact, but that's not the point." Barry was outraged, especially when no one came to his defense. "If somebody had written about the 'Uganda Dinner'—you know, how all the 'niggers' were going to get together—management would have stomped all over them! But in this case, of course, they didn't."

One of the partners rallied to Barry's defense, circulating a memo that urged tolerance. "It was a half-assed effort," Barry says, "but it claimed that 'this firm does not discriminate, that we don't want anyone to discriminate.'" The response from some of the other lawyers was a thinly veiled attack. "This was before New York's civil rights bill was passed," Barry points out, and the partners were well aware of this. A few days after the original memo, one of the litigators responded by circulating a note explaining that "it was perfectly permissible to discriminate on the basis of sexual orientation." He attached a case "so everyone would know that this was perfectly permissible." Barry's attitude at the time was, "Well, I'm not going to let these fuckers get me down."

In 1986 New York passed a nondiscrimination ordinance that Barry hoped would change the atmosphere in the firm. He was quickly disappointed. Barry learned through a junior partner, a woman sympathetic to his predicament, that several of his most vocal critics had been privately told to let the issue rest. "They told these people, after the gay civil rights bill was passed, 'You've got to cut this out, it's against the law.'" But their response, according to Barry's source, was "Fuck the law." Meanwhile, the incidents continued. "I know for a fact that there was one partner who used to take candidates out to lunch and say, 'Oh, you're going to have lunch with Barry? You'd better watch your ass on that one.' One of the partners even told a candidate, 'Oh, that fag, everybody hates him. I wish we could get rid of him.' "

As Barry entered his seventh year with the firm, he knew that his chances for partnership were slim. One of the attorneys was frank with Barry, and told him, 'Look, they hate you so much, not just for being gay, but for being *openly* gay, that even if they're taking money out of their own pockets and throwing it out the window, they're still going to vote against you.' There comes a point when you can play the good boy and it isn't going to make a damn bit of difference, because people really won't even vote their pocketbooks.' "

The final blow came in the summer of 1988. Barry had interviewed a candidate for a summer position and had been impressed by his credentials. "The kid wasn't gay," Barry says, "although he looked as though he *could* have been. He was very mild mannered, very smart, wanted to go into corporate law. If you were stereotyping, there was a good chance he was gay. But he wasn't." Barry recommended that the firm make an offer, but immediately ran into opposition from some of the other attorneys. While the head of the hiring committee was out of town, one of the litigators bypassed the proper channels and told the candidate that no offer would be made. Barry protested, but found he had little support. Although several of the partners admitted that the decision had been a mistake, none would join Barry's effort to have the candidate reinstated. "That's when I realized the firm was going to let this guy get away with what he did—this macho jerk—because everyone else was too much of a wimp to stand up to him and say, 'No, this is wrong.' It was the same kind of thing: nobody would stand up for me either." Barry called an old friend at another firm and told him, "I'm ready to get out of here." He left the firm a few months later.

Even if a man's original goal was to blend in, tactics that politicize his identity inevitably set him apart. Even as he struggles to remove the stigma of his differentness, he cannot help but draw attention to it. The struggle can at times dominate his professional life, rendering it even more different from the normal life initially denied him.[11] Now working at another firm, Barry doesn't regret his decision to confront his employer. "I think one reason I'm kind of militantly out of the closet is that I had a very tough time accepting the fact that I'm gay," he says. "It took me a long time to admit it. I had what I now realize was a nervous breakdown. So I finally said, 'I'm gay, that's it.' What irritates me most is the cowards who came before me, who would not let it be known that they were gay, which made it very difficult for people like me to come out of the closet. So I determined that I would never, *never* be in the closet. Partially it's my own stubbornness, and partially it's because there are people who come in behind me that I feel I owe some kind of duty to."

While Barry became "political" by degrees, some men take a confrontational stance from the moment of disclosure. When a man is politically active outside the workplace, for example, he may find that news of his activism reaches professional circles. Sometimes without meaning to, he becomes known in the workplace for his political activities outside it. Michael found himself in this situation when his involvement with ACT-UP began to attract the attention of clients. In the summer of 1990, he was quoted in an article about AIDS drug trials in the *Philadelphia Gay News*. A few days later, one of Michael's clients seemed to behave oddly. "The following Monday I had a meeting with a client who sort-of didn't want to shake my hand, looked at me strangely all through the meeting, obviously having read the article—though he didn't say anything about it." Michael doesn't know if his client was offended by his involvement with ACT-UP, his role as a spokesman, or the simple news that he is gay.

As Chip took on an increasingly public role with ACT-UP, he tried to preempt an awkward situation by speaking directly to his boss. "I was working with ACT-UP, running some demonstrations during the Bush campaign," he recalls. "I had some friends who had AIDS, and I felt it was the thing to do. I didn't want someone to come up to my boss and say, 'I saw Chip on the news.' So I thought our relationship would be better if I told him directly, to circumvent any of that. And it was. I said, 'I don't want you to be blindsided by this, but this is what I'm going to do.' And my boss said, 'Well, you gotta do what you gotta do.' " Since then, Chip has continued his involvement with ACT-UP, although he says, "I try to keep the politics to a minimum at work."

Even as he spoke to his boss, however, a situation was brewing within the company that Chip ultimately felt demanded a confrontational stance. Chip had told several of his coworkers, shortly after joining the company, that he is HIV positive. Although his health was otherwise good, he was troubled by persistent allergies and began visiting the company nurse for a monthly allergy shot. After one of these visits, she called him aside. "She pulled me in back," he recalls, "and said, 'We don't give shots to HIV positive people.' And so I said, 'Well, why not?' and she said, 'It's company policy.' I asked who was responsible for the policy, and she told me." After thinking it over, Chip confronted the man who wrote the policy. "He explained that they didn't have a throw down bed, which is something they use for people who are going into shock. I said you can get that whether you're HIV positive or not, when you're dealing with allergy shots. And he said, 'The other thing is, there's some risk to the nurse who gives the shot.' "

Chip eventually saw through these transparent excuses. After a series of phone calls and meetings with the head of personnel, Chip learned that it was the company's legal consultants who had recommended against the monthly shots. "They didn't think it was wise to shoot antigens into someone with an immune deficiency. That made sense to me, but it doesn't apply to me because I have a battery of doctors. I have my immune system counted all the time and it's normal; I'm HIV positive, but asymptomatic." The company ultimately relented, and agreed to give Chip his monthly shots. Though HIV status does not necessarily communicate anything about sexual orientation, Chip assumes that his coworkers now "either know, or at least wonder if I'm gay." In either case they know that he is persistent.

The confrontation starts, quite often, when a lesbian or gay employee sets out to right a situation that he or she considers unfair. Coming out, in these instances, may be motivated by a particular grievance, a discriminatory policy or practice they want changed. To voice their concerns, they must first identify themselves. As health insurance and other benefits become an increasingly high priority for lesbian and gay employees, more of them can be expected to identify themselves in his context.

It was this same sort of inequity that ultimately prompted Don to become more political. He was new to the Bay Area when he joined Levi Strauss & Co. in 1980. "My previous job was with a real estate investment firm that was very conservative. I didn't share anything there. I was extremely closeted." When he joined his present employer, he began the transition. "At first I didn't take a real proactive role in enlightening people around my being gay," he recalls. "In the past I tended to just brush over it and to not really get into it with people. I wouldn't *deny* it, if people were talking to me about it, but I wasn't an advocate for being gay in the company."

Two years ago one of Don's coworkers, a woman named Janice, tried to enroll her lesbian partner for company health benefits. She was turned down. Frustrated by this incident, she and Don decided to form an employees' association. The company already had organizations for African American, Hispanic, and Asian employees and tended to look favorably on minority activism. The only question was how to get started. Don and Janice considered sending private invitations to coworkers they knew were gay but quickly decided that this would set a bad precedent. "We realized that we didn't want to start out that way. It would be like this clandestine, secret organization. So we put fliers out everywhere. On every bulletin board we had a flier with our names on it saying, 'Come celebrate our diversity. Join us for this special lunchtime meeting where we'll discuss forming a lesbian and gay employee group.'"

Some sixty people showed up for the first meeting. The national papers got wind of it, and before long Don was thrust into the national spotlight. Today he attends conferences and grants interviews on behalf of the company. In 1991 the company even awarded Don a "community service leave" that allowed him to spend half of his company time on gay-related projects. As cofounder of the company's lesbian and gay organization, he continues to work with upper management on matters of gay visibility and employee benefits. "That's the direction I'm heading," he says. "Every time that I don't say anything or try to skirt over the issue, I've missed an opportunity to help somebody confront the issue. Gay diversity needs to be as visible as other kinds of diversity."

Don's company was receptive to his efforts and seems willing to listen and work with gay and lesbian employees around sensitive issues. It also seems willing to tolerate a certain amount of internal agitation and debate—and in this respect it is unusual. While disagreement and dissent are tolerated in most workplaces, they are kept within bounds. Arguments are confined to specific adversarial situations (a debate, the discussion of a proposal), outside of which professionals are expected to exhibit decorum and to be good team players. There are penalties, in particular, for being difficult or confrontational. Perhaps this is why politicizing strategies often begin with a series of smaller confrontations, leading a man, gradually, to abandon all efforts at accommodation. In many cases one can identify a final straw that broke the camel's back—and in many cases, today, it involves AIDS.

This was the situation faced by Mark. His firm is large and well known, and has about five thousand employees. Mark joined the compensation division several years ago, and the atmosphere, as he describes it, is hostile. "The firm is extremely homophobic," he says. "I only know of one—no, I guess two gay partners. I know one of them quite well, and he's extremely closeted. He was married when he joined the firm and got a divorce about three years later. He was very careful not to be too visibly friendly with me inside the firm and said that he thought it was the kiss of death, as far as career success, to be out. The whole culture is very much directed toward the family, and there are lots of homophobic comments and jokes and gesturing, not only internally but also during client contacts." Under the circumstances Mark adopted an avoidance strategy and concentrated on his work. He was quickly promoted, and received a string of sizable bonuses.

Early in 1986 the situation grew more complicated. Mark's lover had known for several years that he had been exposed to HIV, and his health had gradually begun to fail. Mark had anticipated this situation and had warned his boss, Marcia, before taking the job. "I had worked with Marcia at another firm. Before I started work I told her, 'Luke's sick. There may come a time—and who knows how soon—when I'll have to direct a lot of time and effort to caring for him. I don't want to take this job if that's going to be a problem.' And I was told, 'Oh, no, don't worry, we've been friends for years, I know all about it. The head of our area is wonderful. She really understands, and she wouldn't care. Everything will be fine.' "

By the time Luke got sick, however, Marcia faced problems of her own. She was in the middle of a complicated pregnancy and had been ordered to bed for the duration. She was also up for partner that year, which placed a tremendous strain on her staff, especially Mark. With Marcia home in bed, there were only two senior people remaining. "I guess she decided that it wouldn't look good if I was also out of the office."

As Luke required more and more attention, Mark found himself in a bind. "When Luke got really sick, I started asking for time off to take care of him. Marcia kept putting me off, saying, 'Can't you just get through this project?' 'Finish this proposal and then we'll discuss it.' She kept putting the issue off, and I kept working until midnight five days in a row, going home in the middle of the day to take care of Luke." Eventually the strain became too much for Mark, and shortly before Luke died, he lost his temper:

> About a week before Luke died I came into the office at ten o'clock, after having worked until midnight the night before. On my way home I had dropped a draft of a presentation I was doing with Marcia's doorman so she could review it and give me comments. When I was getting ready to leave for work, Luke had an accident, so I had to change the bed and clean up the bedroom and the bathroom.
>
> I finally got to work at ten. Marcia had the receptionist call her the minute I came in the door. As soon as I reached my office, the phone was ringing. It was Marcia, and she said, "How dare you come prancing into the office at ten o'clock when you've got a major presentation to do on Friday and it looks like shit?" I explained to her what happened and she said, "Well, I thought I told you two weeks ago if you couldn't take care of Luke without having it impact your work, you would have to put him in the hospital or hire a nurse." I reminded her that I had tried hiring a nurse. It drove Luke crazy. "Until he wants one, I'm not going to force one on him. Being independent is really important to him and the de-

ception of his independence is probably part of what's keeping him alive. I'm not going to interfere with his denial mechanisms." She said that I had better not come into the office late again. So I said, "What do you want me to do, leave him lying in a bed of shit?"

Luke died a week later, sitting in an airplane, on his way to visit his sister. "I couldn't get the day off from work to take him," Mark recalls. "That's my biggest regret, because I wanted to tell him I loved him, one more time, before he died." For Mark this episode was the last straw. He was determined not to be taken advantage of again.

About six months later Mark attended a meeting at the gay community center and heard Larry Kramer make a speech about the need for direct action in the fight against AIDS. The meeting was the beginning of ACT-UP, and Mark got involved "quite heavily from the very beginning." He led several of the early demonstrations, and helped organize the famous "zap" against Burroughs-Wellcome, the manufacturer of Retrovir, the first drug approved as a treatment for AIDS. "I came out on the Phil Donahue show," he recalls. "I had come out to the head of my department before that, and some of the other senior people at work found out when Luke died. I didn't think many people would see the show, because it's on during the day and people are at work. I never watch TV myself and didn't think anybody would have taped it."

As it turned out, several of Mark's coworkers saw the show, and the "Donahue" appearance set off a string of events that would make him increasingly visible at work. Shortly after the show aired, Mark took part in several other media events that quickly found their way into the company grapevine. "We did a demonstration in front of the White House," he recalls, "and at the Third International AIDS Conference in the summer of '87. My picture was on the cover of the Week in Review section of the Sunday *Times*. A bunch of people came up to me afterwards and asked, 'Was that you in the *Times*?' Then I started doing a lot of work on homelessness and AIDS, and I kept getting quoted in the paper about this or that. It got to the point where there was no sense trying to hide. Pretty much everybody knew."

Since that time things have been "strained at best." The company was apparently embarrassed by Mark's growing visibility as an activist.

After the Donahue appearance, he was placed on probation and was told he would be fired if he didn't tone down the AIDS activism. "They've done a lot to encourage me to quit. They've given me minimal raises, haven't given me bonuses. They put me on probation recently for 'doing too much AIDS work on company time.' I was told that I had better not make any more AIDS calls and receive or send any AIDS faxes on company time, or I'd be fired immediately. A whole bunch of things like that." Mark continues to work for the company but has since filed a lawsuit.

Facing Discrimination

When he uses an integration strategy, a gay man exposes himself to whatever prejudice, confusion, or apprehension coworkers may have about homosexuality. Integration strategies differ, in this respect, from other strategies. By posing as a heterosexual, a gay man feigns membership in the sexual elite, thus escaping whatever penalties he might otherwise pay. By avoiding sexuality altogether, he tries to make it a nonissue, downplaying its significance and potential consequences. The penalties associated with the use of either strategy result less from the direct experience of homophobia than from the mechanics of the strategies themselves—the energy required, the ethical dilemmas posed, and the feelings of social detachment that often result. Integration strategies, by contrast, expose a man directly to homphobia. The consequence of using such a strategy will depend largely on the environment in which he works.

Evidence of prejudicial hiring, firing, and compensation practices is abundant, documented in countless surveys, autobiographical accounts, legal papers, anecdotal reports in the gay press, and gossip that circulates through extended social networks of gay professionals. In surveys roughly one in three gay men claims he has been the victim of discrimination in the workplace (see Appendix). Twice that number anticipate it at some point in the future. Even when they have not experienced discrimination firsthand, gay men are highly sensitive to its prevalence among their peers. Ask a gay man if he considers discrimination a serious problem and he will usually volunteer a story about a homophobic boss or client—if not his own story, at least one he heard from an entirely reliable source. When asked, most can name a friend who was denied a job, promotion, or security clearance. Many know someone who sued his or her employer. All have read about the thousands of men and women expelled by the U.S. military for being gay or lesbian, or about companies like AT&T and Western Union that have defended themselves against lawsuits *not* by claiming they did not discriminate, but by demonstrating that it is entirely legal to do so.[12] If the abundance of these cautionary tales is any measure of our collective fears, employment discrimination is the number one concern of lesbian and gay professionals.

Consequently, while actual discrimination is common, the fear of potential discrimination is epidemic. Like Damocles' sword, it is a perpetual threat, a fact of life for gay professionals who reveal their sexuality at work. Howard has been active in the Pacific Bell lesbian and gay employee association since it was founded. Although his employer is publicly supportive of the group, Howard knows he is taking a considerable risk, at least in professional terms. In early 1991 the organization lobbied the company to support AB101, the California bill that—had it not been vetoed by Governor Wilson—would have extended workplace protections to lesbian and gay employees. "When you do that kind of thing, as someone with some career aspirations, it's very nerve racking," says Howard. You never know what happens when you walk out of the room and they close the door. What do they say? I've seen enough careers ruined by the perception that you're not playing 'on the team,' as it were. Your reputation is everything, and it has an effect on where you go and what you do. And that, of course, is the $64,000 question for me: What impact does this really have? And it's something I'll never know."

Howard doesn't worry that he will be fired. As a labor negotiator, he knows that his company is too smart to penalize him in an overt way. "Coming out to the level that I have, given the exposure I've had, I'm golden and untouchable. This corporation is never going to try to go after me on the basis of my sexuality because it's so 'out there' that they'd be afraid of being sued." In this sense Howard knows that he is lucky. "It's a curious phenomenon," he says, "knowing that your job is protected by something that might, under other circumstances, put it at risk." Still, while he knows that his job is safe, "that's different than having a warm and fuzzy environment."

The threat of discrimination figures prominently in the decisions gay men make about self-disclosure.[13] While few know for sure how vulnerable they are at work, all use the available evidence to arrive at some kind of guess. Some feel that their jobs are secure, that their performance records or client relationships make them difficult to fire or that another job would be relatively easy to find. Others recognize that they have few protections, performance that is difficult to measure or document, or careers in which mobility is limited and jobs are scarce. When assessing their own vulnerability, gay men take several factors into consideration.

An independent or powerful boss is one sign that a man may be vulnerable.[14] When bosses and clients can hire and fire at will, for example, a man may find it necessary to take certain precautions. "I can't tell the other doctors I'm gay," says Miguel, "because I'm not free yet. If I'm going to specialize in infectious diseases, I'll still depend on these people. I don't know if they'll take someone who's openly gay. I don't know what their mentality is. Once I have my fellowship and my private practice, I won't care. The first person I'll tell will be my secretary. But at this point I can't take that chance." Terry finds himself in a similar situation. The law firm's senior partner, a man in his sixties, is a vocal homophobe. "He makes derogatory comments about homosexuals. He said something not too long ago, when Bush signed the Hate Crimes Bill and several homosexuals came to the signing. He said, 'I like Bush, but it really made me mad the other day when he had all those queers up to the White House.'" Because Terry is entirely dependent on the senior partner for work, he feels safest wearing a disguise at work. "He's the monarch," Terry says, "and he could fire me at will."

Nowhere is a man more vulnerable than when his career depends on the favor of a particular mentor. In many medical residency programs, for example, surgeons come up for renewal at the end of each year, and the "pyramid" structure of these programs ensures that some will be eliminated. Sometimes the dismissals are the result of measurable performance deficits, but Tip claims to know several surgeons in his program who were dismissed from his program due to "personality differences" with the other staff. "In your third year of general surgery they could bump you and say, 'You're not coming back next year.' Then you'd be left, after all these years, with no job. Unless you find a residency program that will take you to finish, you can't work."

Tip's program doesn't use the pyramid formula, however, which he initially hoped would afford him some measure of security. "That's why I chose this hospital, because I knew I'd be accepted from start to finish." But three years into the program, Tip has never felt more vulnerable. "Even now they could get rid of me," he says. He describes his profession as a tight-knit community, and realizes that his boss is one of its most visible members. "The network is strong. The head of surgery, Dr. Thomas, is the head of the society for the whole country for plastic surgery. He knows everyone. To be mobile at all in plastic surgery requires that Dr. Thomas give me his approval—at least for another year and a half." Worse yet, Dr. Thomas has a reputation for bullying the other doctors. Shortly after he joined the program, Tip learned of another doctor, a woman named Mary, who had been forced to leave. "She was a lesbian, and Dr. Thomas, bigot that he is, made her life so miserable that she ultimately chose to do her residency elsewhere." For Tip the solution is to play it straight around Dr. Thomas. "I wouldn't want to set myself up to be eliminated," Tip says. "Being gay would be a very big reason to be eliminated."

Men who work directly with clients or customers would appear to have a more solid economic footing. Their dependence is dispersed across many individuals outside their own organization, so that no single boss or committee is responsible for their livelihood. Especially when they are self-employed, these men are more likely to be openly gay at work.[15] Chris, whose consulting firm is often brought in to restructure or rescue a company that is in trouble, says that all his clients know that he is gay. "I'm usually the boss at these places," he says, "so at least to my face, they can't appear to dislike it. I may be insulated for that reason. I've never had to be concerned about what my boss would think. If I had to get that paycheck to eat the next week, it might have been very different." Michael is also self-employed as a consultant. "The risk levels are not high because no one client is all that important," he says. "If someone doesn't like the mouthwash that I use, or the fact that I'm gay, it doesn't much matter to the business."

With economic freedom comes the ability to take certain risks. Andy says that one of the law firm's senior partners is having an especially profitable year, which has made it easier for the man to be openly gay. "When his practice wasn't as good as it is now, I'm sure he was much more worried," says Andy. "It's fortunate that his practice has gone well, so he can afford to be open." Milton feels the same way. "The thing that protects me—and that doesn't protect one of the women in the firm, who's a lesbian—is that I have my own client base. I have a highly portable piece of the practice. I can always pick up and go someplace else. And I have clients that pay on time and pay well. So they're not going to fuck with me." The strong client base is especially important, Milton says, because he is vulnerable in more ways than one. "It's still risky for me," he says. "My skin is black. We always say in black America that if white America gets a cold, black America gets pneumonia. It's riskier for me than it is for a white fellow in the same position."

A notable exception to this pattern is a man who fears his clients would desert him en masse if they were somehow to learn that he is gay. Darren feels certain that the current hysteria about AIDS would make him unemployable as an openly gay dentist. At the time of our interview, in the summer of 1990, news about Dr. David Acer, a Florida dentist who presumably exposed several of his patients to HIV, was capturing national headlines. In Darren's clinic, conversations about AIDS had become virtually unavoidable. "There was this particular patient, and he had done some kind of charity work for AIDS or something. The other dentists found out about it, and they were hysterical. They wanted to find out if he had an appointment, to make sure that everyone knew that this person could not be handled in our office." Two years later the office policy hasn't changed. The other dentists and hygienists continue to worry that "if any of our patients found out that there were AIDS patients here, we would go out of business." Though Darren considers these fears irrational, he's careful when speaking to patients. "I'm absolutely convinced that if my patients knew I'm gay, they wouldn't come to me. There is no doubt in my mind—I've spoken to many of them about it."

Darren's sense of vulnerability lies in his assumption that his patients are capable of acting as a group, much in the way that a single, powerful employer might fire a subordinate. When asked if the other dentists would try to protect him, Darren shakes his head. "I think I'd lose my job," he says. "I think that the people who are in control of my job would, regretfully, try to find a way to get rid of me. 'We really like him,' they'd say. 'But it's a business decision, and we have to get rid of him.' "

Perceived vulnerability also varies with the degree to which one's job performance is defined in concrete, measurable terms. In occupations that depend heavily on trust, reputation, and other intangibles, gay men tend to assume that they are more vulnerable. Other professions make use of more formal credentialing processes or measures of success, which make job effectiveness easier to document.[16] When a man's performance is measured in sales figures, for example, his track record affords him a certain amount of security; even if he is fired, his record will enable him to find work. "On Wall Street, especially as a trader, if you make money for the firm you can be a serial killer and it wouldn't matter to most of the firms," according to Jerry. "If you can make money in this business, it doesn't matter what you do with your personal life, or what color you are or what your sexual preference is. That's the bottom line on Wall Street."

Unique, irreplaceable skills can also make a man feel more secure. "Nobody knows these systems better than I do," says Ed, who supervises dozens of IBM's largest corporate accounts. "It would take someone new a long time to get up to speed." Chip feels that his experience with the company's accounting software makes him a key asset. "I have more latitude because of what I do than some other people," he says. "It seems to me that people whose jobs are more important are more comfortable about being gay because they feel more indispensable to the company and therefore less likely to be fired."

Mobility within an industry—in particular, the ease with which one can find other work—can also boost a man's sense of security. Occupations characterized by high turnover and transferable skills tend to broaden the options for the future. Being fired is less of a concern, for example, when the industry is too large and disjointed for the job pool to be poisoned by a former boss. Likewise, when the field is characterized by low entry or exit barriers, gay men know they can always pick up and move into some other, related line of work. "You know, I can always be a flight attendant," says George. "I could work eight days a month, make forty thousand dollars a year, and then start a business on the side." Because he's a member of the projectionists union, Barry knows that he could always resume the career he abandoned after law school. "If worst comes to worst, I can go back and make forty dollars an hour projecting movies."

For many gay men, however, career mobility—and thus their sense of security—has been drastically diminished by the specter of AIDS. The epidemic has encouraged many gay men to be conservative when planning their careers. Given the dire penalties that accompany being unemployed and without health insurance, many are unwilling to give up a steady job. Private insurance has become virtually unobtainable without a blood test, anchoring men who are HIV-infected to their current employers and insurance policies. Those who do not know their status or who fear a blood test worry that a career move would force them to confront some frightening realities. "I have not had an AIDS test yet, and I need to do that," says George. "I don't think I've got a reason to be concerned, but I'm not deluding myself. There's still some doubt there. I need to find out if I'm positive or not, because if I have a chance of coming down with AIDS I'd be worried about getting past somebody's blood test in a pre-employment screening. That would keep me at the company in a second."

It is widely assumed, finally, that nondiscrimination policies and laws will encourage gay men to come out at work. Although lesbians and gay men have no protection from employment discrimination at the federal level, some 130 cities and counties have now added sexual orientation to the list of protected categories. Seven states and the District of Columbia have enacted laws that prohibit discrimination by private employers on the basis of sexual orientation. Yet while formal policies play an important symbolic role and provide a platform from which lesbians and gay men can demand other rights and benefits, they contribute relatively little to a man's subjective sense of his own security.[17] More than 25 percent of the men we interviewed were "not sure" if their employers had an explicit policy on sexual orientation; 40 percent knew for a fact that they did not. At least as many were uninformed about local or state protections in their areas. Similarly, a recent survey of 205 professional journalists, conducted by the American Society of News Editors, found that 41 percent did not know if their paper's health insurance plan covered AIDS-related illnesses. Nearly 40 percent of those in newsrooms with union contracts did not know if those contracts prohibit discrimination based on sexual orientation. And 35 percent did not know if their paper had a nondiscrimination clause protecting lesbians and gay men.[18]

Among gay men who are aware of a company policy or law (33 percent of our participants), there is little faith that their function is more than symbolic. Perhaps this is because most gay men realize just how difficult such policies are to enforce. Few are willing to accept a free-fall into an untested legal safety net. "The formal policy is that you don't discriminate," says Mark, whose company surveyed its own clients and found antigay discrimination virtually across the board. "But it's informally known that if you suspect someone may be gay, you should overlook hiring them." Darren confirmed that his dental clinic often refuses to treat patients with HIV. He thought that the policy was probably illegal but assured me that there was little way to enforce the law.

Harry learned this lesson the hard way when he was dismissed from a fund-raising job at a national charity. "One day, my boss just called me in the office and said, 'You have not raised enough money and you have your choice: Either resign or be fired.'" Harry knew that his employer was obligated to give him several weeks' notice and refused to resign. He also knew that his boss was vocally antigay and felt that this had influenced her decision to fire him. Harry was quickly advised, however, that despite the fact that the District of Columbia had a strong civil rights law, a suit would be expensive and fruitless. "They got a bunch of lawyers together and were just going to paper us to death." Overwhelmed by the potential cost, Harry backed down. "I couldn't afford to take them to court. My attorney said it would cost five hundred dollars per hour, we'd probably spend fifty thousand, and we'd be lucky if we got one hundred thousand. So I've had to eat that experience."

Tip is similarly skeptical. Although New York has a municipal ordinance that prohibits discrimination, he is confident that Dr. Thomas could find a way around the law. "It would never be *said*," Tip explains. "It would be a very underhanded thing. They could cite any incident. They could pull scores from tests; every year we have to take a test on improvement of skills. They could say you're not performing well enough and you will not be re-enlisted. The three professors could act in concert, or Dr. Thomas could do it alone. And it wouldn't even be disputed, not at all, unless I chose to fight it. Even if you fought it you wouldn't win. There's no way to win."

The mistrust of these policies highlights the extent to which most professional jobs revolve around the cultivation of relationships. They have an interpersonal dimension that cannot easily be defined; intangibles like rapport and chemistry cannot be legislated. Consequently, even in organizations with aggressive nondiscrimination policies, gay men are reluctant to seek legal solutions to what they perceive are interpersonal problems. A survey of Philadelphians found that 66 percent of the men (and 83 percent of the women) fear employment discrimination *despite* the legal protections provided by the local Fair Practices Act.[19] A marketing executive at Lotus drew the same conclusion. Though his company has a nondiscrimination policy and in 1991 gained national attention as the first large, publicly traded company to offer benefits to the spouses of its lesbian and gay employees, he is reluctant to come out. "I'm still concerned that it could become an issue in very subjective, touchy-feely ways. It could hurt me for a promotion or raise, so I'm still handling that on a one-to-one basis. I have to gauge their reactions before I make any blanket announce-ments."

Indeed, feelings of vulnerability are so deep, rooted as they are in countless experiences from childhood to the present, that no policy or program will easily put them to rest. Quite often one can iden-tify no particular reason for a gay man's sense of insecurity. Al at-tributes his fears to the gloomy economic climate in his firm. "I guess I'm concerned about the economic situation and the fact that it makes it a lot easier for people to come up with excuses to get rid of people, or to not hire people." Andy uses an avoidance strategy for the same reason. Although he made partner several years ago and knows of at least two gay men who have done well at the firm, he fears for his job. "The only reason I would not be open with my partners is fear of my job and career," he says. "If I were more con-fident about my job, less expendable, or if there were more open-ings in the field, I might feel differently. But there are a lot of attorneys out of work. Absent that, I would like to be more open." How would he feel if the economy turned around, or if his client base grew and became more stable? "Two things would push me toward openness," he answers. "Financial security and the desire to reveal a relationship, when I have one."

Compensation

The pervasive fear of discrimination, coupled with low feelings of self-worth, can drive a man to take several steps. Perceiving his job to be at risk, he becomes a star performer, the top salesman, the award-winning agent.[20] Insecure about his personal worth, he tries to be an exemplary professional, the consummate company man. He compensates by working longer and harder than his straight peers, driven by the conviction that he doesn't measure up in other, more personal ways.[21] "It's like women who have to fight a little harder to prove themselves in the workplace," says Geoff. "I think gay men have to do the same thing."

Gay men sometimes stage elaborate displays of professional competence for the benefit of their peers. They effect the image of the model professional: someone who is highly qualified, works well with others, places the company's interests before his own, and is a vigilant guardian of its reputation and assets. Loyalty and worth to the company are made evident in conspicuous displays of initiative, effort, and self-denial.[22] Carter says that this is the reason he takes comfort in his long and profitable list of clients. "I have a burden to produce more than the average person," he says. "I know I'm vulnerable, being up front about being gay. So the more I bring to the hotel, the more I do for the hotel and do for my clients, the more I can be myself and not worry about getting shot down or passed over for promotion." Several of the hotel's senior catering managers, he says, are "older women who don't really care for my life-style. But they depend on me for all their business. I bring a lot of the catering business to them, so it's very civil." The same is true of Carter's boss. "I do a lot for him, so he knows I can be of help."

Derek feels that his sexuality has strongly influenced his professional style. He works long hours and is known for taking the initiative on projects. He even suspects that he is "somewhat of an irritant to senior people because I'm always getting into their soup, always doing things that they see as ego threatening." The aggressive work ethic, Derek says, is just a way of protecting himself. "I wouldn't have to prove as much if I were straight," he says. As it is, "I run circles around everyone else so no one will ever be able to say I don't outperform anybody in the building. And it's not because I have this great desire to do well. I feel I *have* to outperform everybody." Asked why this is the case, Derek shrugs, as if the answer were obvious. "I can't be just 'okay.' I cannot allow average performance from me. Christ, I'm gay. I have to work harder."

Beneath the flurry of professional activity, Derek also has regrets about his personal life. "I don't have anything else to focus my attention on," he says. "For example, I've gotten involved in the arts because I had to have some avenue, not because I'm that crazy about them. Other people are all so excited about their kids, and they *talk* about them. They talk about arguments they had with their wives or their husbands, or the great dinner they had with their wife and husband. I can't do any of that. What I have is my job, and I have the success of my company. If they want to go home because they have something else—that's fine, but then I'm going to do their jobs for them. That's very threatening to them, I think." Derek wonders how his life would be different if he had a family and children. "I'd probably walk out the door at six, just like the rest of them," he says, "if I thought I could."

Derek's boss seems to have figured this out. Shortly after Derek joined the company, he and his boss flew to Washington together and enjoyed a bottle of wine during the flight. Before long the conversation turned to relationships. "He said something like, 'You've got to stop worrying about yourself. Your performance is what I want. I don't care about anything else.' He kept dropping hints, and I said, 'I really don't know what you're talking about.'" Derek's boss made it more explicit. "He explained that he had figured out that I'm gay thirty days after I started working for him, and he was *thrilled* about it because he knew that I was scared to death. That meant I was going to work twice as hard as anybody else would, which meant that he got a great deal. He paid for one guy and he got two guys, and that was fine. He thought that was really neat."

Hearing this, Derek tried to change the subject. "I told him that I was very uncomfortable with the conversation. I didn't know where it was going, and I said I wanted to talk about something else. And he said, 'Well, fine, if you don't want to enjoy the situation, that's fine. But it's your problem if you're uncomfortable, because I'm not uncomfortable.'" Derek hasn't raised the issue since and is not happy with the idea that his boss got "twice what he was paying for" by hiring him. Still, he laughs at the implications of the suggestion. "Maybe the solution for straight business people is to find single male homosexuals who are hung up about it, hire them into corporate positions, and go back and reap the profit."

When a man bears more than one kind of stigma, the need to compensate may be even more acute. Professionals who are marginalized because they are foreign, female, or non-white must manage the competing demands of multiple stigma.[23] Because he speaks with a strong Puerto Rican accent, Miguel worried that he would encounter both racism and heterosexism when he moved to Philadelphia from Puerto Rico. To avoid the latter, he decided to counterfeit a heterosexual identity. "When I went to work in the hospital, and I found the problems I have in terms of the culture and language, I thought, 'I can't put another rock in my way.' I already have enough problems with the language, so I said, 'I can't tell these people I'm gay.' "

Milton learned to compensate long before he knew he was gay. Today his status as a "double minority"—as an openly gay African American—only intensifies the effort. "Achieving blacks are taught, 'You've got to work harder; you've got to stay there later because you will always be perceived as being different. And when you don't know something, people will notice it more; when you *do* know, people will notice it more. Always know more, always work harder.' " Following this advice, Milton has developed a scrupulous work ethic and a heightened attentiveness to his clients. "I work very hard to keep those clients," he says. "I have clients that people are always trying to pick off from me. So I have to make sure that my client contact in those companies will always say, 'Milton does such a bang-up job there really is no reason we shouldn't use him.' "

As he struggles to keep these clients, Milton imagines his life as a balancing act. Bifurcating his world into personal and professional roles, he imagines the two halves to be in opposition; like many professionals he feels that concessions in one realm are necessary for achievements in another. Gay men, in particular, speak of the "sacrifices" and "trade-offs" imposed on the professional by the personal. "I took a big risk in coming out at work," one man explains. "It may ultimately hurt me, but that was the chance I took." When asked how far he will likely rise in the ranks of his company, he is uncertain. "I'm not so sure," he begins, pausing for a moment. "I suppose if that were my main concern, I wouldn't have come out in the first place. I'll probably be fine, but who knows?" Although he couldn't identify a particular boss or client who might penalize him for being openly gay, he nurtures the vague expectation that he will someday pay for his choice of strategy.

Compensation rituals are a hedge against such consequences. By amassing a large and profitable client list, gay professionals console bosses who might otherwise make trouble for them.[24] With extraordinary service they deny a homophobic client any reason to look elsewhere. Their career achievements, in this context, are more than an effort to stand out in a positive way. They are a form of professional armor, an attempt to defuse homophobia by appeasing one's enemies.

Perhaps this is why men who are openly gay at work tend to speak of career success as an uphill battle, as something that happens despite the odds. When they describe their future within a particular company, they speak in tentative terms and downplay their own ambitions as if it were just a bit optimistic to take them too seriously.[25] Often these are men with advanced degrees, personal charisma, and a long list of concrete achievements—men whose credentials give them every reason to expect professional success. But these men are also openly gay in environments that are tolerant, at best, and for many this has radically limited their sense of the possible.

Tokenism

Groups that are numerically scarce face yet another predicament in most work settings. Whenever "the few" must interact with "the many," they often find that their behavior is interpreted symbolically. They become "tokens" and are treated "as representatives of their category, as symbols rather than individuals."[26] For the lone gay among straights, the foreigner among natives, or the occasional black among many whites, token status brings with it several characteristic predicaments.

For their peers, lesbians and gay men symbolize many of our culture's most knotted beliefs about sexuality. The homosexual is a key figure in a number of heated social and moral debates. As Jeffrey Weeks has pointed out, our "attitudes to homosexuality are inextricably linked to wider questions: of the function of the family, the evolution of gender roles, and of attitudes to sexuality generally."[27] In work environments, an openly gay doctor or engineer becomes a lightning rod, a target for his peers' attitudes toward sexuality in general and homosexuality in particular. His mere presence seems to raise "issues" beyond his immediate work performance.

Perhaps this is why gay professionals, once they have come out,

are so often treated as community spokespeople. Once he has identified himself, a gay man is often asked to speak "on behalf of" all
gay people, called upon to supply the "gay perspective." His performance is used to judge the qualifications of gay people as a group.
Even his most mundane behavior begins to have symbolic consequences. He doesn't get along with coworkers: "Gay people are so
argumentative." He sets a new sales record: "He's a credit to the gay
community." Simply by being visible an openly gay man becomes a
surrogate for an entire category of people, a representative for a
point of view, and a participant in a cultural debate he may know
or care little about.

For many tokenism is viewed as an opportunity. In a survey by
Out/Look, 57 percent of lesbians and gay men said that their desire
"to educate others" was a major incentive to come out.[28] Chip says
that "if something happens to me, if I become ill or get run over by
a truck tomorrow," he will look back with pride on the ways he has
helped to educate others. His coworkers "think differently about
gays today than they did before I encountered them." Similarly,
Carter says that he has "a good time" exposing coworkers "to my
life-style and what we do." When asked to describe his ideal job
environment, he says that he'd like to go even further. "It would be
nice to have a cute gay girl so they could see another aspect of gay
life: that there can be a normal-looking lesbian who's not wearing
comfortable shoes. I'm really enjoying showing them some of my
life." Like many gay men Carter finds himself trying to broadcast a
positive message about the gay "community," demonstrating with
his own individual behavior "the way gay people really are."

Some men formalize their token status, volunteering themselves
as delegates from the gay community. When his firm was working
on a new AIDS medication, Sean became the in-house expert on
gay lives and life-styles. In more personal conversations, he encourages coworkers to ask questions about his sexuality, hoping that
they will "come to understand gay people" through their interactions with him. "I've been given the unique opportunity," he says,
"in that I have something that other people don't understand that I
can teach them about. And through my teaching, hopefully, they
will gain a positive image of it, as opposed to getting a negative or

stereotypical image of it. I feel great when people turn around or when they realize—it's just another notch for me every time somebody deals with it in a positive manner." Likewise, Howard's company treats him as its liaison to the gay community. "The company is very interested in fostering connections to the gay community," he says, "because of the political influence and clout the community has with the city and county of San Francisco, the mayor, and so forth. They use me to build those connections."

Not all men are eager to serve as tokens, however. John is routinely called by the bishop, who treats him as the local expert on gay matters. "I'm already very well known in the diocese as 'the gay priest,'" John says. "I get incredible calls from the bishop. Something will be happening in another county or something, and he'll call me. And I say, 'What do I know about it? I'm certainly not the only gay priest you've got. Maybe you should call somebody out there.'" Although Barry is glad he stood up to the homophobic litigators in his firm, he no longer wants to play this role. "I was tired of being the center of attention," he says. "While he is still openly gay at work, his new job allows him to be more anonymous. "I wanted to be someplace where my boss would handle all of the politics, and that would be that." As Russ points out, "One advantage to being closeted is that I don't have to explain gay life to all these people. I'm sure many of them would be very inquisitive, but I don't want to do all that *explaining*."

Sometimes the attention can become patronizing. Jack feels that coworkers often regard him as a symbol, using him in ways that suggest he "stands for" something beyond his own sexuality. Their contact, he says, is weighted with too many levels of significance. "I sense that a lot of my coworkers like to show off that they have liberated views in this area, using me as somebody with whom they can openly talk and joke about sexuality. It comes up probably more than it should, but my closest friends at work all seem to enjoy the opportunity to talk openly with a gay person." Although Jack enjoys the candor, he senses an ulterior motive to these conversations. "Sometimes I feel like a trophy, like they're boasting to themselves and to other people that they have a good friend who is gay."

Consequently, while Jack no longer keeps secrets about his sexuality, he still finds it difficult to "be himself" at work. He enjoys talking with his colleagues about his sexuality, and about homosexuality in general. Yet he finds that even in these open, intimate conversations, he is still performing. He knows that he is exploited as a symbol and bears the burden of responding as such. He knows that when they talk with him, coworkers are at the same time testing and refining their attitudes toward homosexuality in general. As a result Jack feels that he is "on" whenever talking about the subject. His own sexual appetites run toward the rough and dangerous, and he has been arrested more than once for having sex in a public setting. Yet he does not want coworkers to form this impression of all gay men, and is thus reluctant to talk about these incidents at work. He worries that an explicit discussion of his erotic life would be too personal and would overstep the boundaries of good taste. He carefully plans his disclosures, monitoring the way each is received. At all times he is managing.

"It's a bit like being under a microscope," says Derek, who finds that once a coworker learns his secret, he becomes a sort of novelty item. "I'm sure they drive home and think, just like they did in the sixties, 'Isn't it wonderful to have a black friend? Isn't he everybody's favorite Negro?' Today I'm sure they feel almost smugly that, 'Isn't this *wonderful* that we know somebody who's gay? Aren't they wonderful—and aren't they something we didn't think they were?' "

As long as lesbian and gay professionals remain a novelty in the workplace—and as long as the sexual culture of the workplace ensures the hegemony of heterosexuality—coming out will not free a man from the hassles of tokenism and identity management. Integration strategies may bring support; they may eliminate the need for petty deceptions and dodges. After coming out a man may feel more honest and relaxed. But what integration strategies do not bring, in most settings, is treatment as an equal. Even when a man is well received, he is defined by his difference. His coworkers' shows of acceptance bring their own kind of agitation, not normalcy. By definition tokens are not peers. As gay professionals leave the closet and face these more subtle, intractable forms of hetero-sexism, they begin to see the problem in broader terms. Once visi-ble they face essentially the same concerns as women, ethnic minorities, and others who are stigmatized in professional work en-vironments. Concern with the mechanics of sexual self-disclosure is replaced by the struggle for integration. No longer in hiding, they begin the battle for acceptance.

Yet despite the hassles that can accompany a man's exit from the closet—discrimination, stigmatization, tokenism, and pressure to compensate—there is remarkable (and quite surprising) consensus on at least one point. More than half our participants have revealed themselves to one or more of their coworkers. They received a vari-ety of responses, from verbal taunts and pink slips to the mixed blessing of effusive sympathy and support. Yet not one of these men now says that he regrets his decision to come out. Men who suffered both emotionally and financially say that on balance they would do it again. Even men who were severely penalized for their disclosure now point to it with pride. "It's sort of a bittersweet deal, to be honest," says Howard. "I have no regrets about what I've done or how I've conducted myself, but it's a source of a fair level of stress, given the conservative, corporate reaction. Still, the die is cast. There are some deeply closeted people here who are very am-bitious and who have stayed in the closet for that reason. I just couldn't live with myself if I did that. And beyond that, I'm not *that* ambitious. I'm not willing to do what it takes to be chairman of the board."

More than anything these men describe an overwhelming sense of relief that followed the disclosure. They speak of reduced stress, enhanced self-images, and a feeling of liberation. One man ex-plained that it was like "coming up for air after being underwater for twenty-five years." Indeed, among social scientists (as well as gay activists), there is a growing sense that it is harmful for lesbians and gay men to keep their sexuality a secret. There is mounting ev-idence that men who have come out experience less anxiety and de-pression.[29] They have more positive self-concepts and feel more capable of fully experiencing their emotions and interests. "You can take *Outweek* to the office," says Michael, whose firm employs several openly gay people. "People read the *Philadelphia Gay News* at lunch and talk about the guy who delivers the water: 'Isn't he adorable?' Or the Federal Express guy: 'A real hunk.'" John went even further. "I talk about myself a lot these days," he says. "There's a lot of self-disclosure, in the congregation and in meetings. I cry in public places sometimes. I just feel that my goal is to become more and more *myself* in my job. I'm not just a priest; I'm not just my job. It feels really good."

They also speak of friendships that have deepened and doors that were flung open. Milton says that by being openly gay he has tapped a vast network of support in the Washington area. His work with the Whitman-Walker Clinic, a local AIDS service organization, has led to cultural and professional opportunities in other settings. As Milton explains: "I got on the Arena Theater board because of it. I got on the Leadership Washington council because of it. I give speeches all over town because of it. I've been invited to the church of the president of the United States to give a sermon on the second Sunday in February because of it. It hasn't closed any doors for me. It's only opened up opportunities for me, the kind of opportunities that I love. In terms of my law practice, it hasn't shut any doors, but I think it hasn't opened that many either. Wait—not true. One of my biggest clients is openly gay, and I don't think that would have come about if I hadn't been open about who I am."

John found that coming out deepened the quality of his relationships with the men and women in his parish. In 1984, after five years with a wealthy suburban congregation, he accepted a position at a church in downtown Philadelphia that included a large gay following. "I wanted to be in a place where I could be gay, and where my being gay would have some positive influence on the lives of the gay people in that congregation—on the straight people, too." After arriving in Philadelphia, he came out to his congregation and began to involve himself in the local gay community. He encountered some resistance, and several of his critics—including some who were themselves gay—left the congregation. "But that's fine with me," says John. "We all have to make certain choices."

Others describe support networks that materialized, outpourings of warmth and concern. Several years ago at his company's annual retreat, Jack was asked to speak to those in attendance. The company had sponsored a series of workshops on different aspects of its corporate culture, and Jack was asked to lead the workshop on "individual life-styles." "I opened the workshop by saying, 'As most of you know I'm an openly gay recovering alcoholic who has just been named vice president of human resources.' I think that sums up our culture. There aren't many organizations in which you would feel that comfortable doing that. But you can at this company."

Others have followed Jack's example. Last year one of the firm's senior editors became ill, and word soon got around that he had AIDS. "He was an editor, a married man with two children," says Jack. "He was extremely closeted, and he ultimately confided in his manager because he had to explain his absences and all. He came to see me, and we worked together. It was one of the most rewarding experiences I've ever had, to see him gradually open up and sort of blossom like a flower." As the man grew increasingly ill, Jack helped arrange housing and support for him. "By this time his wife and children had moved to a farm in West Virginia. She was panic stricken at the idea of taking care of him. The hospital didn't want him, and he wasn't safe alone since he was suffering from dementia. It was a terribly messy situation. In one of the last conversations that we had, he said it was terrible that he had to come out in this way. But he finally realized that the more open he was at work, the more he told people what was going on in his life, the more love and support he got."

As gay men know only too well, however, the decision to come out cannot be taken lightly. In making it, a man juggles a whole host of concerns. First, there are situational considerations, such as the level of homophobia in a particular industry or company ("What are my coworkers' attitudes toward homosexuality? How are they expressed?"), the company's prevailing ideas about privacy and professionalism ("How much personal sharing do my peers expect?"), as well as the behavior of other lesbian or gay people ("What strate-

gies are others using? With what consequences?"). No less important are personal considerations that influence strategy choice.
Each strategy imposes different social and emotional sacrifices, ethical dilemmas, and levels of anxiety. Each requires a different bun-
dle of skills, such as the ability to invent and remember a
falsehood, the ability to control one's voice, or the confidence to
confront homophobia directly. Even the most mundane decision
about self-disclosure is thus enormously complicated because it involves so many situational, personal, and ethical issues. All of these
considerations may bear on a man's response to a simple, everyday
situation: Someone asks how he spent the weekend. Someone invites him to dinner, telling him to "bring a friend." Someone asks
if he's single.

In describing a man's response to these situations as a "choice," I
imply that gay men are always rational and deliberate about their
public self-presentation. In fact, that is rarely the case. There is no
agreed-upon menu from which gay men make their selections, nor
is there always evidence that they have given the matter any conscious thought. To be sure, some men display a surprising degree of
self-awareness. Some are deliberate and calculating in their decisions, having weighed the risks and benefits with friends, therapists, or career counselors. Some plan a change in strategy well in
advance, carefully orchestrating their entry into or exit from the
closet.

But just as often gay men do not experience these decisions as
choices at all. Their response to a hostile work situation may feel
more like a detested chore, a compromise, a defense—anything but
a choice. Perhaps they adopted a particular strategy by default, unaware that other options were available. Some feel they were forced,
by a particular boss or client, to use one approach or another. Nor
do they usually imagine that the various accommodations and sacrifices they have made are motivated by anything so central as a
"strategy." Whatever clear, specific reasons they now offer to explain their behavior, these post hoc justifications must not be mis-
taken for the choosing itself.

Until recently, the notion of choice was doubly inappropriate
because the closet, whatever its drawbacks, was the only realistic

option for a man who took his professional ambitions seriously. The penalties for coming out were too severe and the protections too few. Self-disclosure was tantamount to corporate suicide, which made it an option only for the financially independent or the professionally unambitious. For men and women who wanted to leave the closet, there were no models of how to go about it. There was no one to demonstrate a different way of thinking about privacy, no one to illustrate how such an exit might be accomplished.

All that is changing. By making themselves visible, lesbian and gay professionals are helping to shatter the presumption that the closet is a necessary, or even desirable, response to heterosexism.[30] Conventions about secrecy are changing as an increasing number abandon it. A 1992 survey of *Out/Look* readers found that 67 percent now work with at least one openly gay person.[31] "You hear about more and more people who are coming out, and I guess that kind of upsets all our assumptions about the closet," says Martin. "If I were just starting my career today, I don't know if I would make the same choice. Or at least I'd see that there *are* choices."

Echoing the changing rhetoric of gay activism, men now speak of their responsibility to provide role models for other gays. Indeed, the current debate about the "outing" of gay celebrities and politicians has centered on the obligation these figures presumably have to serve as role models or community leaders. "I always have those kinds of feelings when I read essays or articles about how everyone should come out, so that the world will be a better place," says Bill. "And then I feel kind of guilty sometimes, because it's true. If everyone who's in the closet agreed to come out, at the exact same time on the exact same day, I might hop on the bandwagon. I just don't have the courage to do it independently."

More and more gay professionals can now point to a gay peer who showed them an alternative to the closet. "My business partner had a dramatic impact on my life in a number of ways," says Carl, who has run the thriving real estate firm alone since the death of his partner. "I think the most significant impact was his ability to present himself in an open way to people. With this guy what you saw was what you got. I learned a lot from him." As Chip explains, "It's very reassuring to me that one of the highest people in our company, a vice president, had his lover come up to the office to show him sheets and towels, to ask if those were the colors he'd like, that kind of stuff." Andy tells a similar story. "One of the partners is quite open," he says. "It blazes a trail for me. It sets an example with other people. It means that the people I'd be looking to for acceptance have already dealt with it once. They already have a policy. In that sense, it will make it easier for me."

To appreciate the difference such people can make, one need only contrast the following story—about a man's first day of work—with my own. When he joined Levi Strauss in 1980, Don was trained by a gay man named Dominic. "He taught me my job, and he was pretty open about his sexuality, so we just got right into the subject. It was obvious that I was in a different environment." Don soon came out to some of the others in his division, many of whom are gay themselves. "It was quite a group of girls," he says.[32] "It was really a lot of fun, people being very gossipy, socializing, and so forth. You just went on breaks with people, chatted with people." The circle expanded until Don found that he was using an integration strategy with all of his peers, his boss, and the managers above him.

A few years later a position became available in the menswear division, and Don jumped at it. The man who held it was being promoted, which Don took as a positive sign. "I felt a little more inclined to try for the job," he says, "because the man who held the position before me was gay. It was definitely a job I wanted, and there was also the hope that the hiring manager wouldn't have any issues, since there had been a gay man in the position before me. It helped that there were some gay footsteps to follow. The minute that I got here, I knew immediately that I didn't need to hide anything. And I never have."

8

Dismantling the Closet

IN 1990 DENNIS BREINING was promoted to the St. Paul headquarters of the Minnesota Mining and Manufacturing Company. "It was my professional dream come true," he says. "I got the promotion I wanted and I bought a house. It was two of my lifelong ambitions." Still, Dennis found himself anxious and depressed at work. His career was moving along nicely, but it no longer seemed to be a source of much happiness. "I had days when I just didn't go to work because I couldn't put on the heterosexual mask," he says. "I had realized all my dreams, but there was this one big lie at the center of my life." Dennis resolved to do something about it, determined to have "a whole, full life, just like everyone else."

Dennis went to the company's telephone directory and scanned through the listings. There he found a number for "employee assistance," which he thought sounded promising, and gave it a try. When a secretary answered, Dennis explained that he was new to 3M and wanted to make contact with the company's lesbian and gay support group. Was there a mailing list? Did she know when the group met? There was silence for a moment, then a nervous, whispered reply: "I'll have to call you back."

When the woman in employee assistance called back, she told Dennis that 3M had no lesbian and gay support group. Still whispering, she explained that she did have a certain friend, however, who might be able to help. She offered to put the two men in touch and took down Dennis's number. Someone phoned him a few days later. "As it turned out there was this monthly lunch group," Dennis says. "They had been meeting for several years at a local restaurant. Most of them were technical people, not managers, and they didn't really talk about gay issues. It was a public place, and everyone was afraid of being overheard."

Dennis suggested that other lesbians and gay men be invited to join the monthly meeting, which before long had outgrown its table at the restaurant. For a time the group used a larger banquet room in the back, but when the staff began making homophobic remarks, it was decided to reconvene the meetings in private homes. Now, as the group expanded and relocated, the friendly dinners gave way to more serious discussion of lesbian and gay employment issues. Although 3M had active employee groups for women, African Americans, and the disabled, the company's lesbians and gay men were largely invisible. They were not included in company training and orientation materials that specifically dealt with diversity issues in the workplace. Personnel policies made no reference to sexual orientation, and the lesbian and gay group had no official standing in the company, which prohibited them even from distributing meeting announcements through company mail. Frustrated by the situation, Dennis and another member volunteered to approach Sandy Bryant, the head of human resources at the corporate level. They scheduled a meeting in which they planned to ask Sandy about the company's policy on sexual orientation.

Sandy said that he was sympathetic to the group's concerns but disagreed about the need for an explicit policy on sexual orientation. As he explained to Dennis, 3M's human resources "principles" statement already prohibited discrimination of any type. A specific policy on lesbian and gay issues would be redundant. Nor did Sandy seem to think that homophobia, however regrettable, was within the company's jurisdiction. As he listened to Sandy's reply, Dennis realized how much work lay ahead for the group. He also noticed several things about Sandy's behavior that troubled him: Sandy was visibly uncomfortable during the meeting, shifting in his seat and looking away nervously. He repeatedly spoke of "this issue" or "matters concerning this subject" without using the word *gay.* He never uttered the word *lesbian.* At several points during the meeting Sandy referred to the fledgling lesbian and gay organization as a "networking group."

In the months that followed, Dennis and the others scheduled a series of meetings with Sandy. They explained that a blanket policy against discrimination was not enough. "Whatever the policy said, something else was happening on the floors," says Dennis. "We explained to Sandy that these were people who could lose their jobs, or their lives, if their sexual orientation were known." To make the point, the group discreetly arranged for closeted lesbian and gay workers to meet with Sandy, to educate him about their special concerns. Dennis described his own situation to Sandy. "I used up all my vacation time so that I could spend time with my lover, who has terminal cancer. When he was rushed to the hospital with a brain hemorrhage, I was denied family emergency leave. I had to borrow vacation time from the company and pay it back."

The group also surveyed 3M's operations outside Minnesota and found that personnel policies varied widely from one facility to the next. Sexual orientation protections had become law in some states and had been written into company policy. At other locations there was no mention of the subject. Sandy agreed that the inconsistency was a problem. But the most compelling argument for a revised policy turned up, somewhat unexpectedly, at a small plant in Missouri. "We found a plant where sexual orientation had been included in the nondiscrimination policy, even though the law didn't require it," Dennis recalls. Sandy called to ask why the policy had been adopted and learned to his surprise that there had been no specific complaints of harassment, no lobbying from a lesbian and gay employee association. "The plant managers told Sandy that it was simply the right thing to do," says Dennis. "For Sandy that was the turning point." In 1991, a year after Dennis first joined the lunch group, Sandy recommended that management revise its personnel policies to include sexual orientation. The change was approved a month later.

Other changes have followed. "It happened so quickly, we were caught by surprise," says Dennis. "The new policy became the basis for us to push for other changes." Shortly after the policy was adopted, Sandy published an article entitled "A Matter of Principle" in *3M Today,* the company magazine, explaining the reasoning behind the change. The lesbian and gay group, which adopted the name 3M PLUS ("People Like Us"), was invited to address the corporate committee that supervises diversity issues. In June 1992 the company had a prominent booth in the lesbian and gay pride parade in Minneapolis, at which Dennis and others handed out copies of the new company policy. Despite some initial resistance, the group also succeeded in having sexual orientation included—along with race, gender, and disability—in the company's diversity training materials. They have also asked for formal recognition as an employee group, which would bring funding and office space. "In the long run," Dennis says, "the company will probably have a pluralism council, and lesbians and gays will be part of it."

The scenario Dennis describes will become an increasingly common one as American business grapples with the issue of sexual diversity. In companies large and small, lesbian and gay workers have begun to step forward and identify themselves, some as individuals and some as members of employee groups. Their concerns about employment, long ignored by the mainstream media and eclipsed even in the gay community by the more immediate tragedy of AIDS, are finding their way onto the agenda. For most employers, meanwhile, sexual diversity issues remain new and unfamiliar turf. When the issue is first brought to their attention, they tend to fall back on familiar, longstanding misconceptions. Believing in the separation of work and sexuality, they remain comfortably, perhaps even willfully, oblivious to heterosexism. They may be aware of some occasional name-calling or a few isolated "problem" employees, but they do not see homophobia as a significant, institutionalized problem. Looking around them, they don't imagine that many of their employees are lesbian or gay. When pressed, they offer one of several characteristic responses: "It isn't a problem, or we already would have heard about it." "Our nondiscrimination policy already covers that." Or, "An employee's sex life is none of my business."

What employers must be shown, of course, is that there are a number of good reasons for a company to combat heterosexism. In some municipalities legal compliance and community relations are good reasons. So is an employer's ethical responsibility to workers, whose civil rights and happiness are often at stake. For some companies eradicating heterosexism may be a way to placate an internal group or pacify an outside organization. All of these are good reasons, of course, but none of them is a business reason. As women, the disabled, African Americans, and other groups have learned, companies are most enthusiastic about combating prejudice when they can be shown the economic incentives for doing so. Given the pressures under which companies operate, only business reasons will supply the necessary long-term motivation.[1]

For lesbian and gay workers, this is good news. The economic case against heterosexism is strong. Whatever employers think about homosexuality as a moral or civil rights issue, they cannot ignore the accumulating evidence that heterosexism is wasteful and expensive.

The Bottom Line

To assess a group's significance in the labor market, one would typically begin with an estimate of its size, an approach that is complicated by the paucity of data on lesbian and gay workers. In all likelihood gay professionals number in the millions and can be found in every industry and region. We have no reason to doubt that they can be just as productive, ambitious, and competent as their heterosexual peers. They are probably late for work just as often.

While we lack hard data, several comparisons are suggestive. As a group lesbians and gay men probably outnumber Hispanics, Asian–Pacific Islanders, the disabled, and others whom we have traditionally classified as minorities. If the standard 10 percent estimate can be believed, their proportion of the professional work force approaches that of African Americans, who represent 12.1 percent of the population (but only 5.6 percent of the professional work force).[2] There is even evidence that gay men are disproportionately drawn to white-collar, professional jobs, further increasing their numbers in corporate America. Surveys of gay men typically locate only a small number who work in blue-collar or manual jobs, a finding that has led some researchers to speculate that gay men tend to avoid work settings that emphasize traditionally masculine traits such as physical aggressiveness.[3] If this is so, gay men may be concentrated in white-collar, professional jobs. So long as heterosexism blocks their career paths, the collective energy of millions may be wasted.

To see how heterosexism directs and diverts the talents of gay professionals, one need only examine their career histories. Consider Duane, who now runs his own oil exploration company. By the time Duane left Houston to begin his freshman year at Columbia, he already had "feelings" for other boys. "I had been interested in banking and finance since I was twelve, and that's what first drew me to New York," he says. "But the main impetus for going to Columbia was the thought that at some point, someday, I'll have to deal with being gay. I'd had these feelings since high school, but nothing was really clear. Well into my thirties, I toyed with the idea of getting married. It frightened me, but I'd read about Greenwich Village in *Time* magazine, and I figured that if there were any decent gay people, they would be in New York City."

Beginning with the move to New York, Duane sees a pattern to the decisions that have shaped his career. After Columbia he found a job on Wall Street that ensured him financial independence and allowed him to remain in New York. He turned down jobs in smaller cities and dreamed of someday opening his own business. It wasn't until he started his own oil and gas exploration company that he returned to Houston. "Being gay, I've always sought out situations where I can work with certain kinds of people, be in control, and protect myself as much as possible. I try, consciously and unconsciously, to get my career in shape so that I'm not dependent on anyone else. I always have my eyes over my shoulder." Now in his forties, Duane says that at any number of points his career might have taken a different turn. "Who knows where I'd be if I were straight. I might be doing something completely different."

It seems that every gay professional tells a version of this story: Perceiving a particular industry or company to be intolerant, he looked elsewhere; aware that certain cities had a reputation for tolerance, he made geography a consideration; feeling vulnerable, he was drawn to positions that ensured him independence or security; or, wanting to protect himself, he accumulated credentials—graduate degrees, board certifications, society memberships—that enhanced his objective worth as a professional. Craig says that the fear of discrimination was behind his decision to leave the army, a move that ultimately led him to a management job at American Express. For John concerns about his own sexuality made the priesthood attractive. Likewise Brent says that his fear of exposure was one of the chief reasons he left his home town in North Dakota to relocate in a "brand-new town where people didn't know me as well."

Examining these career histories, one is struck by the number of decision points at which heterosexism can become a factor. Concerns about discrimination and self-disclosure can influence a man's choice of job, industry, or geographic location. Over time the steps he takes to avoid, prepare for, or respond to heterosexism lead him down career paths that differ substantially from those taken by heterosexual peers. While heterosexism may not *force* him to make any of these decisions, its invisible hand can be felt at all times, guiding the opportunities he pursues, the relationships he nurtures, and the risks he is willing to take. Two job opportunities that would seem comparable to a straight peer may represent vastly different problems and opportunities for a gay man.

Gay careers are thus shaped and diverted by the subtle, persistent tug of heterosexism. In the *Out/Look* survey, 30 percent of respondents said that sexual orientation issues had "probably" or "definitely" influenced their choice of profession. Thirty-two percent said it influenced their choice of company. More than half said it would influence their decisions in the future.[4] Several patterns result. As heterosexism pushes and pulls gay men along their career paths, they find themselves in a number of characteristic situations.

One of these is the ghettoization of gay men. Perceiving his environment to be hostile, a man may seek refuge in a "safe" job or position. He may nestle into a protected corner of a large organization, staying out of the spotlight that accompanies big promotions, high-profile assignments, and broad decision-making responsibilities. He may be drawn to departments that have a reputation for tolerance or in which other lesbians and gay men have already clustered.

Ghettoization is a concern for members of other minority groups, who frequently find themselves sidelined in organizations. Ghettos tend to grow up around jobs that involve little discretion or uncertainty, in which what to do and how to judge its doing are fairly routine.[5] They are typically populated by those who perform "support" functions like public relations, human resources, or maintenance—workers who may not be directly involved in the central operations of the company. They include support staff and salespeople more often than line managers, technical "experts" (who manage the company's computer system, for example), or "skilled workers" (who handle its word processing) rather than broad-based decision makers. In most of these roles the required skills are tangible, and performance can be measured "objectively," in terms of sales figures or concrete tasks accomplished.

Ghettos offer sanctuary and security and can provide an oasis of tolerance in a larger, more homophobic organization. As the supervisor of his company's records management department, Brent is both spatially and organizationally segregated from the other managers. His function is similar to that of the other support staff. "We have a certain number of projects to handle, certain records to manage and reports to generate. We get requests from clients, and try to respond as quickly as we can." On the whole, Brent is comfortable in the department. The staff is small, and he works with at least two other men who are gay. To his knowledge his job is secure. "I fit in pretty well here," says Brent.

Yet even as a ghetto protects, it can imprison. Having found a comfortable niche within an organization, a gay man too often discovers that there are glass ceilings and walls all around him. "Within this group and with my managers, I fit in fine," says Brent. "It's with the company as a whole that I have some reservations. I'm not the kind of person who'll go all the way to the top. Within my group, at my current level and the one above it, I'll be okay. But beyond that, when we get to senior executive management, I won't. It's an entrepreneurial, good-old-boy type company, and I don't fit into that category. I'm not someone who can entertain Arabs or do deals over drinks."

Brent has adjusted his expectations accordingly. As a high school student, he was president of the state chapter of the Future Business Leaders of America, and his professional ambitions were evident in his decision to move to Houston, his choice of college, and his decision to major in business. Yet today he seems resigned, and takes his greatest pleasure in activities that have nothing to do with work. Other men describe a similar attitude toward work. As numerous studies of organizational behavior have demonstrated, people tend to have low aspirations when they think their chances for mobility are low. They "disengage" and write off their companies or careers as something to care about for anything but short-term, monetary reasons. They make peace with limited opportunity, exhibiting low commitment and nonresponsibility at work.[6] For some men, the expectation of failure can even become a self-fulfilling prophecy. Perceiving limited opportunities, they behave in ways that virtually ensure them.

Other men resist being pushed into ghettos, fighting their way out if necessary. Shortly after he came to work for a large New York consulting firm, Mark saw that it had a niche for gay employees. "I don't think that they have a problem with gays or lesbians working for the firm," he says, "provided they're in certain positions. It's clear that the company doesn't want anyone in senior management or in a consulting job who is gay or lesbian, because that isn't the image the firm wants to project. I don't think they have a problem with gay or lesbian support staff or technical staff or clerical staff. There are several male secretaries in the office who are obviously gay."

Several years ago Mark discovered that he had been pushed into one of these fringe positions. After the death of his lover, as Mark's involvement with ACT-UP began to attract publicity, he was quietly removed from several key projects. He was also reclassified from consultant to senior technical specialist, a position of equal rank but less responsibility. At the time it was explained that the change was temporary, that it would give Mark an opportunity to "put his life back together" after Luke's death. "Since that time I was clearly kind of shelved," he says. "I was pretty much written off as someone who would never make partner, and so I became uninvited to any kind of planning meetings or social events." Looking ahead, Mark knew that his career lay elsewhere.

As Mark would soon demonstrate, one alternative to ghettoization is entrepreneurial flight. Rather than accommodate themselves to a safe, secure niche in the corporate world, some men abandon it altogether. They find work in nonprofessional fields or break away to start their own design, financial, travel, or consulting firms. Unable to find a progay work environment, they set out to create one. After he was stripped of his responsibilities at work, Mark began to lay the groundwork for his own company, a real estate development firm that will buy and rehabilitate abandoned Manhattan properties. He now works for himself.

The lure of self-employment is strong in the gay community. Asked to describe the "ideal job environment," gay men consistently speak of small businesses, stores, and not-for-profit firms. Many say that they want greater latitude in their decision making. The don't want a single boss or client on whom they are dependent. "I'll have a private office somewhere," says Tip. "It won't be in a hospital at all—too many peers, too political, too many options for bad things to happen. It will be a private office or a private practice, where I don't have to deal with anybody."

These same ambitions ultimately led Carl to the job of his dreams. In 1980, a friend in the real estate business told him about a small firm in the Castro neighborhood of San Francisco that was on the verge of bankruptcy. He invited Carl to join a three-way partnership that would rebuild the firm. Carl agreed at once. "The company was exclusively gay at the start," he recalls. "It was one of the things that enabled us to become so successful. There was a whole spirit in the Castro in the late seventies and early eighties, a whole feeling of camaraderie and support. Gay people wanted to use gay real estate agents. They wanted to keep their business within the community. Gay men wanted to have a gay dry cleaner, a gay photo developer, a gay lawyer, and a gay grocer. We managed to capitalize on that as we built the company."

Over the next ten years, the company grew into one of the largest real estate firms in San Francisco. "As we expanded and became more legitimate, we began to attract straight people," says Carl. "By 1986 the demographics of the Castro were changing. It was becoming much less ghettoized, more diverse, more nongay people were moving in. Straight people who lived there stopped moving out. The emphasis was off people working with gay realtors. People wanted the realtor who would do the best job." The company diversified and has continued to grow. Some fifty agents now work in its two offices, about two-thirds of them lesbians and gay men. As president, Carl spends most of his time on managerial responsibilities, personally handling only a few select clients. "Working for myself has given me a lot of freedom to do what I want, and be who I want," says Carl. At forty he has no thought of retirement. "I plan to stay with the company until I can't get out of my car to get to the office. 'Until the walker breaks,' as they say."

Self-employment is not for everyone, of course. Some men want the security, resources, and opportunities that come with working for a large company. They may not want the responsibility of running a small business, or they may lack the funding needed to start one. Self-employment may not even be possible in their line of work, given its particular structure and economics. Like other career-choices-as-coping-mechanisms, starting a business also means accepting certain trade-offs. By working for himself, a man often limits his own mobility, making it difficult for him to adapt periodically to changing market conditions or to his own evolving talents and interests. But for some, self-employment is an escape from the pressures of life in large, bureaucratic organizations. "I think that's why I've continuously been moving to smaller companies," says Jeff. "For a long time my best friend and I had it in our heads that someday we would start our own company. He's the first person I told I was gay, and we've always talked about going into business for ourselves."

Heterosexism does much more, however, than influence the career plans of a few lesbian and gay professionals. Its impact is not limited to the scattered men who are lured into ghettos or pressured to leave corporate environments altogether. Indeed, from an economic point of view, ghettoization and entrepreneurial flight are the tip of an iceberg, the surface evidence of a more extensive—if largely unseen—diversion of human resources.

For gay professionals, the drain on productivity should by now be apparent, given the issues of identity management described in earlier chapters. However a man manages his identity at work, his strategy consumes time and personal resources. Men who disguise themselves are preoccupied with the mechanics of deception, inventing the stories and directing the necessary supporting players, worried that at any moment their ruse may be exposed. Men who try to avoid the issue of sexuality altogether find their productivity sapped in a different way. They can become isolated within their organizations, excluded from the social networks they need to do their jobs. They dodge intrusive, personal questions only to find themselves without mentors, advocates, and friends. Finally, gay men who are public about their sexuality encounter even more blatant forms of discrimination. They tell of relationships that soured, rapport that evaporated, and support that never materialized. Not surprisingly, in the 1992 *Out/Look* survey, some 29 percent of gay men (and 38 percent of lesbian women) said that sexual orientation issues were a source of unnecessary stress at work.[7] The impact on productivity can only be negative.

Yet heterosexism can also damage an organization in other, less evident ways. Even as it diverts the energies of lesbian and gay employees into the management of stigma, heterosexism also constricts other kinds of communication. Like all forms of prejudice, heterosexism erects barriers between different groups of individuals. It ensures that they will have a distorted, insufficient understanding of one another's need and talents. On both sides, it encourages mistrust. When Clay lost a friend an to extended illness, his boss encouraged him to take a few days off from work. She attempted to share her condolences, asking Clay how the man had died. Clay responded by being abrupt and mysterious, worried that the cause of the man's death, AIDS, might implicate his own sexuality in some way. In the weeks that followed Clay refused to discuss the issue with his boss, and one can only imagine how the resulting barrier disrupted their work together.

Especially when problems arise, heterosexism can deny coworkers the kind of trust and rapport that would enable frank conversation. Because his professional relationships lack a stable, "personal" footing, a man may be reluctant to discuss even matters that have nothing to do with his sexuality. The result is a "spillover of silence," as habits of communication developed for sensitive, sexual topics are applied to business ones. Justin found that by avoiding personal small talk with the other faculty, he simultaneously lost their collegial input on his writing and research. Likewise, when Dan is asked questions about AIDS in his capacity as the director of a psychiatric clinic, he freezes up. His ability to show compassion and offer useful advice is limited by his own fear of exposure. Finding it impossible to communicate with his boss, Martin resigned his former position at another agency. "He was a real macho type, which is fine, but it meant that I was always on my guard. We just couldn't relate to each other, which made it impossible to do good work." Rather than request a transfer or raise the issue with management, Martin polished his resume.

By viewing male intimacy with suspicion, homophobia also inhibits men from forming close, supportive ties with members of their own sex. Whatever a man's orientation, he is expected to be strong, verbal, and aggressive in professional contexts, and to treat others of his sex accordingly. Standards of "manliness" compel men who might be allies to remain distant, competitive, and independent. Male nurturance and emotionality are devalued and suppressed. For gay and straight men alike, this particular definition of masculinity can become a burden, making them feel that they must constantly take charge of situations, speak their minds, and view accommodation and compromise as signs of weakness.[8]

In environments like these, men learn to suppress ideas and be-haviors that might invite suspicion, to modify their dress and speech, even to join others in the ritual "gay-baiting" of other men. Consider Ralph's frequent, derogatory remarks about a fellow worker, David Miles, who is presumed to be gay by the other men in his office. Or consider Martin, who in meetings at his advertis-ing agency sometimes squelches creative suggestions that involve gay celebrities, humor, or language. Indeed, in such environments, the mere insinuation of homosexuality can be used to stigmatize or silence men (and women) who are perceived as being "different," whether or not they are in fact gay.[9] The loss to the organization in spontaneity, creativity, and solidarity is incalculable.

There is accumulating evidence, in short, that heterosexism is a barrier to effective communication, a solvent to trust, and a hin-drance to productivity. Like other kinds of prejudice, it poisons work relationships, encouraging intolerance and misunderstanding. For gay employees it sets up incentives for a man to deceive, to dis-engage, and sometimes to resign, taking with him whatever invest-ment the company has made in his development.[10] Even for the heterosexual employees it presumably privileges, heterosexism sets up cramped behavioral boxes, thereby stifling ways of thinking and behaving that are inconsistent with strict, traditional gender norms.

The Corporate Response

Some employers have begun to take the loss seriously. In September 1991 the Lotus Development Corporation circulated a memo to all of its U.S. employees. In it, the vice president of human resources, Russ Campanello, announced a dramatic change in company policy. "Since early in its history," the memo began, "Lotus has had a stated policy prohibiting discrimination based on sexual preference. Lotus recognizes that lesbian and gay employees do not have the choice to legalize permanent and exclusive rela-tionships through marriage; thus, they cannot legally share finan-cial, health and other benefits with their significant partners. For this reason, in the interest of fairness and diversity, Lotus will recognize the significance of such relationships by including them in our policies and benefits."

With its change in policy, Lotus became the first major, publicly held American company to extend benefits to the domestic partners of lesbian and gay employees. Four months earlier a similar policy was adopted by Montefiore Medical Center in New York, which with 9,500 employees has three times as many workers as Lotus. Levi Strauss & Co. followed in February 1992, becoming the largest U.S. employer, with 23,000 workers and sixty facilities nationwide, to offer health insurance to lesbian and gay domestic partners. In the two years that followed, a number of large and highly visible companies initiated similar changes in their business practices.

Even employers that do not provide domestic partnership benefits are now taking concrete steps to provide fair, safe, and equitable work environments for lesbian and gay employees. AT&T adopted a nondiscrimination policy in 1975, but it was not until 1990 that the company formally placed lesbian and gay issues under the auspices of its corporate diversity office. In 1989 Xerox employees asked management to add sexual orientation to its nondiscrimination policy. A year later, the company had a new policy and is currently updating its diversity training program to reflect the change. Du Pont moved more slowly, changing its policy in July 1992. Its fledgling lesbian and gay group has now set its sights on a change in Du Pont's benefits policies and training programs.

Workers in dozens of companies tell a similar story. Some employers have formally banned discrimination on the basis of sexual orientation; some have been supportive of lesbian and gay employee associations; and some have added sexuality issues to in-house diversity training programs that already deal with race, religion, and gender. At many there are now newsletters and electronic mail networks for lesbian and gay employees. Other firms have made bold symbolic gestures. In 1992 U.S. West declared June "lesbian and gay awareness month," and added a series of relevant lectures and events to its "pluralism calendar." Levi Strauss withdrew its financial support of the Boy Scouts of America, publicly condemning that organization's policy of discriminating against gay scouts and scout leaders. In November 1992, when Colorado voters rolled back nondiscrimination ordinances in Denver, Aspen, and Boulder, several companies joined a boycott of the state.[11]

On the political front, too, there is slow but certain progress. By January 1993, some 130 municipalities fell under the jurisdiction of laws, municipal ordinances, or executive orders that prohibited employment discrimination on the basis of sexual orientation. Seven states and the District of Columbia had outlawed discrimination in employment, and ten states had similar protections for government employees. The incoming Clinton administration, meanwhile, had just begun its battle to abolish the Pentagon's ban on lesbian and gay service personnel—a fight that continues.

No less important, meanwhile, was a shift in the way lesbian and gay employment concerns were framed in the national media. Today mainstream newspapers and magazines are increasingly willing to report on lesbian and gay employment issues the way they handle other news about employment discrimination, compensation, and policy—as the legitimate business concerns of a minority group, not as gossip about their sexual proclivities. In the national dailies stories about lesbians and gay men now regularly find their way out of the ghetto of the arts and style sections and onto the front page of the business report. The change in coverage also reflects growing attention, within the gay community itself, to employment concerns. In September 1991 several hundred consultants, activists, and managers gathered at the Waldorf-Astoria Hotel in New York. Company representatives spoke about their lesbian and gay employee organizations, and attorneys described the key legal victories and setbacks of recent years. Congressman Barney Frank and Mayor David Dinkins made brief appearances. The conference was entitled Invisible Diversity: A Gay and Lesbian Corporate Agenda, and it was the first meeting of its kind in this country. It precipitated a flurry of news coverage, including major stories in the *New York Times* and the *Wall Street Journal.*

A few months later business leaders witnessed another first. In December 1991 *Fortune* magazine ran an eight-page feature, "Gay in Corporate America." It was the first time a mass-circulation business magazine had run a story of this size or prominence, and its authors took an unambiguously supportive stance. Perhaps startled by his own editorial decision, *Fortune* editor Marshall Loeb included an explanatory statement on the "Editor's Desk" page in the front of the magazine: "Why would *Fortune* ever want to do a cover story about *that?* I suppose a few readers will ask the question. And I admit I was a bit skeptical when reporter Mark D. Fefer proposed that we examine what it's like for gays in corporate America. The answers soon became clear: because they're *there*— sometimes in large numbers. Because they have special concerns on the job. Because business must make the most of everyone's talents and prides itself in managing diversity in the workplace. And because homosexuals surely deserve as much opportunity as any other minority."[12]

In calling homosexuals a "minority group," the *Fortune* article acknowledged how far they have come in the twenty-five years since the Stonewall riots. Even ten years ago, few Americans thought of homosexuality in such terms.[13] By granting lesbians and gay men minority status, we place them in the same category with women, African Americans, and other groups who are now protected by nondiscrimination laws and policies. We accept the women's and civil rights movements as precedents to the movement for gay rights. The tendency to view homosexuality as a moral issue (a sin) or as a medical problem (an illness or perversion) has given way to the understanding that lesbians and gay men are a cultural minority, suffering many of the same predicaments as other oppressed groups. The *New York Times* acknowledged as much, a few months earlier, in its headline to a short article: "Gay Rights, Issue of the 90's." More remarkable than the headline was the story's placement in the business section of the paper.

As more and more companies make this conceptual shift, it will become standard to treat lesbian and gay employees as we do others who are members of "protected" categories. As nondiscrimination policies become the norm, companies without them will begin to stand out. No longer will corporate leaders like Lotus be expected to explain or justify their policies; public attention will turn instead to the shrinking rear guard that has not yet changed its ways. Increasingly, lesbians and gay men will have options in the job market. Job seekers will have a greater incentive to shop around, as it becomes increasingly worthwhile to judge potential employers by their stance on gay issues, their benefits packages, their policies on bereavement leave. Certain companies already stand out from the competition.

All this raises the stakes for employers. Faced with an expanding range of choices, gay professionals have more incentive than ever to favor employers who treat them well. Those who do stand to profit. "I choose to live where my being gay is not a daily issue," says Chris, who takes this into consideration when evaluating potential clients. "In the back of my mind it was probably a factor in my choice of careers, too." Matt says that concerns about sexuality will figure prominently in his next career move. Fifteen years ago, he weighed two competing offers. One was a marketing job at Delta Air Lines. The other offer came from the Ford Motor Company, Matt's current employer. "I accepted this position because I perceived that it would entail more responsibility, and it paid a little more. But knowing what I know today, if I could turn the clock back, I would accept the Delta job. Fifteen years ago the sexuality issues weren't as clear."

In some industries, aggressive nondiscrimination policies have already become standard. Nowhere is this more evident than in the high technology industries. Even as Lotus gained national attention for providing insurance and other benefits to lesbian and gay employees and their partners, many of its competitors were quietly extending them more limited "soft" benefits (such as bereavement leave, household relocation expenses, sick leave to care for unmarried partners, and other benefits that involve little out-of-pocket expense). Trend-setters such as Digital, Microsoft, Apple Computer, Oracle, and countless smaller software firms now have employee organizations and nondiscrimination policies. The incentive for them to be progressive on these issues has become obvious. High-tech companies are painfully aware that their most talented employees can easily move to competitors that provide better benefits and a more tolerant social atmosphere. They also know the high cost of replacing highly trained engineers. As Ron Hayden noted in *The Gay/Lesbian/Bisexual Corporate Letter,* "The new reason for offering domestic partners benefits, inconceivable a year ago, is competition."[14]

Companies that fall behind can expect a talent drain. "I remember a particular interview, before I took this job," says Gary. "I was going in for my initial interview and somebody else had just come out of the office. I overheard the interviewer tell the secretary, 'Well, go find out why this guy's single.' He said this to the secretary right in front of me. So I sat through the whole interview with this constantly on my mind. The interview went well, and I got the offer. But then I thought, 'I don't want to work for this guy. If being married is such an issue, I don't want to work for him.' "

Comments like this give us reason to be optimistic. Because heterosexism is expensive for both employers and employees, market forces may ultimately achieve what appeals to fairness and civil rights will not.[15] The forces that silence, stigmatize, and demoralize lesbian and gay workers are in conflict with the incentive to make money—which means that *someone* stands to profit from their elimination. As the slogan to the Invisible Diversity conference pointed out: "An investment in lesbian and gay Americans is an investment in the bottom line."

Dismantling the Closet

The workplace, in which we spend more than half our waking lives, is rapidly emerging as the frontier of lesbian and gay activism. Yet even as we begin the task of dismantling the corporate closet, we must acknowledge the difficulty of such an undertaking. The closet is a sturdy and enduring feature of organizational life. It satisfies deeply embedded needs, ones that ultimately have little to do with sexuality per se. Indeed, the closet is a response—one of many—to a pressure that is fundamental in large organizations: the pressure to assimilate.

Assimilation has long been a concern in American business. For centuries the "melting pot" has been our culture's metaphor for the way individual differences were presumably erased as people of different races and cultural backgrounds were standardized into a sort of generic "American."[16] In the nation's early factories and offices, the same mentality gave rise to the notion that workers could be homogenized and thus made interchangeable. Early management theories cast workers as undifferentiated units of production, a view that emphasized the ease and efficiency of uniformity, not the value of diversity. Evolving notions of professionalism further advanced the idea that properly trained and socialized workers could (and should) transcend their particular differences when working together.[17] One can even argue that the pressure to conform is inherent in the nature of communal work; it is implicit in our very definition of an organization. Whenever people depend on one another to do a job or perform a task, there must be rules to coordinate their interaction, to make it predictable. Individual differences lead to misunderstandings and mistakes. Variation damages efficiency.

The result in large organizations is pressure to reduce uncertainty by achieving social conformity, a phenomenon that Rosabeth Moss Kanter refers to as "homosocial reproduction." Managers find it easiest to work with those who share their cultural backgrounds, assumptions, and ways of communicating. Having certain social attributes in common, they find one another familiar and predictable. Social heterogeneity is thus an impediment to trust and an obstacle to interaction, prompting managers to hire and promote their social peers. As Kanter has argued, it is the "uncertainty quotient" in managerial work "that causes management to become so socially restricting: to develop tight inner circles excluding social strangers; to keep control in the hands of socially homogeneous peers; to stress conformity and insist upon a diffuse, unbounded loyalty; and to prefer ease of communication and thus social certainty over the strains of dealing with people who are 'different.' "[18]

The personal consequences of such conformity should by now be apparent. Even as it reduces friction and encourages trust, social homogeneity damages an organization in other ways, diverting the energies of its workers from the accomplishment of work to the cultivation of appearances. By promoting homogeneity as a value, a company encourages employees to disguise or suppress traits that set them apart from peers. It forces them to manage the visibility of these traits. And it ensures the need for closets, sexual and otherwise. Before we can do away with closets, then, we must block the forces that push men inside them.

Given that some degree of organizational conformity is unavoidable, however, the relevant question is not if, but when and how (and what sorts of) diversity should be encouraged. If an organization is to function properly, some sort of balance must be struck between total regimentation and total anarchy: Which particular kinds of human variation should be accommodated in our nation's banks, law firms, hospitals, and other professional organizations? Which variations should not? Which are the differences, in other words, that make a difference? For most the answer hinges on our assessment of the relevance of a particular trait to the job at hand. Few would disagree that a man's skills, honesty, and dedication are pertinent to his performance of most jobs. No one would seriously advocate that we tolerate "visual diversity" among those who fly planes or perform brain surgery by arguing that their eyesight is irrelevant to their work. Yet few would argue today that a man's gender, race, or religion have anything to do with his suitability for most jobs. Likewise, there are countless other kinds of human variation that in no way limit an individual's professional competence, provided the job description does not include unwarranted, built-in assumptions about gender, race, sexual orientation, or any other personal characteristic.

Although many have tried, no one has yet established the relevance of sexual orientation to the performance of most jobs (excepting, perhaps, those that require actual sexual contact). Only under exceptional circumstances would the type or intensity of a man's erotic interests interfere with his ability to, say, trade municipal bonds, teach geometry, or design software. Circumstances being what they are, of course, being gay can make it difficult for a man to succeed in any of these roles. His ability to network and schmooze may be limited. He may encounter obstacles placed in his way by others. It might even be argued, as the Pentagon has, that his homosexuality is inherently disruptive, a "threat to good order and discipline." But of course homosexuality is not inherently *any* of these things. When examined, these objections are quickly exposed as the most brutal, circular form of prejudice: A gay man's sexuality is disruptive only because others despise him for it.

As companies grapple with the emerging issue of employee diversity, sexual orientation will ultimately find its place alongside gender, race, national origin, and other traits already targeted by diversity training, recruiting, and retention programs. Indeed, prompted by changes in the labor pool, diversity has of late become a watchword in many companies. The Hudson Institute's 1987 report, "Workforce 2000," demonstrated that "only 15% of the net new entrants to the labor force over the next 13 years will be native white males." Women and ethnic minorities now compose 65% of the labor pool, yet together fill less than 5% of the slots in upper management.[19] Sobered by these reports, a growing number of companies have already turned to consultants, workshops, and training programs to help them cope with a diversifying workforce. Recognizing that white males represent a shrinking proportion of the available talent, employers are working harder to attract and retain top-quality women and ethnic minorities. They are beginning to see the costs of racism and sexism. "Valuing diversity" has become their mission.[20]

Until recently, however, the principle has not been applied to sexuality—a task that is seriously impeded by our inability to "see" organizational sexuality in the first place. Like racism and sexism, heterosexism is deeply embedded in what often appear to be inconsequential behaviors—exclusive information loops, mentoring, rapport, and so forth. Like all forms of bigotry, it leads to explicit, prejudicial outbursts even as it takes its full toll in more subtle, unseen ways. But unlike these other isms, heterosexism can be categorically denied on the grounds that the workplace is—or should be—asexual. Companies can reject the complaint that they discriminate on the basis of sexual orientation by insisting that sexuality has nothing to do with work. Until we learn to see otherwise, we will be blind to the sexual inequities such thinking conceals. Believing deep down that sexuality really has no place at work, gay professionals will acquiesce to its selective suppression. To expose heterosexism, in other words, we must first expose sex.

Despite some progress on lesbian and gay employment issues, there is little sign that beliefs about asexuality are giving way. Indeed, the continuing debate about homosexuals in the U.S. military seems only to demonstrate the intransigence of these beliefs. On Veterans day 1992, in his first major address as president-elect, Bill Clinton renewed his campaign promise to lift the ban on lesbian and gay service personnel. He argued that these soldiers should be judged on their performance, not on what he referred to as their "status." In the absence of any "inappropriate behavior," he said, they should be allowed to serve.[21] The response to Clinton's promise, among lesbians and gay men, was jubilation—and with good reason. Once committed to the task, following Harry Truman's 1948 executive order, the military seriously advanced the cause of racial integration. The ban on homosexuals, like the segregation of white and black troops, has enormous practical and symbolic consequences. By rescinding it the Pentagon would create a ripple effect in its many related and dependent industries.

Yet as the debate unfolded, even the ban's most vocal critics rested their arguments on the myth of asexuality. It quickly became clear that lesbian and gay soldiers would *not* be embraced as complete, sexual people. Even those who strongly support their right to serve spoke of homosexuality as something that must be suppressed if these men and women were to function effectively as soldiers. Both sides agreed that sexual liaisons should not be permitted between shipmates, and there was consensus about the need for tougher penalties for sexual harassment. But beyond these sensible safeguards, there was also the repeated call for a strict new code of military sexual ethics. Gay and straight soldiers alike assured reporters that their sexuality has no rightful place in the trenches, barracks, or cockpits. Gay soldiers, in particular, attacked the ban by insisting that while on duty, they lead the lives of monks. Typically, a bisexual marine sergeant told a *New York Times* reporter: "What I do in my private life I keep totally separate from my work. I'm not going to flaunt my private life in front of them."[22] Far from being discredited, the myth of asexuality was affirmed by assertions such as these.[23]

Even in organizations that strongly value diversity the recognition and acceptance of sexual variation has come slowly. In part, this reflects the profundity of the change that is required. In reconciling the needs of different racial, ethnic, gender, and sexual groups, American business confronts an enormously complex issue—a crisis of identity more than a discrete problem to be solved. Diversity issues force an organization to look squarely in the mirror and rethink basic, underlying assumptions about its objectives, values, and boundaries. Debates about who can participate in an organization inevitably force the larger question of purpose: What is the mission of this organization? To the traditionally white, male, heterosexual club, nontraditional members challenge long-standing assumptions about the way business is done and who gets to do it. And while American business will eventually emerge from this period with a more eclectic membership, and perhaps with new ideas about itself, the transition will not come easily.

In a handful of forward-looking companies, however, one can at least glimpse the prospects for the future. While such innovations were virtually unknown even a decade ago, today many large organizations have a diversity manager, a diversity training program, or a recruitment policy that emphasizes diversity issues. In most large companies, grass-roots employee organizations have sprung up to serve the needs of particular ethnic and cultural groups, and to represent their concerns to management. A "diverse work environment" is even among the attributes some companies now use to entice potential employees. The lesson from these companies is that there is much to be gained when an organization makes room for many different kinds of people.

Nowhere is this better understood than in the computer software industry, in particular at the Microsoft Corporation, the three-billion-dollar company that dominates the market. Just seventeen years after its founding, Microsoft has become a legend, an upstart company known for its intense work ethic and highly motivated work force. Staffers speak with pride about their sixty- and seventy-hour work weeks, jokingly referring to their workplace as "a sweatshop" and "a pressure cooker." "People work very hard here," says Don Pickens, the product manager for the company's popular Word software. "When you're finishing a major project, you practically end up living together. We put in some long hours." The dedication seems to be paying off. In the past six years, Microsoft has more than quadrupled in size. With just fourteen thousand employees, it recently boasted a higher market value than blue-chip rival IBM, with more than three hundred thousand.[24] "Our productivity is what keeps us competitive," says Randy Massengale, the company's diversity manager. "Microsoft got where it is today by hiring people who are smart and work hard. My goal is to make sure that they have what they need to stay productive. Nothing should stand in the way of that goal."

The company's diversity program is an integral part of that strategy. "When people feel unwelcome at work, when they are worried about things outside of work, it becomes a work issue," says Massengale. "We've taken steps to make sure that these things don't stand in the way." The company now has a four-person staff responsible for implementing the company's diversity and HIV/AIDS training programs, updating its benefits policies, and investigating individual cases of harassment and discrimination. The company's Diversity Advisory Council, created last year by Massengale, includes representatives from employee groups for women, the deaf and hard of hearing, blacks, Hispanics, Jews, Native Americans, East Indians, and gay, lesbian, and bisexual workers. It will expand as new groups form. "The groups provide Microsoft with an important service," says Massengale. "They help us formulate policy, identify problems, and create the best possible working environment for our employees—all of our employees."

In addition to making its workers more productive, the company hopes that by creating the right environment it will discourage them from leaving. "Turnover is enormously expensive," says Massengale. "We know how much every individual costs to train, recruit, and promote. When we lose a viable employee, we've probably lost, over the period of that employee's tenure, upward of two million dollars.[25] Others might say less, depending on the industry. But in our case, where people are the lifeblood of the company, their productivity is paramount." Massengale also points to the high cost of absenteeism among employees who are disgruntled or distracted by personal issues. "The situation would be different if we only hired a person's hands or head," he says. "But because we hire a whole human being, we get all of their previous experiences, as well as their current living situation. We have to be aware of that. For example, if someone is overwhelmed by medical expenses or a domestic issue of some kind, they won't be able to work effectively."

But beyond being sensitive to the concerns of a diverse workforce, Microsoft has also learned to view these differences as an asset. "We want to tap into the different needs and backgrounds of our employees, to *use* them," Massengale says. "People here know that the perspectives they bring, based on who they are, will be valued." How does Microsoft "use" these different perspectives? "Our goal is to put a computer on every desk in every home," says Massengale. "In order to do that, we have to know who those people are and what they are like. For example, a company that values diversity will make sure that its products are accessible. It will market them differently and will be sensitive to issues that make it a better corporate citizen." Massengale gives the example of an on-line encyclopedia, Encarta, that is marketed by the company. "You can't sell a product like that unless you know your market," he says. "As a diverse company, we can better sell to a diverse world."

Lesbian and gay issues first became part of Microsoft's diversity agenda in 1990, when the company revised its nondiscrimination policy to include sexual orientation. Informal lesbian and gay lunch groups had met for several years, and an electronic mailing list known as "the alias" already boasted dozens of members. But it wasn't until 1991 that a handful of these employees received formal recognition as Gay, Lesbian, and Bisexual Employees at Microsoft (GLEAM), the company's first—and still its largest—diversity group. Since that time, progress has been rapid. "Microsoft wasn't especially aggressive at first," explains Lee Smith, a software design engineer who joined the company nine years ago when it had fewer than four hundred employees, later becoming one of GLEAM's founding members. "Microsoft has always been a technological leader in the computer software industry, but until recently we've been hesitant to take the lead on human resources issues such as diversity management. Some of our competitors have done a better job. But in the past few years, Microsoft has done an impressive job of catching up. It took a grassroots effort to educate upper management about the benefits of making the work environment one where every employee could be their most creative and productive." Most recently, in the spring of 1993, the company joined Lotus and several other rivals who now extend health benefits to the partners and eligible dependents of lesbian and gay employees. "We're in a better position today," says Smith. "Our policies are among the best in the business." Pickens agrees. "I'm impressed by the change we've seen in the past few years. The diversity program became a vital entity within just a few years."

For lesbian and gay workers the change has brought several tangible benefits. As diversity policies and programs have taken hold, many have found it easier to be frank about their sexuality. Several report that instances of overt homophobia are less common than before. And all are convinced that the change has improved the quality of their work. "Homophobic incidents basically shut people down," says Smith. "They're upset, which means they can't focus on work. You don't see as much of that happening today." A marketing representative in his thirties agrees. Although he continues to use an avoidance strategy at work, he no longer feels "any pressure to invent typical straight activities. I don't feel that I have to hide a hell of a lot. For example, I don't feel uncomfortable if friends meet me at the office to have drinks after work. People don't wonder, 'Why is he going out with these people?' 'Isn't his friend just a bit effeminate?' It's a burden that's been lifted, which lets me concentrate on work."

Others report that they are also more comfortable in the small, intense work groups that characterize the company. "I come in on Monday and banter with my coworker and boss about my weekend and about my boyfriend," says Pickens. "We all kind of joke about it, and it creates a spirit of camaraderie. Someone sent me an e-mail message today, saying she would be at a meeting from 'eight until ten straight.' I wrote back, saying, 'I'll be there from eight until ten, too, but definitely not straight.' So there's a level of camaraderie that's built up, and that's crucial when it's time to put in the extra push to finish a project. When you can talk about your home situation, you can share so much more of yourself with other people. That ultimately makes us a better team."

The change in atmosphere is perhaps most important in times of personal crisis. Kate Robinson, a writer and editor, found herself in a bind last year when her lesbian partner, who has AIDS, required more and more of her attention. She ultimately negotiated a working arrangement that gave her a more flexible schedule. "The diversity office, the people in GLEAM, and my peers were all incredibly supportive," she says. Today, she works out of her home two days per week. "Once the pressure was off, I actually became more productive, which was surprising to me. I got more done, working the same number of hours, especially on projects that required the most concentration. I hadn't realized how much I was dithering until the stress was off and I could quit doing it. You know, you can sit in an office and stare at a terminal and do what looks like work for fifty hours a week—and do maybe fifteen hours of work. I used to sit at work, worried about my lover at home. My new working arrangement lets me be there for her. It helps me think more clearly so that I can be more efficient."

Microsoft's lesbian and gay employees also say that in the long run, the policy will affect the kind of people who are drawn to the company, not to mention those who will stay. "The fact that Microsoft had just added a nondiscrimination clause made a huge difference to me when I was job hunting," recalls Pickens, who joined the company three years ago. "I remember thinking, 'Well, I'm not really planning to be out, waving a flag. But if I'm ever found out to be gay, this won't hinder my promotion path at the company.' I didn't expect it to be an issue, but I knew that if it ever became one, it wouldn't be a problem." More recently, the company's revised policy on health benefits will help it compete with firms that have already extended them to lesbian and gay partners. "The lack of a policy has hurt us in the past," says Smith. "I know people who wouldn't interview with Microsoft because we didn't have domestic partnership benefits, which reduced the size of our recruitment pool." In particular, Smith remembers receiving an e-mail message several years ago in which a candidate asked about the company's policy on benefits for domestic partners. When told that Microsoft didn't have one, the candidate decided to interview elsewhere.

"The atmosphere greatly contributes to my desire to stay here," says Pickens. "And it also raises the level of expectations for other companies. If someone else tried to recruit me, I'd insist on the same kinds of protections, because I expect them now. Otherwise I'd be a very hard recruit. There are people who've been offered cars by other companies, and the question they asked was, 'Do you have sexual orientation protections?' If the answer was no, then forget it." Jeff Howard, a technical writer, agrees. "I could never remain in the closet now," he says. "So a future job would have to be a place in which I could come out. Nor would I take a job where being openly gay would hinder my ability to succeed." Asked if he plans to stay with Microsoft in the long run, he thinks for a moment. "My dedication to the company changed completely when it extended domestic partnership benefits. I don't intend on *using* them, but it really makes me feel I'm paid equally to every other employee. It was symbolic, which meant more to me than the monetary value of the benefit."

While they are quick to point out that the atmosphere is not perfect, most agree that Microsoft has assumed a leadership role on lesbian and gay issues, even when compared to other entrepreneurial, maverick organizations. "The company still has a long way to go," says Pickens. "Just because you have a nondiscrimination clause and diversity groups, you can't assume that everyone is automatically tolerant. People come to Microsoft from all walks of life. That's one reason this is a great company, but it's also a reason that some people are intolerant. The company has to deal with that, which is difficult because we're all so busy." In the future, Pickens hopes that the company will be more aggressive in its anti-homophobia training. GLEAM has urged the company to use its internal policies as a guide for its public activities. They have petitioned Microsoft to oppose more strenuously the so-called hate amendments in Oregon, Colorado, and other neighboring states.[26] They have also argued that its giving programs should include local gay activities, such as those for gay youth. "Microsoft is loath to take a public stand on most issues," says Pickens, "so that will be our challenge in the coming years."

Microsoft is a company, in short, that has made bold, effective, and incomplete strides toward creating the ideal job environment—one that thus far exists largely in theory. In this sense it is not unlike many of its competitors. A time will come when such steps will seem obvious, even conservative; our expectations about what is right and what is fair are rapidly shifting. As they do, the closet will ultimately recede into the realm of the unnecessary and unacceptable, an artifact of an earlier time. "This is the kind of place that's very appealing to stay with," says the marketing representative, who has been with Microsoft now for almost four years. "As I get older, I feel less inclined to hide my sexuality. I'm less tolerant of situations in which I have to do that. So in the long run the environment fits more and more into my ideal. I really feel that here I'm judged on my ability, my drive, and my smartness." Asked if he intends to come out at work, he chuckles and shakes his head. "It may be a long time before I bring a same-sex partner to a company event. But that's just me. Other people do, so it's not the company, it's me." For the time being, he hasn't ruled out the possibility. "I may get around to it yet."

Appendix: The Study

This report grew out of a long and fruitful collaboration. Jay Lucas and I conceived the project early in 1990 as a way of applying our different skills—his in business, mine in cultural studies—to the cause of lesbian and gay employment rights. After a few months of deliberation, we agreed to undertake a study of gay professionals, and spent the next year identifying, screening, and interviewing gay men. With the interviews complete, we worked independently. I set myself to the task of analyzing the data and writing the text, first as my doctoral dissertation at the University of Pennsylvania and then as *The Corporate Closet*. For Jay, meanwhile, the project became the basis for a pioneering firm that specializes in lesbian and gay employment issues: Kaplan, Lucas & Associates. Although we consulted at many points during the writing of the text, I ultimately accept responsibility, for better or worse, for the arguments within.

The Sample

When we began work in the spring of 1990, we immediately encountered a problem familiar to any social scientist studying a population that is difficult to identify or define: How does one locate potential participants? How many of them are there? And just who are "they" in the first place?

When I described our predicament to a friend, a lawyer in his mid-thirties, he volunteered the following anecdote from his childhood: "The first time I bought a gay magazine I remember being struck by this horrible vision," he told me. "I had just hidden it somewhere in the garage when I thought: Larry, now you've done it. Don't you know you're going to be caught? Don't you know that they keep *lists* of people who buy these things? Somewhere, in a giant computer—I was fifteen, so I worried about giant computers in Washington—they've just recorded your name on the master homosexual list. Maybe this is my Jewish background, or maybe it's just that I'm paranoid, but I was convinced: You'll start getting phone calls, then junk mail, then one day they'll round the whole list up."

My friend's paranoia notwithstanding, no one has produced evidence of such a master list, and for researchers this makes sampling a problematic issue. Without a list, there is no way to verify that one has obtained a representative sample of gay men. Indeed, the same conditions that make lesbians and gay men a fascinating subject for research ensure that the exact parameters of the community remain unknown. Because appearances can be managed and manipulated, there is no objective way to identify a gay man. Likewise, such cultural categories as "gay," "straight," and "bisexual" have different subjective meanings to different people. Neither the categories nor the communities can be precisely defined.

Even the term *community* must be used with caution. There are no natural borders around the population in question, no roster of representatives who speak for "our" concerns. As Esther Newton observed more than twenty years ago in her classic study of female impersonators, the community is an abstract category in, around, and against which people align themselves according to their own self-definitions. It permits many different kinds and degrees of participation. "All people who define themselves as 'gay' are placing themselves with other homosexuals as opposed to heterosexuals. However, this by no means implies that homosexuals are united, or that they are prepared to act in unison on any issue whatsoever, be it moral, political, religious, or economic."[1] As the movement(s) for lesbian and gay rights has gathered momentum in the past two decades, its internal fragmentation has become increasingly evident. Indeed, while it is at times fashionable and politically expedient to regard homosexuals as a coherent group—as an ethnicity, community, country, nation, tribe, or people—they are, in fact, none of these things.[2] And more to the point, for purposes of sampling, there is no list of names.

Our solution was to sample for diversity. Unable to draw a random sample, we sought at least to contact men whose personal and professional situations were as varied as possible. We wanted a range of ages, professions, and geographic locations. We also wanted men who represent the extremes of the strategy continuum, from the most secretive to the most public. To cast as wide a net as possible, we also defined *corporate* somewhat broadly. Some of the men we recruited are employed in classic professions like medicine, banking, and the law. Others work as managers, technicians, and administrative assistants in large, white-collar organizations. A handful run their own companies.

While many of their employers are corporations in the legal sense, however, many others are not. Because we wanted to hear about a range of professional experiences we included universities, hospitals, churches, charities, and governmental agencies that— while not usually called businesses—are almost always run like them. When screening a candidate, we insisted only that his workplace share the key attributes of a bureaucratic, professional organization: a management hierarchy, a central office environment in which work is done, and work tasks that necessitate interaction with coworkers. A man who earned a living on a free-lance or at-home basis, such that he was not part of his organization's internal social network, did not meet our criteria. Likewise, we excluded salesmen and field representatives whose only contact with their employers was by phone. Finally, because we wanted participants for whom work was their primary commitment, we also ruled out part-timers, retirees, and students with summer jobs.

We were relatively unconcerned, on the other hand, with the actual sexual practices of our participants. Our questions had less to do with sexual experiences per se than with the communication of sexual identity. Anyone who considers himself gay, however he acts on that conviction, must face the identity issues that we wanted to study. In at least one case this meant that we included a man who had been celibate for almost ten years yet considers himself gay. It also meant that, had any volunteered for the study, we would have excluded men who have sex with other men but have not personally or socially taken on a gay identity.[3]

We also decided early in the project to limit the interviews to men. Although lesbians should find much in the book that is familiar, my discussion has centered on the particular experiences of men. The initial reasons for this were logistical. We located the men through social networking, relying on friends and friends-of-friends to perform the needed introductions. These same friends also served as character references, assuring a candidate (especially one for whom confidentiality was an issue) that we could be trusted. As the recruiting began, however, we quickly discovered that it was difficult for us to locate women of diverse ages, backgrounds, and geographic regions. Closeted lesbians rarely agreed to speak with us, while the men's willingness to trust, and to speak candidly, was enhanced by our alikeness.

We also needed to place some boundaries around the study and knew that the strategies lesbians use to manage their identities at work, as well as the particular trade-offs they face in choosing them, differ in significant ways from those used by men. Lesbians share with gay men the experience of otherness, of being stigmatized for their sexuality, and of making difficult decisions about self-disclosure.[4] Yet there are no "female equivalents" to the men we interviewed.[5] A lesbian's experiences in the workplace inevitably differ from a gay man's, if only because women's experiences differ from men's. Most workplaces are sexist as well as heterosexist, and while lesbians and gay men are both stigmatized as homosexuals, they occupy different strata in the gender hierarchy. Even when sexual orientation has been disguised, gender tends to be self-evident. As a lesbian engineer told me, "Gay men ultimately have male privilege to fall back on. They experience discrimination because they're gay, but they enjoy other entitlements because they're male."

We had little trouble locating potential participants, but our procedure for contacting the men was complicated by several practical considerations. Jay Lucas and I realized at the outset that it would be uninformative to interview friends and acquaintances.

On the other hand, we were wary of contacting complete strangers and feared that many would recoil with suspicion if they received an unexpected call from two gay researchers. We were also afraid that some men would mistake us for members of the press or a political organization with a particular agenda. Even worse, they might be angry to learn that a friend had shared their names and phone numbers without first asking permission. Because it was crucial that we establish rapport with these men, especially those worried about confidentiality, we did not want to startle them with an unwelcome call.

Our solution was to work with "liaisons" who matched us with potential participants, telling the men about the project before we contacted them directly. We began in the summer of 1990 by choosing the five cities—New York, Houston, San Francisco, Philadelphia, and Washington—in which to conduct our fieldwork. In each city we contacted friends who knew gay men and who seemed willing to help us with the footwork. After a careful briefing the liaison would contact potential participants and tell them about the project, our backgrounds, and our procedures for ensuring confidentiality. If a candidate gave permission, we would then call to see if he met our criteria. At this stage we typically asked a few general questions about his personal background and his degree of self-disclosure at work. As the fieldwork progressed, these criteria became increasingly strict, and we were sometimes forced to exclude a candidate whose age, occupation, or self-presentational strategy placed him in an already-filled category.

Because candidates often volunteered the names of other candidates, the initial phone call sometimes set off several further rounds of introductions and telephone calls. Participants in New York and Philadelphia volunteered the names of friends in Washington and San Francisco, and our network of referrals grew geometrically over the course of the year. To secure just five interviews in San Francisco, for example, we ultimately spoke with almost fifty men. As many as five friends-of-friends sometimes linked us to a single qualified participant.

The final sample is described in Figure 1. Between July 1990 and March 1991 we conducted 70 interviews, ultimately speaking to men who lived or worked in ten different states: California, Connecticut, Delaware, the District of Columbia, Maryland, New York, New Jersey, Pennsylvania, Texas, and Virginia. All but a few lived or worked within twenty-five miles of a major urban area. One (Roger) was between jobs, while two (Rodney and Justin) had recently gone on medical disability. In many ways, the sample reflects the somewhat narrow demographics of the professional world. With one exception, all are college educated. All describe themselves as middle to upper middle class. They range in age from twenty-two to sixty-four, from those just out of college to those in senior management. The sample was predominantly white, with two African Americans (Milton and Scott) and one Latino (Miguel). When asked at the beginning of the interview if they considered themselves gay or bisexual, all but two (Eric and Jason) chose the former term. In the years that followed this initial battery of seventy interviews, I have supplemented the database with several additional interviews in an effort to expand and update our initial findings.

While we made every effort to gather a diverse group of participants, our method ensured that certain professions, age groups, and strategies would be better represented than others. Some gay men were more difficult than others for our liaisons to find. By definition certain self-presentational strategies ensured that their users would be less likely to know our liaisons. For men who counterfeit an identity, for example, their inaccessibility may be a sign that the strategy is working. Although we made a special effort to include such men, they are underrepresented in our sample.

Other men, once found, were unwilling to participate. Some made it clear by their words or actions that sexuality was an uncomfortable topic. When asked to take part in the study, a Catholic priest apologized and declined. "I just think I'd be uncomfortable doing that," he said. "I'm sorry, but it's not something I want to talk about." Others, especially those working in organizations that they consider homophobic, were concerned about confidentiality. Military personnel were difficult to find and reluctant to participate. A young engineer at a major defense contractor declined to take part, explaining that he is periodically subject to polygraph tests. "It makes me nervous even thinking about this stuff," he told me, "because that's one more thing that could turn up on the test. It took me six months to get a security clearance, and that would be a disaster. I know other people who've lost their clearance for being gay. The less I say about it, the better."

Others were concerned about their public reputations and the specter of media exposure. A Houston lawyer in his mid-thirties agreed to take part but informed us that despite our assurances, "all of your tapes and notes would turn up in court if you were ever sued." A U.S. congressman told us he'd "love to help" but had been made nervous in recent months by the outing controversy and the unwanted press it had brought several other gay politicians. I had met the congressman several years earlier at a small party in the Philadelphia area, but despite our network of mutual friends, he was wary. As a compromise he agreed to answer a few questions "off the record" and to act as a liaison. "Let me put you in touch with Barney Frank," he suggested. "He loves to talk about this stuff."

Whatever their reasons for being inaccessible, these were the men who got away. The refusal rate was quite low once we had spoken to candidates by phone; fewer than ten declined to participate after speaking with us. But there was a much larger group that never made it to the initial phone conversation. In all likelihood our liaisons approached men they assumed would be willing to participate, eliminating at the outset anyone they feared would be reluctant. Even among those they assumed would agree, the answer was sometimes no. While we made a special effort to appeal to these nervous or hard-to-find men, we did not always succeed.

In the text I have cloaked the men in pseudonyms. I've made every effort to preserve the telling details and circumstances in their case histories, balancing the competing demands of truth and confidentiality, but I have taken several steps to ensure that the men themselves cannot be identified. In most cases, I have invented first names and have disguised all references to specific coworkers. When extended (and potentially recognizable) situations are described, I've changed a few inconsequential details. I've used company names whenever possible, omitting them when a firm was small or a man's position in it difficult to disguise. When company names appear, however, they are accurate. The resulting veil of anonymity—though it clearly frustrates one of the central aims of the project, namely, to foster the recognition that gay men are a large, integrated part of the professional work force—strikes me as a necessary evil. The companies these seventy men represent are among our most respected and familiar; they make products we all use and trust. Although many of the men were willing to see their names in print, however, their stories inevitably involve others who would not feel the same way. That will change in time.

The Interviews

We began with a series of group sessions designed to elicit the vernacular language and conceptual categories gay professionals use when discussing self-disclosure. We asked them to talk about coming out at work, and we heard their own definitions and their own emphasis in explaining them. Then, as the interviews became more structured, we developed specific and closed-ended questions. We began meeting individually with gay men in July 1990.[6]

In the interviews themselves, Jay Lucas and I carefully managed what we revealed about ourselves. We said as little as possible about our own values and work experiences. We avoided terms like *strategy* or *identity management.* When the conversation turned to activist organizations like ACT-UP and Queer Nation—groups perceived by some to be militant—we concealed our own opinions. We also tried to show restraint when a participant provoked a particularly strong positive or negative reaction, as some inevitably did. To the extent possible, we wanted to establish a neutral, supportive environment in which participants felt they could be candid.

We made certain, however, that participants knew we were gay. Most had already assumed as much or had been told by the liaison before our initial phone contact. Even so, at the start of each interview, Jay and I included a specific reference to our own sexuality. We knew that interviewees would be more comfortable and candid when they felt that the person asking the questions had been forthcoming about his own life. We also knew that the so-called "reciprocity effect" is especially powerful in conversations about sensitive subjects.[7] (A friend refers to the mutual exchange of personal information as "trading hostages.") We hoped in particular that our disclosure would facilitate trust and put weight behind our promise to protect their confidentiality. By disclosing our membership in the gay community, we wanted to signal that we knew its rules about self-disclosure and respected its conventions regarding secrecy.

Our self-disclosure improved the interviews in other ways. By revealing that we were gay we established our credentials as "insiders."[8] There are certain experiences one will only share with, and expect to be understood by, others of the same sexual orientation. In his study of sexual diversity among American Indians, for example, anthropologist Walter Williams found that many of his participants had been unwilling to confide in the heterosexual researchers who had preceded him. "If I had been the typical ethnographer, because of the fact that such private behavior is not talked about, I might have concluded that nothing sexual was occurring among these men."[9] Indeed, many of the earliest ethnographic accounts of lesbians and gay men were marred by the insufficient access granted nongay researchers.[10] When the participant has reason to mistrust the researcher, access and understanding will be limited.[11]

Having accepted us as fellow community members, the men treated us with a familiarity and ease unusual among new acquaintances. Participants took conversational shortcuts and assumed we were able to follow. They were liberal in their use of gay argot and such remarks as "you get the idea" and "you know what I mean." Because the men assumed that we had shared (or at least heard about) similar life experiences, stories about sexual awakenings and comings out were often told in schematic terms. As one man explained: "I did the 'coming out' thing in the usual way. I had wet dreams and fantasies about the football captain, misguided attempts with girls, guilt, and a few drunken oh-God-I-was-so-drunk-I-don't-remember-a-thing nights with buddies in college. Then the discos, the self-help books, conversations with my parents. Sound familiar?"

The significance of this rapport was most evident when it was

inadvertently breached. Due to a misunderstanding, one participant assumed through the first part of the interview that we were
heterosexual. He found himself at a loss when trying to explain a
particular scenario, during a complicated story about his unex-
pressed feelings toward a college roommate. When we assured him
that we understood, that we were gay ourselves, he apologized and
started again. "I wasn't going to get into the whole story," he explained, "because I didn't think two straight guys would have any
idea what I was talking about." His initial reluctance underscores
the importance of rapport, as well as the dependence of the interviewer on the trust and candor of the interviewee.

At the same time the very process by which we built rapport be-
trays our vulnerability to the broad class of validity threats called
"interviewer effects." Certain aspects of the interview situation may
have pressured participants to withhold or distort information.
Our encounters with participants generally took the form of a
one-sided conversation in which one party was granted privileged,
non-reciprocal access to information about the other. We asked
participants to divulge information that often signifies intimacy in
our culture—information that is normally reserved for lovers,
friends, priests, or therapists—and claimed the ability to analyze it
in some special fashion. Not surprisingly participants often wanted
to know what we "thought of" their decisions. How did they measure up to the other participants? Did we approve of the decisions
they had made? At other times participants seemed to regard us as
newfound friends with whom they were to spend a few hours of
intimate conversation. They served us drinks and snacks (in one
case an elaborate spread of hors d'oeuvres) and assured us, as we
finished the interview, that we had been pleasant company. Several
offered to "show us around" the city and urged us to let them
know "the next time you're in town." Five men called within a few
days of our meeting to invite me to dinner. During the meal they
inevitably used the opportunity to justify or elaborate on their
comments or to seek my feedback.

After the interviews several men spoke as if they had just taken
part in a therapeutic exercise of some sort. Dan explained that he
rarely thought about these issues. "You asked questions that I've

never really . . . that I've thought about maybe just sporadically, but nothing more than that. It was really thought provoking." Likewise, Eric seemed somewhat shaken up. "You've helped me a great deal, because you've made me bring out some things that I've hidden, about the way I feel about myself and being gay. I think what you're doing is great, and I really respect you for doing this. I think . . . I hope your book is going to be real positive in the marketplace, and that the world accepts it."

In short, despite our efforts, the interviews were not neutral encounters between two "objective" researchers and their respondents. Nor could they have been. A researcher is inevitably a positioned subject.[12] Whether the men viewed us as confidants or authority figures, it is reasonable to assume that most sought our approval or favorable judgment. Consequently it would be inaccurate to say that we collected data on the ways gay men actually behave at work. Our data reflect, rather, what gay men recall and choose to reveal about their own behavior at work. The snapshots we've taken are not exactly candid because "people pose even in their confessions."[13] In at least one case, I learned through independent means that a participant had exaggerated the degree to which he was openly gay at work. Another had misreported by several years the date he came out to his boss. As these subtle distortions remind us, identity management is an endless process—even in interviews on the subject.[14]

Table 1
The Men

Name	Age	Title, Employer
Al	28	Attorney, law firm
Andy	34	Partner, law firm
Arthur	32	Partner, entertainment law firm
Barry	40	Attorney, law firm
Bill	31	Park Ranger, California Park Service
Brent	28	Supervisor, diversified energy company
Burt	41	Legal assistant, diversified hospitality company
Carl	40	President/co-owner, real estate company
Carter	34	Sales manager, Hilton hotels
Charles	56	Travel agent, corporate travel agency
Chip	27	Manager of information systems, investment firm
Chris	40	President/CEO, arts management consulting firm
Chuck	28	Trader, investment bank
Clay	53	Executive secretary, SmithKline Clinical Laboratories
Craig	45	Vice president of finance, American Express
Dan	31	Director, psychiatric clinic
Darren	32	Dentist, medical clinic
Dave	27	Credit manager, fuel supply company
Derek	37	Senior vice president, employment agency
Don	32	Financial analyst, Levi Strauss & Co.
Duane	38	President, entrepreneurial oil and gas company
Ed	39	Regional sales manager, IBM
Eric	51	Marketing officer, division of bank
Gary	36	Director of tax administration, Bell Atlantic
Geoff	33	Construction manager, Catholic college
George	33	Training executive, Europe-based airline
Glen	46	General counsel, diversified energy company
Greg	33	Architect, diversified construction company
Grey	27	Director of marketing, urban shopping mall
Harry	49	Director of development, AIDS service organization
Howard	31	Labor relations representative, Pacific Bell
Jack	61	Vice president of human resources, publishing company
Jason	60	Senior vice president, Johnson & Johnson
Jeff	30	Financial analyst, entrepreneurial investment firm

Table 1 *(continued)*

Name	Age	Title, Employer
Jerry	32	Trader, investment bank
Jim	36	Software engineer, computer equipment supplier
Joel	50	Partner, lobbying and consulting firm
John	39	Priest, Episcopal congregation
Justin	44	Professor, small private college
Keith	27	Senior clerk, diversified energy company
Kirk	31	Obstetrician, Philadelphia hospital
Larry	47	Managing partner, law firm
Les	64	Business manager, technical high school
Louis	43	Partner, law firm
Mark	36	Compensation consultant, consulting firm
Martin	29	Account supervisor, Ogilvy & Mather
Matt	40	Regional supervisor, Ford Motor Company
Michael	41	President/owner, entrepreneurial consulting firm
Miguel	29	Medical resident, Philadelphia hospital
Milton	41	Partner, law firm
Mitch	34	Attorney, law firm
Nick	27	Project manager, consulting firm
Patrick	28	Human resources trainer, hospital
Paul	55	Management supervisor, British Airways
Peter	28	Realtor, real estate firm
Phil	29	Senior manager, consulting firm
Ralph	27	Account executive, oil and gas exploration company
Randy	34	Broker, investment bank
Rob	60	Instructor, private music school
Rodney	27	Trader, Morgan Guaranty
Roger	46	Attorney, Department of Labor
Roland	36	Art director, advertising agency
Roy	38	Vice president, division of Time-Warner
Russ	27	Claims negotiator, insurance company
Scott	33	Sales representative, Blue Cross
Sean	22	Account executive, Manning, Selvage & Lee
Steve	24	Staff accountant, accounting firm
Stuart	32	Attorney, law firm
Terry	34	Attorney, law firm

Table 1 *(continued)*

Name	Age	Title, Employer
Tim	29	Editor, *U.S. News & World Report*
Tip	29	Surgical resident, large Manhattan hospital
Todd	29	Human resources, Bell Atlantic
Tom	42	Teacher, public elementary school
Tony	32	Product development, financial services firm
William	41	Psychiatrist, outpatient clinic

Table 2
Sample description

	Number	Number Using Each Strategy*		
	Total (70)	Counterfeit	Avoid	Integrate
Age				
21–25	2	1	1	1
26–30	17	5	12	6
31–35	19	4	11	9
36–40	12	2	5	7
41–45	7	—	5	3
46–50	5	—	4	2
51–55	3	2	1	1
56–60	3	1	1	2
60+	2	—	1	1
Religion				
"Important"	31	11	19	10
Protestant	17	7	9	5
Catholic	10	4	8	2
Jewish	2	—	1	1
New Age	2	—	1	2
"Not important"	39	2	22	22
Racial Identity				
African American	2	1	1	1
Latino	1	1	—	—
White	67	13	40	31
Marital Status				
Married	2	2	—	—
Divorced	3	—	2	1
Never married	65	13	49	31

*The numbers in these three columns often exceed the number in the total column. Because many gay men use more than one strategy, they are counted more than once.

Table 2 *(continued)*

	Number	Number Using Each Strategy*		
	Total (70)	Counterfeit	Avoid	Integrate
City of Interview				
Philadelphia	23	5	14	9
Houston	16	6	11	4
New York	17	3	9	10
Washington	9	—	6	6
San Francisco	5	1	1	3
Strategy Used with Parents				
Counterfeit	5	5	1	—
Avoid	27	7	23	5
Integrate	35	1	16	27
(Deceased)	3	2	1	—
Lesbian or Gay Coworkers				
Many	18	2	7	14
Some	27	5	17	13
Not aware of any	25	8	17	5
Employer				
Company	55	14	34	25
Self-employed	6	—	3	3
Not-for-profit	2	—	—	2
Government	2	—	2	—
Educational	5	1	2	2
Size of Office				
Fewer than 25	32	9	23	13
25 or more	38	6	18	19

Table 2 *(continued)*

	Number	Number Using Each Strategy*		
	Total (70)	Counterfeit	Avoid	Integrate
Homophobic Incidents or Comments				
Major/often	13	7	4	3
Minor/occasional	24	4	15	12
Rarely/never	33	4	22	17
Expected Consequence of Having Sexuality Revealed				
Fired	4	2	3	—
Harassed	6	3	3	—
Embarrassed	20	6	16	5
None	40	4	19	27
Social Obligations at Work				
Often	21	7	11	11
Sometimes	24	5	12	14
Rarely/never	25	3	18	7
"How often do people at work talk or joke about sex?"				
"Often"	34	10	11	21
"Not too often"	36	5	30	11
Vulnerability to Being Fired				
High	21	8	13	6
Moderate	13	3	9	6
Low	36	4	19	20
"Does your company have a non-discrimination policy that includes sexual orientation?"				
"Yes"	23	5	11	13
"No"	28	9	20	8
"Not sure"	19	1	10	11

Table 2 *(continued)*

	Number	Number Using Each Strategy*		
	Total (70)	Counterfeit	Avoid	Integrate
"With whom do you spend most of your time?"				
Coworkers	34	8	22	12
Clients/customers	36	7	19	20

Table 3
Survey Research on Employment Discrimination

	Location	Sample	Lifetime Rate of Discrimination[1] (percentages)
Gross and Aurand (1992)	Philadelphia	860♂	30
		553♀	24
	Pennsylvania	398♂	33
		265♀	32
Eight in Ten (1989)	Massachusetts	796♂	24
		561♀	23
Gross (1988)	Philadelphia	291♂	25
		146♀	19
	Pennsylvania	170♂	34
		114♀	34
Dallas Gay Alliance (1986)	Dallas	230♂	28[2]
		34♀	
Blumstein and Schwartz (1983)	National	1,887♂	27
		1,514♀	32
Bell and Weinberg (1978)	San Francisco	686♂	26
Weinberg and Williams (1974)	New York and San Francisco	1,057♂	30
Saghir and Robins (1973)	Chicago and San Francisco	89♂	32
Williams and Weinberg (1971)	New York and San Francisco	63♂	29

[1]The "lifetime" rate of discrimination is the percentage of men who have experienced employment discrimination at any point in their careers. However, because these studies define discrimination in different ways, direct comparisons should be made with caution. For a more exhaustive list of studies, see Lee Badgett et al., *Pervasive Patterns of Discrimination Against Lesbians and Gay Men: Evidence from Surveys across the United States* (Washington, D.C.: National Gay and Lesbian Task Force Policy Institute, 1992), which summarizes data from twenty surveys.

[2]This study did not report different rates of discrimination for men and women.

Notes

Chapter 1: Dimensions of the Closet

1. The difficulty in making such estimates begins with the vagaries of the category itself (see my discussion of sampling in the Appendix). Using the data collected in the 1940s and 1950s by Alfred Kinsey and his associates, most lesbian and gay activists claim that some 10 percent of the male population engages primarily in homosexual sex. Although the figure has been the subject of much recent debate, it is the one most often cited by researchers and policymakers. See Patrick Rogers, "How Many Gays Are There?" *Newsweek*, Feb. 15, 1993, p. 46.
2. See Warren Blumenfeld's discussion of heterosexual men who work in nontraditional, "gay" occupations, in *Homophobia: How We All Pay the Price* (Boston: Beacon, 1992), p. 33.
3. Richard Zoglin, "The Homosexual Executive," *MBA*, reprinted in Martin P. Levine, ed., *Gay Men: The Sociology of Male Homosexuality* (New York: Harper & Row, 1979), p. 69.
4. Jeff Yarbrough, "Vanity Fairies," *Advocate*, vol. 598, Mar. 10, 1992, p. 32.
5. Midge Decter, "The Boys on the Beach," *Commentary*, Aug. 1980, p. 40.
6. Reported in *In Full View*, vol. 2, no. 1 (1992), a newsletter published by Overlooked Opinions, 3712 N. Broadway, Suite 277, Chicago, IL 60613. Overlooked Opinions bases these figures on a 1992 survey of 7,500 lesbians and gay men, randomly selected from the firm's national "panel" of respondents. The panel itself was assembled through event marketing (distributing information at marches and conferences), and through referrals by other panel members.

7. The National Gay and Lesbian Task Force Policy Institute maintains a database of surveys on employment discrimination. Twenty of the surveys are summarized in its 1992 report, Lee Badgett et al., *Pervasive Patterns of Discrimination Against Lesbians and Gay Men: Evidence from Surveys Across the United States.* For more information, contact the NGLTF Policy Institute, 1734 14th St. NW, Washington, DC 20009.

8. The Philadelphia sample included 860 males and 553 females. (In suburban and rural areas of Pennsylvania, the rate of discrimination was slightly higher.) See Larry Gross and Steven K. Aurand, *Discrimination and Violence Against Lesbian Women and Gay Men in Philadelphia and the Commonwealth of Pennsylvania: A Study by the Philadelphia Lesbian and Gay Task Force,* 1992, or contact the PLGTF, 1501 Cherry St., Philadelphia, PA 19102.

9. This same argument has been advanced to explain increased levels of antigay violence in recent years. As lesbians and gay men become more visible, we are more likely to bear the full force of homophobia.

10. In their study of lesbian physical educators, for example, Sherry E. Woods and Karen M. Harbeck found that eleven of their twelve participants believed that they would be fired if they were open about their sexual orientation. "Although the twelfth participant stated that she would probably not lose her job, she did admit to engaging in 'passing' behaviors so that her colleagues would assume that she was heterosexual." See Harbeck, ed., *Coming Out of the Classroom Closet: Gay and Lesbian Students, Teachers, and Curricula* (New York: Haworth, 1991), p. 149. (Simultaneously published as the *Journal of Homosexuality,* vol. 22, nos. 3–4).

11. Virginia R. Brooks, *Minority Stress and Lesbian Women* (Toronto: Lexington, 1981), p. 170.

12. Joseph Harry and William B. DeVall, *The Social Organization of Gay Males* (New York: Praeger, 1978), p. 161.

13. The same point can be made about the designation of "hate crimes," which require authorities to make judgments about an alleged criminal's motives. See, for example, James C. McKinley Jr., "Tracking Crimes of Prejudice: A Hunt for the Elusive Truth," *New York Times,* June 29, 1990, pp. A1+.

14. Jay K. Brause, "Closed Doors: Sexual Orientation Bias in the Anchorage Housing and Employment Markets," *Identity Reports: Sexual Orientation Bias in Alaska* (Anchorage: Identity Incorporated, 1989). Cited in Badgett et al., *Pervasive Patterns,* p. 2.

15. The term "symbolic annihilation" was coined by George Gerbner and Larry Gross. See Gross, "Out of the Mainstream: Sexual Minorities and the Mass Media," in Ellen Seiter et al., eds., *Remote Control: Television, Audiences and Cultural Power* (London: Routledge, Chapman, and Hall, 1989), pp. 130–49.

16. As Joseph Neisen has defined it, heterosexism operates in many ways and at many levels. "Heterosexism manifests itself in blatant discrimination against gays and lesbians as well as in more subtle forms of exclusion or lack of acknowledgment. Heterosexism is alive when individuals refuse to rent to gays or lesbians, when the military discharges someone for homosexual behavior or mere suspicion of being homosexual, and when governments prohibit gays and lesbians from marrying legally. Heterosexism also works in more subtle ways, as when television programs and advertisements show only heterosexual couples, when mainstream media underreport gay and lesbian events like the 1987 National March on Washington for Gay and Lesbian Rights, and when magazine articles and obituaries fail to acknowledge the life partners of gay men and lesbians." Each of these examples has an organizational equivalent. See Neisen, "Heterosexism or Homophobia? The Power of the Language We Use," *Out/Look,* vol. 10 (1990), pp. 36–37.

17. The results are from an unpublished survey conducted by *Out/Look* magazine. The questionnaire was bound into the spring 1992 edition of the magazine, and the findings were intended for publication the following fall. Unfortunately the magazine ceased publication in the summer of 1992. See James D. Woods, "Self-Disclosure at Work," *Out/Look,* vol. 16 (1992), pp. 87–88. See also the 1989 survey conducted by Steve Teichner for the *San Francisco Examiner,* which used random digit dialing to reach eight hundred men and women (four hundred of them in the San Francisco Bay Area). In that survey only 15 percent of the men and 19 percent of the women said that sexual orientation had played a major role in their selection of a job or profession. Cited in Badgett et al., *Pervasive Patterns,* p. 13.

18. Likewise, a 1973 survey of eighty-nine gay men in Chicago and San Francisco found that 16 percent had been "fired or asked to resign, or their jobs were threatened due to their homosexuality." Yet when the same men were asked if "homosexuality set limits on their ambitions and imposed restrictions on their choice of career or advancement," the number doubled. See Marcel T. Saghir and Eli Robins, *Male and Female Homosexuality* (Baltimore: Williams & Wilkins,

1973), cited in Martin P. Levine, "Employment Discrimination Against Gay Men," *International Review of Modern Sociology,* vol. 9 (1979), pp. 151–63.

19. Cited in "Approaching 2000: Meeting the Challenge to San Francisco's Families," Mayor's Task Force on Family Policy, June 13, 1990, p. 7.

20. The *Partners* survey included 1,266 lesbian and gay couples, and was reported in the May/June 1990 issue. (Copies can be obtained by writing Partners, Box 9685, Seattle, WA 98109-0685). Also cited in Jennifer J. Laabs, "Unmarried . . . with Benefits," *Personnel Journal,* Dec. 1991, pp. 62–70.

21. Ibid., p. 68.

22. Marny Hall observed a similar effect among the thirteen lesbian professionals in her study: "Though no respondent thought her homosexuality had any impact on work performance, most felt their future options were limited by their lesbianism. They could advance to a certain level but not beyond because they could not project the necessary corporate image. Some seemed not to care; several said, 'I'm not ambitious'; some were resigned: 'I've definitely settled for less.' Others aimed for careers outside the business world, where their lesbianism wouldn't be an obstacle. Several planned to go into business for themselves or to become free-lance consultants. Still others took refuge in technical areas in which they had little interaction with co-workers." See Hall, "Private Experiences in the Public Domain: Lesbians in Organizations," in Jeff Hearn et al., eds., *The Sexuality of Organization* (Newbury Park, CA: Sage, 1989), p. 134.

23. Brendan Lemon, "Man of the Year: David Geffen," *Advocate,* vol. 619, Dec. 29, 1992, p. 38.

24. The term *homophobia* is unfortunate, but has become virtually unavoidable in gay parlance. As John Boswell points out, its origins would have it mean "fear of what is similar," not "fear of homosexuality." (See Boswell, *Christianity, Social Tolerance, and Homosexuality* [Chicago: University of Chicago Press, 1980], p. 46n.) Yet one commonly hears the term used to designate all sorts of cultural prejudice against lesbians and gay men, thus making it possible to say that an institution or situation is "homophobic." (See, for example, Blumenfeld's discussion in *Homophobia,* p. 3.) As I use the terms, *homophobia* falls into the larger category of *heterosexism,* which like racism and sexism denotes an entire class of discriminatory attitudes and behaviors. The awkward *sexual orientationism* would be a more appropriate, parallel term.

25. Most gay professionals can recall what Erving Goffman calls "atrocity stories and exemplary moral tales," illustrating "extreme mistreatment by normals." See Goffman, *Stigma: Notes on the Management of Spoiled Identity* (New York: Simon & Schuster, 1963), p. 25.

26. Loren Ghiglione et al., *Alternatives: Gays & Lesbians in the Newsroom* (Washington, DC: American Society of News Editors, 1990), p. 11.

27. Barry D. Adam, *The Rise of a Gay and Lesbian Movement* (Boston: Twayne, 1987).

28. Syndicated columnist, Sept. 6, 1992.

29. Louie Crew, "Before Emancipation: Gay Persons as Viewed by Chairpersons in English," in Crew, ed., *The Gay Academic* (Palm Springs, CA: ETC Publications, 1978), pp. 3–48.

30. Quoted in *Harvard Business Review,* vol. 68, no. 3 (1990), p. 118.

31. Here I am closely following Rosemary Pringle (1989), who in her book, *Secretaries Talk: Sexuality, Power and Work* (New York: Verso), offers this interpretation of the relationship a female secretary has with her male boss: "No one seriously believes that secretaries spend much time on the bosses' knee. Actual sexual interactions are the exception rather than the norm and, jokes aside, the centrality of work to the boss-secretary relationship is generally conceded. Yet the sexual possibilities color the way in which the relationship is seen. . . . Even if the cruder representations are discounted, the relationship is seen to be oozing with sexuality which is suppressed, sublimated or given limited expression in flirtation and flattery. It bases itself on personal rapport (some bosses call it "chemistry"), involves a degree of intimacy, day-to-day familiarity and shared secrets unusual for any but lovers or close friends, and is capable of generating intense feelings of loyalty, dependency and personal commitment" (p. 159). See also Pringle, "Bureaucracy, Rationality and Sexuality: The Case of Secretaries," in Hearn et al., *The Sexuality of Organization,* p. 162.

32. See Deborah Sheppard, "Organizations, Power and Sexuality: The Image and Self-Image of Women Managers," in Hearn et al., *The Sexuality of Organization,* p. 153.

33. The point was definitely not lost on Dr. Jeffery Collins, formerly an employee of Triton Biosciences, Inc., a division of the Shell Oil Company. In 1985 Collins was dismissed after his secretary stumbled onto a memo Collins had written, and left in the photocopier, outlining the rules for a gay safe-sex party. Collins sued the company, and in June 1991 a California superior court ruled in his favor,

awarding him $5.3 million in damages, the largest award ever made to an individual for a gay employment-bias claim. (The amount was subsequently reduced on appeal.) In her ruling Judge Jacqueline Taber of Alameda County Superior Court noted: "This case presents the relatively new issue of how far a corporation may go in demanding that its managerial staff, in their respective private lives, deport and conduct themselves in a manner acceptable to and meeting the corporation's concept of propriety." At the time of the ruling, Collins was earning about 20 percent of his former salary working as a dog shipper in a veterinary clinic ("Vindicated," *New York Times,* June 23, 1991, p. E7).

34. As Jeffrey Escoffier notes, "Any occupation that must depend on 'trust' or intangible personal qualities will be extremely harsh to homosexual members, because any deviation would be seen to undermine the effective performance of occupational responsibilities —whether this is, in fact, the case or not." See Escoffier, "Stigmas, Work Environment, and Economic Discrimination Against Homosexuals," *Homosexual Counseling Journal,* vol. 2, no. 1 (1975), p. 12.

35. Rosabeth Moss Kanter, *Men and Women of the Corporation* (New York: Basic Books, 1977).

36. This estimate is supplied by Elsie Y. Cross Associates, a diversity management firm in Philadelphia.

37. At times, the metaphor seems virtually irresistible. For example, in an interview with the *Advocate,* a gay newsmagazine, National Organization of Women president Patricia Ireland spoke of her relationships with both her husband of twenty five years and a female companion "who is also very important in my life." She ducked the label "bisexual" and criticized the temptation to "categorize other people by their sexuality." She also insisted that her two relationships had long been a matter of public record. "I've never hidden how I've lived my life," she explained, citing a previous interview in which she had spoken of her female companion. Her interviewer apparently viewed all of this as equivocation, and framed Ireland's comments as a traditional coming-out story. The cover headline read: "America's Most Powerful Woman Comes Out." See Donna Minkowitz, "Patricia Ireland Takes the Reins," *Advocate,* vol. 592, Dec. 17, 1991, pp. 38–44.

38. The same language is often used to describe other sorts of potentially stigmatizing disclosures. Today people can "come out" as soap opera fans, junk food junkies, or sports fanatics. In the fall of 1990, the

late Lee Atwater, then chairman of the Republican National Committee, was criticized for permitting someone on his staff to write a memo accusing Tom Foley of "coming out" of the liberal closet (an innuendo that was also assumed to imply that Foley is gay). Within support groups one sometimes hears individuals "come out" as rape or incest survivors, alcoholics, people with AIDS, or as practitioners of sadomasochism and pedophilia.

39. Marny Hall, "The Lesbian Corporate Experience," *Journal of Homosexuality,* vol. 12, nos. 3–4 (1986), p. 74.

40. These ambiguities were a recurrent nuisance as Jay Lucas and I were recruiting participants for the study (see the Appendix). Before we scheduled an interview, we tried to learn something about a man's degree of self-disclosure at work, which usually made it necessary to use closet language. "How out are you at work?" we asked. "Are there other closeted people at work?" The frequent response from potential participants was confusion: "Well, what do you mean—in the closet to my boss?" Or, "Well, I'm pretty closeted, but not entirely." Other times, when we avoided the metaphor, it was volunteered: "I have a friend who might be right—he's totally closeted at work." Or, "I know a few guys who are out in Houston, let me see if they'll talk to you." Then, in subsequent meetings, we frequently discovered that our terminology had failed us. Several participants told us over the phone that they were "totally out" at work, only to reveal during the interview that they had never discussed their sexuality with anyone at work; neither was there any evidence that coworkers had figured it out. Others said they were closeted at work, but could list a handful of people with whom they spoke candidly about their sexual lives. Clearly we lacked a precise way of talking about sexual self-disclosure.

41. For example, see Sheppard's discussion of the ways women "manage" gender in male-dominated environments, in "Organizations, Power and Sexuality," pp. 139–57.

42. As Goffman has argued, when personal traits are inferred rather than directly perceived, there is always the opportunity for false inferences. *Virtual* social identity, those traits by which we are known to others, can be detached from *actual* social identity, those traits we in fact possess. See *Stigma,* pp. 41–42.

43. As Richard Dyer argues in his study of lesbian and gay film: "No other group is quite so literally socially invisible. Being lesbian/gay does not show—unlike gender, color or disability, it is not physiolog-

ically apparent; unlike class or ethnicity, it is not something the visible markers of which you have to *un*learn if you wish to disguise it; only if you choose to behave in an 'obvious' style is being lesbian/gay in any sense visible. This of course does afford a measure of protection. Coming out is a deliberate decision to do without that mask of invisibility." See Dyer, *Now You See It: Studies in Lesbian and Gay Film* (New York: Routledge, 1991), p. 249.

44. Recently, biomedical research has revived the search for somatic markers (or "causes") of homosexuality by suggesting a link between brain structure and sexual orientation. See *New York Times,* Aug. 20, 1992, p. A1; see also the follow-up letter from William M. Byne, M.D., to the editor, Sept. 19, 1992. For a review of the literature on the biomedical origins of sexual orientation, see Michael J. Bailey and Richard C. Pillard, "A Genetic Study of Male Sexual Orientation," *Archives of General Psychiatry,* vol. 48 (1991), pp. 1089–96. A more general discussion can be found in Chandler Burr, "Homosexuality and Biology," *Atlantic,* Mar. 1993, pp. 47–65.

45. The self-consciousness is characteristic of other stigmatized groups. One sees it in women who navigate male corridors of power, who adapt their appearance and speech to accommodate masculine values, and whose behavior is sometimes calculated to defy prevailing stereotypes about women. One sees it in African Americans who in mixed company avoid words or appearances that might set them apart, who muffle their frustration so as not to appear divisive, and who see themselves as "problems" for some imagined "mainstream." And one sees it in religious, political, and cultural minorities who are routinely called on to justify their beliefs or explain their dissimilarity, who become sources of curiosity or derision for those who are more typical. For a discussion of the different coping strategies used by blacks, Jews, and gay men, see Barry Adam, *The Survival of Domination* (New York: Elsevier, 1978). See also Stanford M. Lyman and Marvin B. Scott, "Paranoia, Homosexuality and Game Theory," *A Sociology of the Absurd* (New York: Appleton-Century-Crofts, 1970), pp. 71–88.

46. See Joseph P. Goodwin, *More Man Than You'll Ever Be: Gay Folklore and Acculturation in Middle America* (Bloomington: Indiana University Press, 1989).

47. In a 1990 survey of professional journalists conducted by the American Society of News Editors, the authors noted: "While nearly three-fifths of survey respondents consider themselves 'out' in

their newsrooms, the issue of being or not being publicly gay carries agonizing import for these journalists. No topic seems to hold more emotional weight for those who commented with their surveys. Respondents struggled over whether to come out, to whom to come out, the impact on their careers (some in dread about it), the impact on their effectiveness as journalists, the yearning to be accepted and the anger when they are not. Clearly, in this respect, newsrooms are a microcosm of the larger society." See Ghiglione et al., *Alternatives,* p. 15.

Chapter 2: The Asexual Professional

1. In her memoir, Power Play: *What Really Happened at Bendix* (New York: Simon & Schuster, 1984), Cunningham protested the limitations we place on romance between coworkers. In it, she wrote: "Men and women who work together will fall in love. And why should this surprise anyone? People who work together come to know each other in a way that is far more meaningful by most standards than meeting in a singles bar. To put these people off-limits to one another is unrealistic. And to presume that such romances are "not worthy of truly ambitious women," as one popular magazine would suggest, is an affront to love based on mutual admiration and respect." The Agees were married in June 1982.
2. David F. Greenberg, *The Construction of Homosexuality* (Chicago: University of Chicago Press, 1988), p. 437–38. See also pp. 434–54.
3. *New York Times,* June 13, 1991, p. D1.
4. Indeed, much of our sexual discourse, over the past century, can be viewed as skirmishes between two opposed camps: those who would liberate sexuality (releasing it *from* society) and those who would regulate, repress, or limit sexuality (protecting society *from* it). In either scenario there is an opposition, some version of which is woven through all of our dominant accounts of sexuality. See Jeffrey Weeks, *Sexuality and Its Discontents* (New York: Routledge, 1985).
5. In his famous essay on bureaucracy, Max Weber notes that one of its primary goals is to "segregate official activity as something distinct from the sphere of private life," and emphasizes that "the executive office is separated from the household, business from private correspondence, and business assets from private fortunes." Though he makes no mention of sexuality per se, Weber implicitly locates it in the relam of the private, the personal, the nonorganizational. Like F.

W. Taylor, Fayol and Urwick, and the many other "founding fathers" of organizational theory, Weber was primarily interested in effectiveness and efficiency, an orientation that tends to render sexuality invisible. See Weber, "Bureaucracy," in H. H. Gerth and C. Wright Mills, eds., *From Max Weber: Essays in Sociology* (New York: Oxford University Press, 1946), pp. 196–244. For a general discussion of sexuality in organizational theory, see Gibson Burrell and Jeff Hearn, "The Sexuality of Organization," in Hearn et al., *The Sexuality of Organization,* pp. 1–28; in the same volume, see Albert J. Mills, "Gender, Sexuality and Organization Theory," pp. 29–44; see also Jeff Hearn and Wendy Parkin, *'Sex' at 'Work': The Power and Paradox of Organizational Sexuality* (New York: St. Martin's, 1987), pp. 17–39.

6. See Gibson Burrell, "Sex and Organizational Analysis," *Organization Studies,* vol. 5, no. 2 (1984), pp. 97–118.

7. See Arlie Russell Hochschild, *The Managed Heart: Commercialization of Human Feeling* (Berkeley: University of California Press, 1983).

8. See Barbara Gutek, "Sexuality in the Workplace: Key Issues in Research and Organizational Practice," in Hearn et al., *The Sexuality of Organization,* pp. 56–70.

9. In *The Work/Life Dichotomy: Prospects for Reintegrating People and Jobs* (New York: Quorum, 1989), Martin Morf addressed this same distinction, noting that work is "imposed by society and done for society. It is collective and public activity. Thus, the work sphere is associated with society rather than the individual" (p. 5). One's "life," he maintains, is suspended when there is a "job" to be done.

10. Andrea Warfield, "Co-Worker Romances: Impact on the Work Group and on Career-Oriented Women," *Personnel,* May 1987, pp. 22–35.

11. Ibid., p. 30.

12. "Romance in the Workplace: Corporate Rules for the Game of Love," *Business Week,* June 18, 1984, pp. 70–71.

13. Letitia Baldrige, *Letitia Baldrige's Complete Guide to Executive Manners* (New York: Rawson, 1985), p. 53.

14. Diane Feldman, "Sexual Harassment: Policies and Prevention," *Personnel,* Sept. 1987, pp. 12–17.

15. See Aaron Groff Cohen and Barbara Gutek, "Dimensions of Perceptions of Social-Sexual Behavior in a Work Setting," *Sex Roles,* vol. 13, nos. 5–6 (1985), pp. 317–27; and Beth Schneider, "Consciousness About Sexual Harassment Among Heterosexual and

Lesbian Women Workers," *Journal of Social Issues,* vol. 38, no. 4 (1982), pp. 75–98.

16. Gutek, "Sexuality in the Workplace," p. 57.
17. As Joan Acker notes, even feminist perspectives on organization tend to reproduce some version of this dichotomy: "Some of the best feminist attempts to theorize about gender and organizations have been trapped within the constraints of definitions of the theoretical domain that cast organizations as gender neutral and asexual." See Acker, "Hierarchies, Jobs, Bodies: A Theory of Gendered Organizations," *Gender and Society,* vol. 4, no. 2 (1990), p. 144.
18. See, for example, Roger E. Quinn, "Coping with Cupid: The Formation, Impact, and Management of Romantic Relationships in Organizations," *Administrative Science Quarterly,* vol. 22 (1977), pp. 30–45. See also Burrell and Hearn, "The Sexuality of Organization," pp. 20–21.
19. As Carole Pateman notes, the "public" and the "private" are the central categories of patriarchal-liberal society, and our culture tends to divide social space along these lines. "The public sphere, and the principles that govern it, are seen as separate from, or independent of, the relationships in the private sphere." See Pateman, "Feminist Critiques of the Public/Private Dichotomy," in S. I. Benn and G. F. Gauss, eds., *Public and Private in Social Life* (New York: St. Martin's, 1983), p. 282.
20. Although I did not study lesbian professionals in a systematic way, anecdotal evidence suggests that they differ from gay men in their relationship to the asexual imperative. For professional women, decisions about maternity and concerns about sexual harassment may tend to heighten their awareness of sexuality in the workplace, breaking down the imagined bifurcation of the world into private and professional spheres. (For example, for a discussion of pregnancy as a sexualized status in the workplace, see Sheppard, "Organizations, Power, and Sexuality," pp. 151–53.) A fruitful topic for future research would be the different ways lesbians and gay men conceptualize these domains.
21. The "asexual organization" is the product of several converging historical and ideological developments. Our prevailing model of "professional" behavior is the product of legal, medical, and religious discourse; Western notions about the distinction between public and private behavior; the domestication of sexuality; and ideologies about rational bureaucratic organization. Its roots can be found in

the paleobureaucracies of medieval Catholicism and the Quaker prisons, workhouses and schools of the seventeenth and eighteenth centuries (see Burrell, "Sex and Organizational Analysis," pp. 97–118); in Western, patriarchal-liberal notions of "privacy" (see Pateman, "Feminist Critiques," pp. 281–303; Jean Bethke Elshtain, *Public Man, Private Woman* [Princeton: Princeton University Press, 1981]; Jeffrey Weeks, *Against Nature: Essays on History, Sexuality and Identity* [London: Rivers Oram, 1981]); in the Puritan restriction of sexuality to procreation and the domestic sphere (see John D'Emilio and Estelle Freedman, *Intimate Matters* [New York: Harper & Row, 1988]; Michèle Barrett and Mary McIntosh, *The Anti-Social Family* [London: Verso, 1982]); and later in Weberian theories of the rational, impersonal bureaucracy (see David F. Greenberg, *The Construction of Homosexuality*).

22. The unthinking tendency to regard sexuality as a paradigmatically private activity can be found in countless essays about sexuality and civil rights. For example, in *Nobody's Business* (New York: Addison-Wesley, 1990), Alida Brill offers this criticism of a gay pride march: "What was wrong with the picture of that spring day? These citizens were undeniably exercising their legitimate rights to speech, to protest, to assembly. Yet there, on the streets, they were also giving up a part of themselves, that most intimate, and in some ways most sacred, part of all humans. They were voluntarily revealing the identity of their sexual souls. . . . This was not the same as a march for the right to vote or to engage in other public activities. Taking to the streets to announce openly and publicly that most inherently private aspect of life—a person's bedroom behavior—they represented a striking paradox" (p. 23). Brill never pauses to question the received wisdom that sexuality is inherently private, intimate, and sacred. For a more philosophical defense of this position, see Richard Mohr's discussion of the "inherent privacy" of sex in *Gays/Justice: A Study of Ethics, Society, and Law* (New York: Columbia University Press, 1987), pp. 94–126.

23. Woods, "Self-Disclosure at Work," pp. 87–88.

24. In one of a series of studies about self-disclosure, Sidney M. Jourard asked eighty female college students to rate twenty conversational topics according to their "intimacy value." The item with the highest intimacy value was "How often I have sexual experiences and the nature of these experiences," followed by "The things in my past or present life about which I am most ashamed" and "The kind of per-

son with whom I would like to have sexual experiences." The items with the lowest intimacy value involved favorite subjects for study, the types of play and recreation enjoyed, and favorite literature, TV shows, and radio programs. See Jourard, *Self-Disclosure: An Experimental Analysis of the Transparent* (New York: Wiley-Interscience, 1971), p. 214.

25. During the interviews, one of our participants, Geoff, explicitly acknowledged the paradox of discussing his sexual life with two total strangers. Asked how much he knew about the sexuality of his coworkers, he replied: "I don't want to get all that close to them. I have a real problem with people knowing that much about me." He paused for a moment, and laughed. "In fact, it's very strange to me, even doing this interview, but I'll never see you guys again, so it doesn't matter."

26. Woods, "Self-Disclosure at Work," pp. 87–88.

27. Patrick invoked the relevance criterion several years ago, while working as a manager in a local department store. Patrick had been told that one of the salesclerks was spreading rumors about his sexuality. "This part-time salesperson (who I think was a huge queen himself) said to someone else, 'He's queer; he's queer as a three-dollar bill.' I overheard it, and I was furious. Working in retail, everyone's gay, but I was closeted there. So I confronted him. I said, 'André, is there something you wanted to say to me?' and he said, 'No, what are you talking about?' I said, 'I'll bet you three dollars that there is.' I said, 'My personal life is none of your fucking business. And if you don't like it, that's too bad. You can transfer to another department or quit.' We never talked about that or much else again."

28. As Deborah Sheppard has observed, advice literature for professional women devotes considerable detail to the control or suppression of female sexuality in work environments. In order to succeed, women are advised to "desexualize" their dress, office decor, and speech. See Sheppard, "Organizations, Power and Sexuality," p. 150.

29. Barbara Gutek's study of professional women found, for example, that most would be insulted by a sexual overture from a man at work (though they imagined that other women would be flattered). As Gutek points out, however, fewer jobs require men to be physically attractive. The backhanded compliment or sexual overture is undoubtedly more insulting and threatening to women because they have traditionally been viewed as sexual objects in a way that heterosexual men have not. See Gutek, "Sexuality in the Workplace," p. 66. In this

respect, women and gay men have much in common; all are judged in terms of an (exaggerated) sexuality that tends to eclipse their other accomplishments. See also Sheppard, "Organizations, Power and Sexuality," pp. 139–57; and Adrienne Rich, "Compulsory Sexuality and Lesbian Existence," *Signs,* vol. 5, no. 4 (1980), pp. 631–60.

30. See, for example, Wendy Parkin's discussion of residential health care organizations. As she notes, these organizations, often called "homes," occupy a sort of intermediate zone, and incorporate elements of both the public world of professional work and the private world of sexuality and the family. See Parkin, "Private Experiences in the Public Domain: Sexuality and Residential Care Organizations," in Hearn et al., *The Sexuality of Organization,* pp. 110–24.

31. According to Greenberg, this is why organizations like the military and the church have shown such an exceptional preoccupation with homosexuality in their ranks. See Greenberg, *The Construction of Homosexuality,* pp. 443–45.

Chapter 3: The Sexual Double Standard

1. As Kath Weston observed in her study of kinship in the lesbian and gay community: "A relative's first reaction [when a lesbian or gay man came out] was often to question this 'change.' Could this be a case of self-delusion? A 'phase'? The person coming out frequently responded by presenting gayness as an essential identity, something that had been there all along but was only recently recognized, a development that made sense of past experiences, like pieces of a puzzle falling into place." See Weston, *Families We Choose: Lesbians, Gays, Kinship* (New York: Columbia University Press, 1991), p. 79.

2. In their 1979 survey, Karla Jay and Allen Young asked gay men if "most people can tell instantly that you are gay?" While a few (5 percent) responded that they could, the majority (78 percent) assumed that they could not. (The remaining 17 percent were not sure). See Karla Jay and Allen Young, *The Gay Report* (New York: Summit, 1979).

3. Andrew Sullivan's appointment as editor of the *New Republic,* in the fall of 1991, is another case in point. Shortly after his promotion, there was a flurry of press coverage, much of which framed Sullivan as an "unlikely" or "surprising" choice as editor. With few exceptions, the "surprise" seemed to be his age (twenty-eight years), and the fact that he was "openly" or "admittedly" gay. See also Joseph A.

DeVito, "Educational Responsibilities to Gay Male and Lesbian Students," in James Chesebro, ed., *Gayspeak: Gay Male & Lesbian Communication* (New York: Pilgrim, 1981), p. 203.

4. In her influential essay "Compulsory Heterosexuality and Lesbian Existence," Adrienne Rich describes the ability of this presumption to render lesbians invisible: "The assumption that 'most women are innately heterosexual' stands as a theoretical and political stumbling block for many women. It remains a tenable assumption, partly because lesbian existence has been written out of history or catalogued under disease; partly because it has been treated as exceptional rather than intrinsic; partly because to acknowledge that for women heterosexuality may not be a 'preference' at all but something that has had to be imposed, managed, organized, propagandized, and maintained by force, is an immense step to take if you consider yourself freely and 'innately' heterosexual." See Rich, "Compulsory Heterosexuality," p. 648.

5. Sol Worth and Larry Gross have used the term "non-sign event" to describe a phenomenon that, because it conveys no new information, is perceived and processed without conscious thought. See Worth and Gross, "Symbolic Strategies," in Gross, ed., *Studying Visual Communication* (Philadelphia: University of Pennsylvania Press, 1981), pp. 134–46.

6. In "Sexuality in the Workplace," Gutek suggests another explanation for the belief that sexuality is private. Drawing on a survey of 1,232 working people in Los Angeles, she suggests that "people tend to think positively about sex; sexual encounters affirm one's sexual desirability and probably indicate that the two people are interested in each other and perhaps already intimate" (p. 58). My own research does not support Gutek's conclusion that most professionals view sexual behavior as something "benign or even positive" (and thus extra-organizational), though this may merely reflect self-evident differences in our research populations. The gay men I interviewed were more circumspect about sex; it was a source of complications and risks, something expected to provoke the censure of others, an indulgence that brought with it a sort of guilty pleasure.

7. Acker, "Hierarchies, Jobs, Bodies," p. 151.

8. Acker has argued that even our notion of "a job"—an abstraction that distinguishes workers from the work processes they dominate—conceals an implicit masculine ethic. Ibid., p. 154.

9. In their study of a factory in the UK, David and Margaret Collinson draw this conclusion: "The evidence indicates that so long as women

were excluded from the shop floor, men's discourses about sexuality, their initiation ceremonies, practical jokes and banter, and displays of 'pin ups' and other pornographic literature were tacitly accepted by managers who could see no major incompatibility between these demonstrations of masculinity and production." See Collinson and Collinson, "Sexuality in the Workplace: The Domination of Men's Sexuality," in Hearn et al., *The Sexuality of Organization,* p. 98.

10. See Acker, "Hierarchies, Jobs, Bodies," p. 142. Richard Dyer has made the same point about race in "White," *Screen,* vol. 29, no. 4 (1989), pp. 44–65.

11. Gutek, "Sexuality in the Workplace," p. 62. See also Jeff Hearn, "Men's Sexuality at Work," in A. Metcalf and M. Humphries, eds., *The Sexuality of Men* (London: Pluto, 1985), pp. 110–28.

12. Gregory M. Herek, "The Context of Anti-Gay Violence: Notes on Cultural and Psychological Heterosexism," *Journal of Interpersonal Violence,* vol. 5, no. 3 (1990), p. 321. See also Weston, *Families We Choose.*

13. The same double standard seems to inform these comments by Seymour Kleinberg: "Like prostitutes, who are most tolerated when they are off the street and behind red lights, homosexuals create anxieties of critical proportions when they insist on being seen and heard. Even people with no special distaste for gays ask why they have to be confronted with gay sexual lifestyle. *I would guess that these people consider heterosexual displays in public just as vulgar and intrusive as homosexual ones.* A longstanding tradition unites decorum and sexual oppression; some people don't want any dissemination of sexual information—of any sort, at any time—outside the bedroom. *Their fear of sexuality may be far more intense than their fear of homosexuals"* (p. 71; emphasis mine). Kleinberg is right, of course, when he says that some people categorically disapprove of sexual displays, but this only returns us to the ambiguity of the category; people who fear any display of sexuality would likely ignore a man and woman holding hands, even as they would be shocked by the sight of two men embracing. See Kleinberg, *Alienated Affections* (New York: St. Martin's, 1980).

14. For a discussion of the "symbolic interactionist" approach to the category of sexuality (and homosexuality in particular), see Kenneth Plummer, ed., *The Making of the Modern Homosexual* (London: Hutchinson, 1975).

15. For example, intramural affairs among heterosexuals are also kept under wraps, especially when either coworker is married. Martin remembers a man and woman at his agency who kept their relationship (and shared apartment), a secret for almost two years, until they finally announced an engagement. Al, a Philadelphia attorney, works with a secretary who became romantically involved with one of the senior partners in his firm. When she became pregnant, there was a deafening silence about her increasingly obvious condition. "She stayed at work through her pregnancy," Al recalls. "Everyone knew they were seeing each other, and everyone knew he was still married to this other associate. People talked about it very cautiously. Nobody was particularly condemnatory, nobody was particularly enthusiastic about it. They just sort of walked around it very carefully. And when his divorce came through and they got married, there was a little congratulatory note in the firm bulletin."

16. Gayle Rubin, "Thinking Sex," in Carole Vance, ed., *Pleasure and Danger: Exploring Female Sexuality* (London: Routledge & Kegan Paul, 1984), p. 279.

17. I owe these observations, about the significance of numbers in work settings, to Rosabeth Moss Kanter, *Men and Women of the Corporation* (New York: Basic Books, 1977), pp. 206–41. See also Kanter and Barry Stein, *A Tale of "O": On Being Different in an Organization* (New York: Harper & Row, 1980).

18. We might also ponder the metaphors implicit in the frequent remarks: "I don't want to rub their noses in it," and "I don't want to shove it down their throats."

19. My discussion follows Kanter's description of this effect with respect to gender. See Kanter, *Men and Women,* especially pp. 210–12.

20. Weeks, *Sexuality and Its Discontents,* p. 221.

21. In her study of female managers, Sheppard identified a similar predicament faced by professional women. As she observes, in male-dominated environments women's sexuality can become a sort of "master trait" that overrides their professional capabilities or organizational status. See Sheppard, "Organizations, Power and Sexuality," p. 154.

22. As Adam has demonstrated, the stereotype of hypersexuality has been applied to other "inferiorized" groups, notably Jews and blacks. See Adam, *The Survival of Domination,* pp. 44–46.

23. Hall, "Private Experiences," p. 125.

24. In *Families We Choose,* Weston cites a typical example of this tendency. One of Weston's informants, a lesbian she calls Misha Ben Nun, found herself in a conversation with her father during which he asked specific questions about her sexual activity: Had she ever kissed a man, touched a man, or had any other sort of heterosexual contact? Misha's response was to talk about the community of women she had found in San Francisco, attempting "to move the discussion in the direction of friendship and kinship, but her father insisted on reducing sexual identity to a matter of sex. When her father elevated (hetero)sexual activity to a signifier of sexual identity by asking Misha if she had had sex with a man, he mixed erotic with nonerotic forms of love" (p. 94).

25. In a *Gaysweek* editorial, David Rothenberg (1979) offered a protest against this tendency: "Someone recently commented to me that gays keep announcing what they do in bed. He then asked, 'Wouldn't it be embarrassing for heterosexuals to do the same?' Another myth. I never tell anyone what I do in bed when I state that I am gay. When a candidate for office parades wife and children into a TV commercial, he is 'coming out' to me as a heterosexual. When a man nibbles on a woman's ear in the seat in front of me at a theater, he is 'coming out' while 'coming on' " (p. 19). In a letter to the *Village Voice* (April 24, 1990), Vito Russo made a similar point: "When I say my brother and his wife are heterosexual, that doesn't mean I'm talking about their sex lives. Likewise, when we say someone is gay, we're talking about *sexual orientation,* not their sexual activity. It's not our fault that every time someone says 'gay,' people think 'sex.' That's *their* twisted problem" (p. 4).

26. In an analogous fashion, mainstream journalism employs the principle of "privacy" to justify the traditional invisibility of lesbians and gay men in the mass media. See Larry Gross, *The Contested Closet: The Politics and Ethics of Outing* (Minneapolis: University of Minnesota Press, 1993).

27. In his study of English chairpersons, Crew offers this analysis of the double standard: "Only a member of the ruling class could enjoy the luxury of saying, 'I am no more concerned with the sex life of my faculty than I am with what brand of underwear they wear, and I would consider their flaunting of either in equally bad taste.' The key here is the word *flaunting.* The heterosexual dictators of our culture have so defined our way of life that heterosexual references to one's wife, husband, children, even in the most academic of settings, are not consid-

ered *flaunting;* yet let a gay professor just quietly place a picture of her wife or his husband on the desk in the office like anyone else . . ." (ellipses his). See Crew, "Before Emancipation," p. 19.

28. This ideal is in striking contrast with the vision of organizational life presented on television. In prime time depictions of professional situations, coworkers are often linked by personal, romantic, and marital ties, and treat one another as a sort of extended "family." As Leah Vande Berg and Nick Trujillo observe in *Organizational Life on Television* (New York: Ablex, 1989), prime time programming "teaches us that it is extremely difficult to separate one's personal life from one's professional life. After all, most prime time organizational members, including managers, professionals, operatives, and service workers alike treat their work as far more than a mere job—it is an important part of who they are" (p. 258).

29. See the definition supplied by Raymond Williams, *Keywords* (New York: Oxford University Press, 1977), pp. 144–46.

30. The point is derived from Jean Lipman-Blumen's discussion of ideology, which continues: "In addition to providing explanations for life's contradictions, institutional ideologies suggest several approaches for dealing with existential paradoxes: accept them as proof of a better life in the hereafter; accept them because they are rooted in human nature; accept them as necessary for the 'collective good'; accept them because they are traditional and unchangeable. This is the message woven into the very fabric of our major ideologies." See Lipman-Blumen, *Gender Roles and Power* (Englewood Cliffs, NJ: Prentice-Hall, 1984), p. 18.

31. For a discussion of the gap between myth and demographic reality in the case of family structure, parental roles, and reproduction, see Stephanie Coontz, *The Way We Never Were: American Families and the Nostalgia Trap* (New York: Basic Books, 1992).

32. See R. W. Connell, *Gender and Power* (Stanford, CA: Stanford University Press, 1987).

33. Michael Denneny, "Chasing the Crossover Audience and Other Self-Defeating Strategies," *Out/Look,* vol. 4 (1989), p. 19.

Chapter 4: Playing It Straight

1. In Orthodox Jewish culture, for example, there is the custom of showing evidence (i.e. bloody sheets) after the wedding night to demonstrate that the couple has consummated the marriage and to

verify the bride's prior virginity. In the novel *Yentl,* by Isaac Bashevis Singer, the groom (who is actually a woman, played in the film by Barbra Streisand) substitutes a cup of red wine. In contemporary settings, however, only the most extraordinary circumstances require that actual sex be performed for the direct inspection of one's public. In some fraternity initiation rites, for example, there is the requirement that one have sex during the ceremony, fully observed by the elder members. However, in most cases it is not sexual performance but sexual enthusiasm and interest that are on display in such rituals, both of which can be faked. (Or, as I discovered during such an initiation, one can accept the lesser humiliation of simply passing out).

2. In *The Survival of Domination,* Adam supplies this composite portrait of the person (whether black, Jewish, or homosexual) who passes: " 'Passing' represents an escape from identity which is not bad faith, but duplicity. It is an escape from identity more for the other than for the self. Allegiance to dominant norms is paid by 'lip service'; a compliant facade is adopted to facilitate social interaction. The actor is likely to be somewhat integrated into the subordinated community; his denial of identity continues on a part-time or ambivalent basis. To other inferiorized people, the actor reveals a more 'authentic' identity, discarding a pseudo-identity constructed for superordinate audiences. The former identity is experienced 'at ease'; the latter is inhibited—an act" (p. 95–96).

3. Fifteen of our seventy participants were currently using counterfeiting strategies at work. Eight men were using them exclusively, while seven were using them in combination with other strategies. As a group the men who counterfeited were demographically similar to those who did not. They ranged in age from twenty-seven to sixty and were at different levels of their organizations' hierarchies. All worked for companies, with two exceptions (both of whom were medical residents). Two were currently married. See Table 2 for a more detailed description of the sample.

4. Woods, "Self-Disclosure at Work," pp. 87–88. There are several reasons to conclude that this figure underrepresents the number of men who actually use this tactic to counterfeit an identity. First, there is inevitably a bias against reporting activities, perceived by many to be deceptive or dishonest, to two researchers who are themselves openly gay. There is also the likelihood that this particular sample—a self-selected group of men who read a gay political magazine and who bothered to complete and return a questionnaire about self-

disclosure—are not representative of the larger gay population. Indeed, the demographics of the *Out/Look* sample suggest that these findings must be generalized with caution. When contrasted with the general population, for example, the sample was highly educated (44 percent reported completing some kind of graduate school, while 22 percent currently worked for an educational institution) and likely to be openly gay at work (64 percent were out to "all" or "most" of their coworkers). As a group they are probably more liberal and politically conscious than their lesbian and gay peers.

5. An episode (Sept. 1991) of "Designing Women" dramatized these same assumptions. The narrative revolved around Julia's new boyfriend, a man whose effeminate behavior led the other characters to assume that he was gay. As it turned out, to the amusement of all, he was not.

6. Richard Dyer, "Believing in Fairies: The Author and the Homosexual," in Diana Fuss, ed., *Inside/Out: Lesbian Theories, Gay Theories* (New York: Routledge, 1991), p. 199.

7. Alfred Kinsey and his associates estimated, for example, that only about one in seven males homosexuals, and one in twenty female homosexuals, are recognizable as such to the general public. See Kinsey, *Sexual Behavior in the Human Male* (New York: W. B. Saunders, 1948). John Alan Lee gives a slightly higher estimate: "As a visit to any gay bar will demonstrate, something less than 20% of all homosexuals fit into that stereotype." See Lee, "Going Public: A Study in the Sociology of Homosexual Liberation," *Journal of Homosexuality*, vol. 3, no. 1, 1977, p. 75.

8. Goffman gives the example of educated blacks who speak "good English" when visiting the rural South, the illiterate who wear eyeglasses, or vagrants who appear to read a newspaper in Grand Central terminal to avoid being molested by the police. See Goffman, *Stigma*, p. 44.

9. In her study of lesbian professionals, Hall describes several situations in which a woman's heterosexual cover fell apart, often because she failed adequately to censor her speech or outward appearance. "Even though the nondisclosure of their homosexuality was crucial, several respondents felt the secret was not always within their control. For example, one woman was showing a friend from work the plans of the new house she and her lover had bought. Pointing out the main bedroom, she accidentally said, 'This is where we sleep.' She was appalled to have revealed the intimate nature of her relationship. Other

respondents felt they revealed their lesbianism through their physical appearance. A lesbian who wore jeans to a clerical job said, 'The way I dress I was in a way forcing it down their throats.' Another woman said, 'At the time they started suspecting, I made a mistake and cut my hair short. That was the tip-off.' " See Hall, "Private Experiences," p. 132.

10. In her study of lesbians, Brooks reports a relationship between stress levels and the ability to hide: "[S]tress increased for respondents as their self-perception of being discreditable (visible) increased: stress was lowest for those who believed only other gay people would think they were gay, higher for those who believed no one would think they were gay. Stress increases, then, with increased fear and anxiety regarding one's undisclosed sociosexual identity." See Brooks, *Minority Stress,* p. 100.

11. As Lee observed in his study of twenty-four gay men, "The greatest cost for those whose current social status is built around the assumption that they are heterosexual is the fear of disclosure, and with it attendant guilt and anxiety." See Lee, "Going Public," p. 61.

12. See Goffman, *Stigma,* p. 14. See also Lyman and Scott, "Paranoia, Homosexuality and Game Theory," pp. 71–88.

13. Woods, "Self-Disclosure at Work," pp. 87–88. When asked, "Which of the following influenced your decision to 'come out' at work," 62 percent of respondents checked the answer, "To avoid the hassle of misleading co-workers."

14. Jennie Livingston describes an experience that will be familiar to many: "When I was about eleven years old I figured out that people who dressed a little funny or walked too hard or too soft *got it* from the other kids, and that I was one of those. Objectionable girls were 'tomboys' or 'dogs,' and boys—before anyone really knew about homosexuality— were 'fags'. . . . We were the ones who couldn't play the gender game right. The boy who couldn't walk tough: *faggy.* The girl who spoke up too many times, too loudly, or who didn't have breasts yet: *doggy.* We didn't know exactly *why* what we were doing was wrong. But we couldn't help committing multiple acts of what was called in Margaret Atwood's *The Handmaid's Tale* 'gender treachery.' See Jennie Livingston, "The Fairer Sex," *Aperture,* vol. 121 (1990), p. 6.

15. A point made by Hall, "Private Experiences," p. 136.

16. Woods, "Self-Disclosure at Work," pp. 87–88.

17. This discussion draws on observations made by Sissela Bok, *Lying: Moral Choice in Public and Private Life* (New York: Vintage, 1978), p. 142.

18. In her study of kinship, Weston makes a similar point about the accusations lesbians and gay men often encounter because they do not form traditional families. As she notes, "Many of the gay men and lesbians I met had become adept at refuting accusations of gay selfishness and irresponsibility." See Weston, *Families We Choose*, p. 158.

19. For example, see Leon Festinger, "A Theory of Social Comparison Process," *Human Relations,* vol. 7 (1954), pp. 117–40. See also Valerian J. Derlega and Janusz Grzelak, "Appropriateness of Self-Disclosure," in Gordon J. Chelune et al., eds., *Self-Disclosure, Origins, Patterns, and Implications of Openness in Interpersonal Relationships* (Washington, DC: Jossey-Bass, 1979), p. 157.

20. Lee, "Going Public," p. 62.

21. See, for example, D. W. Cramer and A. J. Roach, "Coming Out to Mom and Dad: A Study of Gay Males and Their Relationships With Their Parents," *Journal of Homosexuality,* vol. 15, nos. 3/4 (1988), pp. 79–92; and Martin S. Weinberg and Colin J. Williams, *Male Homosexuals: Their Problems and Adaptations* (New York: Penguin, 1974).

22. F. W. Bozett, "Gay Fathers: How and Why They Disclose Their Homosexuality to Their Children," *Family Relations,* no. 29 (1980), p. 175.

23. As Adam explains, in terms of class analysis: "The identity, culture, and values of the inferiorized are to be negated (or at least concealed) for the *promise* or opportunity of improved life chances. Submission to the social rules which preserve the superordinance of the white, Gentile, heterosexual group(s) supposedly mitigates the barriers confining inferiorized existence." See Adam, *The Survival of Domination,* p. 120.

24. See Lee, "Going Public," p. 61.

25. See Larry G. Ehrlich, "The Pathogenic Secret," in James W. Chesebro, ed., *Gayspeak: Gay Male & Lesbian Communication* (New York: Pilgrim, 1981), pp. 130–41.

26. The "green question" drew a wide range of responses. One man feared that his coworkers "would probably think it was Kaposi's sarcoma," a cancer often associated with AIDS. Jerry, a Wall Street broker, laughed. "They'd probably say 'Oooh, he turned *green*. It's probably all that money." Still another group seemed most upset by the prospect of a color-coordination nightmare. "Exactly what *shade* of green?" one man asked. "Are we talking chartreuse or hunter or lime green?"

Chapter 5: Maintaining Boundaries

1. As Adam observed in his study of Jews, blacks, and gay men, such segregations are common among inferiorized groups. To deflect the hostility of some audiences while developing relationships in alternative, in-group, or community audiences, the inferiorized develop different strategies for dealing with each, "shifting from one behavior set to another as the occasion demands (p. 93)." African Americans may adopt a compliant facade in hostile settings, venting their frustration only to other African Americans. Jews may assimilate in public while preserving religious traditions in private, among friends, or in community ghettos. See Adam, *The Survival of Domination*, pp. 93–97. Likewise, it is relatively uncommon for a gay man to use only one of the three basic strategies available to him. More often he avails himself of an entire repertory of strategies and finds it fitting to use different ones in different situations.

2. The practice is a time-honored one in Hollywood. Revisionist biographies have already blown the whistle on celebrities like Rock Hudson, Cole Porter, and their female accomplices (although even in their day rumors were abundant). A more contemporary solution seems to be counterfeit marriages between lesbians and gay men, or so we hear about a number of well-known Hollywood figures. See Gross, *The Contested Closet*.

3. See Margaret Cruikshank, *The Gay and Lesbian Liberation Movement* (New York: Routledge, Chapman & Hall, 1992), chapter 5. See also John D'Emilio, *Sexual Politics, Sexual Communities* (Chicago: University of Chicago Press, 1983); and Adam, *The Rise of a Gay and Lesbian Movement*.

4. Richard Mohr, *Gay Ideas: Outing and Other Controversies* (Boston: Beacon, 1992), p. 29.

5. Ibid., p. 27.

6. See D'Emilio, *Sexual Politics;* Adam, *The Rise of a Gay and Lesbian Movement;* and Cruikshank, *The Gay and Lesbian Liberation Movement*. See also Barbara Ponse, *Identities in the Lesbian World: The Social Construction of Self* (Westport, CT: Greenwood, 1976).

7. For personal recollections of this period, see Eric Marcus's oral history of the lesbian and gay movement, *Making History: The Struggle for Gay and Lesbian Equal Rights* (New York: HarperCollins, 1992).

8. See Roy Cain, "Disclosure and Secrecy among Gay Men in the

United States and Canada: A Shift in Views," *Journal of the History of Sexuality*, vol. 2, no. 1 (1991), pp. 25–45.

9. See Donald Webster Cory, "Take My Word for It," *The Homosexual in America: A Subjective Approach* (New York: Greenberg, 1951), pp. 103–13.

10. See Mohr's philosophical critique of the notion that secrecy is a "right" in *Gay Ideas*, pp. 11–48.

11. Erving Goffman, *The Presentation of Self in Everyday Life* (New York: Doubleday, 1959).

12. An interesting exception is celebrities, to whom lesbians and gay men seem to feel no corollary obligation. Perhaps because these media figures are perceived as being "apart" from the community, its members feel little responsibility to protect their (often highly visible) closets.

13. Although, as Ponse observes in her study of secrecy in the lesbian community: "The veils of anonymity are often as effective with one's own as with those from whom one wishes to hide. Thus, an unintended consequence of secrecy is that it isolates members from one another." See Ponse, *Identities in the Lesbian World*, p. 319.

14. Ibid., p. 319.

15. Ghiglione et al., *Alternatives*, p. 15.

16. Woods, "Self-Disclosure at Work," pp. 87–88.

17. As Goffman observed in his study of stigma, in addition to those who share a stigmatizing trait (the "own"), the stigmatized can usually expect support from "the wise," those who are not similarly stigmatized, but who are accorded a sort of courtesy membership in the clan. See *Stigma*, pp. 28–31.

18. Woods, "Self-Disclosure at Work," pp. 87–88.

19. The assumption of in-group solidarity was evident in a 1992 ad for the Gay and Lesbian Victory Fund, a fundraising organization committed to the election of lesbian and gay politicians. The ad featured a photograph of California governor Pete Wilson, who had recently vetoed a state bill that would have outlawed employment discrimination against lesbians and gay men, and the text: "It's happened again. Another so-called 'friend' of the gay and lesbian community has traded integrity for politics, and sacrificed our rights for political expediency. Once again, we've learned. The only people our community can *really* count on to stand by us are lesbian and gay people themselves." See *Advocate*, vol. 595, Jan. 28, 1992, p. 6.

20. Even for men who are openly gay, questions of loyalty and access can present problems. Roland, for example, feels that he has a "discipline problem" with an openly gay assistant in the advertising agency at which he is the creative director. "I think he takes advantage of the fact that we're both gay, like we're soul sisters or something. I mean, he's very flamboyant in the office, and I personally find that out of character at work. He's making a lot of conversation about his boyfriend and this and that, and I don't see any need to slap it around in front of everyone's face. But he gets that way, and then he manipulates me; he'll come in crying because something happened last night." For Roland this is a breach of office etiquette and an attempt to abuse his loyalty. "I'm *not* his best friend," Roland says. "I don't want him to come in and take advantage of me that way. No one else comes in complaining about their personal problems, so we shouldn't either."

21. The rift has its roots in the earliest years of gay liberation, predating by several decades the current controversies about self-disclosure and exposure. As Ponse observed in 1976, "Over the past several years, with the advent of both gay liberation and the rise of the feminist movement, there has been increasing resentment against the structures of secrecy. An ethos of openness has been developing in certain parts of the gay community." See Ponse, *Identities in the Lesbian World*, p. 334.

22. For example, for a discussion of the debate over the "outing" controversy, see Gross, *The Contested Closet*.

23. As one of Jay and Young's respondents says, one of the attractions of the closet "is the very secrecy of it, the mischief of a secret club, of being what most people are afraid to be . . . I think some of the joy of homosexuality is its deviousness" (*The Gay Report*, p. 160). These comments are also in line with Georg Simmel's observations about the intensity of relationships between secret sharers. See Simmel, *The Sociology of Georg Simmel*, ed. and trans. K. H. Wolff (New York: Free Press, 1950), p. 360.

24. Steve once teased a coworker by threatening to defect. "I met him through a mutual friend who said, 'This is a friend of mine, Glen.' So Glen and I were standing there making small talk and he said, 'Where do you work?' and I said 'United Savings.' He got this big smile on his face." The two men became friends and sometimes ran into one another in the office. As it turned out, Glen had appeared

in a local gay magazine, *Sweat*. "His picture was in one of the gay publications," Steve recalls. "One time we were riding the elevator together, and this lady was in it with us. Glen is a very nice-looking man, very macho, and I looked at him and said, 'So, have you done any more modeling lately?' Later he said, 'I'm going to *kill* you!' "

25. The point is made most forcefully by Mohr in *Gay Ideas,* pp. 11–48.
26. This sort of in-group hostility has long characterized the community. In the first major ethnography of the gay community, published in 1956, Maurice Leznoff and William A. Westley interviewed sixty gay Canadians, whom they then categorized as either "secret" or "overt." The former group feared public exposure, and refused to associate with the latter, for whom exposure was far less of a concern. As one of the "secret" homosexuals explained:

> If someone who is gay wanted to be spiteful they could say something in the wrong quarter. Nobody who cared about himself would say anything. The trouble is that some don't care. I make it a rule to avoid anybody who is perfectly open about himself. It's easy not to become friendly with those people but it's hard to avoid them entirely. You certainly don't want to snub them because that might make them antagonistic. You just don't call them or see them at social gatherings. But you do meet them at bars and that's where you can be introduced to them. If they remember you and continue to say hello to you on the street, you have to acknowledge them or they might feel that you are trying to snub them (p. 260).

The result, according to Leznoff and Westley, was mistrust and hostility between the secret and overt groups. The secret group, intent upon maintaining secrecy, kept their distance from the more overt members of the community. See Leznoff and Westley, "The Homosexual Community," *Social Problems,* vol. 3, no. 4 (1956), pp. 257–63.

27. As Ponse observed in her study of lesbians, women who maintained different degrees of secrecy with different groups often found it unsettling to make the transition, especially when the difference was greatest. Women who were activists in one context, while maintaining secrecy in another were troubled by feelings of disloyalty. "Being secretive among one's friends and at the same time an activist in the gay community was experienced as dissonant by these women." See Ponse, *Identities in the Lesbian World,* p. 328.

Chapter 6: Dodging the Issue

1. Avoidance strategies are perhaps the most common strategies used by gay professionals. More than half of our participants (59 percent) used them at work, sometimes in combination with either counterfeiting (10 percent) or integration (16 percent). One in three men (33 percent) used avoidance strategies exclusively.

2. I should distinguish my use of the term *avoidance,* which concerns the construction of social identities, from another usage that refers to the subjective formation of sexual self-concepts. In several identity-stage models, psychologists and sociologists have described a process by which same-sex interests or experiences are suppressed or "avoided." This kind of avoidance takes several forms, including the inhibition of same-sex interests, the curtailment of exposure to opposite-sex peers, or the adoption of antihomosexual postures. See Richard R. Troiden, *Gay and Lesbian Identity: A Sociological Analysis* (Dix Hills, NY: General Hall, 1988), pp. 47–49. See also Vivienne C. Cass, "Homosexual Identity: A Concept in Need of Definition," *Journal of Homosexuality,* vol. 9, nos. 2–3 (1979), pp. 105–26.

3. See Derlega and Grzelak, "Appropriateness of Self-Disclosure," p. 163.

4. For a discussion of the "reciprocity effect," see Richard Archer, "Role of Personality and the Social Situation," in Gordon Chelune et al., eds., *Self-Disclosure: Origins, Patterns, and Implications of Openness in Interpersonal Relationships* (San Francisco: Jossey-Bass, 1979), pp. 46–55.

5. Beth Schneider observed a similar effect in her study of working lesbians. In interviews with 228 women, she found that larger workplaces were less conducive to self-disclosure than smaller ones (though size of department had an opposite, nonsignificant effect). Although large and small organizations differ in a number of other respects, Schneider proposes that intimacy may be the intervening variable, and concludes that "the size of the organization may diminish the opportunity for the development of intimacy leading to disclosure." See Schneider, "Coming Out at Work: Bridging the Private/Public Gap," *Work and Occupations,* vol. 13, no. 4 (1987), p. 471.

6. See Hall, "Private Experiences," p. 137.

7. In *The Gay Report,* Jay and Young describe a gay man whose physical handicap seems to preclude a homosexual identity (or a heterosexual

one, for that matter). "I have muscular dystrophy," he notes, "and am disabled, so people don't expect me to be anything sexually" (p. 140).

8. The concept is described, in the context of the mass media, in Elisabeth Noelle-Neumann, "The Spiral of Silence: A Theory of Public Opinion," *Journal of Communication*, vol. 24, no. 2 (1974), pp. 43–51. On the subject of social withdrawal and ambiguity, see also Andrew Hodges and David Hutter, *With Downcast Gays: Aspects of Homosexual Self-Oppression* (Toronto: Pink Triangle Press, 1974).

9. Ponse, *Identities in the Lesbian World*, p. 323.

10. Ibid.

11. Woods, "Self-Disclosure at Work," pp. 87–88.

Chapter 7: Coming Out, Moving On

1. In Goffman's language, he is no longer one of the "discreditable" who attempts to withhold "information about the failing." By revealing his secret, he becomes one of the "discredited" who manages instead the "tension generated during social contacts." See Goffman, *Stigma*, p. 42.

2. A third (30 percent) of the men were using integration strategies exclusively, making their sexuality known across the board to bosses, peers, clients, and others. A smaller group (16 percent) used integration strategies with some coworkers while using avoidance tactics with others. Only one of the men was simultaneously counterfeiting, avoiding, and integrating at work. See Table 1 in the Appendix for details.

3. Woods, "Self-Disclosure at Work," pp. 87–88. Contrast these figures to the 38 percent of *Out/Look* readers who claimed, in an earlier survey, that they were "out" to all of their coworkers. See "Coming Out: The Results," *Out/Look*, vol. 10 (1990), p. 86.

4. Weston, *Families We Choose*, p. 67.

5. In his study of gay fathers, Bozett found that some sort of "external" event was usually necessary to motivate a personal disclosure. "No matter how much the gay father wants to make known his 'real self,' this desire alone is usually insufficient to provoke direct disclosure. In most instances he needs an external, social condition to serve as a motivating force and as a vehicle for his disclosure. In this way disclosure of the gay identity becomes part of a larger topic, rather than being the topic itself" (p. 176). Only one of Bozett's eighteen partic-

ipants disclosed to his child directly, without being prompted by an external event. The situations that most commonly supplied an opportunity for disclosure were the father's divorce from the mother and his development of a committed relationship with another man. "Had these social events not occurred, the fathers would not have disclosed, or at least they would not have disclosed when they did" (p. 176–77). See Bozett, "Gay Fathers," pp. 173–79.

6. Troiden describes a strategy that incorporates elements of what I call "minimizing" and "normalizing" (in the section that follows): "Women and men who *cover* are ready to admit that they are homosexual (often because it is obvious or known), but nonetheless take great pains to keep their homosexuality from looming large. They manage their homosexuality in ways meant to demonstrate that although they may be homosexual, they are nonetheless respectable." *Gay and Lesbian Identity,* p. 56.

7. Seymour Sarason, "Jewishness, Blackness, and the Nature-Nurture Controversy," *American Psychologist,* vol. 28 (1973), pp. 962–71.

8. Kanter, *Men and Women,* p. 220.

9. At times the desire for balance seems to give these conversations a mechanical, give-and-take quality. Chuck recalls a conversation in which his own disclosure was directly prompted by a coworker's revelations about his own life. While having dinner with one of the bank's summer interns, he decided it was appropriate to raise the issue. "This kid kept saying, 'There's something I have to tell you, something real important that I have to tell you. But I'd feel better if you told me something about yourself first, because I feel that you're kind of holding things in.' So I thought, 'He's a little younger, maybe he's trying to tell me that he's gay and wants me to tell him that I am first.' So I did. I said, 'Okay, well, I'm gay.' He told me that he thought I was before I said that, but that wasn't what he had to tell me. As it turned out, it was something totally wacko." In this scenario a personal revelation was motivated by an equivalent revelation (or at least the anticipation of one).

10. Barbara Ponse has described women who "aristocratize" homosexual behavior, attaching special significance to homosexual experiences. See Ponse, "Lesbians and Their Worlds," in Judd Marmor, ed., *Homosexual Behavior: A Modern Reappraisal* (New York: Basic Books, 1980), pp. 157–75.

11. See Goffman, *Stigma,* p. 114.

12. See Lee Badgett, "Labor Market Discrimination: Economic and

Legal Issues for Gay Men and Lesbians" (Paper delivered at the Annual Meeting of the American Economic Association, New Orleans, Jan. 3, 1992.) A similar argument was used by Michael J. Bowers, the Georgia Attorney General after he rescinded a job offer to Robin Joy Shahar, a lesbian attorney. See Tamar Lewin, "Judge Affirms Suit by Lesbian over Withdrawal of Job Offer," *New York Times,* March 11, 1992, p. A16.

13. The level of homophobia in a workplace is directly correlated with the strategy choices of its gay employees. (Note that because men often use more than one strategy, the following percentages do not total 100. See Table 2 in the Appendix.) In our own sample, men who had witnessed frequent and specific instances of homophobia (13 men, or 19 percent of the sample) were most likely to counterfeit (54 percent) and avoid (31 percent). Only three of these men (23 percent) used integration strategies. By contrast, men who had witnessed only occasional displays of homophobia (24 men, or 34 percent of the sample) were clustered toward the right of the continuum. These men tended to use avoidance (63 percent) or integration (50 percent) strategies, while a handful used counterfeiting strategies (17 percent). Finally, among those who had witnessed no explicit displays of homophobia in the workplace (33 men, or 47 percent of the sample), the most common strategies were avoidance (67 percent) and integration (52 percent). Only four (12 percent) of these men used counterfeiting strategies at work.

Likewise, men who considered themselves highly vulnerable to being fired or penalized in some other way (21 men, or 30 percent of the sample) tended to use avoidance (62 percent) or counterfeiting (38 percent) strategies, although almost a third (29 percent) used integration strategies. The reverse pattern was observed among men who thought they were only moderately vulnerable (19 percent of the sample), who tended to favor avoidance (70 percent) or integration (46 percent) strategies, with a small number who were counterfeiting (23 percent). Finally, men who thought they would be relatively difficult to fire or penalize (51 percent of the sample) were clustered toward the right of the continuum, using integration (56 percent), avoidance (53 percent), and only occasionally, counterfeiting (11 percent).

These findings are consistent with other reports that have identified a relationship between perceived job security and level of self-disclosure. In her study of 228 professional lesbians, for example,

Schneider found that women who had been fired from a previous job after revealing their lesbianism were 50 percent less likely to come out in subsequent jobs (p. 481). See Schneider, "Coming Out at Work," pp. 463–87. Similarly, Alan P. Bell and Martin S. Weinberg's respondents exercised considerable discretion in disclosing their sexuality to co-workers, and most appeared reluctant to "come out" at work for one of two reasons: fear of endangering job credibility or effectiveness, or fear of job or income loss. See Bell and Weinberg, *Homosexualities: A Study of Diversity Among Men and Women* (New York: Simon & Schuster, 1978).

In their much earlier report Leznoff and Westley reported a similar link between work environment and self-disclosure. Men whom they categorized as "overt" here typically "persons of low socioeconomic status who have jobs where concealment is not a prerequisite" (p. 262). Most were employed either as artists and beauticians, occupations that had "traditionally accepted homosexual linkages in the popular image," or as waiters and servicepeople, fields that "are of such low rank as to permit homosexuals to function on the job." Of the thirteen men with professional jobs, all fell into the category of "secret" homosexual. Though the authors were unable to specify the direction of the influence, they observe that there is "a rough relationship between form of evasion and occupation" (p. 260). See Leznoff and Westley, "The Homosexual Community," pp. 257–63.

14. A strong and supportive boss can also be a source of security. Carter remembers a former job in a Florida hotel: "The owner was gay, and he lived in the penthouse. That's when I really came out. He introduced me to all these rich queens in Florida, who were just dying to meet a new person, an American—the Latin influence is so strong down there. I was real popular, I was new, and I worked for somebody that they liked and respected. That really helped me deal with it, knowing that they couldn't get too down on me at work, because the head guy was gay. He had a lover and all that. But before that I had hid desperately."

15. The six men in our sample who were self-employed, and thus presumably least vulnerable, were evenly divided in their use of avoidance and integration strategies. A similar pattern can be found when one compares men who work primarily with clients to those who spend most of their time with people in their own organizations. Men whose work is centered around clients (52 percent of the sam-

ple) favored the use of avoidance (65 percent) strategies over integration (35 percent) and counterfeiting (24 percent). Conversely, men who spent most of their time with coworkers (49 percent) preferred integration (56 percent) over avoidance (53 percent) and counterfeiting (19 percent). The pattern suggests that gay men are less likely, or less able, to avoid sexual subjects with coworkers. Given the small size of the sample, however, these slight differences must be interpreted with caution. See Table 2 in the Appendix.

16. See Escoffier, "Stigmas, Work Environment," pp. 8–17.

17. Even so, gay men are more likely to come out when they are protected by a company policy. In our own sample, men who thought their employers had nondiscrimination policies (33 percent) favored integration (56 percent) and avoidance strategies (48 percent) over counterfeiting (22 percent). By contrast, when no company policy was in place, the men were clustered toward the center of the continuum, preferring avoidance (71 percent) to counterfeiting (32 percent) and integration (29 percent). Most significantly, however, when men answered that they "weren't sure" (27 percent), they tended overwhelmingly to integrate (58 percent) or avoid (53 percent); only one of these men used a counterfeiting strategy. Given these men's preference for strategies toward the right of the continuum, their ignorance of company policy may simply be a function of their indifference. See Table 2 in the Appendix.

18. Ghiglione et al., *Alternatives,* p. 18.

19. Gross and Aurand, *Violence and Discrimination,* p. 2.

20. Joseph Harry and William B. DeVall suggest that this effect, rather than sampling problems, may explain the high levels of education observed in several surveys of gay men. "Although it is possible that all of these studies suffer from the same deficiency, namely, an undersampling of less-educated male homosexuals, the fact that these studies were from a variety of time periods and places and used various methods of obtaining respondents suggests that male homosexuals probably are more educated than the general population. If this is true, it implies that male homosexuals may have several assets, in addition to their high educational levels, to offset the multiple discriminations they face in the world of work and achievement." See Harry and DeVall, *The Social Organization of Gay Males* (New York: Praeger, 1978), p. 155.

21. Chip hinted at the concerns that may lie beneath his own somewhat strict work ethic:

Most of my areas of discomfort come from feeling like a shame-based person, in that the stuff I do isn't good enough. All the intellectual stuff tells me otherwise, be it my performance reviews or the comments I get from the people I work with. But for me, hearing things like "faggot" since sixth grade, all through my upbringing, created a real sense of core shame in me. So no matter how well I do in whatever I'm doing, I still feel basically like a piece of shit. And I see that manifesting itself in the way I worry that Ron, my new boss, will think I'm a fuck-up.

22. See Adam's discussion of "compensatory overconformity" among Jews, in *The Survival of Domination,* p. 98–99.
23. The same observation has been made about lesbian professionals, who experience what Hall calls "double jeopardy" as both women and homosexuals. See Hall, "Private Experiences," pp. 125–38.
24. For example, in J. Dressler's report on gay teachers, it was those with poor teaching records who were most often disciplined after their sexuality became known. Those with stronger professional records, even in cases of apparent misconduct, were usually left alone. See Dressler, "Survey of School Principals Regarding Alleged Homosexual Teachers in the Classroom: How Likely (Really) Is Discharge?" *University of Dayton Law Review,* vol. 10, no. 3 (1985), pp. 599–620.
25. During the interviews I sometimes sensed a reluctance to speak of careers in terms of years or decades—which may be yet another casualty of the AIDS epidemic. The pervasive environment of illness and death may have discouraged long-term thinking. At times there was even the sense that such conversations would be inappropriate, even cruel. A recent party comes to mind, at which a young entrepreneur, speaking about his growing software company, stopped himself short. "I feel awkward talking about what I'll be doing in five years," he told me. "Some of these guys won't be around then."
26. This discussion draws on Kanter's analysis of tokenism, in particular as it impacts women in male-dominated environments. See Kanter, *Men and Women,* p. 209. See also Kanter and Stein, "A Tale of 'O.' "
27. Jeffrey Weeks, *Coming Out: Homosexual Politics in Britain, from the Nineteenth Century to the Present* (New York: Quartet, 1977), p. 2.
28. Woods, "Self-Disclosure at Work," pp. 87–88.
29. Several studies have identified a correlation between self-disclosure

and positive identity (although they do not resolve the obvious question of causal direction). See Patrick J. Schmitt and Lawrence A. Kurdek, "Personality Correlates of Positive Identity and Relationship Involvement in Gay Men," *Journal of Homosexuality*, vol. 13, no. 4 (1987), pp. 101–9; and G. J. McDonald, "Individual Differences in the Coming Out Process for Gay Men," *Journal of Homosexuality*, vol. 8 (1982), pp. 47–60.

30. For example, in his study of twenty-four gay Canadians, Lee found that involvement in a gay liberation organization became an important precursor of self-disclosure. "At some point in this involvement, the individual found himself in a situation where the group was an important *reference group* for the standards (ethical, moral, political) by which the individual, self-reflexively, assessed his own actions. For each individual, at the point of deciding to go public, the gay liberation movement (in the form, usually, of a specific group, and sometimes a specific individual), became a *more important* reference for behavior than the collegial, professional, or commercial group of which he was part." See Lee, "Going Public," p. 73 (emphasis his).

31. Woods, "Self-Disclosure at Work," pp. 87–88.

32. In gay circles, "girls" is sometimes used as affectionate slang for other gay men.

Chapter 8: Dismantling the Closet

1. My comments follow those made by Roosevelt Thomas, Jr., in "From Affirmative Action to Affirming Diversity," *Harvard Business Review*, vol. 68, no. 2 (1990), pp. 112–17.

2. According to U.S. Census data, in 1990 blacks accounted for 12.1 percent of the total U.S. population and 10.1 percent of the total civilian labor force but held only 6.3 percent of "managerial and professional" jobs and 9.3 percent of "technical, sales and administrative support" positions. See *Statistical Abstract of the United States*, 112th edition (Washington, DC: Government Printing Office, 1990), pp. 392–94.

3. See Henry and DeVall, *The Social Organization*, pp. 155–59.

4. Woods, "Self-Disclosure at Work," pp. 87–88. (See also note 22 in Chapter 1).

5. In her study of professional women, Kanter observed that they tended to find "their management opportunities in low uncertainty, non-discretionary positions that bear the least pressure to close the

circle: closer to the bottom, in more routinized functions, and in 'expert' rather than decision-making roles. They are also found in those areas where least social contact and organizational communication are required: in staff roles that are administrative rather than line management and in functions such as public relations, where they are removed from the interdependent social networks of the corporation's principal operations" (p. 55). See Kanter, *Men and Women.*

6. See ibid., pp. 140–55.

7. Woods, "Self-Disclosure at Work," pp. 87–88.

8. See Blumenfeld, *Homophobia,* p. 37.

9. Ibid., pp. 9–11.

10. As A. O. Hirschman demonstrated in *Exit, Voice and Loyalty: Responses to Decline in Firms, Organizations and States* (Cambridge: Harvard University Press, 1970), people tend to abandon organizations (the "exit" option) when they perceive dialogue (the "voice" option) to be too risky.

11. Several newsletters now track lesbian and gay issues in corporate environments. See, for example, *Working It Out: The Newsletter for Gay and Lesbian Employment Issues,* published by Ed Mickens, P.O. Box 2079, New York, NY, 10108. See also *The Gay/Lesbian/Bisexual Corporate Letter,* published by Arthur Bain, P.O. Box 602, Murray Hill Station, New York, NY 10156-0601. A data base of information on state and local statutes is kept by the National Gay and Lesbian Task Force Policy Institute.

12. *Fortune,* Dec. 16, p. 4.

13. See D'Emilio, *Sexual Politics.*

14. Ron Hayden, "Domestic Partnership Benefits Emerge as Corporate Trend," *The Gay/Lesbian/Bisexual Corporate Letter,* vol. 1, no. 2 (1992), pp. 3–4.

15. See Badgett, "Labor Market Discrimination"; See also Thomas, "From Affirmation Action."

16. An observation made by Ann M. Bohara and Patrick McLaurin in " 'Managing Diversity': A View from Practice" (paper presented at the 1991 Meeting of the Eastern Communication Association).

17. See M. S. Larson, *The Rise of Professionalism: A Sociological Analysis* (Berkeley: University of California Press, 1977).

18. Kanter, *Men and Women,* p. 49.

19. Cited in J. P. White, "Elsie Cross vs. The Suits: One Black Woman Is Teaching White Corporate America to Do the Right Thing," *Los Angeles Times Magazine,* Aug. 9, 1992.

20. See Thomas, "From Affirmative Action."
21. Quoted in the *New York Times,* Nov. 15, 1992, p. 22.
22. Quoted in the *New York Times,* Nov. 16, 1992, p. A10.
23. But of course the military is no less sexual than most workplaces; in all likelihood it is more so. There is a blatant sexual dimension to the military's public imagery, with its sexy, scrubbed, and ostensibly straight sailors and soldiers staring out from recruitment posters. As soldiers left for Somalia in January of 1993 the television featured a parade of images: men and women kissing their loved ones goodbye, talking about their families, waving to their children. Barracks are renowned for their lewd jokes, boasting rituals, and towel-snapping. And the Pentagon assertions notwithstanding, one can even argue that much of what the military calls "good order and discipline" is in fact the channeling and suppression of sexual impulses.

    Recent scandals have thrown cold water on some of the sexist and heterosexist assumptions that pervade military culture. At the 1991 Tailhook Association convention, an annual conference for top Navy aviators, the frat-house atmosphere culminated in a drunken revel during which 83 women (and 7 men) were assaulted, groped, pinched, bitten, and fondled; a number of women, among them several female officers, were forced to "run a gauntlet" of their male peers. In response to the Navy's claim that the scandal was an isolated incident, the Pentagon's own report made it clear that the abuses were not significantly different from those at earlier meetings–behaviors that were widely condoned by the Navy's civilian and military leaders. The report urged the disciplining of 175 navy officers who either witnessed or took part in the incident. (See Michael R. Gordon, "Pentagon Report Tells of Aviators' 'Debauchery,' " *New York Times,* April 24, 1993, p. Al.) Just a few months earlier, 1st Lt. Heidi De Jesus, stationed at Goodfellow Air Force Base in western Texas, had been charged with committing "homosexual acts" and scheduled for discharge. In her three years in the service De Jesus had received numerous positive performance reviews. Her sexual orientation had not been an issue until she was exposed by a male officer, a man whose sexual advances she had rebuffed. (See *Newsweek,* Dec. 28, 1992, p. 8). In this atmosphere, it is hard to take seriously the Pentagon's fear that it is gay soldiers who will "flaunt" their sexuality in the ranks.
24. For a more thorough discussion of Microsofts' work environment and the history of its gay, lesbian, and bisexual employee association,

see "Making Microsoft's Meritocracy Work," The Gay/Lesbian/
Bisexual Corporate letter, vol. 2, no. 1 (winter 1993), pp. 3–6.

25. Massengale estimates a $2 million sales-to-employee ratio over a 7-
year period, which is the basis for this figure.

26. In the November 1992 election, both Oregon and Colorado voted
on referendums that would have overturned local non-discrimina-
tion ordinances that protected lesbians and gay men. Oregon's measure failed; Colorado's passed, and is currently in litigation. Several
other states will vote on similar measures in coming elections.

Appendix: The Study

1. Esther Newton, *Mother Camp: Female Impersonators in America*
(Chicago: University of Chicago Press, 1979), p. 22.

2. Steven Epstein has argued, for example, that gay identity is analogous to "ethnicity," although his characterization applies primarily to
evolving political and academic discourse, not to the subjective experiences of most gay people. Nor does it deny the internal stratifica-
tions and subdivisions that exist within the proposed ethnic category.
In fact, one effect of gay "ethnic" politics is to exaggerate the homogeneity of its constituents. As Epstein notes: "[W]hile affirming a
distinctive group identity that legitimately differs from the larger society, this form of political expression simultaneously imposes a "to-
talizing" sameness *within* the group: it says, this is who we "really
are." A greater appreciation for internal diversity—on racial, gender,
class, and even sexual dimensions—is a prerequisite if the gay movement is to move beyond 'ethnic' insularity and join with other progressive causes." See Epstein, "Gay Politics, Ethnic Identity: The
Limits of Social Constructionism," *Socialist Review*, vol. 17, no. 3–4
(1977), pp. 9–54. For a response, see Ed Cohen, "Who are 'We'?
Gay 'Identity' as Political (E)motion," in Diana Fuss, ed., *Inside/Out:
Lesbian Theories, Gay Theories* (New York: Routledge, 1991),
pp. 71–92.

3. See Thomas S. Weinberg, "On 'Doing' and 'Being' Gay: Sexual
Behavior and Homosexual Male Self-Identity," *Journal of
Homosexuality* 4(2), pp. 143–56; See also Joel D. Hencken,
"Conceptualizations of Homosexual Behavior Which Preclude
Homosexual Self-Labeling," *Journal of Homosexuality*, vol. 9, no. 4
(1985), pp. 53–64.

4. I base these conclusions, in part, on studies of lesbian workers by

Hall ("Private Experiences"), Weston (*Families We Choose*), and Schneider ("Coming Out at Work"). See also Escoffier ("Stigmas," p. 16).

5. In our efforts to balance the one-sidedness of the discourse, we sometimes apply what are essentially male models to female experiences. Yet, while the intent may be to ensure fairness, it is rarely sufficient simply to "add women and stir." As Adrienne Rich noted in an influential essay: "Lesbians have historically been deprived of a political existence through 'inclusion' as female versions of male homosexuality. To equate lesbian existence with male homosexuality because each is stigmatized is to deny and erase female reality once again. To separate those women stigmatized as 'homosexual' or 'gay' from the complex continuum of female resistance to enslavement, and attach them to a male pattern, is to falsify our history" ("Compulsory Heterosexuality," p. 650). See also Marta B. Calás and Linda Smircich, "Re-writing Gender into Organizational Theorizing: Directions from Feminist Perspectives," in Michael Reed and Michael Hughes, eds., *Rethinking Organization: New Directions in Organization Theory and Analysis* (Newbury Park, CA: Sage, 1992), pp. 229–53.

6. The methodology is described in greater detail in James D. Woods, *The Corporate Closet: Managing Gay Identity on the Job* (Ph.D. dis., Annenberg School for Communication, University of Pennsylvania, 1992). For a discussion of the advantages of a two-interviewer team, see Harry V. Kincaid and Margaret Bright, "The Tandem Interview: A Trial of the Two-Interviewer Team," *Public Opinion Quarterly*, vol. 21, no. 2, (1957), pp. 304–12.

7. Commenting on his famous series of experiments on self-disclosure, Sidney Jourard notes that "much of social science is founded on a person's willingness to reveal himself to researchers; the conditions and dimensions of authentic self-disclosure therefore bear directly upon the validity of many 'facts' in the social sciences. See Jourard, (1979) *Self-Disclosure: An Experimental Analysis*," p. 3. Jourard and his colleagues have observed, in particular, that subjects disclosed more with an interviewer who had himself disclosed information of a personal nature. When such information was withheld, participants were less likely to feel they could trust the interviewer. For a review, see Chelune et al., *Self-Disclosure: Origins*.

8. In his study of the gay baths ("Outsider/Insider: Researching Gay Baths," *Urban Life*, vol. 8 [1979], pp. 135–52), J. Styles also makes

the case for "insider" status. As Kenneth Plummer recounts the study: "[Styles] contrasts the earlier phases of his study where he used an *outsider* strategy—'observation without sexual participation, and a correspondingly heavier reliance upon informants as original sources of ideas as well as a means of testing these notions—with an *insider* strategy—'observation and sexual participation in the baths, the heavy use of these as a source of original typologies and images, and the employment of informants as a way of testing, revising and evaluating these typologies and images.' " See Plummer, ed., *The Making of the Modern Homosexual* (London: Hutchinson, 1981), p. 220.

9. Walter Williams, *The Spirit and the Flesh: Sexual Diversity in American Indian Culture* (Boston: Beacon, 1986), p. 106.

10. Susan Krieger notes in her review of the literature on lesbian identity: "[The researchers] have been for the most part nonlesbian. . . . Many of the studies report that access to lesbian populations has been affected by whether or not the researcher was a lesbian; access and trust are viewed as problematic because of the secret and stigmatized nature of many lesbian populations. See Kreiger, "Lesbian Identity and Community: Recent Social Science Literature," *Signs,* vol. 8, no. 1 (1982), p. 228–29.

11. Contrast this to the caveat issued by Hall in the introduction to her study of lesbian professionals: "My embeddedness in the lesbian community—personally, socially and professionally—as well as my gay-affirmative politics precluded an 'objective' method of data gathering or analysis. Instead I employed a naturalistic mode of enquiry. Such an approach, because it emphasizes the multiple, constructed, context-bound nature of reality and acknowledges the intersubjectivity of interviewer and interviewee, was most consonant with my values as a lesbian and feminist" ("Private Experiences," p. 129). See also Plummer's discussion of scientific "objectivity" (*The Making of the Modern Homosexual,* pp. 220–22).

12. Recent work in cultural anthropology has encouraged us to view the researcher as a positioned subject whose very presence shapes the nature of the interview situation. The practice of ethnography, consequently, must be viewed as attempt to represent, in words, the experiences one has lived through or heard described by others, when the stated purpose was to study a culture. See Renato Rosaldo, *Culture and Truth: The Remaking of Social Analysis* (Boston: Beacon, 1989).

13. Hochschild, *The Managed Heart,* p. 57.
14. Even when respondents *intend* to tell the whole truth, they bump into the limitations of their own memories. As researchers we tried to gain access, through verbal means, to a range of interpersonal phenomena that, at the time of their occurrence, were often nonverbal, non-conscious, and unmemorable. The object of our study is thus evanescent: the passing glance, the meaningful comment or gesture, and the practiced social ritual leave no traces for the social scientist to examine; like the other minutiae that comprise human encounters, they are irrecoverable. Those that *can* be recalled often misrepresent the encounter—they were exceptional in some way and for this reason were experienced consciously, remembered, and recalled during the interview.

Bibliography

Acker, Joan. "Hierarchies, Jobs, Bodies: A Theory of Gendered Organizations," *Gender and Society,* vol. 4, no. 2 (1990), pp. 139–58.

Adam, Barry D. *The Survival of Domination.* New York: Elsevier, 1978.

———. *The Rise of a Gay and Lesbian Movement.* Boston: Twayne, 1987.

"Approaching 2000: Meeting the Challenge to San Francisco's Families." Mayor's Task Force on Family Policy, June 13, 1990.

Archer, Richard L. "Role of Personality and the Social Situation." In *Self-Disclosure: Origins, Patterns, and Implications of Openness in Interpersonal Relationships,* edited by Gordon Chelune et al., San Francisco: Jossey-Bass, 1979, pp. 28–58.

Badgett, Lee, "Labor Market Discrimination: Economic and Legal Issues for Gay Men and Lesbians." Paper delivered at the Annual Meeting of the American Economic Association, New Orleans, Jan. 3, 1992.

Badgett, Lee; Colleen Donnelly; and Jennifer Kibbe. *Pervasive Patterns of Discrimination Against Lesbians and Gay Men: Evidence from Surveys Across the United States.* Washington, D.C.: National Gay and Lesbian Task Force Policy Institute, 1992.

Bailey, J. Michael, and Richard C. Pillard. "A Genetic Study of Male Sexual Orientation." *Archives of General Psychiatry,* vol. 48 (1991), pp. 1089–96.

Baldridge, Letitia. *Letitia Baldridge's Complete Guide to Executive Manners.* New York: Rawson, 1985.

Barrett, Michèle, and Mary McIntosh. *The Anti-Social Family.* London: Verso Editions/NLB, 1982.

Bell, Alan P., and Martin S. Weinberg. *Homosexualities: A Study of Diversity Among Men and Women.* New York: Simon & Schuster, 1978.

Benn, S. I., and G. F. Gauss. *Public and Private in Social Life.* New York: St. Martin's, 1983.

Blackwood, Evelyn. "Breaking the Mirror: The Construction of Lesbianism and the Anthropological Discourse on Homosexuality." *Journal of Homosexuality,* vol. 11, nos. 3–4 (1985), pp. 1–17.

Blumenfeld, Warren J., ed. *Homophobia: How We All Pay the Price* (Boston: Beacon, 1992).

Blumstein, Philip, and Pepper Schwartz. *American Couples.* New York: William Morrow, 1983.

Bohara, Ann M., and Patrick McLaurin. " 'Managing Diversity': A View from Practice." Paper presented at the Annual Meeting of the Eastern Communication Association, Pittsburgh, April 22–25, 1991.

Bok, Sissela. *Lying: Moral Choice in Public and Private Life.* New York: Vintage, 1978.

———. *Secrets: On the Ethics of Concealment and Revelation.* New York: Vintage, 1983.

Boswell, John. *Christianity, Social Tolerance, and Homosexuality.* Chicago: University of Chicago Press, 1980.

Bozett, F. W. "Gay Fathers: How and Why They Disclose Their Homosexuality to Their Children," *Family Relations,* vol. 29 (1980), pp. 173–79.

Brause, Jay. "Closed Doors: Sexual Orientation Bias in the Anchorage Housing and Employment Markets." In *Identity Reports: Sexual Orientation Bias in Alaska.* Anchorage, Alaska: Identity Incorporated, 1989.

Brill, Alida. *Nobody's Business.* New York: Addison-Wesley, 1990.

Brooks, Vriginia R. *Minority Stress and Lesbian Women.* Lexington, MA: Lexington Books, 1981.

Burr, Chandler. "Homosexuality and Biology." *Atlantic,* Mar. 1993, pp. 47–65.

Burrell, Gibson. "Sex and Organizational Analysis." *Organization Studies,* vol. 5, no. 2 (1984), pp. 97–118.

———. "Modernism, Post-Modernism and Organizational Analysis 2: the Contribution of Michel Foucault," *Organization Studies,* vol. 9, no. 2 (1988), pp. 221–36.

Burrell, Gibson, and Jeff Hearn. "The Sexuality of Organization." In *The Sexuality of Organization,* edited by Hearn et al., Newbury Park, CA: Sage, 1989, pp. 1–28.

Cain, Roy. "Disclosure and Secrecy among Gay Men in the United States and Canada: A Shift in Views." *Journal of the History of Sexuality,* vol. 2, no. 1 (1991), pp. 25–45.

Calàs, Marta B., and Linda Smircich. "Re-writing Gender into Organizational Theorizing: Directions from Feminist Perspectives." In *Rethinking Organization: New Directions in Organization Theory and Analysis,* edited by Michael Reed and Michael Hughes, Newbury Park, CA: Sage, 1992, pp. 227–53.

Cass, Vivienne C. "Homosexual Identity Formation: A Theoretical Model." *Journal of Homosexuality,* vol. 4, no. 3 (1979), pp. 219–35.

———. "Homosexual Identity: A Concept in Need of Definition." *Journal of Homosexuality,* vol. 9, nos. 2–3 (1984), pp. 105–26.

Chelune, Gordon J., et al. *Self-Disclosure: Origins, Patterns, and Implications of Openness in Interpersonal Relationships.* San Francisco: Jossey-Bass, 1979.

Chesebro, James, ed. *Gayspeak: Gay Male & Lesbian Communication.* New York: Pilgrim, 1981.

Child, J. "Quaker Employers and Industrial Relations." *Sociological Review,* vol. 12 (1964), pp. 293–305.

Clegg, S. "Organization and Control." *Administration Science Quarterly,* vol. 26 (1981), pp. 545–62.

Cohen, Aaron Groff, and Barbara Gutek. "Dimensions of Perceptions of Social-Sexual Behavior in a Work Setting." *Sex Roles,* vol. 13, nos. 5/6 (1985), pp. 317–27.

Cohen, Ed. "Who Are 'We'? Gay 'Identity' as Political (E)motion (A Theoretical Rumination)." In *Inside/Out: Lesbian Theories, Gay Theories,* edited by Diana Fuss. New York: Routledge, 1991, pp. 71–92.

Coleman, Eli. "Developmental Stages of the Coming Out Process." *Journal of Homosexuality,* vol. 7 (1982), pp. 31–43.

Collinson, David L., and Margaret Collinson. "Sexuality in the Workplace: The Domination of Men's Sexuality." *In The Sexuality of Organization,* edited by Jeff Hearn et al., Newbury Park, CA: Sage, 1989, pp., 91–109.

Connell, R. W. *Gender and Power.* Stanford, CA: Stanford University Press, 1987.

Cory, Donald Webster. *The Homosexual in America: A Subjective Approach.* New York: Greenberg, 1951.

Cramer, D. W., and A. J. Roach. "Coming Out to Mom and Dad: A Study of Gay Males and Their Relationships With Their Parents." *Journal of Homosexuality,* vol. 15, nos. 3/4 (1988), pp. 79–92.

318   *Bibliography*

Crew, Louie. "Before Emancipation: Gay Persons as Viewed by Chairpersons in English." In *The Gay Academic,* edited by Louie Crew. pp. 3–48. Palm Springs, CA: ETC Publications, 1978.

Crisp, Quentin. "A Meeting of Manners." *Advocate,* Dec. 1990, pp. 64–66.

Cruikshank, Margaret. *The Gay and Lesbian Liberation Movement.* New York: Routledge, 1992.

Cunningham, Mary. *Power Play: What Really Happened at Bendix.* New York: Simon & Schuster, 1984.

D'Emilio, John. *Sexual Politics, Sexual Communities.* Chicago: University of Chicago Press, 1983.

D'Emilio, John, and Estelle Freedman. *Intimate Matters: A History of Sexuality in America.* New York: Harper & Row, 1988.

Decter, Midge. "The Boys on the Beach." *Commentary,* Aug. 1980, pp. 35–48.

Derlega, Valerian J., and Janusz Grzelak. "Appropriateness of Self-Disclosure." In *Self-Disclosure: Origins, Patterns, and Implications of Openness in Interpersonal Relationships,* edited by Gordon J. Chelune et al., San Francisco: Jossey-Bass, 1979, pp. 151–76

Deutsch, Claudia H. "Gay Rights, Issue of the 90's." *New York Times,* Apr. 28, p. D23.

———. "The Boss Who Plays Now Pays." *New York Times,* June 13, 1991, p. D1.

DeVito, Joseph A. "Educational Responsibilities to Gay Male and Lesbian Students." In *Gayspeak: Gay Male & Lesbian Communication,* edited by James W. Chesebro. New York: Pilgrim, 1981, pp. 197–207.

Denneny, Michael. "Chasing the Crossover Audience & Other Self-Defeating Strategies." *Out/Look,* vol. 4 (1989), pp. 16–21.

Dressler, J. "Survey of School Principals Regarding Alleged Homosexual Teachers in the Classroom: How Likely (Really) Is Discharge?" *University of Dayton Law Review,* vol. 10, no. 3, (1985) pp. 599–620.

Dyer, Richard. *Gays & Film.* Rev. ed. New York: Zoetrope, 1984.

———. "White." *Screen,* vol. 29, no. 4 (1989), pp. 44–65.

———. *Now You See It: Studies on Lesbian and Gay Film.* New York: Routledge, 1991.

———. "Believing in Fairies: The Author and the Homosexual." In *Inside/Out: Lesbian Theories, Gay Theories,* edited by Diana Fuss. New York: Routledge, 1991, pp. 185–201

Ehrenreich, Barbara. *The Worst Years of Our Lives: Irreverent Notes from a Decade of Greed.* New York: HarperCollins, 1991.

Ehrlich, Larry G. "The Pathogenic Secret," In *Gayspeak: Gay Male & Lesbian Communication,* edited by James W. Chesebro. New York: Pilgrim, 1981, pp. 130–41.

Elshtain, Jean Bethke. *Public Man, Private Woman.* Princeton: Princeton University Press, 1981.

Epstein, Steven. "Gay Politics, Ethnic Identity: The Limits of Social Constructionism." *Socialist Review,* vol. 17, nos. 3–4 (1987), pp. 9–54.

Escoffier, Jeffrey. "Stigmas, Work Environment, and Economic Discrimination Against Homosexuals." *Homosexual Counseling Journal,* vol. 2, no. 1 (1975), pp. 8–17.

Feldman, Diane. "Sexual Harassment: Policies and Prevention." *Personnel,* Sept. 1987, pp. 12–17.

Festinger, Leon. "A Theory of Social Comparison Process." *Human Relations,* vol. 7 (1954), pp. 117–40.

Foddy, W. H. "A Critical Evaluation of Altman's Definition of Privacy as a Dialectical Process." *Journal for the Theory of Social Behavior,* vol. 14, no. 3 (1984), pp. 297–307.

Foddy, W. H., and W. R. Finighan. "The Concept of Privacy from a Symbolic Interaction Perspective." *Journal for the Theory of Social Behaviour,* vol. 10, no. 1 (1981), pp. 1–17.

Ghiglione, Loren, et al. *Alternatives: Gays & Lesbians in the Newsroom.* Washington, DC: American Society of News Editors, 1990.

Gleason, Philip. "Identifying Identity: A Semantic History." *Journal of American History,* vol. 69, no. 4 (1983), pp. 910–31.

Goffman, Erving. *The Presentation of Self in Everyday Life.* Garden City, N.Y.: Doubleday, 1959.

———. *Stigma: Notes on the Management of Spoiled Identity.* New York: Simon & Schuster, 1963.

———. *Strategic Interaction.* Philadelphia: University of Pennsylvania Press, 1969.

Goodwin, Joseph P. *More Man Than You'll Ever Be: Gay Folklore and Acculturation in Middle America.* Bloomington: University of Indiana Press, 1989.

Greenberg, David F. *The Construction of Homosexuality.* Chicago: University of Chicago Press, 1988.

Gross, Larry. "Out of the Mainstream: Sexual Minorities and the Mass Media." In *Remote Control: Television, Audiences and Cultural Power,* edited by Ellen Seiter et al. London: Routledge, Chapman & Hall, 1989, pp. 130–49.

Gross, Larry. *The Contested Closet: The Politics and Ethics of Outing.* Minneapolis: University of Minnesota Press, 1993.

Gross, Larry, and Steven K. Aurand. *Discrimination and Violence Against Lesbian Women and Gay Men in Philadelphia and The Commonwealth of Pennsylvania.* Philadelphia: Philadelphia Lesbian and Gay Task Force, 1992.

Gross, Larry; Steven K. Aurand; and Rita Addessa. *Violence and Discrimination Against Lesbian and Gay People in Philadelphia and the Commonwealth of Pennsylvania.* Philadelphia: Philadelphia Lesbian and Gay Task Force, 1988.

Gutek, Barbara A. "Sexuality in the Workplace: Key Issues in Social Research and Organizational Practice." In *The Sexuality of Organization,* edited by Jeff Hearn et al. Newbury Park, CA: Sage, 1989, pp. 56–70.

Hall, Marny. "The Lesbian Corporate Experience." *Journal of Homosexuality,* vol. 12, nos. 3/4 (1986), pp. 59–75.

————. "Private Experiences in the Public Domain: Lesbians in Organizations." In *The Sexuality of Organization,* edited by Jeff Hearn et al. Newbury Park, CA: Sage, 1989, pp. 125–38.

Harbeck, Karen, ed. *Coming Out of the Classroom Closet: Gay and Lesbian Students, Teachers, and Curricula.* New York: Haworth, 1991.

Harry, Joseph, and William B. DeVall. *The Social Organization of Gay Males.* New York: Praeger, 1978.

Hayden, Ron. "Domestic Partnership Benefits Emerge as Corporate Trend," *The Gay/Lesbian/Bisexual Corporate Letter,* no. 1, no. 2 (1992), pp. 3–4.

Hearn, Jeff. "Men's Sexuality at Work." In *The Sexuality of Men,* edited by A. Metcalf and M. Humphries, pp. 110–28. London: Pluto, 1985.

Hearn, Jeff, and Wendy Parkin. *'Sex' at 'Work': The Power and Paradox of Organizational Sexuality.* New York: St. Martin's, 1987.

Hearn, Jeff; Deborah L. Sheppard; Peta Tancred-Sheriff; and Gibson Burrell, eds. *The Sexuality of Organization.* Newbury Park, CA: Sage, 1989.

Hencken, Joel D. "Conceptualizations of Homosexual Behavior Which Preclude Homosexual Self-Labeling." *Journal of Homosexuality,* vol. 9, no. 4 (1984), pp. 53–64.

Herek, Gregory M. "The Context of Anti-Gay Violence: Notes on

Cultural and Psychological Heterosexism." *Journal of Interpersonal Violence,* vol. 5, no. 3 (1990), pp. 316–33.

Hirschman, Albert O. *Exit, Voice, and Loyalty: Responses to Decline in Firms, Organizations and States.* Cambridge: Harvard University Press, 1970.

Hochschild, Arlie Russell. *The Managed Heart: Commercialization of Human Feeling.* Berkeley: University of California Press, 1983.

Hodges, Andrew, and David Hutter. *With Downcast Gays: Aspects of Homosexual Self-Oppression.* Toronto: Pink Triangle Press, 1974.

Hollingsworth, Gaines. "Corporate Gay Bashing." *Advocate,* Sept. 11, 1990, pp. 28–33.

Horn, Patrice D., and Jack C. Horn. *Sex in the Office.* Reading, MA: Addison-Wesley, 1982.

Jay, Karla, and Allen Young. *The Gay Report.* New York: Summit, 1979.

Jourard, Sidney. *Self-Disclosure: An Experimental Analysis of the Transparent Self.* New York: Wiley-Interscience, 1971.

Kanter, Rosabeth Moss. *Men and Women of the Corporation.* New York: Basic Books, 1977.

Kanter, Rosabeth Moss, and Barry A. Stein. *A Tale of "O": On Being Different in an Organization.* New York: Harper & Row, 1980.

Kincaid, Harry V., and Margaret Bright. "The Tandem Interview: A Trial of the Two-Interviewer Team." *Public Opinion Quarterly,* vol. 21, no. 2 (1957), pp. 304–12.

Kinsey, Alfred et al. *Sexual Behavior in the Human Male.* New York: W. B. Saunders, 1948.

Kleinberg, Seymour. *Alienated Affections.* New York: St. Martin's, 1980.

Krieger, Susan. "Lesbian Identity and Community: Recent Social Science Literature." *Signs,* vol. 8, no. 1 (1982), pp. 91–108.

Kronenberger, George. "Out of the Closet." *Personnel Journal,* June 1991, pp. 40–44.

Laabs, Jennifer L. "Unmarried . . . with Benefits." *Personnel Journal,* Dec. 1991, pp. 62–70.

Larson, M. S. *The Rise of Professionalism: A Sociological Analysis.* Berkeley: University of California Press, 1977.

Larson, Paul C. "Sexual Identity and Self-Concept." *Journal of Homosexuality,* vol. 7, no. 1 (1982), pp. 15–32.

Lee, John Alan. "Going Public: A Study in the Sociology of Homosexual Liberation." *Journal of Homosexuality,* vol. 3, no. 1 (1977), pp. 49–78.

Lemon, Brendan. "Man of the Year: David Geffen," *Advocate,* Dec. 29, 1992, pp. 35–40.

Levine, Martin P. "Employment Discrimination Against Gay Men." *International Review of Modern Sociology,* vol. 9 (1979), pp. 151–63.

Lewes, Kenneth. *The Psychoanalytic Theory of Male Homosexuality.* New York: Penguin, 1988.

Leznoff, Maurice, and William A. Westley. "The Homosexual Community," *Social Problems,* vol. 3, no. 4 (1956), pp. 257–63.

Lipman-Blumen, Jean. *Gender Roles and Power.* Englewood Cliffs, NJ: Prentice-Hall, 1984.

Livingston, Jennie (1990). "The Fairer Sex," *Aperture,* vol. 121, pp. 6–10.

"Love at Work" (1986) *Personnel Management,* January, pp. 20–24.

Lyman, Stanford M., and Marvin B. Scott. *A Sociology of the Absurd.* New York: Appleton-Century-Crofts, 1970.

Lynch, Frederick R. "Non-Ghetto Gays: A Sociological Study of Suburban Homosexuals." *Journal of Homosexuality,* vol. 13, no. 4 (1987), pp. 13–42.

Marcus, Eric. *Making History: The Struggle for Gay and Lesbian Equal Rights.* New York: HarperCollins, 1992.

McDonald, G. J. "Individual Differences in the Coming Out Process for Gay Men." *Journal of Homosexuality,* vol. 8 (1982), pp. 47–60.

McKinley, James C., Jr. "Tracking Crimes of Prejudice: A Hunt for the Elusive Truth." *New York Times,* June 29, 1990, p. A1.

Mills, Albert J., and Peta Tancred, eds. *Gendering Organizational Analysis.* Newbury Park, CA: Sage, 1992.

Mills, Albert. "Gender, Sexuality and Organization Theory." In *The Sexuality of Organization,* edited by Jeff Hearn et al. Newbury Park, CA: Sage, 1989, pp. 29–44.

Mohr, Richard. *Gay Ideas: Outing and Other Controversies.* Boston: Beacon, 1992.

———. *Gays/Justice: A Study of Ethics, Society and Law.* New York: Columbia University Press, 1987.

Morf, Martin. *The Work/Life Dichotomy: Prospects for Reintegrating People and Jobs.* New York: Quorum, 1989.

Munyard, Terry. "Homophobia at Work and How to Manage It." *Personnel Management,* June 1988, pp. 46–50.

Neisen, Joseph H. "Heterosexism or Homophobia? The Power of the Language We Use." *Out/Look,* vol. 10 (1990), pp. 36–37.

Newton, Esther. *Mother Camp: Female Impersonators in America.* Chicago: University of Chicago Press, 1979.

Noelle-Neumann, Elisabeth. "The Spiral of Silence: A Theory of Public Opinion." *Journal of Communication*, vol. 24, no. 2 (1974), pp. 43–51.

Olson, Myrna R. "A Study of Gay and Lesbian Teachers." *Journal of Homosexuality*, vol. 13, no. 4 (1987), pp. 73–81.

Parkin, Wendy. "Private Experiences in the Public Domain: Sexuality and Residential Care Organizations." In *The Sexuality of Organization*, edited by Jeff Hearn et al. Newbury Park, CA: Sage, 1989, pp. 110–24.

Pateman, Carole. "Feminist Critiques of the Public/Private Dichotomy." In *Public and Private in Social Life*, edited by S. I. Benn and G. F. Gauss. New York: St. Martin's, 1983, pp. 281–303.

Petrow, Steven. "True Blues: Gay and Lesbian Cops Battle the Closet." *Advocate*, Jan. 29, 1991, pp. 38–40.

Plummer, Kenneth. *Sexual Stigma: An Interactionist Account.* London: Routledge & Kegan Paul, 1975.

———., ed. *The Making of the Modern Homosexual.* London: Hutchinson, 1981.

Ponse, Barbara. *Identities in the Lesbian World: The Social Construction of Self.* Westport, CT: Greenwood, 1978.

———. "Lesbians and Their Worlds." In *Homosexual Behavior: A Modern Reappraisal*, edited by Judd Marmor. New York: Basic Books, 1980, pp. 157–75.

Pringle, Rosemary. *Secretaries Talk: Sexuality, Power and Work.* New York: Verso, 1989.

———. "Bureaucracy, Rationality and Sexuality: The Case of Secretaries." In *The Sexuality of Organization*, edited by Jeff Hearn et al., pp. 158–77. Newbury Park, CA: Sage, 1989.

Quinn, Robert E. "Coping with Cupid: The Formation, Impact, and Management of Romantic Relationships in Organizations." *Administrative Science Quarterly*, vol. 22 (1977), pp. 30–45.

Rich, Adrienne. "Compulsory Heterosexuality and Lesbian Existence." *Signs*, vol. 5, no. 4 (1980), pp. 631–60.

Rogers, Patrick. "How Many Gays are There?" *Newsweek*, Feb. 15, 1993, p. 46.

"Romance in the Workplace." *Business Week*, June 18, 1984, pp. 70–71.

Rosaldo, Renato. *Culture and Truth: The Remaking of Social Analysis.* Boston: Beacon, 1989.

Rothenberg, David. "Oppression and Political Disadvantage," *Gaysweek*, Feb. 5, 1979, p. 19.

Rubin, Gayle. "Thinking Sex." In *Pleasure and Danger: Exploring Female Sexuality,* edited by Carole Vance. London: Routledge & Kegan Paul, 1984, pp. 267–319.

Russo, Vito. Letter to the editor. *Village Voice,* Apr. 24, 1990, p. 4.

Saghir, Marcel T., and Eli Robins. *Male and Female Homosexuality.* Baltimore: Williams & Wilkins, 1973.

Sarason, Seymour. "Jewishness, Blackness, and the Nature-Nurture Controversy." *American Psychologist,* vol. 28 (1973), pp. 962–71.

Schmitt, Patrick J., and Lawrence A. Kurdek. "Personality Correlates of Positive Identity and Relationship Involvement in Gay Men." *Journal of Homosexuality,* vol. 13, no. 4 (1987), pp. 101–9.

Schneider, Beth. "Consciousness About Sexual Harassment Among Heterosexual and Lesbian Women Workers." *Journal of Social Issues,* vol. 38, no. 4 (1982), pp. 75–98.

———. "Coming Out at Work: Bridging the Private/Public Gap." *Work and Occupations,* vol. 13, no. 4 (1987), pp. 463–87.

Sheppard, Deborah. "Organizations, Power and Sexuality: The Image and Self-Image of Women Managers." In *The Sexuality of Organization,* edited by Jeff Hearn et al. Beverly Hills, CA: Sage, 1989, pp. 139–57.

Simmel, George. *The Sociology of Georg Simmel.* Edited and translated by K. H. Wolff. New York: Free Press, 1950.

Styles, J. "Outsider/Insider: Researching Gay Baths." *Urban Life,* vol. 8 (1979), pp. 135–52.

Taylor, N., ed. *All in a Day's Work: A Report on Anti-Lesbian Discrimination in Employment and Unemployment in London.* London: Lesbian Employment Rights, 1986.

Thomas, Roosevelt, Jr. "From Affirmative Action to Affirming Diversity." *Harvard Business Review,* vol. 68, no. 2 (1990), pp. 112–17.

Troiden, Richard R. *Gay and Lesbian Identity: A Sociological Analysis.* New York: General Hall, 1988.

Tucker, Scott. "Our Right to the World." *Body Politic,* vol. 85 (1982), pp. 29–33.

Vande Berge, Leah, and Nick Trujillo. *Organizational Life on Television.* Norwood, NJ: Ablex, 1989.

Warfield, Andrea. "Co-Worker Romances: Impact on the Work Group and on Career-Oriented Women." *Personnel* (1987), pp. 22–35.

Warren, Carol. *Identity and Community in the Gay World.* New York: Wiley, 1974.

Weber, Max. "Bureaucracy." In *From Max Weber: Essays in Sociology,* edited by H. H. Gerth and C. Wright Mills. New York: Oxford University Press, 1946, pp. 196–244.

Weeks, Jeffrey. *Sexuality and Its Discontents.* New York: Routledge & Kegan Paul, 1985.

———. *Sexuality.* London: Tavistock, 1986.

———. *Against Nature: Essays on History, Sexuality and Identity.* London: Rivers Oram, 1991.

Weinberg, Thomas S. "On 'Doing' and 'Being' Gay: Sexual Behavior and Homosexual Male Self-Identity." *Journal of Homosexuality,* vol. 4, no. 2 (1978), pp. 143–56.

Weinberg, Martin S., and Colin J. Williams. *Male Homosexuals: Their Problems and Adaptations.* New York: Penguin, 1974.

Weston, Kath. *Families We Choose: Lesbians, Gays, Kinship.* New York: Columbia University Press, 1991.

Weston, Kathleen, and Lisa Rofel. "Sexuality, Class, and Conflict in a Lesbian Workplace." *Signs,* vol. 9, no. 4 (1984), pp. 623–46.

Westwood, Gordon. *A Minority.* London: Longmans, Green and Co., 1960.

Williams, Walter. *The Spirit and the Flesh.* Boston: Beacon, 1986.

Williams, Raymond. *Keywords.* New York: Oxford University Press, 1977.

Wolfe, Susan J. "The Rhetoric of Heterosexism." In *Gender and Discourse: The Power of Talk,* edited by Alexandra Dundas Todd and Sue Fisher. Norwood, NJ: Ablex, 1988, pp. 199–224.

Woods, James D. "Self-Disclosure at Work." Results of a questionnaire distributed in *Out/Look,* vol. 16 (Spring 1992), p. 87–88. [See chapter 1, note 17.]

———. *The Corporate Closet: Managing Gay Identity on the Job.* Ph.D. dissertation, Annenberg School for Communication, University of Pennsylvania, 1992.

Woods, Sherry E., and Karen M. Harbeck. "Living in Two Worlds: The Identity Management Strategies Used by Lesbian Physical Educators." In *Coming Out of the Classroom Closet: Gay and Lesbian Students, Teachers, and Curricula,* edited by Karen Harbeck. New York: Haworth, 1991, pp. 141–66.

Worth, Sol, and Larry Gross. "Symbolic Strategies." In *Studying Visual Communication,* edited by Larry Gross, Philadelphia: Univ. of Pennsylvania, 1981, pp. 134–46.

Yarbrough, Jeff. "Vanity Fairies." *Advocate,* Mar. 10, 1992, p. 32.

Zedeck, S., and S. Cascio. "Psychological Issues in Personnel Decisions." *Annual Review of Psychology,* vol. 35 (1984), pp. 461–518.

Zoglin, Richard. "The Homosexual Executive." In *Gay Men: The Sociology of Male Homosexuality,* edited by Martin P. Levine. New York: Harper & Row, 1974, pp. 68–77.

Index